Road Accident Statistics

Road Accident Statistics

T. P. Hutchinson

Department of Civil Engineering, University of Adelaide

Rumsby Scientific Publishing

P.O. Box 76, Rundle Mall, Adelaide, South Australia 5000

Published by and available from: Rumsby Scientific Publishing, P.O. Box 76, Rundle Mall,
Adelaide, South Australia 5000.
ISBN 0 7316 0653 1

To the reader:

In this book, I discuss road accident statistics from all over the world, both the process of their collection and the data that results. If I didn't think I'd done a pretty good job, I wouldn't have published it. But be reasonable—it is not realistic to expect me to know as much about any one system as those involved in it daily do. So, perhaps you will detect errors and omissions: if so, write and tell me of them. Perhaps you have researched in the areas dealt with: if so, send me reprints of the publications that resulted. Perhaps you will think of new ways of tabulating your data after reading this book: if so, let me know the results. A book is only part of the cycle of communication. Your feedback is important too.

T. P. Hutchinson

Department of Civil Engineering
University of Adelaide
Box 498, G.P.O.
Adelaide
South Australia 5001

Acknowledgements

Many people have contributed help or information in the course of my research and writing of this book. I hope they will accept that my appreciation is no less than if I had listed their hundreds of names.

I must, however, acknowledge my debt to my mentors during my early training in road safety research at the Transport Studies Group, University College London—the late Professor Reuben J Smeed CBE, the late Dr Geoffrey Grime OBE DSc, and Mr Howard R Kirby.

T. P. H.

Chapters

Contents

Chapter 1

Introduction

1.1 What this book is about

This Chapter has two purposes: to describe the structure and content of this book as a whole, and to emphasise how different the road accident picture is in different countries.

The book is an account of the methods of collecting and processing data about the occurrence and consequences of road accidents, and gives numerous statistical tables as examples of the findings.

In Chapters 1 and 2 are some aggregate statistics from many countries. Chapters 3–7 deal with various aspects of data collected by the police about road accidents, and Chapters 8–13 discuss how medical sources can supplement the police data, especially in respect of the nature of injury sustained. Finally, Chapter 14 examines insurance data. The book concentrates on what can and cannot be found in statistics that are routinely collected—special research studies are outside its scope, though naturally reference will be made to some.

Now to amplify that outline.

Chapters 1 and 2. The chief feature of Chapter 2 is a list of the total numbers of road accident deaths in as many countries of the world as I could find information for. This is supplemented by tables in which the totals are disaggregated by age and by category of road user, and by a bibliography of sources. And it is preceded in Sections 1.2–1.7 by a series of tables emphasising the differences that exist between countries in the relative importance of the several sub-populations among the totality of road deaths.

Chapters 3–7. Chapter 3 gives descriptions of the police accident data capture systems as they operate in a number of jurisdictions, Chapter 4 examines what are the major problems encountered with the data, and includes summaries of empirical studies of the errors present, and Chapter 5 is devoted to how such systems work in developing countries. Chapter 6 turns attention to one of the outputs of the process, the yearbook of statistics on road accidents, and examines what is in the yearbooks of six jurisdictions. Chapter 7 is a collection of data tables—on the effectiveness of seat belts, the effectiveness of crash helmets, the role of alcohol, and other issues.

Chapters 8–13. The core of this part of the book is Chapters 9 and 10, which are concerned with the nature of injury sustained in road accidents—by those killed and those attending hospital respectively. Preceding them, Chapter 8 describes and compares methods of classifying the nature of injury and how severe it is. How does data from the medical statistical systems (i.e. from death certification and from hospitals) compare with police data? That is the concern of Chapter 11. Then Chapter 12 examines data on nature of injury from whatever source it comes (medical, police, insurance), and is distinguished by being organised by country. Chapter 13 looks to the future, when police and hospital data may be integrated, and describes some recent progress to this end.

Chapter 14. This is given over to the special features of data originating in insurance claims made by casualties or vehicle owners.

Perhaps I should justify the use, in the title of this book and at many points within it, of the word "accident". There is a body of opinion which says this should be avoided. The claim is that road crashes and the injuries that result have causes, and that to refer to "accidents" implies that these causes cannot be identified and combatted. While I take the point that many crashes and injuries are caused by particular acts and circumstances, and that there exist countermeasures of known efficacy against many of these, and while I respect the achievements and expertise of those people who decry the accident concept, yet I disagree with them. There are three reasons why I continue to use the word "accident". The first is that it is used in popular language, in ordinary conversation, and by the media. A body of specialists should not separate themselves from the general public by adopting different language, except when justified by a substantial gain in precision. This is especially so in road safety studies, a subject that many of the general public are interested in—and can contribute to, both by political activity and by their own research. The second reason is linguistic: I deny that the main connotation of "accident" is absence of identifiable cause. Instead, I think it is absence of deliberate intent. Certainly this criterion is satisfied by the vast majority of road crashes (the number of murders and suicides committed with motor vehicles is tiny). And even recklessness and negligence (in their ordinary senses) account for only a fairly small proportion of the crash total. The third reason is that, while there are reasons for many of the deaths and injuries on the roads, and these often fall into a stereotyped category, there are numerous cases where the event is a freak one[1], and to always avoid the term "accident" is to miss this important aspect of the total phenomenon.

Finally in this first Section, it is appropriate to offer my sympathy to those readers who have themselves been involved in a serious road accident, or had a relative or friend killed or maimed on the roads. I hope they won't be offended by this book's devotion to impersonal statistics, or think I am insensitive to their individual tragedies.

1.2 Different accident pictures in different countries

The remainder of this Chapter will be devoted to demonstrating that the various types of road casualty occur in very different proportions in different countries. By "types", I mean the categories pedestrian, motorcyclist, pedal cyclist, and vehi-

cle occupant, and also the various ages, children, young adults, the elderly, and other adults. Sections 1.3–1.5 will look at ages of road fatalities, and Section 1.6 at the categories of road user; Section 1.7 will examine changes over time in accident rates in recent years. I shall resist the temptation to speculate on the reasons for the differences found: the point is simply that what is the case is one country may not be so in another—and, correspondingly, the priorities for road safety improvement may be different too.

Before coming to the tables of data, let me point out that both police and certification data will be drawn upon in this Chapter—as, indeed, throughout this book. The former receives much wider use than the latter—because of the greater amount of information about the accident circumstances that it has, and because it includes those injured as well as those killed. The chief advantage of certification data is the coding of nature of injury, and this will be taken up in Chapter 9. Other advantages include the accuracy with which age is recorded, and that such information about the casualty as occupation or ethnic origin may be given. Three studies have caught my attention.

- Baker (1979) used U.S. data for 1976–77 to plot population-based death rates for child vehicle occupants as a function of their age, and to extend this plot to individual months of age for those less than one year old. She found that the death rate for babies less than six months old was triple that for children aged 6–12 years. (This effect does not seem to be present to such a degree in data from England and Wales. In 1982–85, there were 25 deaths of babies under 1 year of age as motor vehicle passengers, only a little more than expected from the 71 deaths of children aged 1–4.)

- In Britain, Keeling et al (1985) found an excess of fatal accidents within a week of the child's birthday, and suggested this was a result of the child's excitement making him or her less careful. (This study used data from the Oxford Record Linkage Study, and I am not sure that a similar study would be possible with routine certification data.)

- Mueller et al (1987) noted that pedestrian death rates in Washington state in 1981–83

---

[1]This is the first and last textual footnote. In their learned work on pedal cyclist casualties in Sweden, Bjornstig and Naslund (1984) report "In all but one of the eight accidents involving animals, the cyclist was exercising a dog. The other cyclist was frightened by an elk and crashed into a ditch."

Table 1.1: Death rates (per 100,000 population in a given age/sex group) for road accidents.

	Total no.	Overall rate	Females 1-4 / 5-14	15-24 / 25-34	35-44 / 45-54	55-64 / 65-74	75+	Males 1-4 / 5-14	15-24 / 25-34	35-44 / 45-54	55-64 / 65-74	75+
Australia 1984	2714*	17.4	5 5	16 9	6 9	11 14	23	8 8	56 28	18 17	15 26	59
Austria 1985	1518*	20.1	3 5	12 6	5 3	10 18	27	7 8	69 26	21 29	31 35	48
Belgium 1984	1959*	19.9	2 5	13 7	8 8	9 15	24	7 11	55 36	28 22	22 37	60
Bulgaria 1984	1124*	12.5	6 5	4 6	6 4	6 11	17	7 6	20 22	18 22	23 29	42
Canada 1984	3973*	15.8	5 5	12 8	8 7	9 11	18	4 8	47 27	19 18	17 20	37
Czechoslovakia 1984	1569*	10.1	2 3	4 3	4 4	5 9	19	4 4	19 17	15 19	23 24	43
Denmark 1983-84	1329	13.0	4 6	9 5	5 7	8 12	21	5 6	35 13	13 15	17 23	47
Finland 1983-84	1131	11.6	4 4	9 3	4 7	9 16	18	4 7	22 14	12 14	20 31	56
France 1984	10973*	20.0	5 5	16 9	9 10	10 13	19	6 7	56 35	27 28	27 32	50
German Dem. Rep. 1984	1995*	12.0	3 4	9 5	4 5	7 10	20	4 5	34 16	14 14	15 19	36
Germany, Fed. Rep. 1985	7978*	13.1	5 5	11 5	3 4	6 11	15	4 6	41 18	13 15	13 21	37
Greece 1984	2091*	21.1	5 4	13 8	7 8	14 19	24	11 7	55 40	28 32	33 36	52
Hong Kong 1984-85	585*	5.4	2 2	1 1	1 4	11 21	25	2 3	7 6	4 5	10 21	31
Hungary 1985	1824*	17.1	3 4	10 5	8 7	9 14	31	6 6	35 28	23 27	35 48	54
Ireland 1983	538*	15.3	4 3	12 6	5 9	8 16	31	4 9	46 19	19 15	27 31	53
Israel 1983-84	849*	10.3	5 3	6 4	3 4	8 21	29	7 5	20 15	17 12	16 25	52
Japan 1985	12456*	10.4	2 1	5 2	3 5	7 13	20	5 4	31 11	10 15	20 29	45
Kuwait 1983, 1985	880*	26.8	15 6	5 6	11 18	27 15	98	30 28	39 33	32 61	111 198	513
Netherlands 1984	1625*	11.3	1 3	8 4	4 4	7 17	14	4 7	28 15	11 14	14 25	51
New Zealand 1983-84	1306*	20.1	7 5	22 8	6 9	10 20	23	10 9	72 31	18 18	15 31	46
Norway 1983-84	873	10.5	2 3	9 3	4 4	5 11	13	6 6	36 14	8 9	12 20	29
Poland 1984	5393*	14.6	4 4	5 4	4 5	6 13	23	5 6	29 28	29 32	28 40	52
Portugal 1985	2597*	25.6	7 5	8 6	8 9	12 20	24	13 12	60 45	42 49	55 65	74
Singapore 1983-85	958*	12.6	1 2	3 3	5 5	13 23	20	2 4	30 20	21 19	26 57	102
Sweden 1983-84	1637	9.8	2 2	7 4	4 4	6 10	10	3 5	29 13	10 10	12 17	34
Switzerland 1984-85	2033	15.7	4 4	11 6	5 7	8 10	23	6 8	46 23	14 16	21 33	58
United Kingdom												
England and Wales 1984	5012*	10.1	2 4	7 3	3 3	5 10	17	4 7	31 15	10 10	10 15	31
Northern Ireland 1983-85	569*	12.1	6 6	7 5	1 7	6 8	15	7 12	33 20	12 16	11 22	36
Scotland 1983-85	1855*	12.0	5 5	7 5	3 4	5 13	20	3 11	29 19	14 15	16 15	37
U.S.A. 1983	43428*	18.6	5 4	17 10	9 9	9 12	16	7 8	50 36	26 22	20 23	42

* Motor vehicle traffic accidents (E810–E819) tabulated, 9th Revision of ICD used. The other 5 countries tabulate motor vehicle accidents, E810–E823 in the 8th Revision of the ICD. See Section 8.3 for clarification of this distinction.

were 2.4 for whites and 3.8 for blacks, per 100,000 population.

Another way certification data differs from police data, which may be an advantage for some purposes, is that it is slightly wider in coverage. It is generally the case that certification figures include, but police figures exclude, deaths occurring between 30 days and 1 year after the accident. And deaths in accidents occurring off the public highway should be included in certification data for motor vehicle non-traffic accidents, but are usually excluded from police data.

1.3 How accident rates depend on age

The data to be discussed is given in Table 1.1. These figures came from the World Health Statistics Annual, published by the World Health Organization, and derive from the death certification and registration process. What is shown is the ratio of the number of deaths from road accidents in a given age/sex group to the number of hundreds of thousands of people in that group.

Detailed discussion of rates of accidents— including the conceptual problems that are especially acute with highly aggregated data, and the practical difficulties in measuring exposure (e.g. distance travelled per annum)—is beyond the scope of this book. Note, though, that the population-based death rate in Table 1.1 tells only part of the story, as it does not take into account the numbers of motor vehicles in the various countries, how far they are driven per year, what type of vehicles they are, what age/sex groups have access to them, and so on. Table 1.1 does give some impression of how the general safety level varies between countries, and also how the dependence on age and sex does.

As to the overall rate, the range of variation in the 30 jurisdictions in Table 1.1 is from 5 deaths per 100,000 population (Hong Kong) to 27 (Kuwait); restricting attention to Western industrialised countries, the range is still from 10 (Sweden) to 26 (Portugal).

Public interest often centres upon people in four age groups: children (especially as pedestrians), adults in their late teens or early twenties (especially as motorcycle riders and car drivers), adults aged (say) 25–64, and the elderly (especially as pedestrians). Of these, the second and fourth are of particular concern because their rates of accidents are higher than average.

How high is the peak rate among males aged 15–24, relative to the minimum rate among adult males (which usually occurs in the 35–44 year age group)? The ratio of these two rates—an indicator of how serious is the young driver problem in a country—varies from over 4 in the case of New Zealand and Norway to under 2 for Finland, Israel, and Portugal (and lower still in countries with fewer privately-owned motor vehicles).

A similar range is found for the ratio of the rate among males aged 75 and over to the minimum rate among adult males—an indicator of how serious a problem is the elderly road user. There are several countries (France, Greece, Poland, Portugal) for which this is under 2, and several for which it is over 4 (Hong Kong, Israel, Japan, Kuwait, The Netherlands, Singapore, Switzerland).

1.4 Which age group is the important problem?

This section and the next continue consideration of the ages of road fatalities. Table 1.2 expresses each of the four age groups (0–14, 15–24, 25–64, and 65 and over) as a percentage of the total. If available, police data has been used in Table 1.2, as it is the best source for most types of information about road accidents, but for some of the countries, certification data has been resorted to. Now let us consider each age group in turn.

Fatalities aged up to 14 years may be as low a proportion of the total as 2% (the figure for Singapore, which I do not find credible) or 6% (9 countries); or they may be 15% or more (Israel, Kuwait, Northern Ireland).

The proportion of fatalities who are aged 15–24 years may be 15% or less (Bulgaria, Hong Kong, Kuwait); or it may be 35% or more (Australia, Austria, Ireland, New Zealand).

As to those aged 25–64, their proportion may be as low as 34% (Canada, Ireland, Norway); or as high as 60% (Yugoslavia).

Finally, fatalities aged 65 years or over are only 4% of the total in Kuwait and 12% in Canada, New Zealand, and Yugoslavia, but are over 25% in Finland, Hong Kong, and Sweden.

1.5 For the young, how important a cause of death is road trauma?

Instead of asking what proportion among all road fatalities are casualties of a certain age, here we ask what proportion among all deaths at a certain age are the result of road trauma. Looked at in this way, it is children and young adults upon whom we should concentrate—adults of 25–64 years have relatively low accident rates, and the elderly die mostly from natural causes. Table 1.3 gives the relevant data, separately for men and women. Certification data has been used here (since police data doesn't concern itself with types of death other than road accidents); those aged under 1 year have been excluded in order to omit perinatal deaths from the denominator.

For children, the range is from under 10% (e.g. Singapore) to over 20% (e.g. Denmark).

For young men (i.e. aged 15–24), the proportion may be 20% or less (Bulgaria, Czechoslovakia, Finland, Hong Kong), or over 50% (Greece, New Zealand). For young women, the range of variation is from below 10% (Bulgaria, Hong Kong,

Table 1.2: Percentages of road fatalities in four age groups. (Source: C = certification, P = police.)

	0-14	15-24	25-64	65+	Source
Australia 1984	9	35	41	15	C
Austria 1985	6	35	41	17	P
Belgium 1984	6	28	47	19	P
Bulgaria 1984	10	13	57	20	C
Canada 1984	8	34	34	12	P
Czechoslovakia 1984	7	17	55	21	P
Denmark 1985	9	28	42	21	P
Finland 1984	7	20	43	30	P
France 1985	6	29	51	15	P
German Dem. Rep. 1984	7	31	41	21	P
Germany, Fed. Rep. 1984	6	34	39	22	P
Greece 1984	6	25	50	19	C
Hong Kong 1984	10	14	48	28	P
Hungary 1984	6	16	58	20	P
Ireland 1984	13	35	34	18	P
Israel 1984	15	... 62* ...		23	P
Japan 1985	6	25	45	23	C
Kuwait 1985	24	14	58	4	C
Netherlands 1984	8	28	40	23	P
New Zealand 1984	10	43	35	12	P
Norway 1984	9	34	34	24	P
Poland 1983	8	18	59	16	P
Portugal 1985	8	23	50	19	C
Singapore 1985	2	28	53	17	C
Sweden 1984	6	28	38	28	P
Switzerland 1985	6	29	42	23	P
United Kingdom					
Great Britain 1984	9	31	37	22	P
Northern Ireland 1983-85	17	31	36	17	C
U.S.A. 1985	7	32	48	13	P
Yugoslavia 1984	10	17	60	12	P

* For Israel, certification data reveals the proportions in the 15–24 and 25–64 year age groups to be 21% and 42% respectively.

Singapore) to 40% (New Zealand).

1.6 Categories of road user

Table 1.4 is analogous to Table 1.2, but classifies road fatalities by their mode of transport instead of by age. It uses police data (certification data is rarely classified in this way and certainly not in the

WHO and similar compilations).

The proportion who are occupants of motor vehicles (riders of two-wheeled motor vehicles being excluded) may be under 30% (Hong Kong, Singapore), or over 70% (Canada, U.S.A.).

How high a fraction motorcyclists are (this term includes riders of mopeds and motor scooters) varies from under 10% (Finland, Hong Kong, Israel) to 30% or more (East Germany, Singapore).

Table 1.3: Percentages of deaths within given age/sex groups that are due to road accidents.

	Females		Males		
	1-14	15-24	1-14	15-24	
Australia 1984	21	36	23	46	*
Austria 1985	17	28	21	48	*
Belgium 1984	12	32	25	49	*
Bulgaria 1984	10	8	9	18	*
Canada 1984	18	32	19	38	*
Czechoslovakia 1984	8	11	11	19	*
Denmark 1984	27	36	25	40	
Finland 1984	16	24	23	20	
France 1984	17	33	17	42	*
German Dem. Rep. 1984	11	20	12	30	*
Germany, Fed. Rep. 1985	18	32	18	43	*
Greece 1984	18	37	26	56	*
Hong Kong 1985	7	5	8	16	*
Hungary 1985	13	22	15	29	*
Ireland 1983	12	33	19	42	*
Israel 1984	8	17	13	21	*
Japan 1985	8	18	13	41	*
Kuwait 1985	20	18	34	37	*
Netherlands 1984	12	28	20	41	*
New Zealand 1983	23	40	23	51	*
Norway 1984	11	28	20	35	
Portugal 1985	13	15	18	40	*
Singapore 1985	1	8	7	27	*
Sweden 1984	17	24	23	39	
Switzerland 1985	13	24	22	36	
United Kingdom					
England and Wales 1984	14	24	19	39	*
Northern Ireland 1983-85	22	23	29	34	*
Scotland 1985	19	20	24	33	*
U.S.A. 1983	16	34	19	37	*

* Motor vehicle traffic accidents (E810–E819) tabulated, 9th Revision of ICD used. (The other 5 countries tabulate motor vehicle accidents, E810–E823 in the 8th Revision of the ICD.)

As to pedal cyclists, their proportion varies from 2 or 3% (Australia, Canada, Israel, U.S.A.) to 22% (The Netherlands).

Pedestrians make up only 13% of the total in The Netherlands, but over 40% in Israel and Poland, and 61% in Hong Kong.

1.7 Trends in recent years

The World Health Statistics Annual expresses road fatalities as a rate per 100,000 population. I have extracted the figures for 1980 and 1984, and calculated the annual percentage rates of change over this period. The results are in Table 1.5.

"Little change may be expected in road accident rates within the next 5–10 years because al-

Table 1.4: Percentages of four categories of road fatalities.

	Motor vehicle occupants	Motor cyclists	Pedal cyclists	Pedest- rians
Australia 1985	65	14	3	18
Austria 1985	54	19	6	21
Belgium 1984	59	13	11	18
Canada 1984	72	10	3	14
Czechoslovakia 1984	42	11	11	36
Denmark 1984	51	15	15	19
Finland 1984	48	9	16	27
German Dem. Rep. 1984	31	30	9	30
Germany, Fed. Rep. 1984	53	15	10	22
Hong Kong 1984	27	6	7	61
Hungary 1984	35	15	13	36
Ireland 1984	45	13	9	34
Israel 1984	50*	2*	2	45
Netherlands 1984	51	14	22	13
New Zealand 1984	59	19	5	18
Norway 1984	59	10	5	26
Poland 1983	32	18	7	42
Singapore 1984	22	35	8	35
Sweden 1984	54	13	14	19
Switzerland 1985	49	24	7	21
United Kingdom Great Britain 1985	44	15	6	35
U.S.A. 1985	72	10	2	16

* For Israel, motorcycle passengers have been included with motor vehicle occupants, not with motor-cyclists.

terations in the behaviour of road users and improvements in the environmental infrastructure of roads can come about only gradually." (WHO, 1979a.) Happily, this prediction has turned out to be overly pessimistic: of the countries in Table 1.5, 22 are showing a fall and 6 an increase, the median rate of change being a 14% decline per 5 years. There are, however, wide cross-national variations: some countries are reducing their accident rate by 8 or more percent per annum— Canada, West Germany, and Hong Kong. In others, the rate is increasing—Greece, Hungary, Japan, New Zealand, Norway, Singapore.

Rather than include all ages, it is arguable that a better indicator of the safety of the roads them-selves is provided by the accident rate to the relatively safe age groups. Consequently, figures for those aged 35–44 years are also given in Table 1.5. The highest rates of decline (10% or more) are achieved by Australia, Finland, West Germany, Hong Kong, and Northern Ireland. New Zealand and Singapore have substantial rates of increase.

Table 1.5: Road fatality rates per 100,000 population in 1980 and 1984, and their corresponding annual percentage rates of change.

	All ages			Ages 35-44			
	Rates		A.P.R.	Rates		A.P.R.	
	1980	1984		1980	1984		
Australia+	24	17	- 7	18	12	-10	*
Austria	25	20#	- 4	20	13#	- 8	*
Belgium	23#	20	- 3	18#	18	- 0	*
Bulgaria	13	13	- 0	15	12	- 5	*
Canada	23	16	- 8	18	13	- 7	*
Czechoslovakia	13#	10	- 7	11#	9	- 4	*
Denmark	14	13	- 2	9	9	+ 0	
Finland	12	11	- 3	9	6	-12	
France	20	20	- 1	17	18	+ 1	*
Germany, Fed. Rep.	20	13#	- 8	14	8#	-10	*
Greece	17	21	+ 6	17	17	+ 1	*
Hong Kong	9	5#	-10	6	2#	-17	*
Hungary	16	17#	+ 1	14	15#	+ 1	*
Ireland	17	15#	- 3	16	12#	- 8	*
Israel	10	10	- 1	9	9	+ 2	*
Japan	10	10#	+ 1	7	7#	- 2	*
Kuwait	32	27#	- 3	30	30#	+ 0	*
Netherlands	13	11	- 4	9	8	- 5	*
New Zealand	19	21	+ 2	11	13	+ 3	*
Norway	9	11	+ 4	5	6	+ 1	
Portugal	27	26#	- 1	27	24#	- 2	*
Singapore	10	11#	+ 2	8	10#	+ 5	*
Sweden	11	10	- 2	9	7	- 6	
Switzerland	19	14	- 7	12	9	- 6	
United Kingdom							
England and Wales	12	10	- 4	7	7	- 1	*
Northern Ireland	18	13#	- 7	12	7#	-10	*
Scotland	14	12#	- 4	12	11#	- 3	*
U.S.A.	23	19#	- 7	20	17#	- 6	*

* Motor vehicle traffic accidents (E810–E819) tabulated, 9th Revision of ICD used. (The other 5 countries tabulate motor vehicle accidents, E810–E823 in the 8th Revision of the ICD.)
# Variations in the time period considered: Austria 1980–85; Belgium 1979–84; Czechoslovakia 1981–1984; Germany, Fed. Rep. 1980–85; Hong Kong 1980–85; Hungary 1980–85; Ireland 1980–83; Japan 1980–85; Kuwait 1980–85; Portugal 1980–85; Singapore 1980–85; U.K., Northern Ireland 1980–85; U.K., Scotland 1980–85; U.S.A. 1980–83.
+ The undercount of Australian deaths in 1984 (see footnote to Table 2.1) means the annual percentage reduction is overstated by a small amount.

Chapter 2

How many road deaths?

2.1 A Chapter of Tables

Table 2.1 lists the total numbers of road accident deaths in most of the countries of the world. It has already been said in Chapter 1 that for many countries there are two sources of such data, the police and the death registration authorities: Table 2.1 includes both if available. Tables 2.2–2.4 classify the deaths by the age and the category of the person killed. Section 2.7 is a bibliography of sources, i.e. a list of the titles and publishers of the statistical serials where these numbers were found, and which in many cases give numerous data tables about the accident circumstances, events, and consequences. (Chapter 6 will examine in detail how some of these present their information.)

Although the idea of a "road accident death" may seem a simple one, there are many subtleties of definition involved. Detailed discussion of these will wait till later; suffice it to say here that they are much more acute in the case of road accident victims who are injured but not killed, so no compilation of statistics of the injured is attempted here.

2.2 Police data

A problem when comparing police figures for different countries is that not all countries use the same time-limit: the most common choice is to say that those dying within 30 days as a result of the accident are to be included in the figures, but that any subsequent deaths are to be excluded. However, the time limit can be as long as 12 months (in the case of some Canadian provinces), or as short as 24 hours (e.g. Japan). Where a country is known to have a definite time-limit in force, its length is indicated in Table 2.1. As the 30 day

limit is widely accepted, it is probable that it is used in many other countries besides those shown. The 30 day limit does not apply to death certification data, to be discussed next; Chapter 11 will go into more detail about this and other differences between the sources.

2.3 Death certification data

As will be discussed in Section 8.3, International Classification of Diseases E codes are used to define categories of external cause of injury. There are three main categories applicable to road trauma: motor vehicle accidents, motor vehicle non-traffic accidents, and other road vehicle accidents. To complicate matters, two Revisions of the ICD are currently in use, the 1965 8th Revision, and the 1975 9th Revision. The most important of the differences between them that concern us is that with the 8th Revision, it is usual for motor vehicle traffic and non-traffic accidents to be treated as one group in the published tables, but with the 9th Revision, it is the number of motor vehicle traffic accidents that is normally given. Hence the coverage is narrower by a few per cent. (For how many per cent, see Table 8.2.)

2.4 Developing countries

Due to a lack of organisation and funding, the data-capture systems of many developing countries are inadequate, resulting in incomplete coverage. (Chapter 5 will take up the issue of developing countries.) Where coverage is known to be patchy (as for Burma, Iran, and Turkey, where only major towns and cities are included), this is indicated in the notes accompanying Table 2.1. Even where there is no indication that coverage is incomplete, the possibility of this being so should be borne in mind when interpreting data from any developing country.

2.5   International compilations

Unfortunately, no worldwide compilations include details of both death certification and police data.

As to data deriving from police reports, there are three main annual publications that reprint official statistics on road accidents from a number of different countries.

Statistics of Road Traffic Accidents in Europe. Published by the U.N. Economic Commission for Europe, Geneva. The edition for 1984 contains information from 27 countries, mostly from Western or Eastern Europe, but including also the U.S.A. The main information given is in two tables:

- The numbers of accidents, according to their nature (6 categories—collision between moving vehicles, collision with pedestrian, single-vehicle accident, etc.), with the numbers occurring in built-up areas being given separately.

- The numbers of persons killed and the numbers injured, classified simultaneously according to their age group (9 categories) and the type of vehicle (if any) they were using (5 categories, plus 4 more not subclassified by casualty age), with the numbers who were drivers being given separately.

Statistical Report on Road Accidents. Published by the European Conference of Ministers of Transport, and distributed by the Organisation for Economic Cooperation and Development Publications Office, Paris. The edition for 1983 contains information from 23 countries, mostly from Western Europe, but including also Australia, Canada, Japan, the U.S.A., and Yugoslavia. There are 11 pages of commentary, plus 10 tables, of which the most detailed classify fatalities and casualties according to the type of vehicle (if any) which they were using.

World Road Statistics. Published by the International Road Federation, Geneva and Washington. The 1984 edition contains accident information from 68 countries. The data given is less detailed than in Statistics of Road Traffic Accidents

in Europe, being confined to little more than the total numbers of killed and injured, and the corresponding rates per 100 million vehicle kilometres travelled. Much of this publication is taken up by statistics on non-safety aspects of roads.

As to data deriving from the death certification process, there are two main international compilations.

Demographic Yearbook. Published by the United Nations, New York. The 1983 edition contains cause-of-death information from 69 countries. The information is confined to the total numbers of road accident fatalities.

World Health Statistics Annual. Published by the World Health Organization, Geneva. The 1986 edition contains cause-of-death information from 49 countries. Road accident fatalities are classified according to their age (11 categories) and sex.

In addition, the following contains a little information from both types of source:

Statistical Yearbook for Asia and the Pacific. Published by the U.N. Economic and Social Commission for Asia and the Pacific, Bangkok. The 1983 edition has entries for 39 countries. Of these, 19 give some road accident data (often, only the total number killed) deriving from the police and/or from death certification.

It is valuable to have two or more sources of statistics: if the numbers of road deaths are similar in both, it does not prove that both are approximately right, but certainly if they are very different it is a warning to investigate why that is so and determine which is the more reliable.

2.6   The Tables

2.6.1   Main Table

Generally, countries are arranged in alphabetical order which, together with their spellings, is based on British Standard BS 5374: 1981, Specification for Codes for the Representation of Names of Countries. Each country is also given a running number; a suffix x merely indicates the country is an extra one added after preparation of the main list.

Where there is a strong connexion between entities (e.g. England, Great Britain, Northern Ireland, Scotland, and Wales with the U.K.), these have been listed together, as have countries (usually dependent territories) whose figures are included in another's national publication.

For each entity, the latest available certification figures and police figures are both included, for two years where possible, as a check on the validity of data collection methods.

Certification figures refer to motor vehicle accidents (usually, using the 8th Revision of the ICD), except where indicated by an asterisk, where they refer to motor vehicle traffic accidents (usually, using the 9th Revision of the ICD).

Where it is known, the police time-limit is stated. (In some cases, the evidence I have for the operation of a 30-day time limit may be no more than the absence of anything to the contrary appearing in Statistics of Road Traffic Accidents in Europe.)

In a few cases, different figures were found in different sources. I have tended to prefer a more recently published figure to an earlier (because the earlier is likely to have been provisional and the later revised), a bigger to a smaller (because I suspect errors of omission to be more likely than errors of commission), and a national source to an international compilation (because the former is closer to the raw data).

The final column indicates the type of publication in which data for each country can be found. Capital letters refer to the international publications, a key for which is given in Section 2.7.1, and lower case letters to national publications. These are categorised into seven types and also have an explanatory key (Section 2.7.2).

Where necessary, notes on certain entries have been included, and these appear at the end of the Table. The reader will appreciate, however, that neither here nor in other tables in this book has it been practicable to include all details on the scope of the statistics or the definitions in use—for these, reference must be made to the primary sources.

The bibliography (Section 2.7) is arranged in the same order as the main table, the number at the beginning of each entry being the same as the running number in the main Table.

2.6.2 Supplementary Tables

There are three of these, which give a slightly more detailed picture than that presented in the main Table.

The first two Tables give details of the ages of those dying in road accidents (for both death certification and police data); four age groups are shown.

The third details the categories of road users killed, derived from police figures. The categories comprise pedestrians, and drivers and passengers of pedal cycles, motor cycles, and motor vehicles. The category "motor cyclists" includes those on mopeds or scooters. The category "motor vehicle occupants" includes those in cars, buses, coaches, and commercial vehicles. (For many countries, it encompasses everyone who was not a pedestrian, pedal cyclist, or motorcyclist.)

2.6.3 Omissions

Even though coverage is greater than for any other compilation, there are omissions. Little data has been found for the U.S.S.R. or the People's Republic of China. Few figures are available for countries which have recently suffered major revolutions or wars, such as Cambodia, Laos, and Vietnam.

2.6.4 An international databank

Bruhning et al (1987) report progress with the establishment of a computerised databank of casualty and exposure-related figures. The countries included: 14 in number (Austria, Belgium, Denmark, Federal Republic of Germany, France, German Democratic Republic, Great Britain, Italy, Japan, The Netherlands, Spain, Sweden, Switzerland, U.S.A.); the years: 1970–86, plus 1965; the data: population (with a breakdown by age groups), vehicles (with a breakdown by type), mileage (classified by network area and vehicle type), injury accidents (classified by network area), fatalities (classified by category of road user, age group, and network area), network length (classified by network area), modal split, area of the state, and various risk values (per population, mileage, and so on).

Section 2.7, the bibliography of sources, follows Table 2.4.

Table 2.1: Total numbers of road deaths.

No.	Country (Certification sources; police sources; police time-limit)	Year	Cert. fig.	Police fig.
1	Afghanistan (J)	1978 1984		100 443
2	Angola (Adf; df)	1972 1973	338 442	574
3	Antigua (B)	1977 1983	1 9*	
4	Argentina (Af)	1980 1981	3783* 3750*	
5	Australia# (ABEbef; DEaef; 30)	1984 1985	2714* 2933*	2821 2942
6	Austria (ABd; CDad; 3)	1984 1985	1816* 1518*	1620 1361
7	Bahamas (ABbd; Id)	1981 1982 1983	20* 42*	32 31
8	Bahrain (d)	1979 1980		84 70
9	Bangladesh# (Edf)	1981 1982		928 1009
10	Barbados (ABf; I)	1983 1984	31* 24*	34
11	Belgium (ABbdf; CDadf; 30)	1983 1984	2271* 1959*	2090 1893
12	Belize (BF; g)	1976 1977 1978 1982	1 12	26 38

Table 2.1: (continued).

No.	Country	Year	Cert. fig.	Police fig.
13	Berkina Faso (D)	1982 1983		51 45
14	Bermuda (BFd)	1975 1978	17 4	
15	Bolivia (Df)	1981 1982		660 629
16	Botswana (D)	1981 1982		96 24
17	Brazil# (Bd; Dad)	1979 1980 1982 1983	20799* 19835*	4056 4209
17x	British Virgin Is. (I)	1983		2
18	Brunei (E; E)	1982 1983 1984	42 25	63 47
19	Bulgaria (ABDd; Dd)	1982 1983 1984	989* 1124*	1229 1123
20	Burma# (BEd)	1977 1978	311 330	
21	Cameroon, United Rep. (Df)	1980 1981		671 781
22	Canada (ABbe; ae; #)	1983 1984	4156* 3973*	4216 4120
23	Cape Verde (ABf)	1975 1980	16 8	
24	Cayman Islands (BF)	1974 1979	11 19	

Table 2.1: (continued).

Table 2.1: (continued).

No.	Country	Year	Cert. fig.	Police fig.
25	Chile	1982	1167*	1274
	(ABd; Dd)	1983	972*	1552
25x	China (People's Rep.)	1986		42000
	Beijing	1982		414
	(g)			
26	Colombia	1975	3274	
	(ABFdf; Ddf)	1977	3676	
		1980		2275
		1981		2383
27	Congo (People's Rep.)			
	(D)	1977		120
28	Cook Islands	1979	6*	
	(#)			
29	Costa Rica	1977		371
	(ABd; ad)	1978		349
		1982	285*	
		1983	200*	
30	Cuba	1976	1134	
	(B)	1977	1484	
31	Cyprus	1983		105
	(CDadf; 30)	1984		111
32	Czechoslovakia	1983	1757*	1605
	(CDd; Ad; 30)	1984	1569*	1466
33	Denmark	1984	662	665
	(ABGbdf;CDGacdf; 30)	1985	763	762
	Faeroe Islands	1983	5	
	(Gbd)	1984	10	
	Greenland	1983	2	
	(Gbd)	1984	6	
34	Dominica	1981	5*	
	(B; I)	1982	5*	
		1983		10#
35	Dominican Republic	1977		185
	(Dd; Dd)	1978	398	
		1980		262
		1982	541*	
36	Ecuador	1978	1817	
	(ABd)	1980	2123*	

No.	Country	Year	Cert. fig.	Police fig.
37	Egypt	1979	1252	
	(ABbd; Dd)	1980	2645*	
		1981		4024
		1982		5092
38	El Salvador	1983	724*	
	(ABdf)	1984	713*	
39	Ethiopia	1982		1029
	(Dd)	1983		1016
40	Falkland Is. (Malvinas)	1974	0	
	(F)	1978	1	
41	Fiji	1978		59
	(AEbd; dg)	1982	41	55
		1983	38	
42	Finland	1983	609	604
	(ABGdf; CDGacdf; 30)	1984	522	541
43	France	1983	10990*	
	(ABf; CDd; 6)	1984	10973*	11525
		1985		10447
44	French Guiana	1977	15*	
	(B)	1979	14*	
45	Gabon	1980		1962
	(Df)	1981		209
46	German Dem. Rep.	1983	1968*	1821
	(ABd; Cd; 30)	1984	1995*	1842
47	Germany, Fed. Rep.	1984	9756	10199
	(ABd; CDad; 30)	1985	7978*	8400
48	Gibraltar	1979	1	
	(#)	1980	0	

Table 2.1: (continued).   Table 2.1: (continued).

No.	Country	Year	Cert. fig.	Police fig.
49	Greece	1983	2164	1586
	(ABdf; CDdf; 3)	1984	2091*	1704
50	Grenada	1977	3	
	(B; I)	1978	4	
		1980		6
51	Guadeloupe	1978	95	
	(A)	1979	31*	
52	Guatemala	1980	1307*	
	(ABd)	1981	916*	
53	Guyana	1983		183
	(I)			
53x	Haiti	1980		1600#
	(I)			
54	Honduras	1977	13	
	(Bd)	1978	16	
55	Hong Kong	1983		340
	(ABE; Daef; 30)	1984	294*	322
		1985	291*	
56	Hungary	1983		1591
	(ABbdf; cdf; 30)	1984	1636*	1590
		1985	1824*	
57	Iceland	1983	21*	
	(ABGfg; CDGfg; 30)	1984	24*	27
		1985		23
58	India#	1982		30010
	(Jdf)	1983		30471
59	Indonesia	1983		10862
	(DJd)	1984		10015
60	Iran#	1983#		2084
	(Bd; J)	1984	1975	
		1985	3341	

No.	Country	Year	Cert. fig.	Police fig.
61	Iraq	1977	68	525
	(df; df)	1979		368
62	Ireland	1983	538*	
	(ABbd; CDad; 30)	1984	488*	
		1985		410
		1986		386
63	Israel#	1983	443*	436
	(ABd; Dadf)	1984	413*	399
	Gaza	1983		59
	(d)	1984		74
	Judea/Samaria	1983		74
	(d)	1984		98
64	Italy	1981	10349*	
	(ABbdf; CDadf; 7)	1983	9977*	7685
		1984		7184
65	Ivory Coast	1981		571
	(Df)	1982		552
66	Jamaica	1970	107	
	(AFd; Id)	1971	153	
		1981		257
		1983		323
67	Japan	1983		9520
	(ABEHbd;DEaf; 24hrs)	1984	12432*	9262
		1985	12456*	
68	Jordan	1978	262	
	(d; Dcd)	1979	232	
		1984		495
		1985		524
69	Kenya	1979	1661	
	(d; Dd)	1980	2228	
		1982		1462
		1983		1515
70	Kiribati	1975		8
	(E)	1976		9
71	Korea, Republic	1984		7468
	(DEJd)	1985		7522
72	Kuwait	1982		402
	(AB; Dd)	1983	416*	330
		1985	464*	

Table 2.1: (continued).

No.	Country	Year	Cert. fig.	Police fig.
73	Lesotho	1982		157
	(Dd)	1983		195
74	Liberia	1980		118
	(D)	1981		97
75	Libyan Arab Jamahiriya	1978		1262
	(ad)	1979		1171
76	Liechtenstein	1978	6	13
	(d; d)	1983		5
77	Luxembourg	1984	71*	70
	(ABd; CDad; 30)	1985	84*	108
78	Macau	1979	11	
	(df; f)	1982	18	
		1985		12
		1986		11
79	Malawi	1977		303
	(g)			
80	Malaysia			
	Peninsular	1983	634	2282
	(EH; Dafg)	1984	650*	3344
	Sabah	1982	211	
	(EH; Dafg)	1983	243	174
		1984		150
	Sarawak	1982	24	
	(EH; Dafg)	1983	37	101
		1984		143
81	Malta	1983		18
	(ABdf; df; 30)	1984	6*	17
		1985	8*	
82	Martinique	1968		39
	(A; #)	1981	6*	
		1982	24*	
83	Mauritius	1982		99
	(AB; Dd)	1983		101
		1984	10*	
		1985	18*	
84	Mexico	1980		8266
	(Ad; d)	1981	17242*	
		1982	15722*	

Table 2.1: (continued).

No.	Country	Year	Cert. fig.	Police fig.
85	Morocco	1982		2232
	(Dd)	1983		2108
86	Mozambique	1974	31	50
	(f; a)	1975	24	25
87	Nepal	1984		177
	(J)			
88	Netherlands	1983	1689*	1756
	(ABbd; CDad; 30)	1984	1625*	1615
89	Netherlands Antilles	1976		51
	(B; d)	1977		53
		1981	13*	
	Aruba	1976		34
	(d)	1977		19
	Curacao	1976		17
	(d)	1977		34
90	New Zealand	1983	625*	644
	(ABEbe; DEacde; 30)	1984	681*	668
91	Nicaragua	1977	394	
	(f)	1978	168	
92	Niger	1982		167
	(Dad)	1983		112
93	Nigeria	1979	6375	
	(g; Dadfg)	1980	7197	
		1984		8830
		1985		9221
94	Niue	1975	2	
	(g)	1979	1*	
95	Norway	1983	428	409
	(ABGbd; CDGacd; 30)	1984	445	407
96	Oman	1980		376
	(d)	1981		406

Table 2.1: (continued).   Table 2.1: (continued).

No.	Country	Year	Cert. fig.	Police fig.
97	Pakistan	1983		4434
	(Da)	1984		4721
98	Panama	1982		299
	(ABd; Dad)	1983	352*	
		1984	346*	
99	Papua New Guinea	1980	26*	269
	(B; J)	1981		291
100	Paraguay	1980		241
	(ABd; d)	1983	178*	
		1984	201*	
101	Peru	1977	909	
	(ABd)	1978	889	
102	Philippines	1978	2284	
	(ABEHd; DJd)	1980	2093*	
		1982		1288
		1984		1119
103	Poland	1982		5535
	(ABdf; Cdf; 30)	1983	5953*	5561
		1984	5393*	
104	Portugal	1984	2749	1902
	(ABd; CDd; #)	1985	2597*	1946
	Azores	1981		35
	(d)			
	Madeira	1981		44
	(d)			
105	Reunion	1969	82	
	(A)			
106	Romania	1982		1624
	(C; 30)	1983		1510
107	St. Helena	1978	1	
	(#)	1979	2	
108	St. Kitts-Nevis-Anguilla	1982	1*	
	(B; Ig)	1983	9*	4

No.	Country	Year	Cert. fig.	Police fig.
109	Saint Lucia	1980	3*	
	(B)	1981	17*	
110	St. Vincent/Grenadines	1978	2	
	(Bd; d)	1979	2	
		1981		9
		1982		10
111	Samoa	1978		34
	(E; E)	1979		18
		1981	1	
		1982	12	
112	San Marino	1979	9	
	(d)	1980	4	
113	Saudi Arabia	1982#		2953
	(Dd)	1983#		2900
114	Senegal	1980		429
	(Df)	1981		160
115	Seychelles	1975		10
	(B; g)	1976		7
		1981	7*	
		1982	6*	
116	Sierra Leone	1977		131
	(f)	1978		156
117	Singapore	1983		298
	(ABEHdf; EJdf)	1984	343*	327
		1985	292*	
118	Solomon Islands	1977	33	
	(g; E)	1981		16
		1982		2
119	South Africa#	1978	4506	
	(ADb; Dadef)	1983		9121
		1984		9621
120	Spain	1979	6562	
	(ABd; CDad; 24 hrs)	1980	6146*	
		1983		4666
		1984		4827

Table 2.1: (continued).

Table 2.1: (continued).

No.	Country	Year	Cert. fig.	Police fig.
121	Sri Lanka	1980	629*	1106
	(E; Eacg)	1981	799*	1247
122	Suriname	1981	55*	
	(B; I)	1982	69*	
		1983		71
123	Swaziland	1977		140
	(d)	1978		152
124	Sweden	1983	804	779
	(ABGbdf; CDGadf; 30)	1984	833	801
125	Switzerland	1984	1109	1097
	(ABd; CDad; 1 year)	1985	924	908
126	Syrian Arab Republic	1976		1373
	(Bd; d)	1977		1320
		1980	177*	
		1981	155*	
127	Taiwan, Prov. of China	1984		3540
	(Df)	1985		3564
128	Tanzania	1979		1016
	(g)	1980		1007
129	Thailand	1984	5655*	2772
	(BEHd; DEJdf)	1985	4315*	2700
130	Togo	1982		186
	(Df)	1983		142
130x	Tokelau	1982	0	
	(g)			
131	Trinidad and Tobago	1974	217	
	(ABbd; d)	1977	238	
		1982		259
		1983		224
132	Tunisia	1984		996
	(Ddf)	1985		1114

No.	Country	Year	Cert. fig.	Police fig.
133	Turkey#	1978	2184	
	(Bd; CDad; 30)	1979	1562	
		1983		5200
		1984		5677
134	Turks and Caicos Is.	1973	3	
	(Fd)			
134x	Tuvalu	1982	0	
	(g)			
135	United Arab Emirates	1978		352
	(d)	1979		384
	Abu Dhabi	1978		199
	(d)	1979		200
	Ajman	1979		7
	(d)			
	Dubai	1979		81
	(d)			
	Fujeira	1979		20
	(d)			
	Ras Al-khaima	1979		22
	(d)			
	Sharjah	1979		46
	(d)			
	Umm Al Qiwain	1979		8
	(d)			
136	United Kingdom	1983		5618
	(CDadf; 30)	1984		5788
	Channel Islands	1978	8	
	(Adf)	1979	9	
	England and Wales	1983		4820
	(ABbdf; adf; 30)	1984	5090	5000
		1985	4914	
	Great Britain	1984		5599
	(adf; 30)	1985		5165
	Guernsey	1983	6	6
	(A; #; 30)	1984	5	5
	Jersey	1983	3	11
	(A; g; 30)	1984	3	2
	Isle of Man	1979	9	
	(A; #)	1980	23	
		1984		13
		1985		11
	Northern Ireland	1982		216
	(ABdf; adf; 30)	1983		173
		1984	178	
		1985	197	
	Scotland	1983		625
	(ABbdf; adf; 30)	1984	612	599
		1985	609	

Table 2.1: (continued).

No.	Country	Year	Cert. fig.	Police fig.
137	United States of America (ABbd; CDad; 30)	1982	44713*	
		1983	43428*	
		1984		44241
		1985		43795
	American Samoa	1979		18
	(Eg; Eg)	1981	1	
		1982	12	
	Guam	1983	29	
	(Ad)	1984	25	
	Pacific Islands (A)	1978	12	
	Puerto Rico	1982	487*	480
	(ABd; a)	1983	533*	514
	U.S. Virgin Islands	1973	16	
	(F)	1977	19	
138	Uruguay	1983	296*	
	(Ad)	1984	269*	
138x	U.S.S.R.	1986		39000
	Latvia	1983		650
	(g)			
139	Venezuela	1980	5211*	
	(Af)	1983	4801*	
140	Yemen, North	1982		641
	(D)	1983		738
141	Yugoslavia	1981	5030*	
	(ABd; CDd; 30)	1982	4772*	
		1983		4517
		1984		4501
142	Zaire	1976		252
	(g)	1977		217
143	Zambia	1982		750
	(f)	1983		747
144	Zimbabwe	1979	790	
	(Af; af)	1982		977
		1983		1038

* Motor vehicle traffic accidents (E810–E819) tabulated, 9th Revision of ICD used.

See numbered country note below:

5 As for many other countries, Australian death statistics are normally tabulated by year of registration, not year of occurrence of death. The certification figures for 1984 and 1985 were respectively artificially depressed and raised by small amounts, owing to abnormal delays in the registration process in New South Wales in 1984, the backlog being cleared in 1985. The number of motor vehicle traffic accident deaths occurring in 1984 was 2837 according to the registration authorities.

9 According to WHO (1983b), "the annual number of road deaths appears to be approximately 3000; the numbers of casualties is not clear because of the absence of satisfactory recording systems".

17 Under-reporting of certification figures varies from region to region. Police figures refer to accidents on Federal roads only, perhaps 10% of the total.

20 Figures refer to main towns and cities only.

22 Police time-limit generally 12 months, with the exception of Quebec (7 days), Newfoundland, Ontario, and Saskatchewan (30 days in each case).

28 Bibliographic details not known.

34 The figure marked # is stated to be approximate.

48 Bibliographic details not known.

53x The figure marked # is stated to be approximate.

58 Absurdly low certification figures not included. Police figure also unreliable.

60 Figures are for cities only. Police data is for 21.3.83 to 21.3.84.

63 Certification figures include East Jerusalem and the Golan sub-district.

82 Bibliographic details not known.

104 Police figures are for deaths at scene of accident or immediately after.

107 Bibliographical details not known.

113 Police figures are for 1402AH to 1403AH. (1402AH began 28.10.81.)

119 Publications do not state whether tribal homelands are or are not excluded from the figures.

133 Certification figures are for provincial capitals and district centres only.

134 Police figures for Guernsey and the Isle of Man were supplied in unpublished form by the relevant police authorities.

Table 2.2: Numbers of road deaths by age group, according to death registration authorities. (Totals include casualties of unknown age.)

No.	Country	Year	Total	0-14	Age group 15-24	25-64	65+
4	Argentina	1981	3750*	482	581	2051	593
5	Australia	1985	2933*	248	1033	1260	392
6	Austria	1985	1518*	79	523	606	310
7	Bahamas	1983	42*	5	14	19	4
10	Barbados	1984	24*	3	4	14	3
11	Belgium	1984	1959*	126	534	899	400
12	Belize	1982	12*	3	2	6	1
17	Brazil	1980	19835*	2886	6336	8649	1763
19	Bulgaria	1984	1124*	110	147	642	225
20	Burma	1977	330	61	64	155	24
22	Canada	1984	3973*	307	1337	1844	481
23	Cape Verde	1980	8	3	2	3	0
25	Chile	1983	972*	128	174	573	95
26	Columbia	1977	3676	779	700	1849	319
29	Costa Rica	1983	200*	24	45	106	24
30	Cuba	1977	1484	183	243	847	210
32	Czechoslovakia	1984	1569*	123	244	857	345
33	Denmark	1985	763	71	205	311	176
	Faeroe Islands	1984	10	1	... 7 ...		2
	Greenland	1984	6	1	... 5 ...		0
35	Dominican Republic	1982	541*	78	116	263	81
36	Ecuador	1980	2123*	394	396	1068	247
37	Egypt	1980	2645*	613	424	1505	103
38	El Salvador	1984	713*	116	119	371	95
41	Fiji	1978	28	7	8	12	1
42	Finland	1984	522	43	107	213	159
43	France	1984	10973*	627	3089	5429	1828
46	German Dem. Rep.	1984	1995*	130	599	835	431
47	Germany, Fed. Rep.	1985	7978*	437	2682	3221	1638
49	Greece	1984	2091*	126	526	1038	401

Table 2.2: (continued).

No.	Country	Year	Total	0-14	15-24	25-64	65+
					Age group		
52	Guatemala	1981	916*	123	192	507	88
54	Honduras	1978	16	1	2	10	3
55	Hong Kong	1985	291*	24	47	125	95
56	Hungary	1985	1824*	102	312	980	430
57	Iceland	1984	24*	3	6	10	5
60	Iran	1981	2874	497	608	1437	272
62	Ireland	1983	538*	51	181	198	108
63	Israel	1984	413*	55	86	175	97
64	Italy	1983	9977*	578	2301	4703	2395
67	Japan	1985	12456*	724	3142	5660	2923
68	Jordan	1979	232	51	36	116	25
72	Kuwait	1985	464*	108	61	268	17
77	Luxembourg	1985	84*	4	33	35	12
80	Malaysia						
	Peninsular	1979	284	44	71	131	33
	Sabah	1977	70	4	14	46	5
81	Malta	1985	8*	1	3	2	2
82	Martinique	1982	24*	3	6	15	0
83	Mauritius	1985	18*	2	3	12	1
84	Mexico	1982	15722*	2646	3629	7609	1500
88	Netherlands	1984	1625*	131	445	648	401
90	New Zealand	1984	681*	66	285	243	87
91	Nicaragua	1978	168	24	35	95	8
95	Norway	1984	445	36	141	149	119
98	Panama	1984	346*	34	68	190	46
100	Paraguay	1984	201*	32	46	99	20
101	Peru	1978	889	167	145	452	77
102	Philippines	1977	2045	526	402	917	179
103	Poland	1984	5393*	436	909	3098	950
104	Portugal	1985	2597*	206	592	1310	489

Table 2.2: (continued).

No.	Country	Year	Total	Age group 0-14	15-24	25-64	65+
109	Saint Lucia	1980	3*	0	1	1	1
112	San Marino	1980	4	0	0	2	2
117	Singapore	1985	292*	7	80	152	49
120	Spain	1980	6146*	551	1337	3114	1143
121	Sri Lanka	1977	432	78	74	218	62
122	Suriname	1982	69*	19	13	29	8
124	Sweden	1984	833	55	223	317	238
125	Switzerland	1985	924	63	266	369	226
126	Syrian Arab Republic	1981	155*	51	24	66	14
129	Thailand	1985	4315*	456	1210	2347	238
131	Trinidad and Tobago	1977	238	33	53	121	31
133	Turkey	1979	1562	311	239	815	169
136	United Kingdom						
	Great Britain	1984	5789*	531	1759	2145	1354
	Jersey	1984	3	0	2	0	1
	Northern Ireland	1985	195*	33	65	73	24
	Scotland	1985	609*	64	155	249	141
137	United States of America						
		1983	43428*	3172	14067	20650	5513
	Guam	1984	25	1	13	11	0
	Puerto Rico	1983	533*	45	117	278	90
138	Uruguay	1984	269*	23	47	145	52
139	Venezuela	1983	4801*	679	1392	2393	320
141	Yugoslavia	1982	4772*	383	736	2867	781

* Motor vehicle traffic accidents (E810–E819) tabulated, 9th Revision of ICD used.

Table 2.3: Numbers of road deaths by age group, according to the police. (Totals include casualties of unknown age.)

No.	Country	Year	Total	Age group			
				0-14	15-24	25-64	65+
5	Australia	1985	2942	326*	1041*	1087*	483*
6	Austria	1985	1361	84	473	555	232
11	Belgium	1984	1893	114	530	872	354
17	Brazil	1983	4209	540*	949*	1970*	165*
22	Canada	1984	4120	315	1369	1900	471
31	Cyprus	1984	111	4	29	51	27
32	Czechoslovakia	1984	1466	109	246	796	305
33	Denmark	1985	772	71	215	326	160
39	Ethiopia	1975/76	925	120*	.. 721* ..		84*
42	Finland	1984	541	39	107	234	161
43	France	1985	10447	616	2963	5266	1540
46	German Dem. Rep.	1984	1842	126	563	756	385
47	Germany, Fed. Rep.	1984	10199	563	3476	3957	2200
49	Greece	1983	1586	89	379	820	292
55	Hong Kong	1984	322	31	46	155	90
56	Hungary	1984	1590	90	261	915	324
57	Iceland	1984	27	3	10	8	6
62	Ireland	1985	410	49	133	152	64
63	Israel	1984	399	55	.. 220 ..		80
64	Italy	1983	7685	388	1849	3561	1508
67	Japan	1983	9520	790	2464	4340	1926
71	Korea, Republic	1985	7522	1619	1045	4130*	728*
72	Kuwait	1978	380	95	55	205	25
77	Luxembourg	1984	70	2	24	34	10
80	Malaysia	1983	2557	368*	849*	1062*	278*
	Peninsular	1983	2282	322*	766*	932*	262*
	Sabah	1983	174	32*	54*	78*	10*
	Sarawak	1983	101	14*	29*	52*	6*
81	Malta	1984	17	2	3	3	4
88	Netherlands	1984	1615	133	458	651	373

Table 2.3: (continued).

No.	Country	Year	Total	Age group			
				0-14	15-24	25-64	65+
90	New Zealand	1984	668	64	287	231	79
95	Norway	1984	407	36	138	137	96
102	Philippines	1984	1119	45	218	804	52
103	Poland	1983	5561	428	988	3268	877
106	Romania	1983	1510	230	154	883	243
119	South Africa	1978	6550	893*	1634*	3675*	343*
120	Spain	1984	4827	300	1256	2561	625
124	Sweden	1984	801	49	223	307	222
125	Switzerland	1985	908	54	264	383	207
133	Turkey	1983	5200	1086	716	2427	320
136	United Kingdom	1984	5788	555	1795	2154	1246
	Great Britain	1984	5599	521	1735	2079	1226
	Northern Ireland	1982	216	32	71	83	30
137	United States of America						
		1985	43795	3124	13845	20995	5555
141	Yugoslavia	1984	4501	369	650	2270	464

* Variations in age groups tabulated:

- Australia 0–16, 17–25, 26–59, 60 and over;

- Brazil 0–17, 18–27, 28–67, 68 and over;

- Ethiopia 1–16, 17–50, 51 and over;

- Korea, Republic 25–60, 61 and over;

- Malaysia 0–15, 16–25, 26–60, 60 and over;

- South Africa 0–13, 14–24, 25–59, 60 and over.

Table 2.4: Numbers of road deaths to the several categories of road user, according to the police.

No.	Country	Year	Total	Motor vehicle occs.	Motor cyc- lists	Pedal cyc- lists	Pedes- trians
5	Australia	1985	2942	1906	405	83	538
6	Austria	1985	1361	740	253	88	280
7	Bahamas	1982	32	10	3	3	16
11	Belgium	1984	1893	1112	243	204	334
17	Brazil	1983	4209	. . .	2853	. . .	1356
22	Canada	1984	4120	2986	420	122	592
31	Cyprus	1984	111	55	24	3	29
32	Czechoslovakia	1984	1466	623	154	165	524
33	Denmark	1984	665	340	99	98	128
42	Finland	1984	541	259	47	86	148
43	France	1985	10447	6857	1607	426	1557
46	German Dem. Rep.	1984	1842	562	561	169	550
47	Germany, Fed. Rep.	1984	10199	5406	1548	979	2266
49	Greece	1983	1586	776	357	18	435
53	Guyana	1977	219	70	21	29	99
55	Hong Kong	1984	322	86	18	21	197
56	Hungary	1984	1590	555	234	208	573
57	Iceland	1984	27	19	0	1	7
59	Indonesia	1977	6432	2864	2165	112	1291
62	Ireland	1985	410	183	50	39	138
63	Israel	1984	399	201*	9*	9	180
64	Italy	1983	7685	4003	1670	573	1432
66	Jamaica	1977	380	127	60	20	173
67	Japan	1984	9262	3417	2322	947	2576
77	Luxembourg	1984	70	50*	4*	0	13
79	Malawi	1977	303	133	13	36	121
80	Malaysia	1983	2557	718	1044	284	511
	Peninsular	1983	2282	589	999	262	432
	Sabah	1983	174	98	17	3	56
	Sarawak	1983	101	31	28	19	23

Table 2.4: (continued).

No.	Country	Year	Total	Motor vehicle occs.	Motor cyc- lists	Pedal cyc- lists	Pedes- trians
81	Malta	1984	17	5	5	0	7
87	Nepal	1984	177	89	49	29	10
88	Netherlands	1984	1615	818	225	360	212
90	New Zealand	1984	668	393	125	31	119
95	Norway	1984	407	241	42	19	105
102	Philippines	1984	1119	561	181	65	312
103	Poland	1983	5561	1802	1026	380	2353
104	Portugal	1970	1702	438	613	115	536
106	Romania	1983	1510	474	44	185	788
108	St. Kitts-Nevis-Anguilla	1971	9	1	0	0	8
110	St. Vincent/Grenadines	1979	8	6	0	0	2
117	Singapore	1984	327	71	116	26	114
119	South Africa	1984	9621	4558*	377*	375	4311
120	Spain	1984	4827	3157	544	102	1024
121	Sri Lanka	1980	1106	306	114	110	563
124	Sweden	1984	801	431	107	111	152
125	Switzerland	1985	908	442	215	60	191
133	Turkey	1980	3722	2194	41	28	1445
136	United Kingdom	1984	5788	2506	985	358	1932
	England and Wales	1983	4820	1966	899	299	1656
	Great Britain	1985	5165	2294	796	286	1789
	Guernsey	1984	5	1	3	0	1
	Northern Ireland	1982	216	119	21	9	67
137	United States of America						
		1985	43795	31452	4570	890	6800
141	Yugoslavia	1984	4501	2413	273	357	1418
143	Zambia	1977	750	370	22	61	297

* Non-standard categories: for Israel, Luxembourg, and South Africa, motorcycle passengers have been included with motor vehicle occupants, not with motorcyclists.

2.7 Bibliography of sources

2.7.1 International compilations

A. Demographic Yearbook. New York: United Nations.

B. World Health Statistics Annual. Geneva: World Health Organization.

C. Statistics of Road Traffic Accidents in Europe. Annual. Geneva: United Nations Economic Commission for Europe.

D. World Road Statistics. Annual. Geneva and Washington, D.C.: International Road Federation.

E. Statistical Yearbook for Asia and the Pacific. Bangkok: United Nations Economic and Social Commission for Asia and the Pacific.

F. Health Conditions in the Americas 1973-1976. (Scientific Publication No. 364.) Washington, D.C.: Pan-American Health Organization.

G. Yearbook of Nordic Statistics. Stockholm: Nordic Council, and Copenhagen: Nordic Statistical Secretariat.

H. SEAMIC Health Statistics. Tokyo: Southeast Asian Medical Information Center.

I. Joint HQ/PAHO Workshop on the Prevention and Care of Motor Vehicle Injuries in the Caribbean. Report on a WHO meeting, held at Bridgetown, June 1984. World Health Organization.

J. United Nations Economic and Social Commission for Asia and the Pacific Seminar on Road Traffic Accident Recording and Analysis, held in Bangkok, 1985.

2.7.2 National publications

Classification:
a. Road accident statistics.
b. Vital statistics.
c. Transport statistics.
d. Statistics annual of a general nature.
e. Yearbook, primarily descriptive rather than statistical in nature.
f. Quarterly or monthly statistical summary.
g. Other.

2 d Annario Estatistico/Annuaire Statistique [Statistical Yearbook]. Luanda: Direccao dos Servicos de Estatistica.

  f Boletim Mensal [Monthly Bulletin]. ibid.

4 f Boletin de Estadistica [Statistical Bulletin]. Buenos Aires: Dirrecion General de Estadistica y Censos.

5 a Road Traffic Accidents Involving Fatalities, Australia. Monthly. Canberra: Australian Bureau of Statistics.

  a Road Traffic Accidents Involving Casualties (Admissions to Hospitals), Australia. Quarterly. ibid.

  b Causes of Death, Australia. Annual. ibid.

  e Yearbook Australia. ibid.

  f Monthly Summary of Statistics. ibid.

6 a Strassenverkehrsunfalle mit Personenschaden [Traffic Accidents Involving Personal Injury]. Annual. Vienna: Osterreichisches Statistisches Zentralamt.

  d Statistiches Handbuch fur die Republik Osterreich [Statistical Handbook for the Austrian Republic]. Annual. ibid.

7 b Commonwealth of the Bahamas Vital Statistics Report. Annual. Nassau: Department of Statistics, Ministry of Finance.

  d Commonwealth of the Bahamas Statistical Abstract. ibid.

8 d Statistical Abstract. Annual. Manama: Directorate of Statistics, Ministry of State for Cabinet Affairs.

9 d Statistical Digest of Bangladesh. Annual. Dacca: Bureau of Statistics.

  f Monthly Statistical Bulletin of Bangladesh. ibid.

10 f Quarterly Digest of Statistics. St. Michael: Statistical Service.

11 a Accidents de la Circulation sur la Voie Publique avec Tues ou Blesses [Accidents on the Public Roads Resulting in Death or Injury]. Annual. Brussels: Institut National de Statistique.

  b Statistique des Causes de Deces [Statistics of Causes of Death]. ibid.

d Annuaire Statistique de la Belgique [Statistical Yearbook of Belgium]. ibid.

d Annuaire Statistique de Poche. [Pocket Yearbook]. ibid.

f Bulletin de Statistique [Statistical Bulletin]. Monthly. ibid.

12 g Traffic and Transport in Belize: A Report to the Permanent Secretary of the Ministry of Energy and Communications of Belize. London: Richard Barrett Traffic and Transportation Associates, 1980.

14 d Annual Abstract of Statistics. London, Bermuda: Central Statistical Office.

15 f Boletin Estadistico [Statistical Bulletin]. La Paz: Instituto Nacional du Estadistica.

17 a Anuario Estatistico de Acidentes de Transito [year] [Statistical Yearbook of Transport Accidents]. Rio de Janeiro: Departamento Nacional de Estradas de Rodagem, Diretoria de Transito.

d Anuario Estadistico do Brasil [Statistical Yearbook of Brazil]. Brasilia: Instituto Brasileiro de Estatistica.

19 d Statistical Yearbook. Sofia: Central Statistical Office of the Council of Ministers.

20 d Statistical Yearbook. Rangoon: Central Statistical and Economic Department.

21 f Bulletin Mensuel de Statistique [Monthly Bulletin of Statistics]. Yaounde: Direction de la Statistique et de la Comptabilite Nationale.

22 a Motor Vehicle Traffic Accidents. Annual. Ottawa: Statistics Canada Transport and Communications Division.

b Causes of Death. Annual. Ottawa: Statistics Canada Health Division, Statistics and Disease Registration Section.

e Canada Yearbook. Annual. Ottawa: Ministry of Supply and Services.

23 f Boletim Trimestral de Estatistica [Quarterly Bulletin of Statistics]. Praia: Servicos de Administracao Civil, Seccao de Estatistica.

25 d Sintesis Estadistica [Statistical Survey]. Annual. Santiago: Division Biblioteca y Informaciones.

25x g News item in The Advertiser (Adelaide), 9.June.87, derived from an Associated Press despatch.

g Report on the Seminar on the Prevention of Road Traffic Accidents, held in Manila, February 1983. Manila: Regional Office for the Western Pacific of the World Health Organization.

26 d Anuario General de Estadistica [Annual General Statistics]. Bogota: Departmento Administrativo Nacional de Estadistica.

f Boletin Mensual de Estadistica [Monthly Bulletin of Statistics]. ibid.

29 a Accidentes de Transito en Costa Rica. [Traffic Accidents in Costa Rica]. Bi-annual. San Jose: Direccion General de Estadistica y Censos and Instituto Nacional de Seguros.

d Anuario Estadistico de Costa Rica [Statistical Yearbook of Costa Rica]. San Jose: Direccion General de Estadistica y Censos.

31 a Statistics of Motor Vehicles and Road Accidents. Nicosia: Statistics Research Department, Ministry of Finance.

d Statistical Abstract. Annual. ibid.

f Quarterly Statistical Digest. ibid.

32 d Statisticka Rocenka Ceskoslovenske Socialisticke Republiky [Statistical Yearbook of the Socialist Republic of Czechoslovakia]. Prague: Federalini Statisticky Urad.

33 a Faerdselsuheld [Road Traffic Accidents]. Annual. Copenhagen: Danmarks Statistik.

b Befolkningens Bevaegelser [Vital Statistics]. ibid.

b Dodsarsagerne i Kongeriget Danmark [Deaths in the Kingdom of Denmark]. Annual. Copenhagen: Sundhedsstyrelsen.

c Vejtransporten i Tal og Tekst. [Road Transport in Facts and Figures]. Annual. Automobil-Importorernes.

d Statistisk Arbog [Statistical Yearbook]. Copenhagen: Danmarks Statistik.

f Statistisk Manedsuversigt [Monthly Review of Statistics]. ibid.

35 d Republica Dominica en Cifras [Dominican Republic in Figures]. Annual. Santo Domingo: Oficina Nacional de Estadistica.

36 d Cuadernos de Estadistica. Quito: Direccion General de Estadistica y Censos.

37 b Vital Statistics. Annual. Cairo: Department of Statistics and Census.

d Annuaire Statistique [Statistical Yearbook]. ibid.

38 d Anuario Estadistico [Statistical Yearbook]. San Salvador: Direccion General de Estadistica y Censos.

f Boletin Estadistico [Statistical Bulletin]. Quarterly. ibid.

39 d Ethiopia Statistical Abstract. Annual. Addis Ababa: Central Statistical Office.

41 b Vital Statistics in Fiji (Statistics of Births, Deaths and Marriages). Occasional. Suva: Bureau of Statistics.

d Annual Statistical Abstract. ibid.

g Report of the Seminar on the Prevention of Road Traffic Accidents, held in Manila, February 1983. Manila: Regional Office for the Western Pacific of the World Health Organization.

42 a Road Traffic Accidents [year]. Annual. Helsinki: Central Statistical Office of Finland.

c Auto ja Tie: Tilastoa [Automobiles and Highways in Finland: Statistics]. Annual. Helsinki: Suomen Tieyhdistys.

d Suomen Tilastollinen Vuostikirja [Statistical Yearbook of Finland]. Helsinki: Tilastokeskus.

f Tilastokatsavksia [Bulletin of Statistics]. Quarterly. ibid.

43 d Annuaire Statistique de la France [Statistical Yearbook of France]. Paris: Institut National de Statistique et des Etudes Economique.

f Bulletin Mensuel de Statistique [Monthly Bulletin of Statistics]. ibid.

45 f Bulletin Mensuel de Statistique [Monthly Bulletin of Statistics]. Libreville: Service National de la Statistique.

46 d Statistisches Jahrbuch der Deutschen Demokratischen Republik [Statistical Yearbook of the German Democratic Republic]. Berlin: Central Statistical Board.

d Statistical Pocket Book of the German Democratic Republic. Annual. ibid.

47 a Verkehr. Reihe 3: Strassenverkehr. 3: Strassenverkehrsunfalle [Transport. Series 3: Road Transport. 3: Road Accidents]. Monthly and annual. Wiesbaden: Statistisches Bundesamt.

d Statistisches Jahrbuch fur die Bundesrepublik Deutschland [Statistical Yearbook of the Federal Republic of Germany]. ibid.

49 d Statistical Yearbook of Greece. Athens: National Statistical Service of Greece.

f Monthly Statistical Bulletin. ibid.

52 d Guatemala en Cifras [Guatemala in Figures]. Annual. Guatemala City: Direccion General de Estadistica.

54 d Annuario Estadistico [Statistical Yearbook]. Tegucigalpa: Dirrecion de Estadisticas y Censos.

55 a Annual Traffic Accident Report. Hong Kong: Royal Hong Kong Police.

e Hong Kong [year]: A Review of [previous year]. Annual. Victoria: Hong Kong Government Information Services.

f Hong Kong Monthly Digest of Statistics. Victoria: Census and Statistical Department.

56 b Demografiai Evkonyv. Annual. Budapest: Kozponti Statistikai Hivatal.

c Transport and Communications Yearbook. Budapest: Central Statistical Office.

d Statistical Pocket Book of Hungary. Annual. ibid.

d Statistical Yearbook. ibid.

f Monthly Statistical Bulletin. ibid.

57 f Statistical Bulletin. Monthly. Reykjavik: Icelandic Statistical Office.

g Hagitiundi [Statistical Journal]. Annual. ibid.

58 d Statistical Abstract: India. Annual. Delhi: Manager of Publications.

f Monthly Abstract of Statistics. ibid.

59 d Statistik Indonesia. Annual. Jakarta: Biro Pusat Statistik.

60 d Statistical Yearbook. Tehran: Iranian Statistical Center.

61 d Statistical Abstract. Annual. Baghdad: Ministry of Planning, Central Statistical Organisation.

f Quarterly Bulletin of Statistics. ibid.

62 a Road Accident Facts [year]. Annual. Dublin: An Garda Siochan.

b Vital Statistics. Annual. Dublin: Central Statistical Office.

d Statistical Abstract of Ireland. Annual. ibid.

63 a Road Accidents with Casualties. Annual. Jerusalem: Central Bureau of Statistics and Economic Research.

d Statistical Abstract of Israel. Annual. ibid.

f Statistical Bulletin of Israel. Monthly. ibid.

64 a Statistica degli Incidenti Stradali [Statistics of Road Accidents]. Annual. Rome: Istituto Centrale di Statistica.

b Annuario di Statistiche Sanitarie [Yearbook of Health Statistics]. ibid.

d Annuario Statistico Italiano. [Statistical Yearbook of Italy]. ibid.

d Compendio Statistico Italiano [Compendium of Italian Statistics]. Annual. ibid.

f Bollettino Mensile di Statistica [Monthly Bulletin of Statistics]. ibid.

65 f Bulletin Mensuel de Statistique [Monthly Bulletin of Statistics]. Abidjan: Direction de la Statistique.

66 d Statistical Yearbook of Jamaica. Kingston: Department of Statistics.

67 a Statistics [year]. Road Accidents Japan. Annual. Tokyo: International Association of Traffic and Safety Sciences.

b Vital Statistics Japan. Volume 3. Annual. Tokyo: Ministry of Health and Welfare.

d Statistical Abstract. Annual. Tokyo: Statistics Bureau of the Prime Minister's Office.

d Statistical Yearbook. Tokyo: Statistics Bureau, Management and Coordination Agency.

f Monthly Bulletin of Statistics. Tokyo: Statistics Bureau.

68 c Transport Statistics. Annual. Amman: Traffic Department.

d Statistical Yearbook. Amman: Department of Statistics.

69 d Statistical Abstract. Annual. Nairobi: Central Bureau of Statistics.

71 d Korea Statistical Yearbook. Seoul: Government Publications Centre.

72 d Annual Abstract of Statistics. Kuwait: Central Statistical Office.

73 d Annual Statistical Bulletin. Maseru: Bureau of Statistics.

75 a Statistics of Road Accidents. Annual. Tripoli: Secretariat of the Interior, Department of Traffic and Licences.

d Statistical Abstract. Annual. Tripoli: Census and Statistical Department.

76 d Statistiches Jahrbuch: Furstentum Liechtenstein. Annual. Vaduz: Amt. fur Volkswirtschaft.

77 a Les Accidents Caporels de la Circulation Routiere: Indicateur Rapide, Serie F [Road Accidents: Information Bulletin, Series F]. Monthly. Luxembourg: Service Central de la Statistique et des Etudes Economiques.

d Annuire Statistique du Luxembourg [Statistical Yearbook of Luxembourg]. ibid.

78 d Anuario Estatistico [Statistical Yearbook]. Macau: Reparticao dos Servicos de Estatistica.

f Boletim Mensal de Estatisticas [Monthly Bulletin of Statistics]. ibid.

79 g Annual Report of the Malawi Police Force. Zamba: Government Printer.

80 a Statistical Report: Road Accidents West Malaysia. Annual. Kuala Lumpur: Traffic Branch, Royal Malaysia Police.

f West Malaysia Statistical Bulletin. Monthly. Kuala Lumpur: Department of Statistics.

g Low Yew Hong (1985). General situation on road traffic accidents in Malaysia and police/rtd enforcement in relation to road safety. In Proceedings of National Workshop on the Prevention and Control of Road Traffic Accidents in Malaysia, pp. 60–70. Kuala Lumpur: Ministry of Health.

81 d Annual Abstract of Statistics. Valletta: Central Office of Statistics, Information Division.

f Quarterly Digest of Statistics. ibid.

83 d Bi-annual Digest of Statistics. Port Louis: Central Statistical Office.

84 d Annuario Estadistico de Los Estados Unidos Mexicanos [Statistical Yearbook of the United States of Mexico]. Mexico City: Dirrecion General de Estadistica.

85 d Annuaire Statistique du Maroc [Statistical Year Book of Morocco]. Rabat: Division du Plan et des Statistiques.

86 a Estatisticas dos Veiculos Automoveis [Statistics of Motor Vehicles]. Annual. Laurenco Marques [now Maputo]: Dirrecao dos Servicos de Estatistica.

f Boletim Mensal de Estatistica [Monthly Bulletin of Statistics]. ibid.

N.B. Both the above ceased publication after the cessation of Portuguese rule.

88 a Statistiek van de Verkeersongevallen op de Openbare Weg [Statistics of Road Traffic Accidents]. Annual. The Hague: Centraal Bureau voor Statistiek.

b Monthly Bulletin of Health Statistics. ibid.

d Statistisch Zakboek [Statistical Yearbook]. ibid.

89 d Statistisch Mededelingen: Nederlandse Antillen [Statistical Yearbook: Netherlands Antilles]. Willemstad: Bureau voor de Statistiek.

90 a Motor Accidents in New Zealand: Statistical Statement. Annual. Wellington: Ministry of Transport.

b New Zealand Health Statistics Report. Annual. Wellington: Department of Statistics.

c Transport Statistics Report. ibid.

d New Zealand Pocket Digest of Statistics. ibid.

e New Zealand Official Yearbook. ibid.

91 f Boletin Estadistico [Statistical Bulletin]. Managua: Ministerio de Economia.

92 a Report sur les Accidents de la Circulation Routiere [Road Accidents Report]. Niamey: Gendarmerie Nigerienne.

d Annuaire Statistique [Statistical Yearbook]. Niamey: Commissariat General du Plan.

93 a Road Traffic Accident Data in Nigeria. Annual. Lagos: Nigerian Police Force.

d Annual Abstract of Statistics. Lagos: Federal Office of Statistics.

f Digest of Statistics. Quarterly. ibid.

g Owosina, F A O (1981). The traffic scene in Nigeria—an African example. W.H.O./ O.E.C.D./World Bank Conference on Road Traffic Accidents in Developing Countries, held in Mexico City.

g Akoto, K A, and Wiredu, Y K S (1986). Road accident statistics of the various states of Nigeria. In J O Asalor, E A Onibere, and G C Ovuworie (Editors), Road Traffic Accidents in Developing Countries. Volume 1, pp. 3–20. (Proceedings of the First International Conference, held in Benin.) Lagos: Joja Educational Research and Publishers.

94 g Country Health Information Profile, Niue Islands. Manila: Regional Office for the Western Pacific of the World Health Organization. (This cites as its source the Annual Report of the Department of Health, Niue.)

95 a Veitrafikkulykker [Road Traffic Accidents]. Annual. Oslo: Statistisk Sentralbyra.

b Dodsarsaker [Causes of Death]. ibid.

b Helsestatistikk [Health Statistics]. ibid.

c Samferdsels-statistikk [Transport and Communications Statistics]. ibid.

d Statistisk Arbok [Statistical Yearbook]. ibid.

96 d Statistical Yearbook. Muscat: Directorate General of National Statistics.

97 a Accident Statistics of Pakistan. Annual. Islamabad: National Transport Research Centre.

98 a Situacion Social: Accidentes de Transito [Social Situation: Transport Accidents]. Annual. Panama City: Direccion de Estadistica y Censo.

d Panama en Cifras: Compendio Estadistico [Panama in Figures: Statistical Compendium]. ibid.

100 d Anuario Estadistico del Paraguay [Statistical Yearbook of Paraguay]. Asuncion: Direccion General de Estadistica y Censos.

101 d Anuario Estadistico del Peru [Statistical Yearbook of Peru]. Lima: Oficina Nacional de Estadistica y Censos, Ministerio de Economia y Finazias.

102 d Statistical Handbook of the Philippines. Annual. Manila: Bureau of the Census and Statistics.

103 d Rocznik Statystyczny [Statistical Yearbook]. Warsaw: Gtowny Urzad Statystyczny.

f Biuletyn Statystyczny [Statistical Bulletin]. ibid.

104 d Anuario Estatistico: Continente, Acores e Madeira [Statistical Yearbook: Mainland, Azores and Madeira]. Lisbon: Instituto Nacional de Estatistica.

108 g Annual Report on the Royal St. Christopher Nevis Anguilla Police Force. Basseterre: Royal St. Christopher Nevis Anguilla Police Force.

110 d Digest of Statistics for the Year...Annual. Kingstown: Statistical Unit.

112 d Annuario Statistico 1972/80, Vol. 2 [Statistical Yearbook]. San Marino: Ufficio Statale di Statistica, 1980.

113 d Statistical Yearbook. Riyadh: Central Department of Statistics, Ministry of Finance and National Economy.

114 f Bulletin Statistique et Economique Mensuel [Monthly Economic and Statistical Bulletin]. Dakar: Direction de la Statistique.

115 g Annual Report of the Police Department for the Year...Annual. Victoria: Seychelles Police Department.

116 f Statistical Bulletin. Freetown: Central Statistics Office.

117 d Yearbook of Statistics. Singapore: Department of Statistics.

f Monthly Digest of Statistics. ibid.

118 g Country Health Information Profile, Solomon Islands. Manila: Regional Office for the Western Pacific of the World Health Organization. (This cites as its source the Review of the Health Situation, Solomon Islands.)

119 a Road Traffic Accidents. Annual. Pretoria: Department of Statistics.

a Statistical News Releases: Road Traffic Accidents. Weekly. ibid.

b Report on Deaths. Annual. ibid.

d South African Statistics. ibid.

e South Africa [year]: Official Yearbook of the Republic of South Africa. Pretoria: Department of Foreign Affairs and Information.

f South African Bulletin of Statistics. Quarterly. Pretoria: Central Statistics Services.

120 a Boletin Informativo: Accidentes [year] [Information Bulletin: Accidents]. Annual. Madrid: Direccion General de Trafico, Ministerio del Interior.

d Espana Annuario Estadistica [Spanish Statistical Yearbook]. Madrid: Ministerio de Economica, Instituto Nacional de Estadistica.

121 a Police Department Road Accident Statistics for the Year... Annual. Columbo: Police Department.

c Transport Statistics in Sri Lanka, 1974–1981. Columbo: National Planning Division, Ministry of Finance and Planning, 1982.

g Sayer, I, and Hitchcock, R (1984). An analysis of police and medical road accident data: Sri Lanka 1977–81. Supplementary Report 834, Transport and Road Research Laboratory, Crowthorne.

123 d Annual Statistical Bulletin. Mbabane: Central Statistical Office.

124 a Vagtrafikolyckor med Personskada [Road Traffic Accidents with Personal Injury]. Annual. Stockholm: Statistika Centralbyran.

b Dodsorsaker [Causes of Death]. ibid.

d Statistiskarsbok [Statistical Abstract of Sweden]. ibid.

f Allman Manadsstatistik [Monthly Digest of Swedish Statistics]. ibid.

125 a Strassenverkehrsunfalle in der Schweiz/ Accidents de la Circulation en Suisse [Road Accidents in Switzerland]. Annual. Bern: Bundesamt fur Statistik Schweiz.

d Statistisches Jahrbuch der Schweiz/Annuaire Statistique de la Suisse [Statistical Yearbook of Switzerland]. ibid.

126 d Statistical Abstract. Annual. Damascus: Office of the Prime Minister, Central Bureau of Statistics.

127 f Monthly Statistics of the Republic of China. Taipei: Directorate General of Budget, Accounting and Statistics.

128 g Education on road safety—Tanzanian experience. W.H.O./O.E.C.D./World Bank Conference on Road Traffic Accidents in Developing Countries, held in Mexico City, November 1981.

129 a Road Accident Statistics. Bangkok: Royal Thai Police, Ministry of Interior.

d Statistical Yearbook Thailand. Bangkok: National Statistical Office, Office of the Prime Minister.

f Quarterly Bulletin of Statistics. ibid.

130 f Bulletin Mensuel de Statistique [Monthly Bulletin of Statistics]. Lome: Direction de la Statistique.

130x g Country Health Information Profile, Tokelau. Manila: Regional Office for the Western Pacific of the World Health Organization. (This cites as its source the Annual Report on Health Services, Tokelau.)

131 b Population and Vital Statistics Report. Annual. Port-of-Spain: Ministry of Finance, Central Statistical Office.

d Annual Statistical Digest. ibid.

132 d Annuaire Statistique de la Tunisie [Statistical Yearbook of Tunisia]. Tunis: Secretariat d'Etat au Plan et a l'Economie Nationale.

f Bulletin Mensuel de Statistique [Monthly Statistical Bulletin]. ibid.

133 a Road Traffic Accidents. Occasional. Ankara: State Institute of Statistics.

d Statistical Pocket Book of Turkey. Annual. ibid.

d Statistical Yearbook of Turkey. ibid.

134 d Turks and Caicos Islands: Report for the Year. Occasional. London: Foreign and Commonwealth Office, H.M.S.O.

134x g Country Health Information Profile, Tuvalu. Manila: Regional Office for the Western Pacific of the World Health Organization. (This cites as its source the Annual Report of the Health Division, Ministry of Social Services, Tuvalu.)

135 d Annual Statistical Abstract. Abu Dhabi: Central Statistical Department, Ministry of Planning.

136 a Death and Injury Road Accidents in Northern Ireland. Annual. Belfast: Royal Ulster Constabulary.

a Road Accidents Great Britain. Annual. London: H.M.S.O.

b Mortality Statistics, Accidents and Violence. (Series DH4.) Annual. London: H.M.S.O.

b Annual Report of the Registrar General Northern Ireland. Belfast: H.M.S.O.

b Annual Report of the Registrar-General Scotland. Edinburgh: H.M.S.O.

d Annual Abstract of Statistics. London: Central Statistical Office, H.M.S.O.

d Northern Ireland Annual Abstract of Statistics. Belfast: H.M.S.O.

f Monthly Digest of Statistics. London: H.M.S.O.

g Chief Officer's Annual Report. St. Helier: States of Jersey Police.

137 a Fatal Accident Reporting System: A Review of Information on Fatal Traffic Accidents in the U.S. Annual. Washington, D.C.: U.S. Department of Transportation, National Highway Traffic Safety Administration.

a Highway Safety. Annual. Washington, D.C.: U.S. Department of Transportation, National Highway Traffic Safety Administration.

b Vital Statistics of the United States. Annual. Washington, D.C.: U.S. Department of Health, Education and Welfare, Public Health Service.

d Statistical Abstract of the United States. Annual. Washington, D.C.: U.S. Department of Commerce, Bureau of the Census.

d Guam Annual Statistical Report. Agana: Office of Vital Statistics.

g Annual Report from the Governor of American Samoa to the Secretary of the Interior. Washington, D.C.: Superintendent of Documents, Government Printing Office.

138 d Annuario Estadistico [Yearbook of Statistics]. Montevideo: Direccion General de Estadistica.

138x g Scherer, J L (Editor). U.S.S.R. Facts & Figures Annual. Volume 9, 1985, p. 28. Gulf Breeze, Florida: Academic International Press. (This cites as its source Sovetskaia Latvia, 4.Feb.84.)

g Associated Press despatch, quoting Izvestia, 20.June.87.

139 f Boletin Mensal de Estadistica [Monthly Bulletin of Statistics]. Caracas: Direccion General de Estadistica.

141 d Statisticki Godisnjak S.F.R.J. [Statistical Yearbook of the Federal People's Republic of Yugoslavia]. Belgrade: Savezni Zavod za Statistiku.

142 g Shako, D, et al (1979). Etude de la dynamique des accidents du trafic routier dans la population Kinoise. Medecine d'Afrique Noire, 26(2).

143 f Monthly Digest of Statistics. Lusaka: Central Statistical Office.

144 a Traffic Safety in Zimbabwe. Occasional. Harare: Traffic Safety Board.

f Monthly Digest of Statistics. ibid.

f Quarterly Digest of Statistics. ibid.

Chapter 3

Collection and processing of data from the police

3.1 Introduction

Sections 3.2–3.13 examine a number of slightly different ways of organising the collection of mass accident data using police reports as the principal source. Attention will be confined to advanced industrialised countries (specifically, Great Britain, Australia, Japan, The Netherlands, and the U.S.A.); for the developing world, see Chapter 5. Section 3.14 describes tabulation by computer of the dataset that results, and Section 3.15 expands this by considering the integration of several datasets (e.g. of accidents, vehicle registrations, highway details) into a single system.

The ultimate source of the information is the person who tells the policeman what happened. If that person was involved in the accident, he or she may have a motive for misrepresenting events. (In order to elicit honest responses, in some places the accident report form is not admissible as evidence in court. An example is British Columbia—Mercer, 1987a.) And even the most impartial witness is unlikely to have been trained in observation, or to have a perfect memory. Not much can be done about that, except to base policy on data elements that are as factual as possible, rather than a matter of opinion—and to use a healthy dose of common sense when interpreting the statistics. But a good deal can be done from the stage of the policeman's report onwards. We shall be examining issues like what items different jurisdictions include on their report forms, what categories are used within each item, how the forms are laid out, and so on, later in this and various other Chapters; here, let it just be said that it must not simply be assumed that police officers can automatically fill out an accident report form correctly—they must be trained

to do so. Thus Hambley (1978) mentions that one police force gave its probationary constables basic training in this, and achieved satisfactory processing of the forms, whereas another force undertook no training at all, and the forms suffered a 30–40% reject rate during editing.

3.2 Great Britain

The following description of the collection of road accident data by the police in Great Britain is based upon that in Chapman and James (1973). See also Burr and Brogan (1976) for a description of the flow of information in one particular local government area (the West Midlands). The form used for data capture, known as the Stats 19 form, has been revised several times since then, and the administrative arrangements for processing the data have been modified from time to time, but the basics remain the same.

What accidents are included? Those involving injury which are reported to the police. (The relation between this sample and the totality of injury accidents is a complex one, discussion of which is postponed to Chapter 11.) Any damage-only accidents that are reported to the police are not forwarded under the national (Stats 19) procedure, but in some places the information does get passed on to the local government authority, for use especially in accident location analysis—e.g. in the West Midlands, damage-only accidents were accounting for nearly two-thirds of the total in the databank at the time of the paper by Burr and Brogan (1976).

Where does data capture take place? In the case of the more serious accidents, at the accident site, by the policeman attending. This often happens for slight accidents too, but sometimes an accident will be reported by a driver or other person involved to a police station some time after the event.

How is the information collected? The police officer completes an accident report booklet. This is physically small enough to fit into a pocket or glove compartment of a car, and has a cover of card to give some support when being filled in. A version adapted and slightly simplified for use in developing countries is reproduced as Appendix 3 of Jacobs et al (1975). It includes space for factual information, a narrative description of the accident (including sketch), and statements by persons involved and witnesses.

How is the information coded? Back at the police station, a "Stats 19" form is completed (Figure 3.1), based upon the factual material in the report booklet.

What happens to the Stats 19? Often, several copies are made—for police use, for local government use, and for national government use. One common procedure is for most of the processing to be carried out by the County Surveyor's department, which has responsibility for monitoring traffic safety and making improvements in their local area; they send a machine-readable copy to the Department of Transport, who collate all the counties' records together into a national accident file. ("National" here means England, Wales, and Scotland, i.e. Northern Ireland is not included.) Both at local and national level, certain automatic checks are performed on the input data—e.g. hour of day must be in the range 00–23, and sex of casualty must be coded as 1 or 2; also, there are some cross-checks of the consistency of variables with each other.

There are descriptions in the Guidelines for Accident Reduction and Prevention (IHT, 1986) and the Accident Investigation Manual (DTp, 1986) of the Stats 19 system and how the data is used to plan and evaluate safety improvement measures. These descriptions emphasise the local government context. Thus we find in them recommendations for data that is desirable at local level though not required by national government, in particular a clear language description of the location and circumstances of the accident. (It is clear that the narrative is intended to be part of the computer input, but not whether sophisticated automatic

searching of the texts for repeating factors—as has been done in North Carolina, see Section 3.11.5—is envisaged.)

What of the future? Periodic revisions of the Stats 19 form are made by a committee on which the police, local government, national government, and researchers are represented. One of the most important failings of the present Stats 19 is its omission of vehicle make and model. In the early 1970's this was coded; Thompson (1985) envisages it may be again in the future, through inclusion of the vehicle registration number and comparison with data held in vehicle registration records.

For many years, the design of the Stats 19 form has been oriented towards matters of fact, de-emphasising matters that are necessarily subjective opinions of the police officer. In particular, no attempt is made to record what in casual language would be described as the "causes" of the accident—excessive speed, inattention, inexperience, or whatever. The advantage is the higher reliability of the data that results. I do wonder, though, whether this has been taken too far—though many accidents do not have a single cause, and even when they do, it may not always be discovered by the police, nevertheless there remain some in which the officer does have a soundly-based opinion as to why the accident occurred, or what could be done to prevent a recurrence; such opinions are at present being lost. Certainly, many other jurisdictions collect data of this kind, and they presumably consider it useful. Some police forces do code causation or contributory factors, this variable being used at local government level but not nationally. For example, Burr and Brogan (1976) mention that a list of 92 possibilities is used in the West Midlands.

3.3 South Australia

3.3.1 Mid-1970's

The collection and recording of road accident data in South Australia in the mid-1970's is described by Howard et al (1979, Appendix A). The system has changed since then, but this remains a clear and detailed description of one way of organising things.

The accidents which at that time should have

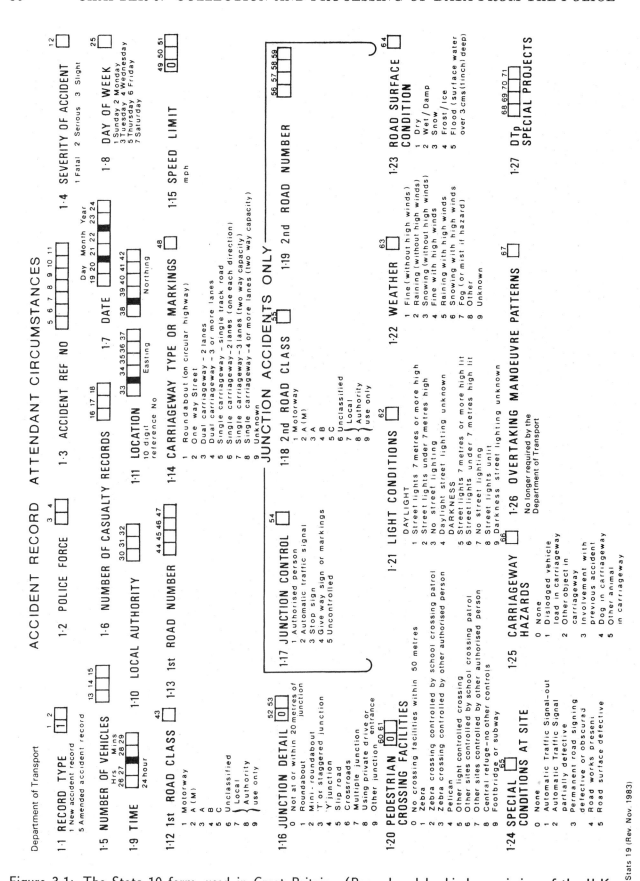

Figure 3.1: The Stats 19 form, used in Great Britain. (Reproduced by kind permission of the U.K. Department of Transport.)

FIGURE 3.1 37

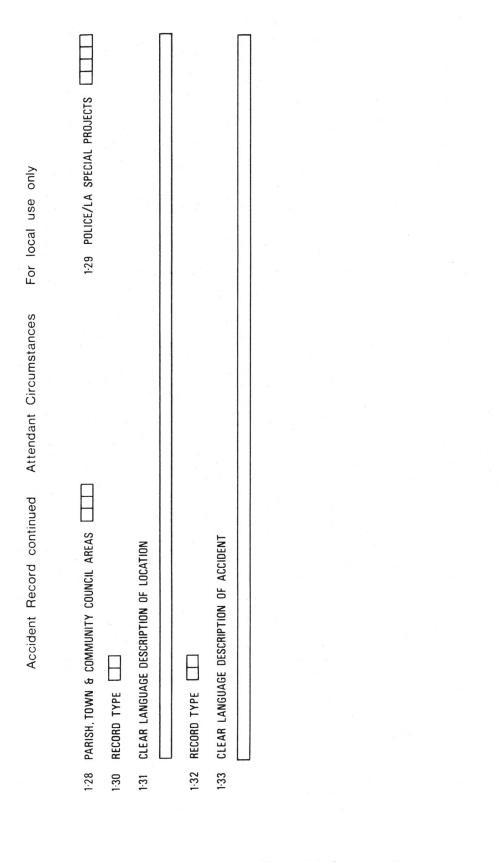

Figure 3.1: (continued).

Stats 19 (Rev. Nov. 1983)

VEHICLE RECORD

2·1 RECORD TYPE [2] (1,2)
1 New vehicle record
5 Amended vehicle record

2·2 POLICE FORCE (3,4)

2·3 ACCIDENT REF NO (5,6,7,8,9,10,11)

2·4 VEHICLE REF NO (12,13,14)

2·5 TYPE OF VEHICLE (15,16)
01 Pedal cycle
02 Moped
03 Motor scooter
04 Motor cycle
05 Combination
06 Invalid Tricycle
07 Other three-wheeled car
08 Taxi
09 Car (Four wheeled)
10 Minibus/Motor caravan
11 PSV
12 Goods not over 1½ tons UW (1.52 tonnes)
13 Goods over 1½ tons UW (1.52 tonnes)
14 Other motor vehicle
15 Other non motor vehicle

2·6 TOWING AND ARTICULATION (17)
0 No tow/articulation
1 Articulated vehicle
2 Double/multiple trailer
3 Caravan
4 Single trailer
5 Other tow

2·7 MANOEUVRES (18,19)
01 Reversing
02 Parked
03 Waiting to go ahead but held up
04 Stopping
05 Starting
06 U Turn
07 Turning left
08 Waiting to turn left
09 Turning right
10 Waiting to turn right
11 Changing lane to left
12 Changing lane to right
13 Overtaking moving vehicle on its offside
14 Overtaking stationary vehicle on its offside
15 Overtaking on nearside
16 Going ahead left hand bend
17 Going ahead right hand bend
18 Going ahead other

2·8 VEHICLE MOVEMENT COMPASS POINT (20,21) From To
1 N
2 NE
3 E
4 SE
5 S
6 SW
7 W
8 NW
or 0 Parked - not at kerb
9 Parked - at kerb

2·9 VEHICLE LOCATION AT TIME OF ACCIDENT (22,23)
01 Leaving the main road
02 Entering the main road
03 On main road
04 On minor road
05 On service road
06 On lay-by or hard shoulder
07 Entering lay-by or hard shoulder
08 Leaving lay-by or hard shoulder
09 On a cycleway
10 Not on carriageway

2·10 JUNCTION LOCATION OF VEHICLE AT FIRST IMPACT (24)
0 Not at junction (or within 20 metres/22 yards)
1 Vehicle approaching junction/vehicle parked at junction approach
2 Vehicle in middle of junction
3 Vehicle cleared junction/vehicle parked at junction exit
4 Did not impact

2·11 SKIDDING AND OVERTURNING (25)
0 No skidding, jacknifing or overturning
1 Skidding
2 Skidded and overturned
3 Jacknifed
4 Jacknifed and overturned
5 Overturned

2·12 HIT OBJECT IN CARRIAGEWAY (26,27)
00 None
01 Previous accident
02 Road works
03 Parked vehicle - lit
04 Parked vehicle - unlit
05 Bridge (roof)
06 Bridge (side)
07 Bollard/refuge
08 Open door of vehicle
09 Central island of roundabout
10 Kerb
11 Other object

2·13 VEHICLE LEAVING CARRIAGEWAY (28)
0 Did not leave carriageway
1 Left carriageway nearside
2 Left carriageway nearside and rebounded
3 Left carriageway straight ahead at junction
4 Left carriageway offside onto central reservation
5 Left carriageway offside onto central reservation and rebounded
6 Left carriageway offside crossed central reservation
7 Left carriageway offside
8 Left carriageway offside and rebounded

2·14 HIT OBJECT OFF CARRIAGEWAY (29,30)
00 None
01 Road sign/Traffic signal
02 Lamp post
03 Telegraph pole/Electricity pole
04 Tree
05 Bus stop/Bus shelter
06 Central crash barrier
07 Nearside or offside crash barrier
08 Submerged in water (completely)
09 Entered ditch
10 Other permanent object

2·15 VEHICLE PREFIX/SUFFIX LETTER (31)
PREFIX/SUFFIX LETTER or one of the following codes –
0 More than twenty years old (at end of year)
1 Unknown/cherished number/not applicable
2 Foreign/diplomatic
3 Military
4 Trade plates

2·16 FIRST POINT OF IMPACT (32)
0 Did not impact
1 Front
2 Back
3 Offside
4 Nearside

2·17 OTHER VEHICLE HIT (VEH REF NO) (33,34,35)

2·18 PART(S) DAMAGED (36,37,38)
0 None
1 Front
2 Back
3 Offside
4 Nearside
5 Roof
6 Underside
7 All four sides

2·19 NO OF AXLES (39)
0 Not goods vehicle
2 2 axles
3 3 axles } Goods Vehicles only
4 4 axles
5 5 or more axles

2·20 MAXIMUM PERMISSIBLE GROSS WEIGHT (40,41) Metric tonnes (Goods vehicle only)

2·21 SEX OF DRIVER (42)
1 Male
2 Female
3 Not traced

2·22 AGE OF DRIVER (43,44) (Years, estimated if necessary)

2·23 BREATH TEST (45)
0 Not applicable
1 Positive
2 Negative
3 Not requested
4 Failed to provide
5 Driver not contacted at time

2·24 HIT AND RUN (46)
0 Other
1 'Hit and run'
2 Non-stop vehicle not hit

2·25 DTp SPECIAL PROJECTS (47,48,49,50)

Stats 19 (Rev. Nov. 1983)

Figure 3.1: (continued).

FIGURE 3.1   39

CASUALTY RECORD

3·1 RECORD TYPE   [3]   (1 2)
   1 New casualty record
   5 Amended casualty record

3·2 POLICE FORCE   (3 4)

3·3 ACCIDENT REF NO.   (5 6 7 8 9 10 11)

3·4 VEHICLE REF NO.   (12 13 14)

3·5 CASUALTY REF NO.   (15 16 17)

3·6 CASUALTY CLASS   (18)
   1 Driver or rider
   2 Vehicle or pillion passenger
   3 Pedestrian

3·7 SEX OF CASUALTY   (19)
   1 Male
   2 Female

3·8 AGE OF CASUALTY   (20 21)
   (Years, estimated if necessary).

3·9 SEVERITY OF CASUALTY   (22)
   1 Fatal
   2 Serious
   3 Slight

3·10 PEDESTRIAN LOCATION   (23 24)
   00 Not pedestrian
   01 In carriageway crossing on pedestrian crossing
   02 In carriageway crossing within zig-zag lines approach to the crossing
   03 In carriageway crossing within zig-zag lines exit the crossing
   04 In carriageway crossing elsewhere within 50 metres of pedestrian crossing
   05 In carriageway crossing elsewhere
   06 On footway or verge
   07 On refuge or central island or reservation
   08 In centre of carriageway not on refuge or central island
   09 In carriageway not crossing
   10 Unknown

3·11 PEDESTRIAN MOVEMENT   (25)
   0 Not pedestrian
   1 Crossing from drivers nearside
   2 Crossing from drivers nearside - masked by parked or stationary vehicle
   3 Crossing from drivers offside
   4 Crossing from drivers offside - masked by parked or stationary vehicle
   5 In carriageway stationary - not crossing (standing or playing)
   6 In carriageway stationary - not crossing (standing or playing) - masked by parked or stationary vehicle
   7 Walking along in carriageway facing traffic
   8 Walking along in carriageway back to traffic
   9 Unknown

3·12 PEDESTRIAN DIRECTION   (26)
   Compass point bound
   1 N
   2 NE
   3 E
   4 SE
   5 S
   6 SW
   7 W
   8 NW
   or 0 - Pedestrian - standing still

3·13 SCHOOL PUPIL CASUALTY   (27)
   0 Not a school pupil
   1 Pupil on journey to/from school
   2 Pupil NOT on journey to/from school

3·14 SEAT BELT USAGE   (28)
   0 Not car or van
   1 Safety belt in use
   2 Safety belt fitted - not in use
   3 Safety belt not fitted
   4 Child safety belt/harness fitted - in use
   5 Child safety belt/harness fitted - not in use
   6 Child safety belt/harness not fitted
   7 Unknown

3·15 CAR PASSENGER   (29)
   0 Not car passenger
   1 Front seat car passenger
   2 Rear seat car passenger

3·16 PSV PASSENGER   (30)
   0 Not a PSV passenger
   1 Boarding
   2 Alighting
   3 Standing passenger
   4 Seated passenger

3·17 DTp SPECIAL PROJECTS   (31 32 33 34)

Figure 3.1: (continued).

been reported to the police were those involving injury or property damage of $100 or more, except that there was no need to report it if the only damage was to one's own property. Police generally only attended the accident scene if there was personal injury, a criminal offence was suspected, or if the damaged vehicles were a traffic or fire hazard. The accident report form, when completed, was passed to the Police Accident Records Section; if there were two or more reports on the same accident (by the two or more drivers involved, perhaps made at different police stations), they were matched together. Top copies went to the Police Adjudication Section, who made the decision about the need for any legal action; that being completed, the forms returned to Accident Records to be microfilmed. Carbon copies went to the Highways Department, where editing and coding took place; this was done directly on to the police form, using red ink, creating a "most likely" composite if there were two or more accounts of the accident and there is any discrepancy. From the Highways Department, the coded form went to the Adelaide office of the Australian Bureau of Statistics (ABS), where the information was transferred onto a transcription form and then to magnetic tape. The ABS kept one copy of the tape and sent another back to the Highways Department.

Another account is by Park (1980), who adds that the average time to complete the report form is 15 minutes. He also describes the location coding method: for urban areas this consists of main road number (3 digits), coding area (4 digits), intersection number within coding area (2 digits), and type of location (e.g. intersection or not, 1 digit); for rural areas it is main road number and distance (in tenths of kilometres) from a reference point.

3.3.2   Update

At the time of writing (early 1987), the Road Safety Division of the Department of Transport has recently taken over responsibility for road accident statistics from the Highways Department, and arrangements are in a transitional stage. A description is in the report by Computer Power (1986), who were asked to advise on how best the computing requirements of the Road Safety Division would be satisfied.

The data sources are still, of course, the police

accident report forms—that used for injury accidents is known as the PD 83 and that for property damage only accidents is the PD 81. The PD 83 is shown in Figure 3.2. The PD 81 is almost identical, the chief differences being the omission of the sections describing the injured person(s) and pedestrian movement, and that giving witnesses' names and addresses. PD 83 is usually completed by the police, PD 81 by persons involved in the accident.

The threshold for including damage-only accidents in the dataset is now $300. Having checked that the form refers to an accident that should be included, the Road Safety Division carries out a number of clerical operations—principally, the coding of the location, interpreting what is written on the form (especially necessary for those not completed by the police) and resolving any ambiguities and omissions, and transcription for keying into the computer. (This takes on average some 20 minutes per form.) This done, the forms are filed in five sequences:

- Fatals: by date.

- Adelaide city accidents: by numerical sequence of accident location.

- Other metropolitan accidents: as for Adelaide city.

- Country town accidents: as for Adelaide city.

- Other country accidents: by road number and road running distance within road number.

There are three main components to the computerised dataset:

- The Accident Detail Master File, which has items such as location, number of casualties, speed limit, etc.

- The Accident Unit Master File, which has details of the vehicles, objects, and persons involved.

- The Intersections Statistics File, which stores statistics on accidents at the recorded intersection.

FIGURE 3.2 41

P.D. 83

SOUTH AUSTRALIA POLICE

ROAD TRAFFIC ACCIDENT

S.A. POLICE

A.R. No. ....

INSTRUCTIONS:

1. If handwritten, use BLACK biro only.
2. Use BLOCK letters only.
3. Where alternatives are shown, place an 'X' in the appropriate box.

   e.g.   Yes ☐1   No ☒

4. Complete both sides of form.

Station: ....

Place an 'X' in the appropriate box.

FATAL ☐1   GOVT. DEPT. ☐2
DEPARTMENTAL ☐3   HIT RUN ☐4
INJURY ☐5   ARREST ☐6
MANNER DANGEROUS ☐7   D.U.I. ☐8
EXCEED P.C.A. ☐9

If person arrested or reported, state offence:

....
ARRESTED/REPORTED

TIME

Date of accident: ..../........./19.......   Time: ....   am ☐1   pm ☐2

Day of week: Mon ☐1   Tues ☐2   Wed ☐3   Thurs ☐4   Fri ☐5   Sat ☐6   Sun ☐7

LOCATION

What was accident between?   e.g. car and truck, 2 cars, car and fence etc. ....

Where did accident happen?   (name intersection, roads etc.) ....

Town or Suburb: ....

If accident not at intersection or junction, name of nearest side street or landmark: ....

If accident not at intersection or junction, the point of impact is ....   ☐1 metres   ☐2 kilometres

N ☐1   S ☐2   E ☐3   W ☐4   from the nearest side street

Did Police attend at scene?   Yes ☐1   No ☐2   Area speed limit: ....km/h.

UNIT 1

Registration number: ....   Year, make and type of vehicle, or type of property: ....

Name of road travelled on: ....

Direction of travel: N ☐1   NE ☐2   E ☐3   SE ☐4   S ☐5   SW ☐6   W ☐7   NW ☐8

Driver's full name: ....   surname   christian names   Sex: M ☐1   F ☐2

Address: ....   Occupation: ....

Age: ....years   If Juvenile—D of B ..../........./19.......   Driver's licence number: ....

Licence: (1) State of issue: ....   (2) Codes: ....   (3) Type: Learners ☐1   Probationary ☐2   Full ☐3

Driving experience in type of vehicle involved in accident: ....years   Total driving experience: ....years

If vehicle was towing a trailer, caravan etc., state type and registration number: ....

Estimated speed of Unit 1 immediately prior to the accident. ....km/h.

UNIT 2

Registration number: ....   Year, make and type of vehicle, or type of property: ....

Name of road travelled on: ....

Direction of travel: N ☐1   NE ☐2   E ☐3   SE ☐4   S ☐5   SW ☐6   W ☐7   NW ☐8

Driver's full name: ....   surname   christian names   Sex: M ☐1   F ☐2

Address: ....   Occupation: ....

Age: ....years   If Juvenile—D of B ..../........./19.......   Driver's licence number: ....

Licence: (1) State of issue: ....   (2) Codes: ....   (3) Type: Learners ☐1   Probationary ☐2   Full ☐3

Driving experience in type of vehicle involved in accident: ....years   Total driving experience: ....years

If vehicle was towing a trailer, caravan etc., state type and registration number: ....

Estimated speed of Unit 2 immediately prior to the accident. ....km/h.

DAMAGE

DAMAGE—UNIT 1

Estimated cost of repair: $ ....

Was damage?   slight ☐1   moderate ☐2   extensive ☐3

Was vehicle towed from scene?   Yes ☐1   No ☐2   Unknown ☐3

DAMAGE—UNIT 2

Estimated cost of repair: $ ....

Was damage?   slight ☐1   moderate ☐2   extensive ☐3

Was vehicle towed from scene?   Yes ☐1   No ☐2   Unknown ☐3

Total Damage: $ ....

INJURIES

Full Name, Occupation and Address	Type of Road User	Vehicle Unit No.	Sex	Age	Position in Vehicle	Injury Details (1 2 3)	Treatment (1 2 3)
1.	☐ Driver ☐ Rider ☐ Pass. ☐ Ped.	☐1 ☐2	☐M ☐F			☐☐☐ Head ☐☐☐ Chest/Body ☐☐☐ Multiple ☐☐☐ Internal ☐☐☐ Shock ☐☐ Limbs ☐☐ Neck ☐☐ Other	☐☐☐ Not Treated ☐☐☐ By Private Dr ☐☐☐ Treated at Hospital ☐☐☐ Admitted to Hospital ☐☐☐ Fatal HOSPITAL
2.	☐ Driver ☐ Rider ☐ Pass. ☐ Ped.	☐1 ☐2	☐M ☐F				
3.	☐ Driver ☐ Rider ☐ Pass. ☐ Ped.	☐1 ☐2	☐M ☐F				

Figure 3.2: Form PD 83, used in South Australia.

STATISTICAL DATA

TYPE OF LOCATION

INTERSECTION ETC.

1. Interchange
2. + Cross
3. Y Junction
4. T Junction
5. Multiple
6. Rail Crossing

BETWEEN INTERSECTIONS

1. Crossover
2. Rail Crossing
3. Divided
4. Not divided
5. One way street
6. Freeway
7. Ramp—on
8. Ramp—off
9. Pedestrian Crossing
10.

ROAD FEATURES

1. Straight road
2. Curve or bend
3. Bridge, Culvert or Causeway

ROAD CONDITIONS

1. Sealed
2. Not sealed

1. Wet
2. Dry

WEATHER

1. Raining
2. Not raining

LIGHTING

1. Daylight
2. Dawn/Dusk
3. Night

TYPE OF ACCIDENT

1. Rear end
2. Hit fixed object
3. Side swipe
4. Right angle
5. Head on
6. Hit pedestrian
7. Roll over
8. Right turn accident
9. Hit parked vehicle
10. Hit animal
11. Hit object on road
12. Left Rd out of control
13.

VEHICLE MOVEMENT

1. Right turn
2. Left turn
3. 'U' turn
4. Swerving
5. Reversing
6. Stopped on road
7. Straight ahead
8. Enter private driveway
9. Leave private driveway
10. Parked
11. Parking—angle
12. " —parallel
13. Unparking—angle
14. " —parallel
15. Overtaking—on right
16. " —on left
17.

TRAFFIC CONTROLS

1. Traffic signals
2. Railway Crossing—Boom
3. — Flashing signals
4. — No control
5. Stop signs
6. Give way signs
7. No control
8. Round-a-bout
9.

APPARENT ERRORS

1. Excessive speed
2. Fail to stand
3. Fail to keep left
4. Change lanes to danger
5. Fail give way right
6. Incorrect turn
7. Reverse w/o due care
8. Follow too close
9. Overtake w/o due care
10. Disobey traffic lights
11. " — stop sign
12. " — give way sign
13. " — police signal
14. " — rail signal
15. Incorrect or no signal
16. Inattention
17. No error indicated
18. Other
19. Dangerous driving
20. D.U.I.

PEDESTRIAN MOVEMENT

1. Walk on footpath
2. On Pedestrian Crossing
3. Within 20 m Crossing
4. Alight parked vehicle
5. Walk between parked vehicle
6. Walk on road
7. " against traffic
8. Pushing or Work on vehicle
9. Playing on road
10. Crossing w/o control
11.

BLOOD ALCOHOL CONTENT ALCOTEST

U.1 U.2
1. Refuse Alcotest
2. Nil Reading
3. Alcohol Ind — Under PCA

NOT TESTED

4. Outside 2 Hour Period
5. Injured
6. Other ....

BREATH ANALYSIS

7. Refuse Test
8. Tested — Under PCA
9. Tested — Charged PCA
Result
1. ....% 2. ....%

10. Charged DUI
11. Blood Test
12. Nil Reading
Result
1. ....% 2. ....%

RESPONSIBILITY

1. Driver/Rider
2. Passenger
3. Pedestrian
4. Animal
5. Other

" " Police Reg/Div where accident occurred

WITNESSES—DO NOT INCLUDE THOSE INJURED

Name: .... Address: .... Tel: ....

Name: .... Address: .... Tel: ....

Name: .... Address: .... Tel: ....

Name: .... Address: .... Tel: ....

BRIEF DESCRIPTION OF ACCIDENT:

SYMBOLS FOR PLAN

Street Intersection

Curved Street

Persons

Vehicle 1

Vehicle 2

(Direction of travel indicated by arrow in symbol)

INDICATE NORTH WITH AN ARROW

Reported to or at .... by .... at .... hours on .... / .... /19 ....

Date: .... / .... /19 ....

Signature of Member   Rank   I/D No.

B9094

Figure 3.2: (continued).

3.4 Victoria

Corben and Ashton (1984) give an account of road accident reporting in Victoria, Australia. There, reports to the police must be made if anyone is injured, or any property is damaged and the owner is not present. Both a brief (always used) and a detailed (for serious accidents) report form were in use. These were referred to as Forms 512 and 513 respectively; in 1986, a single form (510) replaced them—see Figure 3.3. The form is sent to the Police Traffic Department, who forward a photocopy of it to the Road Traffic Authority.

At the time of Corben and Ashton's account a change-over was being made from a node/double-node system of coding location to the use of the Australian Map Grid. By the former, I mean each intersection ("node") is allocated a number; mid-block accidents are located by the two intersections between which they occur. The numbering of intersections in turn has four components: the map number, the horizontal grid number, the vertical grid number, and a serial number within the square thus defined.

The report form is carefully examined and if there are omissions or ambiguities the form is returned to the police or a telephone enquiry is made. The appropriate road user movement code (see Section 6.4.5 and Figure 6.3) is determined; and the usual factual data about the accident also coded. The information thus acquired is used to expand and update the computerised State Traffic Accident Record. Certain changes of procedure are being introduced during 1987, with police becoming involved in the initial computer entry of the data.

3.5 Western Australia

The collection, processing, analysis, and distribution of road accident data in Western Australia is described by Willett (1981). Traffic accidents were required to be reported if (a) they occurred in a public place and any person was killed or injured, (b) they occurred on a public road and property damage exceeded $300, or (c) they occurred on a public road and the owner of damaged property was not present. If an accident not legally required to be reported nevertheless is reported, the details are still processed and recorded. If a policeman does not attend the accident and take particulars, each driver involved is required to independently report it to a Road Traffic Authority office. Consequently, as in South Australia, it is often necessary to match together two or more reports on the same accident. The Road Traffic Authority then forward the forms to the Main Roads Department.

Staff of the Main Roads Department code items concerning location, vehicle and pedestrian movements, and objects struck, and enter the accidents into the computerised database. The accident data file is part of an integrated system, and potentially can be linked to driver licence, vehicle registration, traffic control device, and road inventory files. Not only can it potentially be done, the linkage actually is done routinely for the vehicle registration data. (The success rate of the matching is around 80%.) Consequently, the database has an extensive list of information for each of the vehicles (if registered in Western Australia). The data items are listed in Table 3.1.

3.6 ACRUPTC's recommendations (Australia)

3.6.1 Background

The several states and territories of Australia have separate systems for collecting and processing road accident statistics. They have never even been able to agree on a common report form. The long (and, to date, unsuccessful) efforts towards this end were recounted by Johinke (1978). In the same publication, Bagley (1978) gives a description of the situation then from the viewpoint of the Australian Bureau of Statistics. As Lane (1972) remarked, however sound the proposals may be, the real problem lies in getting them actually implemented by the various states and territories. See, for instance, Watkins (1972) and TPR (1973) for ideas on what data should be collected and what categories the variables should be divided into. (Watkins' proposal for classifying type of accident will be given in Table 6.6.)

A different tactic was tried when the issue was revived in 1976–77: instead of aiming for complete uniformity, perhaps a common core of data items could be achieved?

STATION COPY

VICTORIA POLICE
V.P. Form 510

ACCIDENT REPORT
(Rev 1986)

TACO NUMBER

STATION A B NO

TYPE OF ACCIDENT (Circle appropriate number)

FATAL	1	STRUCK M/CYCLE	1
INJURY	2	STRUCK PEDESTRIAN	2
NON–INJURY	3	STRUCK CYCLIST	3
		STRUCK MOTOR VEH	4
SPEED ZONE		OTHER VEHICULAR*	5
	KPH	NON VEHICULAR*	6
		*SPECIFY	

TRAFFIC DEPT FILE NO

DATE OF ACCIDENT / /

TIME OF ACCIDENT (24 HRS)

TOTAL NO OF VEHICLES INVOLVED

TOTAL NO OF PERSONS INVOLVED

OCCURRED ON — NAME OF STREET, ROAD OR HIGHWAY — MUNICIPALITY — FOR COUNTRY — IN TOWN OF OR BETWEEN TOWNS OF AND

FOR METRO — (DISTANCE) — FROM — N/S/E/W — NAME OF INTERSECTING STREET, ROAD OR HIGHWAY — MELWAY REF — (DISTANCE) — FROM — N/S/E/W — (HIGHWAY ONLY) NEAREST KILOMETRE POST (INSERT NUMBER) — (NON HIGHWAY) NEAREST LANDMARK

COMPLETED DETAILS OF EACH VEHICLE INVOLVED

	VEHICLE "A"	VEHICLE "B"	VEHICLE "C"
NAME			
ADDRESS			
	POSTCODE	POSTCODE	POSTCODE
STATUS (OWNER, DRIVER, PERSON IN CHARGE)			
DATE OF BIRTH / / — S/B/H — SEX — INJURY — DAMAGE			
TYPE OF VEHICLE — PR/LAMPS — TOWING 1 YES 2 NO			
REGISTRATION NO — STATE — DATE OF EXPIRY			
LICENCE/PERMIT NO — STATE — DATE OF EXPIRY — TYPE			

OTHER PERSONS INVOLVED INCLUDE OWNERS OF PROPERTY (NOT VEHICLES) DAMAGED

NAME	ADDRESS	STATE-MENT	VEH	POS	S/BELT HELMET	AGE YRS	SEX (M/F)	INJURY

INJURED TAKEN TO (NAME & INITIALS) — NAME OF HOSPITAL — VEHICLES TOWED FROM SCENE (Reg. No.) — WHERE TO

INDEPENDENT WITNESSES (NOT PASSENGERS)

NAME	ADDRESS	VIEWED ACCIDENT FROM	WRITTEN STATEMENT

SKETCH OF LOCALITY

SHOW NORTH WITH ARROW

OBJECT HIT (Specify)	TRAFFIC CONTROL
LIGHT	ATMOS/CON
SURFACE CONDITION	SURFACE TYPE
PED. MOVEMENT	CAUGHT FIRE

SUMMARY OF CIRCUMSTANCES

		VEH A	VEH B	VEH C
SECTION 80 MCA COMPLIED WITH?	0. N/A 1. YES 2. NO			
PRELIMINARY BREATH TEST TAKEN?	0. N/A 1. YES 2. NO			

POLICE ACTION TAKEN OR PROPOSED

T I N NO (OR BRIEF) — OFFENCE CODE

SIGNATURE — RANK — NUMBER — DISTRICT — STATION — CHECKED BY

NAME (BLOCK LETTERS) — DATE / /19 — DID POLICE ATTEND SCENE 1. YES 2. NO — RANK — NO

2701(F4)

Figure 3.3: Form 510, used in Victoria.

FIGURE 3.3   45

CODING GUIDE

To be used for all entries where * is marked.

SEATBELT/CRASH HELMET

1 SEATBELT WORN
2 SEATBELT NOT WORN
3 CHILD RESTRAINT WORN
4 CHILD RESTRAINT NOT WORN
5 SEATBELT/RESTRAINT NOT FITTED

6 CRASH HELMET WORN (for motorcycle, pillion passenger & bicycle)
7 CRASH HELMET NOT WORN
8 NOT APPLICABLE TO VEHICLE TYPE
9 NOT KNOWN

INJURY

1 KILLED OR DIED WITHIN 30 DAYS
2 INJURED ADMITTED TO HOSPITAL
3 OTHER INJURED REQUIRING MEDICAL TREATMENT
4 OTHER INJURED NOT REQUIRING MEDICAL TREATMENT
5 NOT INJURED

DAMAGE

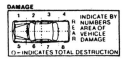

INDICATE BY NUMBERS AREA OF VEHICLE DAMAGE
() – INDICATES TOTAL DESTRUCTION

LICENCE TYPE

1 LEARNER
2 PROBATIONARY
3 CONDITIONAL
4 PROB. & COND.
5 STANDARD
6 DISQUALIFIED
7 UNLICENCED
8 INAPPROPRIATE
9 NOT KNOWN

POSITION (POS)

Blank – PEDESTRIAN (DO NOT CODE)
PL – PILLION PASSENGER
OR – OTHER REAR PASSENGER – INCLUDES LUGGAGE AREA OF STATION WAGON REAR OF GOODS CARRYING VEHICLE BUS. TRAM ETC.
NK – NOT KNOWN

LF	CF	
LR	CR	RR
	OR	

STATEMENT

1 WRITTEN STATEMENT MADE
2   "   "   NOT MADE

VEHICLE (VEH)

INSERT A.B.C. ETC
OR P FOR PEDESTRIAN

TYPE OF VEHICLE

1 CAR
2 STATION WAGON
3 TAXI
4 UTILITY
5 PANEL VAN
6 ARTICULATED VEHICLE (Semi)
7 TRUCK (excluding semi)
8 BUS COACH
9 MINI BUS (9–13 seats)
10 MOTOR CYCLE
11 MOPED
12 MOTOR SCOOTER
13 BICYCLE
14 HORSE DRAWN, HORSE RIDDEN
15 TRAM
16 RAILWAY TRAIN/TROLLEY
17 EMERGENCY SERVICE ON CALL
18 OTHER VEHICLE (specify)
99 NOT KNOWN

LIGHT CONDITIONS

1 DAYLIGHT
2 DUSK OR DAWN
3 DARK—STREET LIGHTS ON
4 DARK—STREET LIGHTS OFF
5 DARK—NO STREET LIGHTS
6 DARK—STREET LIGHT DETAILS NOT KNOWN
9 NOT KNOWN

PEDESTRIAN MOVEMENTS

0 NOT APPLICABLE
1 CROSSING CARRIAGEWAY
2 WORKING, PLAYING, LYING OR STANDING ON CARRIAGEWAY
3 WALKING ON CARRIAGEWAY WITH TRAFFIC
4 WALKING ON CARRIAGEWAY AGAINST TRAFFIC
5 PUSHING OR WORKING ON VEHICLE
6 WALKING TO, FROM OR BOARDING TRAM
7 WALKING TO, FROM OR BOARDING OTHER VEHICLE (specify)
8 NOT ON CARRIAGEWAY (e.g. footpath)
99 NOT KNOWN

ATMOSPHERIC CONDITIONS

1 CLEAR
2 RAINING
3 SNOWING
4 FOG
5 SMOKE
6 DUST IN THE AIR
7 STRONG WINDS
9 NOT KNOWN

CAUGHT FIRE

0 NOT APPLICABLE
1 YES
2 NO
9 NOT KNOWN

WERE PRESCRIBED LAMPS ALIGHT?

HEAD. TAIL NUMBER PLATE BRAKE CLEARANCE (TRUCKS ONLY) PARKING. (INDICATORS IF TURNING)
0 NOT APPLICABLE
1 YES
2 NO
9 NOT KNOWN

ROAD SURFACE CONDITION

1 DRY
2 WET
3 MUDDY
4 SNOW
5 ICY
9 NOT KNOWN

TRAFFIC CONTROL

0 NOT APPLICABLE
1 INTERSECTION SIGNALS OPERATING STOP GO
2 INTERSECTION SIGNALS FLASHING
3 CONTROL OUT OF ORDER/ MALFUNCTIONING
4 PUSH BUTTON PEDESTRIAN SIGNALS NOT CONTROLLING INTERSECTION
5 PEDESTRIAN CROSSING
6 RAILWAY X ING GATES, BOOMS
7 RAILWAY X ING FLASHING LIGHTS/ BELLS ONLY
8 RAILWAY X ING NO AUTOMATIC SIGNALS.
9 ROUNDABOUT SIGN
10 STOP SIGN
11 GIVE WAY SIGN
12 SCHOOL CROSSING WITH FLAGS
13 SCHOOL CROSSING WITHOUT FLAGS
14 POLICE
15 OTHER (SPECIFY)

ROAD SURFACE TYPE

1 PAVED
2 UNPAVED
3 GRAVEL
9 NOT KNOWN

Figure 3.3: (continued).

Table 3.1: Items recorded in the road accident database of Western Australia.
Accident variables

- Accident file number.
- RTA attended.
- Day.
- Date.
- Time.
- Intersection or not.
- Key road.
- Off-road location type.
- Cross road 1.
- Cross road 2.
- Straight line kilometre distance.
- Distance error.
- Local Government Authority.
- Accident location on road reserve.
- Accident unit number of colliding or non-collision vehicle.
- Origin of colliding or non-collision vehicle.
- Non-collision accident type.
- Accident unit number of target vehicle or pedestrian.
- Target vehicle or pedestrian origin.
- Target vehicle or pedestrian destination.
- Target vehicle movement type.
- Pedestrian movement type.
- Target vehicle impact point.
- Object 1.
- Object 2.
- Object 3.
- Traffic control.
- Road feature.
- Road alignment.
- Road condition.
- Road gradient.
- Road surface.
- Atmospheric conditions.
- Lighting.
- Extent of damage.
- Accident nature.
- Accident type.
- Accident severity.
- Accident scope.

Table 3.1: (continued).
Vehicle variables

- Accident unit number.
- Driver or pedestrian name.
- Driver or pedestrian initial.
- Driver or pedestrian address.
- Driver or pedestrian sex.
- Driver or pedestrian date of birth.
- Driver's licence number.
- Vehicle registration number.
- Unit type.
- Towing required.
- Year of manufacture.
- Make.
- Registration body type.
- Colour 1.
- Colour 2.
- Power.
- Fee type.
- Tare weight.
- Aggregate weight.
- Fuel type.
- Number of cylinders.
- Number of axles.
- Annual fee.
- Locality.
- Postcode.

Enforcement variables

- Enforcement type.
- Enforcement details.

Casualty variables

- Vehicle number.
- Casualty age.
- Casualty sex.
- Casualty road user type.
- Extent of injury.

Table 3.2: The core data items recommended by ACRUPTC.

Environment and general variables

- When?
    - Day.
    - Date.
    - Time of day.
- Features of roadway.
    - Intersection design: crossroads; T junction; Y junction; multiple; interchange.
    - Non-intersection features: crossover, median opening; railway level crossing; bridge, causeway, or culvert.
    - Road alignment (non-intersection): straight; curve or bend.
    - Road type: divided; undivided.
- Location.
    - Local government area.
    - Speed limit.
- Accident type.
    - Vehicle-vehicle collision on carriageway: vehicles in traffic; vehicles parked.
    - Single-vehicle collision on carriageway: overturned; struck object; struck pedestrian; struck animal; passenger accident.
    - Single-vehicle collision off carriageway: without colliding; struck object; struck pedestrian; struck animal; struck vehicle.
    - Others.

Table 3.2: (continued).

Vehicle variables

- Registration no.
- Type: passenger car, utility, panel van, or station wagon; motorcycle; other motor vehicle; pedal cycle; train; tram; other.
- Make.
- Year of manufacture.
- Damage: towed; not towed.

Road user variables

- Type.
    - Whether driver or passenger or pedestrian.
    - Whether vehicle occupied or ridden was: passenger car, utility, panel van, or station wagon; other motor vehicle (not a motorcycle); motorcycle; pedal cycle; other.
- Age.
- Sex.
- Injury severity: killed (or died within 30 days); admitted to hospital; other injury requiring medical treatment; injury not requiring medical treatment.
- Licence: full; learner; probationer; no licence; licence not appropriate to class of vehicle driven; cancelled, disqualified, etc.
- Number of occupants (whether injured or not).

Table 3.3: Data recommended by ACRUPTC to be on driver licence or vehicle registration records.
Driver licence records

- Name.

- Address.

- Date of birth.

- Sex.

- Licence number.

- Vehicle class(es), including whether automatic only.

- Date first obtained licence in state of licence.

- Year of first licence in another state or overseas.

- Suspension or disqualification.

- Conditional (or disability) licence.

Vehicle registration records

- Registration no.

- Make.

- Body-style.

- Year of manufacture.

- Model (only for passenger car, utility, panel van, or station wagon).

3.6.2 Summary of the report

At its meeting in March 1976, ATAC (Australian Transport Advisory Council) gave its ACRUPTC (Advisory Committee on Road User Performance and Traffic Codes) the task of re-examining the question of uniformity of road traffic accident statistics. The report that resulted (ACRUPTC, 1978) has four main aspects to it:

- Recommended core data items for state and territory road accident reports. See Table 3.2.

Table 3.4: ACRUPTC's recommendations for an Australian VIN system.
Basic minimum

- Make.

- Model.

- Body-style.

- Year of manufacture.

- Engine type/capacity.

Additional items desirable

- Colour.

- Weight.

- Brakes (front/rear).

- Transmission.

- Seating capacity.

- Items recommended for inclusion in driver licence and vehicle registration records. See Table 3.3.

- Items recommended for inclusion in an Australian Vehicle Identification Number system. See Table 3.4.

- Recommendations for coding vehicle damage data.

3.6.3 Coding of vehicle damage data

ACRUPTC felt improvement to vehicle damage data to be particulary important. As seen in Table 3.2, damage as reflected by whether or not the vehicle had to be towed from the accident scene is included as a core data item. But ACRUPTC considered it desirable to go beyond this, and recommended that the location and extent of damage be recorded, using the following method.

- Location to be specified by the 16 categories: Back; Left side back; Left back door; Left front door; Left side front; Front left; Front centre (chiefly for collisions with narrow objects such as poles and trees); Front right; Right side front; Right front door; Right back door; Right side back; Bonnet; Roof; Boot; Undercarriage.

- Extent to be classified as slight, moderate, or extensive.

3.7 The NAASRA fatal accident report form (Australia)

This is described by Jarvis (1986). The background is that the Road Authorities of the various Australian states have procedures for investigating fatal accident sites. These differ in detail. Arguments in favour of standardising investigation and reporting include:

- Engineers studying a particular site cannot be instinctively aware of all the features and factors that might assume importance when totalled at the national level of analysis.

- Even with regard to site-specific aspects of the crash, the forms that had been in use often had general headings only, relying heavily on the visiting engineer's judgment as to what data was relevant. A well-structured form, as well as being a data-capture instrument, would act as a check list, or aide memoire, and ensure that all factors were considered at the site.

In consultation with the members of NAASRA (National Association of Australian State Road Authorities), the Australian Road Research Board developed a common form, reproduced as Figure 3.4.

Jarvis emphasises a number of desiridata in the design of the form:

- As self-explanatory as possible and easy for the engineer to complete on site.

- Packaged so as to be readily usable and robust in the field.

- Requiring a minimum of additional preparation for computer input.

To achieve these standards, the form has the following physical features:

- It uses paper that is resistant to tearing and water.

- Printing is in two colours to distinguish codings such as column numbers from the content.

- Each form set is housed in a ring binder, hard-backed to provide support for writing.

- A set of instructions is displayed on the inside front cover of the binder.

- A large layout was chosen in order to be clear and easy to use in the field.

My own opinion is that in this last respect, the form is a failure—the print is too small, the alternative answers are too far away from the questions, the structure is not sufficiently clear, the overall result is aesthetically unattractive.

A 6-month trial of the form was carried out in the first half of 1983 in all Australian states with the exception of Queensland but including the Northern Territory. Not all regions of all states participated, in particular there was not a significant response from the metropolitan areas within New South Wales and Victoria. Subsequent to the trial, the Highways Department of South Australia adopted the form as their standard method of reporting engineering examinations of accident sites.

The trial revealed few problems with the form. Three are worth mentioning: the absence of a code for a cyclist being involved; there should be more detail about the manoeuvre being carried out at the time of the accident; road classification was often not known.

Jarvis remarks that on occasions engineers made imaginative attempts to report unusual accidents within the given form structure. This happens with police data too, and limits the amount of automatic cross-checking of variables that can be done—extraordinary things happen from time to time, and apparently-impossible combinations of codes result. The two examples that Jarvis gives, however, are not impossible code combinations but misleading ones:

- Fatal accident, single vehicle, motorcycle involved, struck roadside object, tree...a typical motorcycle accident? No, the tree blew down in high winds and struck the rider on the head as he rode past.

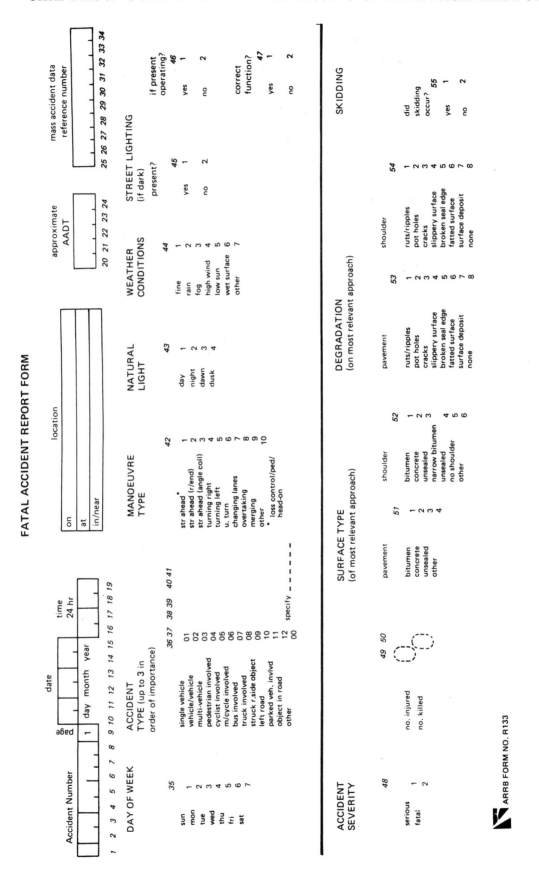

Figure 3.4: The fatal accident report form developed by NAASRA and ARRB, Australia. (A sixth page, for additional notes, is also provided.)

FIGURE 3.4   51

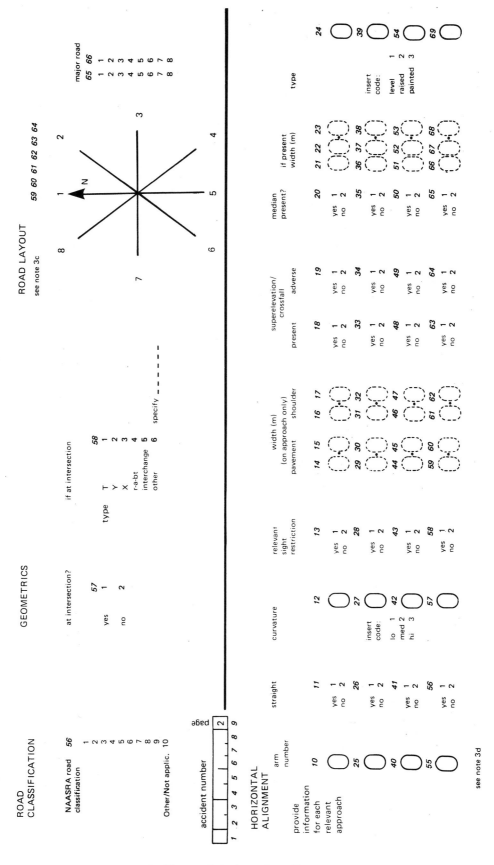

Figure 3.4: (continued).

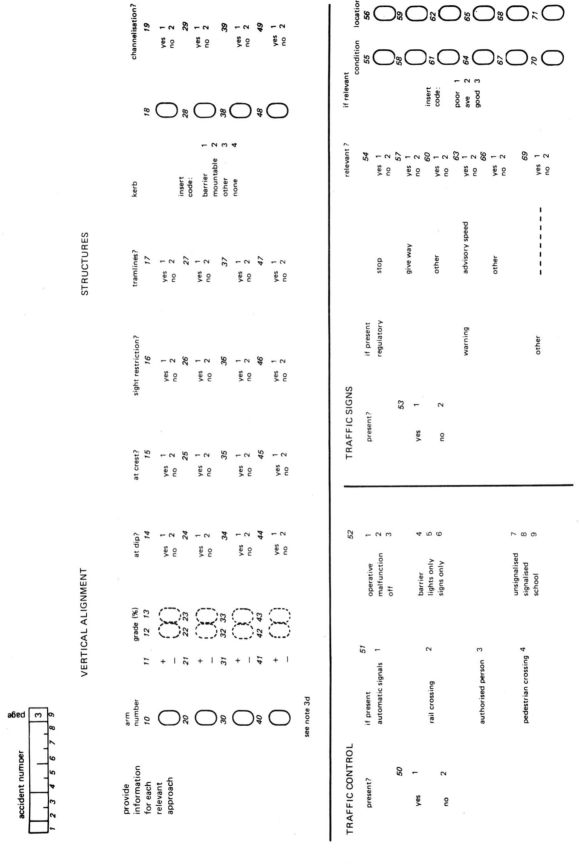

Figure 3.4: (continued).

FIGURE 3.4 53

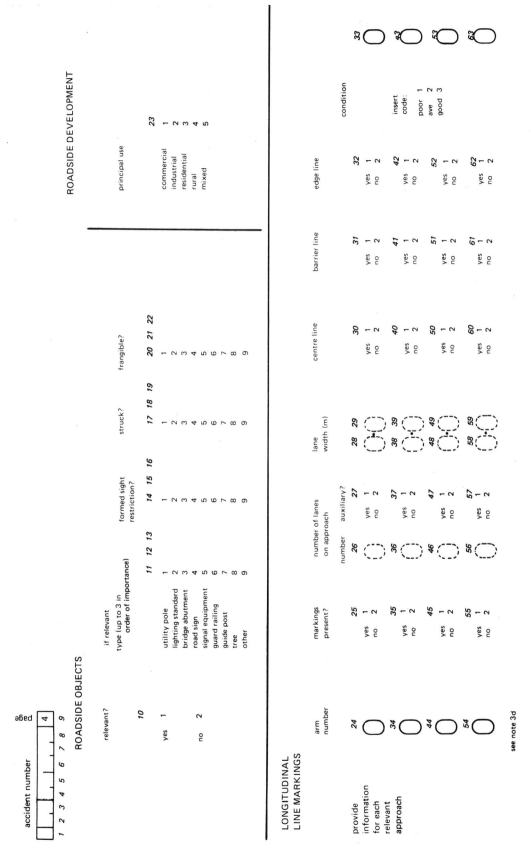

Figure 3.4: (continued).

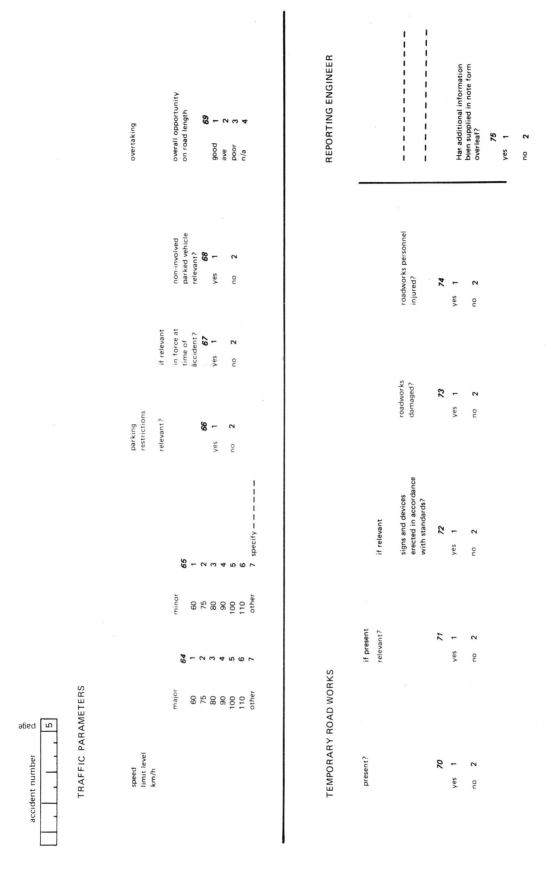

Figure 3.4: (continued).

● Fatal accident, single vehicle, truck involved, struck roadside object, utility pole. In this one, a man standing on the roof of half a house being carried by a low-loader was electrocuted when he came in contact with overhead power lines.

Jarvis consequently makes a key point about form design: "An opportunity should be provided for those reporting to indicate if they feel exceptional circumstances exist which prejudice the sense of the coding used."

3.8   Japan

This account of traffic accident investigation in Japan is based on that of Tomike et al (1982).

Damage-only accidents on ordinary roads: no police accident report filed unless requested by one of the parties for insurance purposes. When requested, the police report is a one-page summary of the facts and the parties involved.

Injury accidents on ordinary roads: different levels of investigation are performed according to whether the accident is a serious one or not. A serious accident is one in which someone is killed or receives injuries requiring 30 days or more medical treatment. (Presumably this is estimated by the investigating officer at the scene.) It is stated in Road Accidents Japan that serious injury means 30 days or more of hospitalisation, but Tomike et al describe it as "all treatment" taking 30 days or more. I do not know which is right.

Expressway accidents: serious accidents receive additional attention, as on ordinary roads, but minor injury and damage-only accidents receive a higher level of attention than on ordinary roads.

The basic investigation report form (Sheet A) describes the accident and the injuries to the two principally-involved persons; Sheet C supplements this for additional injured persons; Sheet B is a supplement used for expressway accidents. The numbers of data items on the sheets is given in Table 3.5, classified into five groups. Table 3.6 gives some examples of the data items, with the numbers of alternative responses available for selection. Figure 3.5, taken from IATSS (1986), lists the main items on the traffic accidents record.

Local police departments send investigation reports to the central police headquarters of their prefecture, where computer-coding takes place. Much accident analysis and safety improvement work is conducted at prefecture level; a copy of the computerised data is sent to the National Police Agency, which summarises national statistics for use by national government in policy formulation and analysis.

3.9   The Netherlands

In The Netherlands, registration of traffic accident data takes place in the following stages: recording by the police; processing of the forms by the Road Accident Records Office; publication of the national figures by the Central Bureau of Statistics. Maas and Harris (1984) report that frequently witnesses of an accident call in medical aid only, i.e. do not inform the police, and whether the police get to know about the accident depends on whether those involved want them to. The public are not very eager to tell the police in cases where the injured person is quite evidently responsible for the accident and there is no appreciable damage to other traffic participants.

Lindeijer (1987) reports on a feasibility study of linking accident and vehicle registration records, using the vehicle registration number as the common item. The reliability and validity of the matching were checked by going to the police reports and finding whether the make and model conformed with the vehicle registration information, and found to be over 95%. However, this study was limited to fatal accidents, and there was a drop-out rate of 12% (principally, foreign-registered vehicles, or the registration number not being recorded by the police).

3.10   U.S. states

Descriptions of the procedures for collecting and processing data may be found in some of the publications cited in Section 4.2.5 below, for instance, Zegeer (1982). There is a collection of the accident report forms used in the 50 U.S. states, plus the District of Columbia, Puerto Rico, and the U.S. Virgin Islands, in NHTSA (1986).

Among the 17 state road accident statistical yearbooks which I have to hand, I find only one prints the report form, so I have chosen that one (South Carolina) to illustrate in Figure 3.6.

 1. **Prefectural police code**
 2. **Form number**
 3. **Municipality code**
 4. **Road classification:**
      Ordinary road, expressway
 5. **Nature of accident**
      Fatal, serious injury, slight injury, property damage
 6. **Number of fatalities**
 7. **Number of seriously injured persons**
 8. **Number of slightly injured persons**
 9. **Data and time of accident**
      year _____ month _____ day _____ hour _____ minute _____
10. **Daytime or nighttime**
11. **Day of week**
12. **Weather conditions**
      Clear, cloudy, raining, fog, snow, etc.
13. **Route code**
14. **Nationality by party concerned**
15. **Area of residence by party concerned**
16. **Occupation code by party concerned**
17. **Age by party concerned**
18. **Sex by party concerned**
19. **Classification of accident**
      Ordinary accident, Special accident (User of amphetamines and other drugs, hazardous concerted action, hit and run, vehicle fire, fit, car starting on its own, opening and closing door, emergency vehicle, unreported, multiple accident)
20. **Road surface conditions**
      (Paved/unpaved) × (dry, wet/slippery, ice, snow on road, other)
21. **Type of area**
      Built-up area of buildings (offices, commercial businesses, factories, residences, multi-storied residences), dispersed buildings, no building
22. **Geographical features**
      Urban (densely populated area, other), non-urban area
23. **Road format**
      Intersection (major, medium-sized, minor), non-intersection (near intersection, tunnel, bridge, other), railway crossing (Type 1, 2, 3, 4), other
24. **Linear formation of road**
      (Uphill, downhill, flat) × [Curve (left/right), sharp bend (left/right), straight], other
25. **Railway crossing**
      Japanese National Railway (J.N.R.), private railroad, not applicable
26. **Intersection format**
      3-way intersection, 4-way intersection (regular, other), 5-way intersection, 6-way or more, not applicable
27. **Vehicular width**
      Less than 3.5m, more than 3.5m, more than 4.5m, more than 5.5m, more than 7.5m, more than 9.0m, more than 13.0m, more than 19.5m, other
28. **Median strip facilities, etc.**
      Guard fence, chatter bar (lane dividing pole) etc., center line. None.
29. **Separation of sidewalk and vehicular road**
      Yes (guard fence, curbing, block, etc., side-strip). None.
30. **Traffic signals**
      Yes (malfunctioning, off-light, flashing). None.

Figure 3.5: Contents of the traffic accidents record in Japan. (Reproduced by kind permission of the IATSS.)

FIGURE 3.5   57

31. Zone
   Living zone, school zone, living-school zone, other. Not applicable.

32. Speed limit
   20km/hr or less, 30km/hr or less, 40km/hr or less, 50km/hr or less, 60km/hr or less, 70km/hr or less, 80km/hr or less, 100km/hr or less, not applicable.

33. Parking and stopping regulations
   24-hour, within permitted hours, outside permitted hours, other.

34. Traffic regulation code

35. Type of vehicle
   Passenger vehicle (bus, microbus, regular, light), truck (special large, large, trailer, regular, regular light van, light), two-wheeled vehicle [motorcycle (small, light, Type 2 moped), moped], special vehicle (agricultural use, large, small), street car, other (train, bicycle, light vehicle) pedestrian, parked vehicle (unmanned), property, no other party involved, no information.

36. Purpose of vehicle use
   Business [regular bus service, chartered bus, hired vehicle, taxi (corporation, private), transport of earth and sand, transport of hazardous materials, garbage truck, concrete-mixer, refrigerated truck, cooled truck, container truck, regular-route cargo transport, local cargo transport, other], private (rented car, bus, school bus, transport of earth and sand, transport of hazardous materials, garbage truck, concrete mixer, refrigerated truck, cooled truck, container truck, other passenger vehicle, other freight truck), motorcycle, moped (family use, other), bicycle, no information, not applicable.

37. Type of accident
   <u>Person vs. vehicle</u> [moving toward vehicle, moving away from vehicle, crossing (crosswalk, near corsswalk, near pedestrian bridge, other), playing on the road, working on road, stopping at roadside, moving on footpath, moving on side strip, other]
   <u>Vehicle vs. vehicle</u> [head on collision (passing or overtaking, other), rear-end collision (moving, stopping or parking), front-end collision, passing/overtaking, making U-turn, moving backwards, changing course, moving past each other, turning left or right, other]
   <u>Single vehicle</u>   collision with structure (electric pole, road sign, pedestrian island, guard fence, house and fence, bridge, other), running off road (rolling down, other), collision with unmanned parked vehicle, overturning, other
   <u>Railway crossing</u>   (crash through crossing gate, ignoring warning signal, moving through immediately prior to gate closure, other)

38. Type of action
   Vehicle [starting, passing/overtaking, making U-turn, backing, crossing, changing course, turning left or right, stopping suddenly, stopping, parking, moving straight ahead (accelerating, slowing, other) other], walking, no information, not applicable.

39. Speed immediately before accident
   20km/hr or less, 30km/hr or less, 40km/hr or less, 50km/hr or less, 60km/hr or less, 80km/hr or less, 100km/hr or less, 120km/hr or less, 121km/hr or more, no information, not applicable.

40. Driving frequency
   Daily, frequently, occasionally, seldom, no information, not applicable.

41. Hours of driving

42. Accident pattern
   Entanglement, drag, run over, knock off, knock down, crash, contact, other.

43. Purpose of travel
   Professoinal driving; business purpose, commuting to work or school, leisure (sightseeing, sports, drive, walking, other), other private purpose (shopping, visiting, going to class, eating or drinking, returning to hometown, other), no information, not applicable.

44. Destination
   Travel within area, from within area to another area, from another area to within area, through traffic, no information, not applicable.

45. Type of driver's license
   Large Type 2, regular Type 2, large special Type 2, large, regular; large special, motorcycle (unrestricted, medium, small), small special, moped, no driver's license, no information, not applicable.

46. Driving qualifications
   Licensed [temporary license (large, regular), record of past revocation, other], Not licensed [revoked (period of ineligibility), suspended; unqualified, issuance procedure not completed, improper license, expired license (within six months), other forms of unlicensed driving, provisional license violation, violation of license conditions], no information, not applicable.

Figure 3.5: (continued).

47. **Appointment of company safe driving supervisors.**
    Appointed safe driving supervisor or operation supervisor, not appointed, no information, not applicable.
48. **Insurance**
    Insured [voluntary (including compulsory) (less than ¥20 million, ¥20 million or more, ¥30 million or more, ¥50 million or more, ¥70 million or more, ¥100 million or more; compulsory only], not insured, no information, not applicable.
49. **Vehicle inspection**
    Vehicle inspection required [(one year, two years) × periodical inspection received/not required], not required, no information, not applicable.
50. **Self protection**
    Used [seatbelt (two-point, three-point, other), helmet (meets standards, other)], not used, not equipped, no information, not applicable.
51. **Degree of vehicle damage**
    Heavy, medium, light, slight, fire, immersed in water, no information, not applicable.
52. **Number of years elapsed since licence acquisition**
53. **Number of years of experience with type of vehicle involved in accident**
54. **Code of each primary violation**
55. **Code of each secondary violation**
56. **Code of vehicle manufacturer**
57. **Model year**
58. **Code of total engine displacement**
59. **Defective vehicle parts**
    Primary: _____   Secondary: _____
60. **Classification of causes**
    Primary cause _____   Secondary cause _____
    Tertiary cause _____
61. **Degree of bodily injury**
    Death, serious injury, slight injury, no information, not applicable.
62. **Part of body injured**
    Head, face, neck, chest, abdomen, back and spinal column, arm, leg, other, no information, not applicable.
63. **Condition of part of body injured**
    Amputation, bone fracture, deep cut, internal injury, drowning, burns, head concussion, whiplash, dislocation, sprain, laceration, confusion, abrasion, bruise, other, no information, not applicable.
64. **Object involved in bodily injury**
    Vehicle interior (thrown from vehicle, steering wheel, window glass, instrument panel, door, pillar, ceiling, seat, luggage, pedal, lever, other), Vehicle body [front (bonnet), bumper, other), side (luggage rack, front wheel, rear wheel, other), rear, luggage, other], motorcycle or bicycle (front wheel, handle bars, other), property, other (electric pole, road sign, pedestrian island, road surface, guard fence, house, fence, other), no information, not applicable.
65. **Hours required to transport injured person from scene of accident to hospital**
66. **Hospital**
    Designated energency hospital, other.
67. **Starting point of crossing made by pedestrian**
    From behind another vehicle (parked vehicle, stopped vehicle, moving vehicle), from behind a building, from behind a structure, from an alley, other from roadside, not applicable.
68. **Quasi-pedestrians, pedestrians**
    In wheelchair, pushing wheelchair, in pram, pushing pram, infant's vehicle, pushing two-wheeled vehicle, other quasi-pedestrian, ordinary pedestrian, not applicable.
69. **Place of accident involving child going to or leaving school**
    (Going to/leaving) (on route to school) (off route to school), no information, not applicable.
70. **Companion of infant**
    Father, mother, grandparent, sibling, friend, other, infant alone, not applicable.
71. **Distance from home (cyclist, pedestrian)**
    Less than 50m, 50m or more, 100m or more, 500m or more, 1,000m or more, 2,000m or more, no information, not applicable.

Figure 3.5: (continued).

FIGURE 3.5   59

72. **Place where bicycle was moving**

    Bicycle crossing zone, crosswalk, exclusive bicycle path, bicycle path, vehicle roadway (left side, right side, other), sidewalk (where bicycle traffic is permitted, other), side strip, exclusive road for pedestrians and bicycles, other, no information, not applicable.

73. **Type of bicycle**

    Two-wheeled [ordinary, sport, mini-cycle, supplementary wheel (installed/not installed)], tandem, other, three-wheeled, no information, not applicable.

74. **Handle bars**

    Ordinary, drop, eagle, other, no information, not applicable.

75. **Brake system**

    Rod, wire (carry bar/disc), other, no information, not applicable.

76. **Gear system**

    Installed [less than 5-speed, 5-speed or more, 10-speed or more, 15-speed or more], not installed, no information, not applicable.

77. **Indicators**

    Installed (on/off, continuous, other), not installed, no information, not applicable.

78. **Reckless driving**

    (Motorcycle or car gang, other than motorcycle or car gang) × (moving in a group/moving alone), no information, not applicable.

79. **Type of load**

80. **Maximum load**

    Less than 1 ton, 1 ton or more, 2 tons or more, 3 tons or more, 5 tons or more, 6.5 tons or more, 8 tons or more, 10 tons or more, 12 tons or more, no information, not applicable.

81. **Overloading**

    Less than 50%, 50% or more, 100% or more, 150% or more, 200% or more, no information, not applicable.

82. **License conditions for physical handicaps (vehicle)**

    Automatic, manual, other, no information, not applicable.

83. **License conditions for physical handicaps (person)**

    Hearing aid, physical aid (artificial hand, artificial leg), other, no information, not applicable.

Figure 3.5: (continued).

TOTAL # MOTOR VEH.   ORIGINAL

SOUTH CAROLINA
UNIFORM TRAFFIC COLLISION REPORT
(FOR INVESTIGATING OFFICERS)
D.H.P.T. FORM TR-310 REV. 3/85

M.V.D. USE ONLY

SHEET   OF   SHEET(S)

FATALITY =

DATE   COUNTY   DAY OF WEEK   S M T W T F S   TIME :   AM PM   ON 1 - INTERSTATE 4 - SECONDARY / 2 - US PRIMARY 5 - COUNTY / 3 - SC PRIMARY 6 - OTHER   ROUTE OR ROAD NO. (Also Street Name. If Any)   MILE POST

INTERSECTION OF ROUTE OR ROAD NUMBER (Also Street Name. If Any) AT   IF NOT AT INTERSECTION: 1 - FEET / 2 - MILES   N E S W   OF   ROUTE OR ROAD NO. (Also Street Name. If Any)

IN   CITY OR TOWN   CONTROLLED ACCESS HIGHWAY LOCATION (Circle One)   1 - MAIN ROAD / 2 - FRONTAGE RD.   3 - MAIN ROAD AT INTERCHANGE   4 - ENTRANCE RAMP / 5 - EXIT RAMP   N E S W   1 - BOUND LANE / 2 - SIDE

IF OUTSIDE CITY LIMITS   MILES N E S W OF   CITY OR TOWN   R R CROSSING I.D. #

UNIT #   DRIVER'S FULL NAME   UNIT #   PED.   DRIVER OR PEDESTRIAN'S FULL NAME

STREET OR R.F.D.   BIRTH DATE   SEX   RACE   STREET OR R.F.D.   BIRTH DATE   SEX   RACE

CITY AND STATE   ZIP   DRIVER LICENSE CLASS 1 2 3 4 / B - BEG. PER.   N - NONE   CITY AND STATE   ZIP   DRIVER LICENSE CLASS 1 2 3 4 / B - BEG. PER.   N - NONE

DRIVER LICENSE NUMBER   STATE   DRIVER LICENSE NUMBER   STATE

LICENSE RESTRICTION   RESTRICTION COMPLIED WITH   Y - YES   N - NO   MEMBER OF ARMED FORCES   Y - YES   N - NO   LICENSE RESTRICTION   RESTRICTION COMPLIED WITH   Y - YES   N - NO   MEMBER OF ARMED FORCES   Y - YES   N - NO

DRIVER WEARING SAFETY BELTS   Y - YES   N - NO   MOVING VIOLATION(S) INDICATED   SPEED LIMIT   MPH   ESTIMATED SPEED   MPH   DRIVER WEARING SAFETY BELTS   Y - YES   N - NO   MOVING VIOLATION(S) INDICATED   SPEED LIMIT   MPH   ESTIMATED SPEED   MPH

YEAR   BODY   MAKE & VEHICLE IDENTIFICATION NUMBER   YEAR   BODY   MAKE & VEHICLE IDENTIFICATION NUMBER

LICENSE PLATE NUMBER   STATE   YEAR   CIRCLE POINT OF INITIAL IMPACT   LICENSE PLATE NUMBER   STATE   YEAR   CIRCLE POINT OF INITIAL IMPACT

VALIDATION NUMBER   TOTAL OCCUPANTS THIS UNIT   VALIDATION NUMBER   TOTAL OCCUPANTS THIS UNIT

OWNER'S NAME   OWNER'S NAME

STREET OR R.F.D   CITY AND STATE   STREET OR R.F.D.   CITY AND STATE

INSPECTION CERTIFICATE   1 - CURRENT   3 - NONE / 2 - EXPIRED   4 - UNKNOWN   ZIP   INSPECTION CERTIFICATE   1 - CURRENT   3 - NONE / 2 - EXPIRED   4 - UNKNOWN   ZIP

DAMAGE SEVERITY 1 - SLIGHT 2 - MODERATE 3 - SEVERE   AREAS DAMAGED (CODES)   APPROX. COST TO REPAIR $ VEHICLE TOWED AWAY Y - YES   N - NO   DAMAGE SEVERITY 1 - SLIGHT 2 - MODERATE 3 - SEVERE   AREAS DAMAGED (CODES)   APPROX. COST TO REPAIR $ VEHICLE TOWED AWAY Y - YES   N - NO

VEHICLE TOWED BY WHOM   VEHICLE TOWED BY WHOM

DIRECTION OF TRAVEL   N E S W   UNIT   1   1 2 3 4   UNIT   2   1 2 3 4   INDICATE NORTH   DESCRIBE WHAT HAPPENED (Refer to units by number):

MAIL ORIGINAL REPORT TO S. C. DEPT. OF HIGHWAYS & PUBLIC TRANSPORTATION, BOX 1498, COLUMBIA, S. C. 29216-0040

WITNESS FULL NAME   ADDRESS   ZIP   AGE   SEX

SUMMONS NUMBER   NAME OF PERSON CHARGED   MOVING VIOLATION CODE(S)   DAMAGE TO PROPERTY OTHER THAN VEHICLE   APPROX. AMOUNT $

SUMMONS NUMBER   NAME OF PERSON CHARGED   MOVING VIOLATION CODE(S)   PROPERTY OWNER'S NAME

POLICE AGENCY NOTIFIED AM PM   POLICE ARRIVED AM PM   AMBULANCE ARRIVED AM PM   PHOTOS TAKEN BY OFFICER Y - YES   N - NO   TRAFFIC FLOW RESTORED AM PM   ADDRESS   ZIP

VICTIMS

NAME 1   ADDRESS   ZIP

NAME 2   ADDRESS   ZIP

NAME 3   ADDRESS   ZIP

NAME OF INVESTIGATING OFFICER   BADGE NUMBER   POLICE AGENCY   DATE

NAME OF OTHER OFFICER(S) AT SCENE   BADGE NUMBER   POLICE AGENCY

Figure 3.6: Form TR-310, used in South Carolina.

FIGURE 3.6 61

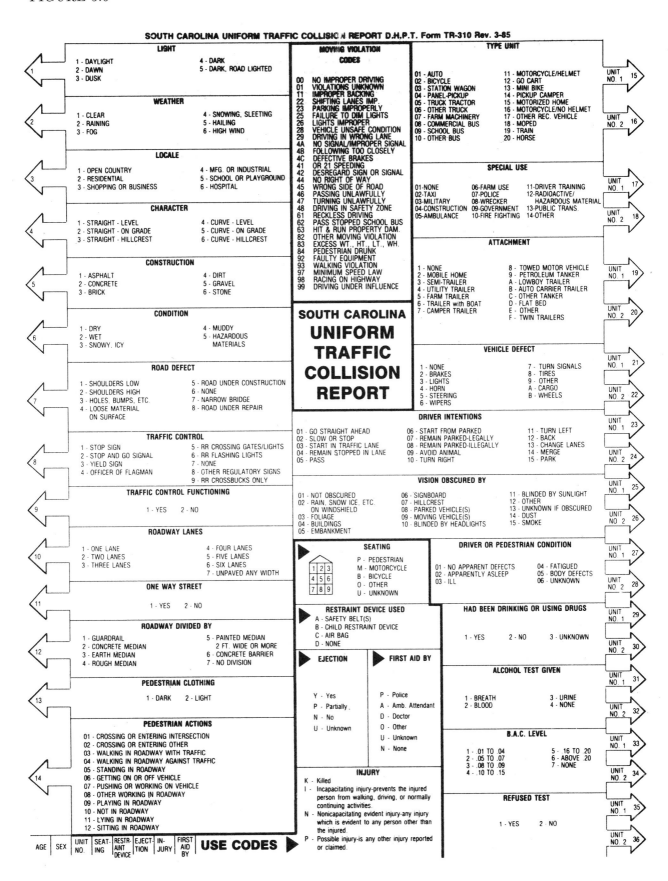

Figure 3.6: (continued).

Table 3.5: Numbers of items within each of five groups on the three Japanese accident investigation sheets.

	A	Investigation sheet B (Expressway supplement)	C (Casualty supplement)
General summary	12	11	5
Date, time, weather	7	0	0
Location description	21	3	3
Human	26	3	15
Vehicle	21	2	9

Table 3.6: Examples of the data collected by the Japanese police, with the numbers of alternative categories available.

	Number of alternative categories
Description of collision and its results:	
Type of collision	41
Vehicles and objects involved	32
Vehicle movements	18
Damage to vehicles	8
Injuries received:	
Overall severity	5
Part of body	10
Type of injury	17
Object causing injury	34
Restraint and helmet usage	9
Cause of accident:	
Primary violation or contributing factor	98
Secondary violation or contributing factor	98
General causes of the accident (up to 3, to be ranked)	5
Detailed causes of the accident (up to 3, to be ranked)	418

3.11   North Carolina

Campbell (1978) makes several interesting points in describing data from North Carolina.

3.11.1   Supplementary surveys

Campbell emphasises the potential in supplementing the standard report form with a short extra questionnaire designed to capture data on a topic of current interest. He gives four examples, on tyre condition (tread depth), occupant characteristics (whether there were passengers, and, if so, their race, sex, and age), restraint system availability and use, and vehicle safety features.

3.11.2   Exposure data

Having data on the population at risk is very important in order to interpret crash data correctly.

Thus tread depth was measured on cars stopping at petrol stations for comparison with tread depth on crash-involved cars, and data on occupant characteristics were collected in the course of a routine origin-and-destination survey.

3.11.3 Vehicle Identification Numbers

The VIN is a multi-character alphanumeric code enabling such things as car make and model to be identified (plus production sequence, factory, engine, etc.). It is interesting firstly because it is such a valuable piece of information to have; and secondly because it is so difficult to use—there are so many characters that mistakes in reporting it are common, different manufacturers use different formats, the formats change from time to time.

Since Campbell wrote his paper, the use of VIN's has become easier: see Section 6.4.6 and Marsh (1985).

3.11.4 Vehicle deformation

An attempt is made to grade the amount of vehicle damage in a crash. This is done by having a manual of photographs, each page representing a type of damage (e.g. "front concentrated", "front distributed", "left front corner", etc.), and on each page three photos depicting successively higher levels: these photos are assigned grades 2, 4, and 6, and grades 1, 3, 5, and 7 may also be used for cases in between those shown or more extreme than them. Such a scale is not perfect—inevitably there is an element of subjectivity in the assessment, and, moreover, a stiffly constructed car yields a somewhat lower rating than one more crushable—but is probably better than an officer's estimate of speed and certainly shows promise as a statistical control variable.

3.11.5 Searching a narrative

The narrative description of the accident is a potential gold-mine of information. However, it is not normally stored in computer-readable form; and if it were, it would be difficult to process. But since 1971, narratives have been stored on computer tape in North Carolina, and the Highway Safety Research Center of the University of North Carolina has developed software to make use of

them. The analyst defines words and phrases that might be used to describe an event (e.g. a type of vehicle defect), and these are searched for in the descriptions. (Often, they should be compared with a test accident data file first, to check that they are producing "hits" and not too many "false alarms", e.g. when searching for vehicle fires using the word "fire", that not too many fire hydrants or fire trucks are found.) This summary is based upon Campbell (1981) as well as Campbell (1978).

Though it is not done at present, the inclusion of a verbal description of the accident in the computerised dataset, and the ability to analyse it with a text-retrieval package, was considered desirable by South Australia's Road Safety Division when planning their future procedures (Computer Power, 1986). As has been mentioned in Section 3.2, some British local authorities include a free-text account of the accident in their database.

3.11.6 Feedback to police

Campbell feels feedback to the police is so important that he published a monthly bulletin, The Accident Reporter, distributed to each police officer in the state. Feedback was generally one of three types:

- Specific admonition about problem areas, or specific instruction on new reporting procedures, and praise, too.

- Reports on special projects that involved the police, such as the supplementary surveys described above.

- More general information about related research, to broaden the officer's understanding.

(I believe publication of The Accident Reporter has ceased, due to shortage of money.)

3.12 The U.S. National Accident Sampling System (NASS)

The U.S.A. does not collect nationwide statistics on all traffic accidents—each state has its own system for collecting and analysing such data, though many do send summary figures to the National

Safety Council in Chicago. What there is instead (since 1979) is the National Accident Sampling System. In 1984, about 12,000 accidents were reported through this (out of a total of 5,900,000 that were reported to the police, which in turn are a subset of the 18,800,000 reported to all sources).

NASS teams located in 50 areas of the U.S.A. investigate a random sample of the police-reported accidents in their area. Estimates of the total numbers are based on scaling up using the known features of the sampling procedure. Because the sampling is random, estimates can also be made of the accuracies (standard errors) of the totals.

The sample design is described in Appendix 2 of NASS (1985). In brief:

- The U.S.A. was divided into 1279 primary sampling units (PSU's), each consisting of a large city, a county, or a group of contiguous counties, having a total population of at least 50,000; these were grouped into 50 categories described by geographic region, degree of urbanisation, per capita service station sales, per capita road miles, and population per square mile; one PSU was then selected from each category.

- The police agencies within a PSU are classified by the number and type of traffic accident reports they process. Sample police agencies are then selected from each category.

- Finally, to avoid the sample being overwhelmed by the great number of minor accidents and to get enough serious accidents in the sample, different severities and categories of accident (e.g. pedestrian, motorcycle, truck, car) have different probabilities of being investigated.

When an accident is selected in the sample, the police accident report serves as a starting point for the NASS investigation. The researchers find the vehicles involved, assess and measure the damage, and locate interior and exterior impact points that caused injuries. They survey the scene of the accident, and reconstruct what happened from clues such as skid marks, impact points, vehicle damage, etc. They interview the people involved, and obtain official records such as vehicle and driver records, and medical or coroner's reports. Such procedures are by now conventional enough in accident research. What is unusual about NASS is the combination of the detail of investigation and the size of sample collected (along with the careful data collection procedures and quality control checks that the involvement of 50 teams necessitates). Figure 3.7 lists the data collected by the NASS.

For a lengthier discussion of the philosophy of the NASS (written while it was still at an advanced stage of planning), see Kahane et al (1977). Some recent developments are described by Nash and McDonald (1985). These include microcomputers for data entry and editing, use of the CRASH 3 program to aid accident reconstruction, and a vehicle contour gauge for damage measurement.

3.13 The U.S. Fatal Accident Reporting System (FARS)

FARS data are gathered on all motor vehicle accidents occurring on roadways customarily open to the public that result in someone's death within 30 days. (Any resulting from natural disasters are excluded.) FARS data is transmitted to the National Center for Statistics and Analysis of the NHTSA (National Highway Traffic Safety Administration) by the states, who use documents such as police accident reports, hospital medical reports, and death certificates as their sources. Because the state records vary in their content, the availability of some FARS data elements varies between states, too.

The forms—for the accident, the vehicle and its driver, and persons involved—are reproduced as Figure 3.8.

An annual report is published (e.g. FARS, 1987); in addition, special analyses can be performed by NHTSA or the computer tapes purchased in order to carry out one's own analyses.

3.14 Computerised tabulation of accident data

3.14.1 Survey analysis packages

The result of the collecting and coding of road accident information is a computer file in which each

FIGURE 3.7 65

DRIVER LEVEL ELEMENTS (For Each Driver Involved)

Vehicle Number
Number of Occupants This Vehicle
Driver Presence in Vehicle
Months Driving Experience This Class of Vehicle
Estimated Mileage This Vehicle
Total Mileage All Vehicles
Type of Operation or Carrier
Federal Safety Regulated
Driver Classification
Driver Education
Frequency Driving Road
Actions Prior to Avoidance Maneuvers (3)
Attempted Avoidance Maneuver
Accidents Within Past 12 Months
Traffic Violation Charged Against This Driver
    Speeding
    Driving While Intoxicated (DWI or DUIL)
    Reckless Driving
    Driving with Suspended or Revoked License
    Failure to Yield Right-of-Way
    Following too Closely
    Running a Traffic Signal or Stop Sign
    Other Violation Charged
    Unknown Violation Charged
Police Reported Alcohol Presence
Alcohol Test Result

License Source
Compliance With License Restrictions
Driver License Status (for this Vehicle)
Driver License Type Compliance
Driver License Restrictions
Additional Driver License Restrictions
Previous Speeding Convictions
Previous Other Harmful Moving Violation Convictions
Previous Driving While Intoxicated or DUIL Convictions
Previous Recorded Suspensions and Revocations
Previous Recorded Accidents
Number of Travel Lanes
Median Width
Median Type
Access Control
Trafficway Flow
Left Shoulder Type
Right Shoulder Type
Roadway Alignment (Horizontal)
Roadway Profile (Vertical)
Roadway Surface Type
Roadway Surface Condition
Speed Limit
Traffic Control Device Functioning
Traffic Control Device
Other Driver Related Factors (3)
Other Environmental Related Factors

OCCUPANT LEVEL ELEMENTS (For Each Occupant Involved)

Vehicle Number
Occupant Number
Age
Sex
Height
Weight
Role
Seat Position
Entrapment
Ejection
Ejection Area
Ejection Medium
Medium Status
Treatment-Mortality
Hospital Stay

Working Days Lost
Manual Restraint System Availability
Manual Restraint System Use
Automatic Restraint System Availability
Automatic Restraint System Function
Relation of Interviewee to Occupant
O.I.C. Body Region (6)**
Aspect (6)**
Lesion (6)**
System/Organ (6)**
AIS. Severity (6)**
Injury Source (6)**
Source of Data (6)**
Injury Severity (Police Rating)
Time of Death

PEDESTRIAN AND NON-MOTORIST LEVEL ELEMENTS
(For Each Pedestrian and Non-motorist Involved)

Pedestrian or Non-motorist's Number
Type
Age
Sex
Height
Weight
Months Cycling Experience
Location
Treatment-Mortality
Hospital Stay
Working Days Lost
Relation of Interviewee to Pedestrian or Non-Motorist
O.I.C. Body Region (6)**

Aspect (6)**
Lesion (6)**
System/Organ (6)**
AIS Severity (6)**
Injury Source (6)**
Source of Data (6)**
Injury Severity (Police Report)
Traffic Violation Charged
Police-Reported Alcohol Involvement
Alcohol Test Result
Time of Death
Other Pedestrian/Non-motorist Related Factors (3)

---

*This element occurs at all levels.
**Indicates that up to six injuries are coded when appropriate.
***Only these data elements are coded for non-towaway accidents.
+Trucks over 10,000 lbs only.
++Indicates that up to four events are coded when appropriate.

Figure 3.7: Data items collected by the U.S. National Accident Sampling System.

On the following two pages is a list of the data elements available on the 1984 NASS automated files. For more complete information, consult the NASS Analytical User's Manual, available through the National Center for Statistics and Analysis (NRD-30), National Highway Traffic Safety Administration, 400 7th Street, S.W., Washington, D.C. 20590.

ACCIDENT LEVEL ELEMENTS

Primary Sampling Unit Number*
Case Number*
Stratification*
Primary Sampling Unit Weight*
National Weight*
Ratio Weight*
Day of Week
Month
Year
First Harmful Event
Manner of Collision
Relation to Roadway
  (Location of First Harmful Event)
Number of Vehicle Forms Submitted
Number of Non-Motorist Forms Submitted
Police-Reported Accident Severity
Hit and Run
Time of Day
Light Conditions
Atmospheric Conditions
Land Use (Urban/Rural)
Federal Aid System
Class Trafficway

Roadway Function Class
Relation to Junction
School Bus Related
Right or Left Turn on Red Related
Number of Travel Lanes
Median Type
Median Width
Access Control
Trafficway Flow
Interchange Geometry
Shoulder Presence
Roadway Alignment (Horizontal)
Roadway Profile (Vertical)
Roadway Surface Type
Roadway Surface Condition
Traffic Control Device
Traffic Control Device Functioning
Accident Occurrence in School Zone (Yes/No)
Speed Limit
Restriction of Roadway at Scene
Additional Restrictions to Roadway at Scene

VEHICLE LEVEL ELEMENTS (For Each Vehicle Involved)

Vehicle Number***
Number of Occupant Forms Submitted***
Vehicle Role***
Manner of Leaving Scene***
Vehicle Model Year***
Vehicle Make***
Vehicle Model***
Body Type***
Towed Trailing Unit
Cab Configuration
Seating Capacity/Truck Vocation
Tractor with Dromedary+
Number of Axles+
Type of Brakes+
Gross Vehicle Weight Rating+
Event Number, this Vehicle (4)++
Object Contacted (4)++
Direction of Force (4)++
Deformation Location (4)++
Specific Logitudinal or Lateral Location (4)++
Specific Vertical or Lateral Location (4)++
Type of Damage Distribution (4)++
Deformation Extent Guide (4)++
Event Number, in Accident (4)++
Vehicle Identification Number
  (Excludes Production Number)

Registration of Vehicle
Vehicle Special Use
Odometer Reading
Passenger Compartment Integrity
Passenger Compartment Intrusion
Magnitude of Intrusion
Fire Occurrence
Type of Most Severe Impact
Role of Other Contacted Vehicle, Object or Person
Rollover Involvement
Jackknife Involvement (Yes/No)
Submission of Potential Safety Problem
Hazardous Cargo
Vehicle Curb Weight
Vehicle Cargo Weight
Source of Cargo Weight
Basis for Total Delta V
Total Delta V
Longitudinal Component of Delta V
Lateral Component of Delta V
Energy Absorption
Crash Damage Data for Highest Delta V
Police Reported Travel Speed
Other Vehicle Related Factors

Figure 3.7: (continued).

FIGURE 3.8

67

US Department of Transportation
National Highway Traffic Safety Administration

1987 Fatal Accident Reporting System (FARS)
ACCIDENT LEVEL

Form Approved thru
O.M.B. No. 2127-0006

CODED BY: _____

DATE CODED: _____

STATE CASE NO: _____

CASE NUMBER STATE (GSA CODES)	1 2	3	6	TRANSACTION CODE	7 8	CARD NO.	9

11 – Original Submission   13 – Delete
12 – Update or Change   14 – List

CARD NO. **1**   **1**

CITY	COUNTY	MONTH DAY YEAR	TIME

14   17   18   20   DATE   21   26   **8 7**   TIME   27   30
Military Time
9999 – Unknown

Number of Vehicle Forms Submitted	31 32	Number of Person Forms Submitted	33 34	FEDERAL-AID SYSTEM	35

1 – Interstate
2 – Federal Aid Primary (other than interstate)
3 – Federal Aid Urban
4 – Federal Aid Secondary (rural only)
5 – Non Federal Aid
9 – Unknown

ROADWAY FUNCTION CLASS   36   37

RURAL
01 Principal Arterial - Interstate
02 Principal Arterial - Other
03 Minor Arterial
04 Major Collector
05 Minor Collector
06 Local Road or Street
09 Unknown Rural

URBAN
11 Principal Arterial - Interstate
12 Principal Arterial - Other
13 Other Principal Arterial
14 Minor Arterial
15 Collector
16 Local Road or Street
19 Unknown Urban

99 UNKNOWN

ROUTE SIGNING   38

1 - Interstate
2 – U.S. Highway
3 – State Highway
4 – County Road

LOCAL STREET
5 – Township
6 – Municipality
8 – Other
9 – Unknown

TRAFFICWAY IDENTIFIER   39   48

Actual Posted Number, Assigned Number, or Common Name (if No Posted or Assigned Number)
Except: Nine Fill if Unknown

MILEPOINT   49   53

Actual to Nearest .1 Mile (Assumed Decimal)
Except: 00000 – None
99999 – Unknown

SPECIAL JURISDICTION   54

0 – No Special Jurisdiction
1 – National Park Service
2 – Military
3 – Indian Reservation
4 – College/University Campus
5 – Other Federal Properties
8 – Other
9 – Unknown

FIRST HARMFUL EVENT   55   56

(See Instruction Manual)

MANNER OF COLLISION   57

0 – Not Collision with Motor Vehicle in Transport
1 – Rear-End
2 – Head On
3 – Rear-to-Rear
4 – Angle
5 – Sideswipe, Same Direction
6 – Sideswipe, Opposite Direction
9 – Unknown

RELATION TO JUNCTION   58

1 – Non-Junction
2 – Intersection
3 – Intersection Related
4 – Interchange Area
5 – Driveway, Alley Access, etc.
6 – Entrance/Exit Ramp
7 – Rail Grade Crossing
8 – In Crossover
9 – Unknown

RELATION TO ROADWAY   59

1 – On Roadway
2 – Shoulder
3 – Median
4 – Roadside
5 – Outside Right-of-Way
6 – Off Roadway – Location Unknown
7 – In Parking Lane
8 – Gore
9 – Unknown

TRAFFICWAY FLOW   60

1 – Not Physically Divided (Two Way Trafficway)
2 – Divided Highway, Median Strip (Without Traffic Barrier)
3 – Divided Highway, Median Strip (With Traffic Barrier)
4 – One Way Trafficway
9 – Unknown

NUMBER OF TRAVEL LANES   61

Actual Value Except:
7 – Seven or more lanes
9 – Unknown

SPEED LIMIT   62   63

Actual Miles Per Hour Except:
00 – No Statutory Limit
99 – Unknown

ROADWAY ALIGNMENT   64

1 – Straight   9 – Unknown
2 – Curve

ROADWAY PROFILE   65

1 – Level
2 – Grade
3 – Hillcrest
4 – Sag
9 – Unknown

ROADWAY SURFACE TYPE   66

1 – Concrete
2 – Blacktop (Bituminous)
3 – Brick or Block
4 – Slag, Gravel or Stone
5 – Dirt
8 – Other
9 – Unknown

ROADWAY SURFACE CONDITION   67

1 – Dry
2 – Wet
3 – Snow or Slush
4 – Ice
5 – Sand, Dirt, Oil
8 – Other
9 – Unknown

TRAFFIC CONTROL DEVICE   68   69

(See Instruction Manual)

TRAFFIC CONTROL DEVICE FUNCTIONING   70

0 – No Controls
1 – Device Not Functioning
2 – Device Functioning - Functioning Improperly
3 – Device Functioning Properly
9 – Unknown

HIT AND RUN   71

0 – No Hit and Run
1 – Hit Motor Vehicle in Transport
2 – Hit Pedestrian or Non-Motorist
3 – Hit Parked Vehicle or Object

LIGHT CONDITION   72

1 – Daylight
2 – Dark
3 – Dark but lighted
4 – Dawn
5 – Dusk
9 – Unknown

ATMOSPHERIC CONDITIONS   73

1 – No Adverse Atmospheric Conditions
2 – Rain
3 – Sleet
4 – Snow
5 – Fog
6 – Rain and Fog
7 – Sleet and Fog
8 – Other: Smog, Smoke, Blowing Sand or Dust
9 – Unknown

CONSTRUCTION/MAINTENANCE ZONE   74

0 – None
1 – Construction
2 – Maintenance
3 – Utility
4 – Work Zone, Type Unknown

NOTIFICATION TIME EMS   75   78

Military Time Except:
0000 – Not Notified
9999 – Unknown

ARRIVAL TIME EMS   79   82

Military Time Except:
0000 – Not Notified
9999 – Unknown

EMS TIME AT HOSPITAL   83   86

Military Time Except:
0000 – Not Notified
9999 – Unknown

SCHOOL BUS RELATED   87

0 – No
1 – Yes

RELATED FACTORS   88 89 90 91 92 93

RAIL GRADE CROSSING IDENTIFIER   94   100

(See Instruction Manual)

CARD NO.	9	ADDITIONAL STATE INFORMATION (See Instruction Manual)	14	24	33	Number of Non-Motorist Forms Submitted	34 35

CARD NO. **2**

HS Form 214 (Rev. 12/86)

☆U.S. Government Printing Office: 1987—718-163/00825

Figure 3.8: The forms used by the U.S. Fatal Accident Reporting System.

Form Approved thru
O.M.B.-No. 2127-0006

CODED BY: _____

DATE CODED: _____

STATE CASE NO: _____

US Department of Transportation
National Highway Traffic Safety Administration

1987 Fatal Accident Reporting System (FARS)
VEHICLE/DRIVER LEVEL

| CASE NUMBER STATE (GSA CODES) | 1 | 2 | CONSECU-TIVE NUMBER | 3 | | 6 | TRANSACTION CODE 21 – Original Submission 22 – Update or Change | 7 | 8 | CARD NO. | 9 | VEHICLE NUMBER (Assigned by Analyst) | 10 | 11 |

Transaction code: **2**, Card No. **1**

VEHICLE MAKE (See Instruction Manual) 14 15 — **VEHICLE MODEL** (See Instruction Manual) 16 17 — **BODY TYPE** (See Instruction Manual) 18 19 — **MODEL YEAR** Actual Value except: 99 – Unknown 20 21

VEHICLE IDENTIFICATION NO. Actual Value except: Zero Fill if no VIN Nine Fill if Unknown — 22 23 24 25 26 27 28 29 30 31 32 33 34 35 36 37 38

REGISTRATION STATE 39 40
GSA CODES Except:
00 – Not Applicable
92 – No Registration
93 – Multiple State Reg., In-State
94 – Multiple State Reg., Out-of-State
95 – U.S. Government Tags
96 – Military Vehicle
97 – Foreign Countries
98 – Other Registration
99 – Unknown

ROLLOVER 41
0 – No Rollover
1 – First Event
2 – Subsequent Event

JACKKNIFE 42
0 – Not an Articulated Vehicle
1 – No
2 – First Event
3 – Subsequent Event

TRAVEL SPEED 43 44
Actual Miles Per Hour Except:
00 – Stopped Vehicle
97 – Ninety-seven MPH or Greater
99 – Unknown

HAZARDOUS CARGO 45
0 – No
1 – Yes
9 – Unknown

VEHICLE TRAILERING 46
0 – No
1 – Yes, One Trailing Unit
2 – Yes, Two Trailing Units
3 – Yes, Three or More Trailing Units
4 – Yes, Number of Trailing Units Unknown
9 – Unknown

SPECIAL USE 47
0 – No Special Use
1 – Taxi
2 – Vehicle Used as School Bus
3 – Vehicle Used as other Bus
4 – Military
5 – Police
6 – Ambulance
7 – Firetruck
9 – Unknown

EMERGENCY USE 48
0 – No
1 – Yes

IMPACT POINT – INITIAL 49 50
00 – Non-Collision
01-12 – Clock Points
13 – Top
14 – Undercarriage
15 – Underride
16 – Override
99 – Unknown

IMPACT POINT – PRINCIPAL 51 52
00 – Non-Collision
01-12 – Clock Points
13 – Top
14 – Undercarriage
15 – Underride
16 – Override
99 – Unknown

EXTENT OF DEFORMATION 53
0 – None
2 – Other (Minor)
4 – Functional (Moderate)
6 – Disabling (Severe)
9 – Unknown

VEHICLE ROLE 54
0 – Non-Collision
1 – Striking
2 – Struck
3 – Both
9 – Unknown

MANNER OF LEAVING SCENE 55
1 – Driven
2 – Towed Away
3 – Abandoned
9 – Unknown

FIRE OCCURRENCE 56
0 – No Fire
1 – Fire Occurred in Vehicle During Accident

NUMBER OF OCCUPANTS 57 58
Actual Value if Total Known
96 – 96 or more
97 – Unknown – Only Injured Reported
99 – Unknown

RELATED FACTORS 59 60 61 62
See Instruction Manual "Related Factors – VEHICLE LEVEL"

VEHICLE MANEUVER 63 64
(See Instruction Manual)

MOST HARMFUL EVENT 65 66
(See Instruction Manual)

Card No. 9, Transaction code **2**

DRIVER PRESENCE 14
1 – Driver Operated Vehicle
2 – Driverless
3 – Driver Left Scene
9 – Unknown

LICENSE STATE GSA CODES 15 16
Except:
94 – Military
95 – Canada
96 – Mexico
97 – Other Foreign Countries
99 – Unknown

DRIVER LICENSE STATUS (Irrespective of Vehicle Driven) 17
NO VALID LICENSE
0 – Not Licensed
1 – Suspended
2 – Revoked
3 – Expired
4 – Cancelled or Denied
VALID LICENSE
5 – Single Class License
6 – Multiple Class License
7 – Learner's Permit
8 – Temporary
9 – Unknown

DRIVER LICENSE TYPE COMPLIANCE (For This Class Vehicle) 18
0 – Not Licensed
1 – No License Required for This Class Vehicle
2 – No Valid License for This Class Vehicle
3 – Valid License for This Class Vehicle
9 – Unknown

COMPLIANCE WITH LICENSE RESTRICTIONS 19
0 – No Restrictions
1 – Restrictions Complied With
2 – Restrictions Not Complied With
3 – Restrictions, Compliance Unknown
9 – Unknown

VIOLATIONS CHARGED
0 – None
1 – Alcohol or Drugs
2 – Speeding
3 – Alcohol or Drugs and Speeding
4 – Reckless Driving
5 – Driving with a Suspended or Revoked License
6 – Other Moving Violation
7 – Non-Moving Violation
8 – Violation, Type Unknown or Other Violation
9 – Unknown

20

PREVIOUS RECORDED ACCIDENTS 21 22
Actual Value Except:
00 – None
99 – Unknown

PREVIOUS RECORDED SUSPENSIONS AND REVOCATIONS 23 24
Actual Value Except:
00 – None
99 – Unknown

PREVIOUS DWI CONVICTIONS 25 26
Actual Value Except:
00 – None
99 – Unknown

PREVIOUS SPEEDING CONVICTIONS 27 28
Actual Value Except:
00 – None
99 – Unknown

PREVIOUS OTHER HARMFUL MV CONVICTIONS 29 30
Actual Value Except:
00 – None
99 – Unknown

DATE OF LAST ACCIDENT, SUSPENSION, OR CONVICTION 31 34
Mo. Yr.
00 – No Record
99 – Unknown

DATE OF FIRST ACCIDENT SUSPENSION, OR CONVICTION 35 38
Mo. Yr.
00 – No Record
99 – Unknown

DRIVER ZIP CODE 39 40 41 42 43
Actual Value Except
Nine Fill if Unknown

RELATED FACTORS 44 45 46 47 48 49
See Instruction Manual "Related Factors – DRIVER LEVEL"

HS Form 214A (Rev. 12/86)

U.S. Government Printing Office: 1987–718-162/00824

Figure 3.8: (continued).

FIGURE 3.8 69

U.S. Department of Transportation
National Highway Traffic Safety Administration

1987 Fatal Accident Reporting System (FARS)
PERSON LEVEL

O.M.B. No. 2127-0006
CODED BY: _____
DATE CODED: _____
STATE CASE NO: ____ ____ ____

| CASE NUMBER STATE (GSA CODES) | 1 | 2 | CONSECU-TIVE NUMBER | 3 | 6 | TRANSACTION CODE | 7 | 8 | CARD NO. | 9 | VEHICLE NUMBER (Assigned by Analyst) | 10 | 11 | PERSON NUMBER | 12 | 13 |

TRANSACTION CODE
31 — Original Submission
32 — Update or Change
3

CARD NO. 1

VEHICLE NUMBER (Assigned by Analyst)
00 — Non-Motorist

PERSON NUMBER (Assigned by Analyst)

NON-MOTORIST STRIKING VEHICLE NUMBER 14 15
Assigned Vehicle Number
Except:
99 — Unknown

AGE 16 17
Actual Value
00 — Up to One Year
97 — Ninety-Seven Years or Older
99 — Unknown

SEX 18
1 — Male
2 — Female
9 — Unknown

PERSON TYPE 19
1 — Driver of a Motor Vehicle in Transport
2 — Passenger of a Motor Vehicle in Transport
3 — Occupant of a Motor Vehicle Not in Transport
4 — Occupant of a Non-Motor Vehicle Transport Device
5 — Non-Occupant — Pedestrian
6 — Non-Occupant — Bicyclist
7 — Non-Occupant — Other Cyclist
8 — Non-Occupant — Other or Unknown
9 — Unknown Occupant Type in a Motor Vehicle in Transport

SEATING POSITION 20 21
00 — Non-Motorist
11 — Front Seat — Left Side (Driver's Side)
12 — — Middle
13 — — Right Side
18 — — Other
19 — — Unknown
21 — Second Seat — Left Side
22 — — Middle
23 — — Right Side
28 — — Other
29 — — Unknown
31 — Third Seat — Left Side
32 — — Middle
33 — — Right Side
38 — — Other
39 — — Unknown
41 — Fourth Seat — Left Side
42 — — Middle
43 — — Right Side
48 — — Other
49 — — Unknown
50 — Sleeper Section of Cab (Truck)
51 — Other Passenger in Enclosed Passenger or Cargo Area
52 — Other Passenger in Unenclosed Passenger or Cargo Area
53 — Other Passenger in Passenger or Cargo Area, Unknown Whether or Not Enclosed
54 — Trailing Unit
55 — Riding on Vehicle Exterior
99 — Unknown

MANUAL (ACTIVE) RESTRAINT SYSTEM — USE 22
0 — None Used - Vehicle Occupant / Not Applicable - Non-Motorist
1 — Shoulder Belt
2 — Lap Belt
3 — Lap and Shoulder Belt
4 — Child Safety Seat
5 — Motorcycle Helmet
8 — Restraint Used — Type Unknown or Other including Other Helmet
9 — Unknown

AUTOMATIC (PASSIVE) RESTRAINT SYSTEM — FUNCTION 23
0 — Not Equipped or Non-Motorist
1 — Automatic Belt in Use
2 — Automatic Belt Not In Use
3 — Deployed Air Bag
4 — Non-deployed Air Bag
9 — Unknown

NON-MOTORIST LOCATION 24 25
00 — Not Applicable — Vehicle Occupant
01 — Intersection — In Crosswalk
02 — Intersection — On Roadway, Not in Crosswalk
03 — Intersection — On Roadway, Crosswalk Not Available
04 — Intersection — On Roadway, Crosswalk Availability Unknown
05 — Intersection — Not on Roadway
09 — Intersection — Unknown
10 — Non-Intersection — In Crosswalk
11 — Non-Intersection — On Roadway, Not in Crosswalk
12 — Non-Intersection — On Roadway, Crosswalk Not Available
13 — Non-Intersection — On Roadway, Crosswalk Availability Unknown
14 — Non-Intersection — In Parking Lane
15 — Non-Intersection — On Road Shoulder
16 — Non-Intersection — Bike Path
17 — Non-Intersection — Outside Trafficway
18 — Non-Intersection — Other, Not on Roadway
19 — Non-Intersection — Unknown
99 — Unknown

EJECTION 26
0 — Not Ejected
1 — Totally Ejected
2 — Partially Ejected
9 — Unknown

EXTRICATION 27
0 — Not Extricated
1 — Extricated
9 — Unknown

METHOD OF ALCOHOL DETERMINATION (By Police) 28
1 — Evidential Test (Breath, Blood, Urine)
2 — Preliminary Breath Test (PBT)
3 — Behavioral
4 — Passive Alcohol Sensor (PAS)
5 — Observed
8 — Other (e.g. Saliva test)
9 — Not Reported

POLICE REPORTED ALCOHOL INVOLVEMENT 29
0 — No (Alcohol Not Involved)
1 — Yes (Alcohol Involved)
8 — Not Reported
9 — Unknown (Police Reported)

ALCOHOL TEST RESULT 30 31
Actual Value (Decimal Implied before First Digit) (0.xx)
95 — Test Refused
96 — None Given
97 — AC Test Performed, Results Unknown
99 — Unknown

DRUGS NOTED IN TOXICOLOGY REPORT (Other than alcohol) 32
0 — No blood test given
Blood Test given, results known
1 — No drugs reported
2 — Drugs reported (excluding nicotine, aspirin)
3 — Not tested for drugs
Blood Test given, results unknown
7 — Test for drugs, results unknown
8 — Unknown if Tested for Drugs
9 — Unknown if blood test given

INJURY SEVERITY 33
0 — No Injury (0)
1 — Possible Injury (C)
2 — Nonincapacitating Evident Injury (B)
3 — Incapacitating Injury (A)
4 — Fatal Injury (K)
5 — Injured, Severity Unknown
6 — Died Prior to Accident
9 — Unknown

TAKEN TO HOSPITAL OR TREATMENT FACILITY 34
0 — No
1 — Yes
9 — Unknown

DEATH DATE 35 40
000000 — Not Applicable
999999 — Unknown
MONTH DAY YEAR

DEATH TIME 41 44
Military Time Except:
0000 — Not Applicable
9999 — Unknown

RELATED FACTORS 45 46 47 48 49 50
See Instruction Manual
"Related Factors — PERSON LEVEL"

HS Form 214B (Rev. 12/86)

☆ U.S. Government Printing Office: 1987—181-772/53393

Figure 3.8: (continued).

accident is a case, and contains a number (perhaps several hundreds) of variables describing the accident. The numerical values of these variables constitute codes whose meanings can be found by reference to some key.

Numerous computer packages for the convenient and efficient processing of such data exist. They are generally referred to as survey analysis packages. Among the best-known are SPSS (Statistical Package for the Social Sciences) and OSIRIS (Organised Set of Integrated Routines for Investigation by Statistics). Packages like these include a tabulation program among their features. Some examples of how such a program can be used with road accident data will now be given; these will use the syntax of OSIRIS (see also Skelton, 1973), but the changes needed to use SPSS or another package would be fairly minor.

3.14.2 The OSIRIS dataset

OSIRIS programs accept and generate data in a common format, known as the OSIRIS dataset. The cases in the data are stored in this by rows, or records in the file; the variables thus become the columns, or fields within those records. The OSIRIS dataset has two parts, the data itself, and a file called the dictionary. The dictionary describes each variable in turn: each is assigned a unique number, and the user references the variable by that number in the control cards for an OSIRIS program. The program then retrieves from the dictionary such information as the alphabetic name of the variable (both for labelling of printed output and to provide the user with a check that the correct variable is being used), the location of the variable field within each data record, the missing data codes, etc. The dictionary needs to be generated only once; thereafter it is retained as part of that OSIRIS dataset. Any subsequent generation of new but derived data as output from an OSIRIS program will also yield an OSIRIS dataset, with dictionary, as part of normal program operation. The user is then freed from the tedious and error-prone process of describing the full data format with each job.

OSIRIS is particularly flexible in the recoding of variables and the selection of subsets of data during the execution of the program. The next two Sections briefly describe these features, and then an example of a TABLES program is given. Finally, some comments on weaknesses in this type of package are given.

3.14.3 Recoding

When processing each case (accident), the variables may be transformed (recoded) before they are tabulated and cross-tabulated. Some examples of how this is done in OSIRIS will now be given. In recode statements, variables from the input dataset are prefixed V (e.g. V15 for variable 15), whereas those that are the result of a prior recode operation are prefixed R.

$$R1=V329$$
$$R2=V26+13$$
$$R3=R2*(V18+V21)$$

The result variable on the left of an equals sign takes on the value, case by case, of the expression on the right. In the last expression above, for instance, variables 18 and 21 from the input dataset are added together and multiplied by recoded variable no. 2, the result being called recoded variable no. 3.

The next example shows a way of reducing the number of categories a variable is divided into. It uses the BRAC operation.

$$R4=BRAC(V73,00-14=1,15-24=2,$$
$$25-64=3,65-98=4,99=9)$$

This supposes that V73 is age of casualty in years, and it is desired to condense this into categories for children, young adults, most adults, and the elderly. As is usual, missing data is identified by the variable field being filled with 9's, so code 99 becomes 9.

Normally, the operation of all the recode statements proceeds sequentially from first to last. However, this can be modified by a GO TO statement. This specifies the next operation is to be that of a statement with a specified label.

Another very useful statement available with the recode facility determines program action according to logical tests. The general format is:

IF logical-expression THEN
statement-A ELSE statement-B

The logical expression consists of variables and constants which are compared with each other in pairs using such relations as EQ (equal to) and LT (less than). These simple relations may be joined by AND and OR:

V42 GE 399
V5 LT 2 AND V6 LT 3

Statement-A and statement-B in the IF statement may assign a value to a variable or may be a GO TO:

    IF V5 EQ 1 THEN R1=V6+1
    ELSE GO TO 35

3.14.4 Filtering

Most OSIRIS programs provide a global filter to enable selection of cases before data is processed by the program. Some programs, including TABLES, also provide local filters of a similar kind: these operate during only some of the program's use of the data.

A filter statement must begin with either INCLUDE or EXCLUDE, which specifies what to do with data cases that satisfy the logical conditions given next in the statement. For each variable which determines the selection of cases, the variable number is given, along with an equals sign and the specific values to be used in deciding whether to keep or to reject the case. These simple expressions may be joined by AND or OR to form a more elaborate statement. Thus the following example signifies that any data case in which variable V8 has the entry 7 and variable V38 has the entry 47 is to be kept:

    INCLUDE V8=7 AND V38=47*

(The asterisk here merely shows the end of the statement.) A list of values may be given in the expression for any variable, separating values by commas and using a dash to indicate a range of values, e.g.:

    EXCLUDE V98=5,6,7,9 OR
    V91=6 AND V2=32-34*

3.14.5 Example of a simple TABLES program

The example is shown in Figure 3.9. Here is the explanation of the lines shown there:

3–5: V40 is the age of the casualty in years. R1 is therefore the age group, individual years for children, by decades for adults.

7: This restricts the cases to pedestrian casualties (V36=0) occurring in the first three months (V5=01–03).

8: Title.

9: BADD=SKIP specifies that when non-numeric characters are found in numeric variables, the program should skip the case. TABL=FIXED specifies that the table description lines (see below) will be in fixed format, not keyword format.

10: Subset specification. The first 8 characters on this line are a label by which it is referred to on a table description line. It may be used in either of two ways: (i) as a local filter, in which case one table is produced that includes cases for which V39 is 2 or 4; (ii) as a repetition factor, in which case two tables are produced, one for cases in which V39 is 2 (female) and one for which V39 is 4 (male).

11: This indicates that table description lines now follow.

12: Table description line. The row variable number is given, and the column variable number. Recoded variables are denoted by a minus sign. Thus this card specifies a table of R1 vs. V39.

13: Table description line. This specifies that a univariate table is to be produced for each of the variables listed on the following line. Each table will be repeated for each category of the repetition factor SEXOFPED.

14: Variable list line for the preceding table description line.

One frequently wants to cross-tabulate three or more variables at once. Inevitably, there are difficulties in presenting the result on two-dimensional paper. The two most common ways round this are to make the row and/or the column variable a combination of two or more variables (e.g. of sex and age group by setting R2=100*V39+R1), or to use the repetition factor facility to repeat the tabulation for each of a number of categories (e.g. as in line 13 above).

3.14.6 Weaknesses and problems

In a university environment—which is where I've done accident data processing—the main weakness of this type of package is its handling of the hierarchical structure of the data. That is, some analyses are carried out at the accident level, some

```
Line
No.
   1    $RUN TABLES
   2    $RECODE
   3         R1=BRAC(V40,00=00,01=01,02=02,03=03,04=04,05=05,06=06,
   4       C 07=07,08=08,09=09,10=10,11=11,12=12,13=13,14=14,15-19=15,
   5       C 20-29=16,30-39=17,40-49=18,50-59=19,60-69=20,70-98=21,99=99)
   6    $SETUP
   7    INCLUDE V36=0 AND V5=01-03*
   8    PEDESTRIAN ACCIDENTS BY AGE,SEX,HOUR,DAY, & MONTH. JAN-MCH 1973
   9    TABL=FIXED,BADD=SKIP*
  10    SEXOFPED INCLUDE V39=2,4*
  11    TABLES
  12           -1    39                               SEXOFPED
  13    UNIVA
  14    V6,V29,V5*
```

Figure 3.9: A simple OSIRIS TABLES program.

at the vehicle level, some at the casualty level. Handling the connexions between these is clumsy. The straightforward way of organising the processing is to provide for a fixed number of variables in each accident, allowing sufficient space for up to (for instance) 3 vehicles and 4 casualties; when there are fewer than the maximum, the allocated space is filled with missing data codes; when there are a greater number, information on the excess ones is thrown away. Having a fixed record length is wasteful of space, and does not address the second part of the problem, how to count at the vehicle or casualty level. To make a count of vehicle drivers, separate tables can be produced for the three vehicles and these added together manually. An alternative is to prepare a new file, with each case being a vehicle (not an accident), and carry out the analysis on that file.

In a public service department responsible for the publication of official statistics, two further factors are important. The first of these is economic—university computing is typically free, government computing is typically expensive. Even the time taken to read in an accident case for processing can cost a lot of money when tens of thousands of accident cases are involved, as they are for a single year's data in many jurisdictions. So choosing a package that is cheap to run is important. The second is the presentation of the output. It is a great convenience—and avoids tran-

scription errors—if the tables are printed in a form suitable for direct photographic reproduction, laid out clearly and attractively, with columns and rows appropriately labelled.

3.14.7 Microcomputers, with special reference to developing countries

Hills and Kassabgi (1984) outline the selection of microcomputer hardware and the development of accident analysis software to run on it, for the Cairo police. At the time of their paper, the facilities in the package were as follows:

- NEWACCS. Used by typists to enter new accidents.

- NEW FILE. Creates new (but empty) accident file.

- COPY FILE. Makes backup copies of master file.

- FILEHAND. Used to ADD new accidents to master file, and to INSPECT, CHANGE, or DELETE accident records.

- SELECT. Lists code numbers of accidents satisfying some selection criterion.

- TABULATIONS. (STANDARD or NON-STANDARD; ACCIDENT, CASUALTY, or VEHICLE numbers).

- GRAPHICS. Histograms of accidents on a major route, accident map, stick diagrams.

By the time of the paper by Hills and Elliott (1986), the package was being evaluated in five other countries besides Egypt. (Their paper is also noteworthy for the clear account it gives of the uses of accident analysis at both national and local levels.) Hills and Elliott are optimistic about the interactions with humans of both the software and the hardware: "The most encouraging finding of this research to date is that developing country staff with no previous experience of computers are entirely capable of running the Microcomputer Accident Analysis Package. This has already led to a far greater insight into the accident problems of the study areas in which the system has been tested... Some minor hardware maintenance problems have occurred, but with the rapid influx of micros into virtually all developing countries, local maintenance expertise is growing and these problems should eventually become insignificant."

On the other hand, the most significant problem encountered was the need for "institution building": that is, in getting adequate staff, funds, and facilities allocated to the work and in forging the necessary links between traffic police, highway engineers, and other road safety interests.

Daffin et al (1986) report the development of a more general package. The authors say this is "a very powerful data entry and tabulation package for handling sample survey and census data... It is able to deal with data from surveys with complex hierarchical structures, yet it is written in such a way that it is fully interactive and easy to use. It is able to produce clearly labelled tables suitable for immediate photographic reproduction... There are attractive table manipulation facilities."

There have been a number of papers in the recent American literature on using microcomputers to process and analyse road accident records—for instance, in Transportation Research Record No. 910, we find papers by Brown and Colson (1983), Kelsh (1983), Stenzel (1983), and Pfefer and Reischl (1983). These are all oriented to the opportunities available to relatively small cities and counties in which automated accident analysis

was not previously carried out. Enthusiasm about the potential must be tempered by realism about the practicalities, however, as this quotation from Stenzel (1983) emphasises: "It is clear that within the next decade most agencies concerned with the use of accident and law-enforcement records will, regardless of their size, have access to computers for the storage and analysis of data. What is also likely is that the process of acquiring and using these automated systems will not be as easy as advertised. The lack of data-processing experience among the personnel of small agencies, coupled with dramatic changes in the marketplace, will make the automation of record systems a risky and difficult process for many agencies. However, if agency administrators are alert to the pitfalls cited in this paper, the task of automation can be accomplished with realistic expectations and maximum payoff to the agency." Stenzel also argues that, when the problem is correctly diagnosed, automation may sometimes be seen as an incorrect prescription: "In many smaller agencies, manual record systems have evolved haphazardly without any overall plan or direction. Automation is often mistakenly viewed as a way to fix record system problems. In many agencies, however, the most pressing need is not to implement an automated system but rather to make a realistic assessment of what problems exist in the current system, what the system is used for, and what alternative solutions (including automation) exist. Preliminary investigations by the Northwestern University Traffic Institute suggest that well-designed manual systems can handle the traffic record needs for approximately 80 percent of all police agencies in the United States. For another 15 percent of departments, the decision whether to automate depends on a number of factors, including the number and kinds of reports wanted, the availability of existing hardware, and anticipated growth patterns for the jurisdiction." Only for the largest 5 percent of police agencies was automation clearly recommended. (The three groups of agencies were those having less than 4000 accidents and citations reported per year, those having 4000–10000, and those having 10000 or more.) While agreeing that traditional methods can be very effective, and noting that care is needed so that computerisation does not lessen the contact between the investigator and the crash, nevertheless I would take a rather more positive line than Stenzel: true, it would be possible for some other technology to accomplish the same task, but microcomputers and their software are the natural choice, as they are becoming so familiar to the majority of people.

3.15 Comprehensive Computerized Safety Recordkeeping Systems

A workshop on this subject was held in May 1985 in Virginia; it is reported in TRC (1985). A Comprehensive Computerized Safety Recordkeeping System (CCSRS) is a state-administered system of computerised files of data on road accidents, drivers, vehicles, and highways, that are linked by variables that are common to the accident file and at least one other file. Thus the driver licence number links the driver licence file to the accidents file, the vehicle registration number or the VIN links the vehicle registration file to the accidents file, and a location reference links the highway inventory and traffic volume files to the accidents file.

Three ways of organising a CCSRS are distinguished in TRC (1985):

- Keep each file separate; each user has to program the merging of data from two or more files.

- Merge some files together, and have (for example) a merged driver file (from the accident and driver licence files) and a merged highway file (from the accident and highway inventory files).

- Merge all files into a database.

The second and third alternatives involve progressive extra investments in storage and routine management of data, for the benefit of less retrieval programming and hence quicker and cheaper results.

TRC (1985) goes on to discuss the local and research uses of a CCSRS, the costs and benefits, the technical and institutional obstacles that need to be overcome in developing a CCSRS, and what research is needed to improve CCSRS's.

Benjamin (1987) reports on what linkage of this type is practised in eleven countries. His account

Table 3.7: Benjamin's survey of the matching of accident data with other information in eleven countries*.

	Driver	Vehicle Highway	
Australia	F,P	F	N
Canada	Y	F	L#
Denmark	P-1986	Y	Y
France	N	L	L
Germany, Fed. Rep.	N	L-rural	L
Netherlands	N	N	F,P-1986
New Zealand	P	Y	Y
Sweden	Y	L-rural	Y
Switzerland	Y	P-1990	N
U.K.	N	L	L
U.S.A.	L	N	N

* Y = Yes, linkage is performed for all injury accidents, or at least is common practice. L = A very limited amount of linkage is performed (e.g. a random or regional sample that is a small proportion of the total). F = Fatalities only are linked. P = Planning of such linkage is under way (with the intended start date, if any, being shown), or the feasibility is under study. N = No, linkage is not carried out (or, at least, not more than occasionally).
# Common practice in British Columbia and Quebec; other provinces plan to follow.

is unclear in some respects (due, no doubt, to ambiguities in the responses he received to the questionnaire he sent out), but I believe Table 3.7 is an adequate summary of his findings.

Chapter 4

Major deficiencies of police data

4.1 Introduction

Society owes much gratitude to the police for the care taken in investigating road accidents, and compiling the relevant statistics. Without these efforts, which have extended over a long period of years, research would have been greatly hampered and many programmes and campaigns to improve road safety would have been poorly aimed or suffered lengthy delays. However, any data-capture system directed at such a complex event as a road accident will possess a number of quirks and idiosyncracies which need to be researched and communicated to those attempting to interpret the accident figures. Such quirks may include simple matters like a tendency to record a driver's age to the nearest 10 years, subtleties like variations in the definitions of what constitutes a "serious" as distinct from a "slight" injury, and substantial biases in what types of accident are represented. The general picture is that factual information is much more reliable than that requiring the exercise of subjective judgment on the part of the police officer.

To interpret police data properly, it is necessary to examine the report form being used, and to ask a number of questions about the data collection process (Storms, 1983):

- Are the categories on the report form incomplete or overlapping?

- Is there an "unknown" category? How often is it used?

- Who fills out the form?

- What training in using the report form do police officers receive?

- Is there a manual of rules explaining the definitions of the categories?

- How long after the accident is the form typically completed?

- What training is received by the personnel responsible for tabulating the statistics?

- How long do they stay in the job? Is it seen as a responsible one?

- Are there incentives for doing the job well? Opportunities for career advancement?

- How is the process of tabulation supervised? Are checks for errors routinely made?

- What use is made of the data? Are statistics published for the public?

This Chapter will be organised as follows. First, the major deficiencies in police data will be summarised. Second, empirical evidence about errors in police data in a number of jurisdictions will be reviewed. Third, some results comparing insurance claims with police data will be presented. (Comparisons of police data with medical data are left to Section 11.4.) Fourth, the method of ascertaining the number of accidents at a spot by examining debris on the road will be outlined.

4.2 Summary of the major deficiencies in police data

4.2.1 The frequent exclusion of the uninjured

In many jurisdictions, accidents which do not involve death or personal injury are excluded. Either they are not reported to the police in the first place, or if they are, the police do not pass on the reports to the organisation responsible for collating the statistics. Furthermore, there is frequently a dearth of information about people who escape injury in accidents in which someone else is injured. It is natural for there to be less concern with property damage only accidents, but it can be as important to know why people are not injured as it is to know why they are. To overcome this, one can use such information as there is on people who are uninjured in injury accidents, one can search for a jurisdiction that is otherwise similar but in which damage-only accidents are reported, or one can turn to insurance data.

4.2.2   Poor information about nature and severity of injury

Mortality and hospital-based statistics can to some extent ameliorate this problem. They are discussed at length in Chapters 8–13.

4.2.3   No information about crash speed

The speeds at which the vehicles were moving prior to the accident and at the moment of impact are obviously crucial to understanding both the causation of the crash and the injuries which resulted, yet the police in most jurisdictions do not attempt to estimate this routinely. This is because of the difficulty of doing so. (Some data from Nevada, North Carolina, and New Zealand will, however, be given in Chapter 7.) There is probably no complete solution to this problem; one tactic that can help is to compare the injuries of several people involved in the same accident, so that even though the speed is unknown, it is known that it was the same for all those people (and consequently differences in their injuries may be compared with differences in their protection, e.g. whether they were wearing seat belts).

4.2.4   Frequent absence of vehicle design information

Information about the vehicles involved is generally lacking in detail, for instance, the make and model of cars is absent. Quite why this should be I do not know. Sometimes it is said recording this is very time-consuming for the police, and the result is error-prone. I find this difficult to accept—police are trained to record facts, and are good at it, it is when they are required to make a subjective judgment that trouble starts. And it surely cannot be beyond the wit of man to design the form in such a way that (say) the twenty most common models can be easily coded. Whatever the reason, the result is that we have no idea what is the effect on safety of even such a major feature of car design as (for instance) whether it is front-wheel-drive or rear-wheel-drive. In some countries, information on the accident records of different types of vehicle is available through insurance claim statistics.

4.2.5   Location

Keeping up the quality of accident location details is a time-consuming task all over the world. In the 1960's Rotman was complaining about this, and such improvements as have been made since then have not eliminated the problem. The TRRL's Overseas Unit goes so far as to recommend that accident location information be duplicated, by being recorded according to both a grid coordinate system and a node/link/cell system. See Hills and Elliott (1986), who also reproduce part of a specially coded map of Islamabad that was commissioned by TRRL in the course of a study there.

At first, this difficulty may seem surprising, as a location is a fact, with little room for error due to subjectivity of judgment. There are a number of reasons; many can be categorised as either lack of information or inability to communicate it. By lack of information, I mean such things as not knowing or mistaking the name of the street, confusing one name with a similar one, not knowing which direction is N, S, E, or W, being unable to estimate distances from landmarks correctly, and (in rural areas) there not being a suitable landmark nearby to identify the site. I was surprised to read (in Sach, 1976) that as late as 1976 and in a country so developed as Australia the lack of accurate up-to-date road maps was a serious hindrance to the traffic engineer. By failure to communicate information, I mean chiefly that a landmark that is very obvious to people at the crash site can be totally unknown and unhelpful to a coder in the highways office, but also problems like poor handwriting, mis-spellings, and the use of abbreviations can be included here. The particular forms that these classes of errors take vary from city to city and county to county according to their geographical and physical features. The specifics of how to limit their number correspondingly vary, but generalities like the importance of experienced motivated staff with knowledge of the locality, good relations between the police and the traffic engineers, and a quick flow of paperwork so ambiguities can be checked while someone remembers the answer, are true everywhere.

An account of the paper by Decker and Hawkins (1982) is appropriate here. There are three main aspects: (i) A summary of a 1978 survey of 10 American states as to the methods used for coding accident locations. The mileposition concept was found to predominate, rather than coordinate (northing and easting) or link-and-node. (ii) A description of a project to expand the existing mileposting system in North Carolina to include the rural secondary highway system as well as the primary network. (iii) A description of a project to improve the efficiency of location coding in Kentucky. Central to the studies in both states was the use of a computerised inventory file to convert the location information provided by the police officer into the code required: e.g. the county, a proper name for a road or street, and a distance from an intersection or other feature, into a route number and mileposition. See Datta and Rodgers (1980) for a report on developing a comprehensive street index for Michigan, used in the generation of a computerised description of accident locations directly from the physical location information observed and reported by the police. For more details of U.S. practices, see Chapter 2 of Zegeer (1982). That Chapter is organised as follows: types of reference methods (including sign-oriented, document-oriented, coordinate, link-and-node, and others); status of the use of reference methods (i.e. which states have referenced how much of their highways); accuracy of accident location reporting, in which it is mentioned that West Virginia codes not only the location but also an estimate of the precision of the location; computerised highway networks, including the Michigan method; the impact of location reference method on computerised processing of the accident reports.

Burr and Brogan (1976) describe how accident locations are coded in the West Midlands (i.e. the Birmingham conurbation) of the U.K. There is also advice in IHT (1986).

4.2.6 Accident rates

Very often there is interest in accident rates, as well as in accident numbers. To calculate a rate, one needs a measure of exposure, for instance the number of million miles driven by the category under consideration, and this requires some sort of survey of travel patterns. Thus we see the necessity for good compatibility between definitions used by the police in recording accidents and those used in exposure surveys. An alternative is to use an "induced exposure" model in analysing accident data—expressed briefly, this involves knowing the relative numbers of single- and two-vehicle accidents, and assuming the former is proportional to dangerousness and the latter is partly proportional to dangerousness and partly to exposure.

4.2.7 Other problems

Here, I note recurring problem-areas that I feel in some way are not quite so fundamental as those above.

- Biases in the data collected. The under-reporting of accidents varies with accident type, e.g. tends to be greater for low-severity accidents, for single-vehicle crashes, and for those involving pedestrians and cyclists. One way of overcoming this is to turn to hospital information on casualties—see Chapter 11. Though this is certainly a "fundamental" problem with police data, I place it in the second rank of importance because most people working with a particular dataset become expert in interpreting it, get to know its own quirks, and can compensate for them if not by a formal statistical model then at least by a good dash of common sense.

- So many different combinations of vehicle movements can occur that devising a coding scheme to accommodate them all is a perennial problem. (We will see some efforts in Section 6.4.5.)

- Assessing whether alcohol played a part is difficult to do accurately. Even if we move away from requiring the police officer to use his judgment in saying if a driver was "in-toxicated" (or "under the influence", or "impaired") to the collection of objective data based on blood or breath analysis, obtaining the required sample is frequently beset with procedural, legal, and medical problems. Some data from Texas and British Columbia on the accuracy of the officer's judgment will be referred to in Section 7.7 below.

- Whether a seat belt was worn is often difficult for the reporting officer to know.

Many of the above issues will be returned to in the Sections below.

4.3 Empirical studies of errors in police data

4.3.1 South Australia: Accidents attended by the police

Howard et al (1979) studied the error rates in police reports of accidents by (with police cooperation) attending accident scenes, making their own reports independently of the investigating officers, and subsequently comparing the details as recorded by themselves and by the police officer. They only recorded such information as could be determined with a high degree of certainty; they did not interview anyone concerned with the accident, so the type of information they could collect was limited. Howard et al were confident it wasn't the survey team that was making the mistakes (except for a few variables, see below) for the following reasons.

- The team was drawn from a group of three professional engineers and one draughtsman, all of whom had previous experience in field data collection surveys.

- The need for accuracy was emphasised and team members were instructed to leave blank any data item which could not be recorded with a high degree of certainty.

- All team members were issued with a set of instructions describing how the form and the codes on it were to be interpreted. (It is noteworthy that the police themselves had no such document.)

Table 4.1: Data from South Australia on the percentage error rates of accident variables.

	Percentage error
Date	0
Registration number	6
Number of units	9
Unit type	4
Unit make	6
Unit colour	8
Sex of driver	3
Time of day	3
Day of week	0
Severity	16
Police attendance	10
Speed limit	2 *
Intersection type	24 #
Road features	8
Road grade	17
Sealed/unsealed road	0
Wet/dry road	8
Controls upon road	26
Controls erected	16
Type of accident	13
Vehicle movement 1	16
Vehicle movement 2	7
Safety belt (driver)	0
Weather	2
Lighting	15
Traffic conditions	23

* Plus an omission rate of 8%.
\# Plus an omission rate of 2%.

The survey team attended 112 accidents. 98 of these appeared on the Highways Department computer tape in due course; 7 were not recorded by attending police because they were minor, and 7 were recorded by police but not coded by the Highways Department for the same reason. Nevertheless, on the basis of the survey team's data, some of the 14 missing ones were sufficiently severe that they ought to have been included in the official records.

Results are given in Table 4.1. Some comments on individual variables are as follows.

- Registration number. Though the error rate is only 6%, even this would be of concern if it were to be used to access other vehicle characteristics from registration records. In 8 of the 9 cases, the error lay with the police, in 1 with incorrect coding by the Highways Department. (Chapter 7 of Howard et al takes this issue further, and concludes that 11% of vehicle registration numbers on the Highways Department tape are in error, the proportion being the same whether or not the police attended the accident.)

- Number of units involved. It might be the survey team in error here, some vehicles having left the scene before their arrival.

- Unit make. Coding of this specifies light/medium/heavy as well as make as such, and these categories are ill-defined.

- Unit colour. Most errors occurred at night, especially under sodium vapour lights.

- Sex of driver. The few errors may have been by the survey team.

- Severity. The discrepancy was consistently that of the official report indicating injury and the survey team specifying damage-only. It was probably the latter who were in error, through injured people having left the scene or having recovered before the team's arrival.

- Speed limit. This is sometimes omitted, presumably because it is thought to be implied by location (metropolitan area).

- Type of location. High error rate, partly because some categories shade into each other (e.g. T- into Y-junctions), and partly because many accidents that occur at or near an intersection do so through circumstances unconnected with that fact, so there is a temptation to record it as "between intersections".

- Road features, grade, and wetness, lighting, traffic conditions. Some errors due to the subjective nature of the categories, e.g. "straight" vs. "slight curve", "level" vs. "slight grade".

- Road features, controls upon road, controls erected. Sometimes the police mark two or more categories for these items. As the computer tape format provides for only one, loss of information is inevitable, even if a degree of consistency is obtained by the Highways Department coders using an order of preference to select one from two or more.

- Type of accident, vehicle movements. There are so many things that can happen in accidents that it is always difficult to devise categories that can be selected unambiguously.

4.3.2 South Australia: Accidents not attended by the police

At the time of the study by Howard et al (1979), some 80% of reported accidents were not attended by the police, but were known to them through one or more of the drivers coming to a police station. (For reported casualty accidents, the 80% figure becomes 40%.) Consequently, Howard et al made a study of how well the two forms agreed when two drivers made separate reports. Table 4.2 gives their results. It will be seen that many of the reasons for discrepancies are similar to those already mentioned above. Results were much the same for the 30 casualty accidents in the sample of 127 as for the 97 damage-only ones.

4.3.3 Indiana

Shinar et al (1983) compared police reports of 124 accidents (involving 207 drivers) with in-depth accident investigations conducted by Indiana University's Institute for Research in Public Safety (IRPS). All occurred in Monroe County, Indiana, between 1971–75. Tables 4.3–4.5 summarise the results.

Of the information describing accident circumstances (Table 4.3), injury severity, speed limit, and vertical character of the road had the greatest number of errors by the police.

The picture is considerably worse for variables describing driver and vehicle characteristics (Table 4.4): the police do not notice (or do not record) many vehicle defects, and the situation for personal conditions limiting the driver's performance and for road-related difficulties is hardly any better.

As to causes of the accident (Table 4.5), the police are conservative, as the false alarm rate

Table 4.2: Data from South Australia on the percentages of omissions, ambiguities, and contradictions between two reports of an accident, and the likely reasons.

| | Omissions, ambiguities, contradictions* | | | | | Likely reasons# |
	OR1	OR2	AR1	AR2	CR	
Location	0	0	0	0	13	8
Year of manufacture	75	7	0	0	36	7
Make	18	0	0	0	6	7
Registration number	17	0	2	0	11	7
Colour	13	0	0	0	28	7
Damage estimate	30	6	0	0	77	7
Type of location	5	2	28	13	35	4
Grade	4	0	0	0	9	2, 6
Road conditions	4	0	0	0	23	2, 6
Controls upon road	24	2	9	0	42	5, 8, 9
Controls erected	27	7	8	2	15	5, 8, 9
Type of accident	8	1	0	0	24	4
Vehicle movement	7	0	3	0	28	1, 3, 5
Apparent errors	31	4	9	0	39	1, 5
Weather	6	0	0	0	5	2, 8
Visibility	12	0	1	0	10	6
Lighting	6	1	2	0	20	2, 5
Traffic conditions	10	0	1	0	42	2
Safety belt (driver)	64	8	0	0	3	7

* OR1: Percentage of cases in which the data item was omitted from one report. (The number of cases was usually 127, the number of accidents in the sample, but in some cases was the number of relevant units.) OR2: Percentage of cases in which the data item was omitted from both reports. AR1: Percentage of cases in which the data item was recorded ambiguously or illegibly in one report. AR2: Percentage of cases in which the data item was recorded ambiguously or illegibly in both reports. CR: Contradiction rate, i.e. the proportion of times the answers were contradictory, given that the data item was answered clearly on both reports.

Coded as follows:

1 The item is subjective, and one or both drivers may wish to conceal the truth, or may honestly hold different opinions resulting from their different viewpoints, e.g. apparent errors, vehicle movements.

2 Choice of a category involves a subjective judgment, but it is unlikely that either driver will wish to mislead, e.g. when does daylight become dusk, or dusk become night? When is the grade of the road level, slight, or steep? When are traffic conditions light, medium, or heavy? Is light drizzle rain or not rain?

3 The item is inherently a complex one, and different choices as to which option best fits the event might be equally reasonable, e.g. vehicle movement.

4 Inadequate knowledge of accident item definitions, e.g. if there is a minor road junction which is irrelevant to the accident, does this count as an "intersection" accident? When does an "approx. right angle" collision become a "side-swipe"?

5 The layout of the form required a single response when the options were not mutually exclusive and perhaps more than one was relevant.

6 The choice appropriate to each driver may genuinely have been different, but one choice would inevitably be lost in processing the accident record because space is provided for only one.

7 The limited knowledge that a driver has about the characteristics of the other vehicle.

8 Lack of knowledge or forgetfulness.

9 Failure by police to mark the "none" option.

Table 4.3: Data from Indiana on the numbers of omissions and misidentifications by the police—accident variables* (124 accidents).

	Misident-ifications	Omissions
Month	1	0
Day of month	6	0
Year	1	0
Day of week	6	2
No. of traffic units	2	0
No. of passenger units	3	0
No. of trucks	1	0
No. of motorcycles	0	0
No. of parked units	1	0
Accident severity	38	0
Converging trajectories	14	0
Speed limit	28	21
Horizontal character	9	4
Vertical character	38	13
Surface composition	13	1
Road ambience	7	0
Weather ambience	7	1
Light ambience	6	1
Location	1	0

* Errors of commission were impossible for these variables.

(probability of reporting a cause, given that it was not truly a cause) is low, typically around 0.01, with the probability of reporting a cause given that it was truly a cause being typically around 0.5. (However, there was a vastly greater number of cases in which any particular cause was in fact absent compared to those in which it was present, so the ratio of omission to commission errors by the police is only about 3 to 1.) Shinar et al point out the different concepts of cause that a policeman and a researcher have: "Part of the policeman's role is to determine the most legally culpable driver in an accident. Thus, a priori, his orientation is to find some fault with one or both of the drivers. On the other hand, the IRPS investigators attempted to identify cause-and-effect relationships which led to the accident regardless of the legal culpability involved. Thus, discrepancies between the police and the IRPS investigations are likely to be a result of: (1) differences in the focus of attention and the definition of the accident cause, and (2) the relative accuracy of the police investigations."

The recommendations which Shinar et al made will come as no surprise to anyone who has worked with police accident data, but, coming as they do from a thorough empirical study of police accuracy, they deserve special weight: "(1) The generally poor police performance indicated by this assessment provides a strong argument for improving the training and motivation of police officers in traffic accident reconstruction and investigation. Significantly, many of the errors were recorded for factors which clearly do not require high levels of expertise to correctly assess...(2) This assessment also demonstrates a need to periodically monitor and report the accuracy of police agencies. Such evaluation can be of benefit both in motivating law enforcement personnel, and through helpful feedback, in better informing them as to problem areas or errors they may be making...(3) Some of the problems detected emphasise the need for improved design of accident report forms...In addition, police agencies should also monitor the rate of missing information, and take corrective action when missing value rates exceed reasonable levels."

4.3.4 New Mexico

Hall (1984) examined the reliability of the accident record system in New Mexico, concentrating on how it serves the needs of the traffic engineer seeking to identify and rectify high accident locations and hazardous roadway features. He commented adversely on the design of the accident report form then in use, pointing out that much of the administrative information that it requests is redundant, as matters like driver's address and date of birth can be determined from driver's name and licence number using existing record systems, and that it is too long and detailed, this resulting in poor attention to accuracy in completing it, and many omissions and errors.

Three other significant comments that Hall made are: (i) That it should be unnecessary for the police officer to record characteristics of the site such as speed limit, road surface type, traffic control devices, and geometrics. Instead, the traffic engineer should determine these from the identification of the site location and the inventory of the roadway and its traffic control devices

Table 4.4: Data from Indiana on the numbers of errors of omission, commission, and misidentification by the police—driver/vehicle variables* (207 driver/vehicle units).

	Misident-ifications	Disagreements		Agreements	
		Police commissions	Police omissions	Absence	Presence
Age	24		1		
Sex	1		0		
Model year	11		20		
Alcohol	6	5	6		
Brakes defective		0	90	113	4
Lights defective		0	40	162	0
Steering defective		0	76	131	0
Other vehicle defects		0	168	37	2
Attention diverted		6	17	181	3
Drinking		3	7	195	2
Eyesight defective		0	87	120	0
Hearing defective		0	1	206	0
Illness		0	3	204	0
Fatigue		1	8	198	0
View obs. (hill crest)		2	5	197	3
View obs. (embankment)		3	5	199	0
View obs. (growth)		1	8	196	2
View obs. (other)		7	15	176	9
Foreign substance on road		14	3	187	3
Shoulder defective		1	9	194	3
Other road defects		0	17	189	1
Make of vehicle	2		4		

* Blanks indicate non-applicability: with one exception, variables were either of the type where errors of commission were impossible, or of the present/absent type where misidentification was impossible; in this latter case, it is important to keep in mind what the true present/absent numbers were, so the numbers of cases where the police and IRPS data agreed are shown.

that is maintained routinely. (ii) The high incidence of inaccuracies and mistakes in specifying the location of the crash. (iii) Highway defects are cited as a principal factor in only 0.5% of crashes; this is implausibly low, as demonstrated by the success of many improvements in highway design and management of operation in reducing accidents; it results from the police being trained to look for driver error and not for highway defects.

As to (i), we have met the same idea in Section 3.15: it holds out the hope of simultaneously reducing the data collection burden on the police and improving the quality of the site characteristics component of the accident records. But two things weigh against it: firstly, the quality of site location is commonly poor (as Hall himself says); secondly, matching up two or more computer files would cause substantial problems unless they were designed from the first to be compatible. Nevertheless, it might sometimes be practicable, and (as in Section 3.15 and TRC, 1985) one can even imagine it as part of a more ambitious scheme: given good quality site location data, site characteristics could be added from the road inventory to the accident record; given good quality date and casualty identification data (name would be best, but there might be adequate substitutes if medical ethics prevent its use), injury details could be added from hospital patient files to the accident record; given good quality vehicle registra-

Table 4.5: Data from Indiana on the numbers of errors of omission and commission by the police—accident causes* (207 driver/vehicle units).

	Disagreements		Agreements	
	Police commissions	Police omissions	Absence	Presence
Vehicular causes	2	9	191	5
Inadequate brakes	2	3	198	4
Tyre problems	0	7	200	0
Other vehicle causes	1	1	205	0
Direct human causes	4	33	73	97
Speed too fast	8	8	181	10
Failed to yield right-of-way	8	1	166	32
Drove left of centre	7	3	193	4
Improper overtaking	6	2	193	6
Passed stop sign	1	1	201	4
Followed too closely	5	0	202	0
Made improper turn	1	2	200	4
Other improper driving	8	56	121	22
Indirect human causes	3	10	192	2
Had been drinking	2	1	202	2
Fatigue	1	2	204	0
Driver inexperience	0	2	205	0
Other indirect human causes	0	8	199	0
Environmental causes	1	60	135	11
Slick roads	2	12	189	4
View obstructions	0	30	176	1
Other highway-related causes	0	17	189	1
Ambience-related causes	1	12	190	4
All causal factors	52	168	-	-

* As well as the two types of errors, the numbers of the two ways in which police could agree with the IRPS data are also shown: agreement on the cause being absent, and being present.

tion number data, vehicle characteristics could be added from registration records to the accident record.

As to (ii), see Section 4.2.5 above.

As to (iii), we may recall the similar comment of Baker (1983a), "The reason we have heard so often that '90 per cent of all crashes are caused by human error' is not that other factors aren't equally important, but that it is the business of the police to collect data on 'human error'." Mercer (1987a) has also confronted this issue. He compared po-

lice and coroners' reports on the causes of fatal traffic accidents in British Columbia. His findings were that the comparison "revealed substantial differences between the two data sets. Generally, the police portrayed these accidents as primarily the driver's fault, in terms of dangerous and illegal driving behaviours, with a high proportion of the accidents being alcohol-related. On the other hand, coroners' reports tended to characterise these fatalities as more of a product of circumstances, less as the driver's fault, and less as a consequence of alcohol impairment." Mercer is aware that "The police probably have more of a legal-offence oriented point of view, which may tend to bias their perceptions", but suggests "As the police have more experience in accident investigation and have standardised accident investigation protocols and forms, it is likely their data are more reliable than the coroners' written text." If Hall is going so far as to suggest the police should be alive to subtle deficiencies in road design or traffic control, I think that is unreasonable. Gross defects they may be able to detect, but intersection control being inadequate for an increased volume of traffic, or a reduced skid resistance, that is the engineer's province, not the policeman's.

Hall finds that "The common thread which ties together the errors and omissions in the accident record system is the failure of the reporting officers to understand the use which is made of the data they collect...What is needed is a stronger effort to show the officer how the accident data are used... The engineer must describe his limited data needs, indicate their use, and stress the need for their accurate reporting...It would seem beneficial to keep the officers apprised of specific applications of their data, such as site selection and before-and-after studies. This communication effort also provides the opportunity to praise good work of some individuals and to gently mention common problems or errors." I would just add that much use of police accident statistics is made at national level too, and feedback from this arena to the police is equally important.

4.3.5   Mississippi

McGuire (1973) compared the number of accidents admitted to at interview by a sample of drivers with the number found in official records: the latter were some 42% of the total that should have been reported. McGuire also investigated the biases in the official records by breaking down this percentage according to age, sex, occupation, and race of the drivers, but as the total sample size was only 110 accidents, the results were too inconclusive to be worth repeating.

4.3.6   Michigan

In the words of Carroll and Scott (1971), "The reporting (notification) decision is a complex pro-

cess, not at all adequately described by legal requirements alone. While fatalities are recorded reliably, minor injury and property damage accidents are significantly underreported. Drivers involved in an accident may or may not be aware of the state and local statutes. They are, however, subject to other concerns and pressures. These may involve operators licence sanctions, considerations of culpability, degree of intent to repair damage, characteristics of insurance coverage and practices in the area, as well as the individual mores of the drivers. Undoubtedly other factors which have not been listed also play an important role." Carroll and Scott go on to note that police practices may not be in line with statutory requirements, and cite the inclusion in the state accident files of California and Michigan of minor damage-only accident reports not legally required. Conversely, the Detroit Police Department, when faced with insufficient manpower and steadily increasing work loads, adopted a policy in 1968 of not responding to accidents if no person was injured, the vehicles could be moved under their own power, alcohol or the use of drugs was not involved, and it was not a hit-and-run, even though the state (Michigan) requirement was reporting of all crashes with apparent damage of $200 or more.

Another point made by Carroll and Scott, which we have seen also elsewhere in this Chapter, is that subjective information (such as what are viewed as the primary contributing circumstances or the probable causes of accidents) is more likely to be in error than factual data.

For more results from this study, see Sections 8.10.2, 8.12.1, and 8.12.3 below.

4.3.7   Victoria

Daltrey (1983) reviews problems with the accident report form. Many of his comments are similar to those already made above, and they will not be repeated, but it is worth giving his list of factors affecting the level of reporting of crashes, some of his comments on specific variables, and general recommendations on report form design.

- Reporting of crashes is affected by:

  - Type of accident, i.e. single-vehicle accidents (especially if alcohol is involved) are less likely to be reported.

- Locale, i.e. whether urban or rural.

- Time of day, as the likelihood of an independent witness being present depends on this (but at peak periods there may be an emphasis on minimising traffic jams, rather than reporting the accident).

- Age of persons involved (young drivers drive cheaper vehicles and any insurance claim would be for a smaller amount).

- Type of vehicle, accidents involving motorcycles or bicycles being poorly reported.

- On specific variables:

  - Speed. In 1981, the Victorian police provided estimates in 85% of accidents. The data indicated that 76% of accidents occurred in the range of speeds 21–60 km/h, but only 14% in the speed range (61–80 km/h) immediately above the speed limit, this suggesting a high arbitrary estimate of speed is specified where there is clear evidence of speed and otherwise a value less than the speed limit is given.

  - Vehicle damage. To record this accurately requires time and expertise not possessed by most police officers.

  - Control at intersection. Sometimes this is taken as meaning some form of active control, so "Stop" and "Give Way" signs are reported as "No control".

  - Road user movement. See Section 6.4.5 and Figure 6.3 for the coding system. Codings by police of the specific (i.e. two-digit) movement type was incorrect in 54% of cases, and of the general (i.e. one-digit) accident type was incorrect in 36% of cases. (The sample size was 65, and the police-assigned codes were checked against those decided upon by the Road Safety and Traffic Authority, who are responsible for processing the police accident data.)

- In designing an accident report form, one should:

  - Maximise operational efficiency, by separating person-oriented data from location description and road furniture codes.

  - Make coding and editing easy by placing related fields adjacent to each other.

  - Remove from the police copy of the form all cells that do not have to be completed. The reporting officer can therefore quickly cross check that all data items have been completed.

  - Remove ambiguous, subjective, and unanswerable questions.

  - Ensure the instructions are clearly expressed.

  - Ensure that only the minimum number of questions are asked. The more there are, the poorer the quality of response.

  - Allow descriptive flexibility.

  - Lay it out for ease of comprehension.

4.3.8 Alabama

A study of accident reporting in the cities and counties of Alabama was described by Turner and Mansfield (1983) and Willis et al (1983). The chief finding was that in some 28% of Alabama cities and counties, there was erratic fluctuation of accident numbers within a 5-year period. (Note that this refers to all road accidents, not necessarily to those involving injury.) Rural irregularities tended to be not as severe as for cities; this was ascribed to rural accident reporting being chiefly by troopers of the Alabama Department of Public Safety, which has statewide programs of training in accident investigation, whereas city police may or may not have had such training. (Bear in mind that most Alabama "cities" are very small, half of them having populations of under 1000.) Cities reporting appreciably more or fewer accidents than would be expected on the basis of their population were identified, and surveys carried out to determine factors in common. As a result, thirteen recommendations were made aimed at alleviating the existing problems and guarding against their recurrence.

Table 4.6: Data from Sydney on the percentages* of crashes included in official statistics ("coded"), reported to the police but not coded, and not reported to the police.

	Coded	Reported	Unreported
All claims	25	43	32
Casualty accidents#	60	35	4

* Based upon the total excluding those for which it could not be determined whether the crash was coded, reported, or unreported, which comprised 8% of the total.

Casualty accidents made up 11% of the total.

4.4 Comparison of insurance claims with police data

The major means of determining the representativeness of accident data collected by the police has been by comparing it with hospital records of casualties. Discussion of such studies will be left until Section 11.4, after death certification and hospital statistics have been examined in Chapters 9 and 10. Another means is to use insurance data for the comparison, and results from two such studies will now be given. Most discussion of insurance material will be in Chapter 14.

4.4.1 Sydney, N.S.W.

Searles (1980) reports taking a sample of claims from the files of an insurance company, and comparing them with the list of accidents that constitutes the basis of official statistics. The study was carried out in Sydney and at the time (1975) all crashes resulting in personal injury or in property damage exceeding $50 were, by law, reportable to the police; the official statistics excluded damage-only accidents in which no vehicle had to be towed from the scene, however. Briefer reports on the study are included in Searles and Jamieson (1983) and Searles et al (1986).

Table 4.6 shows that the proportion of crashes getting into official statistics was 25%, and there were another 43% which the claimant stated were notified to the police but which did not appear

Table 4.7: Data from the Sydney insurance sample on the types of crashes, and the proportions found in the official statistics.

	Percent -age within the sample	Percent -age which were coded	Percent -age of casualty accidents which were coded
Right-angle	22	36	64
Change lanes	7	11	60
Head-on	2	53	66
Rear-end	36	20	52
Acute angle	9	19	65
Parked vehicle	8	22	70
Right turn	6	40	58
Run off road	3	17	57
Fixed object	5	15	67
Other*	2	42	78

* Includes crashes with pedestrians, bicycles, motorcycles, and animals. These are grossly underrepresented in the insurance sample because they cause little damage to the car.

in the official statistics. For crashes involving injury, the figures were 60% and 35%. Table 4.7 disaggregates the information according to type of crash: the first column of data shows the relative frequencies in the sample of insurance claims, and the other two columns show what proportion of each type appeared in the official statistics.

4.4.2 Ostergotland, Sweden

Nilsson (1984) reports a little data from Ostergotland for two weeks in March 1982. In this period, insurance companies received information on 229 accidents. Of these, 49 were also registered by the police; for 39, statistical information was passed on to the road authority. For damage-only crashes, about 1-in-10 were reported by the police if the parties agreed about the question of fault, whereas if the parties disagreed, the proportion was 3-in-10. The more severe the accident, the greater the likelihood of the police knowing about it: thus they knew of about half of the towaway crashes, and almost all those involving injury.

4.5 The debris on road method

Another method of finding out about the occurrence of accidents not known to the police is to visit sites periodically, and collect debris from damaged vehicles, e.g. fragments of coloured plastic or glass from broken lights. One such study was reported by Faulkner (1968), and there was at least one other unpublished one by the same author. Table 4.8 gives some notes on the method used.

For 16 of the 17 roundabouts in the study, police accident reports for the period of the survey were examined; 6 injury and 13 damage-only accidents were identified, but debris had been found for 65 accidents. Only 5 of the police-reported accidents seemed to be among these 65. Thus the total of accidents of this type (i.e. at roundabouts) is some 13 times the police-reported injury accident number.

Table 4.8: Faulkner's debris survey.

- Sites inspected: 17 roundabouts.

- Frequency of inspection: weekly, for 9 weeks.

- Debris collected: amber or red plastic or glass fragments (the identity of clear glass fragments was not always certain).

- Collection method: by two pedestrians, without any form of traffic control.

- Where debris found: mostly at the outside edge of the roundabout, not in the middle of the road or near the centre island.

- Could more than one accident at any one site in any one week be inferred? Yes, if the debris occurred on different sections of the roundabout.

- How to avoid counting two accidents on the same section as one? Not possible to be sure of this; perhaps it would have been better to visit the sites twice per week.

- How to avoid counting the same accident twice? By setting a minimum amount of debris to be considered acceptable evidence for a new accident.

- Wet weather: made the fragments difficult to see.

Nilsson could also make a three-way comparison of statistical sources. Of a total of 40 persons (who were probably all car occupants, though the language is not clear on this point), 18 were in insurance company records, 23 in police statistics, and 22 in hospital records. 7 casualties were in all three sources of information. (For Nilsson's results with the hospital data, see Section 11.4.3.)

Chapter 5

Special features of developing countries

5.1 A WHO conference

In November 1981, the World Health Organization held in Mexico City an International Conference on Road Traffic Accidents in Developing Countries. A report of this meeting was subsequently published (WHO, 1984a); that the 3rd of its 13 chapters should be on "Development and improvement of national reporting systems" demonstrates the importance of road accident statistics. In the words of the report, "Without adequate data sources and facilities for data collection, analysis, and interpretation, there could be no efficient countermeasures, evaluations, strategies, and—perhaps most importantly—no clear case to put to national policy-makers charged with allocating scarce resources to different sectors of the economy."

The Conference agreed that data collection systems should take police records as their starting point, and emphasised the importance of giving individual police officers proper training in accident reporting and providing them with suitable tools for the job (by which it presumably meant well-designed accident report forms, adequate administrative support, and access to computing facilities). It also urged that links should be forged between the police and medical authorities at local and national levels, in view of the value of analysing accident and injury data together. However, concerning injury severity, the Abbreviated Injury Scale (AIS: see Section 8.7) was felt to be too complex for satisfactory use in developing countries, and length of stay in hospital was suggested as a simply proxy. (Even so, there was evidently some wishful thinking. Neither length of hospital stay nor AIS is available in police statistics in advanced countries, let alone developing ones.)

5.2 A survey by TRRL

Probably the most impressive body of work on road safety in developing countries is that of the Overseas Unit of the U.K. Transport and Road Research Laboratory. Over the years, they have conducted many studies both with a wide perspective (e.g. calculations of crude accident rates for many countries) and with a narrow one (e.g. consideration of how the safety of a particular category of road users in a particular city can be improved). It is one of their studies that provides a convenient starting point for this Chapter. It is reported by Jacobs et al (1975).

In 1972, information was requested from 42 developing countries on the extent to which road accidents are reported and analysed, by which organisations, and what kind and quantity of statistical information was acquired as a result. Copies of documents used for the reporting and analysis of road accidents were also requested. 34 countries replied. Most of the countries in the survey were Commonwealth ones.

Jacobs et al distinguish between (i) documents used by the police for reporting road accidents, and (ii) those used for the analysis of road accident data. By (i), they mean the equivalent of the British accident report booklet, a document bound in book form and small enough to be carried either in the police officer's pocket or in the glove compartment of a car; sometimes this is not a booklet, but a form or file cover instead. By (ii), they mean something similar to the British Stats 19 form, a coded sheet on which information is entered as a tick or numerical code (from which input to a computer is easy, if one is used). The police report form used in Kenya is shown as Fig-

THE KENYA POLICE—TRAFFIC DEPARTMENT   POLICE 41

Charge Reg. No.................

ACCIDENT REPORT

Acc. Reg. No.................

O.B. No.................

Reporting Officer .... Division .... Station ....

Location of Accident ....

Highway Authority ....

Date .... Day .... Time ....

	Types of Vehicles concerned	Registration Numbers	Names and Addresses of Owners and/or Drivers (state which)	Brief details of damage
1				
2				
3				

	If in order state "Yes" If endorsed or not in order give details overleaf		
	1.	2.	3.
Certificate of Competency			
Driving Licence			
Road Tax			
Insurance			
T.L.B. Licence			
P.S.V. or Taxi Licence			

Name and Address of injured persons	Class of person	Age	Sex	Fatal Serious Slight	From Vehicle No.	Tribe or Nationality

Class of Person: "P" Pedestrian. "D" Driver. "MC" Motor Cyclist. "PS" Passenger. "C" Cyclist. "PP" Pillion Passenger. "O.P." Other Person.

In case of Fatal Accident give Date of Death.

Names and Addresses of witnesses:—

....
....
....
....

Nationality or Tribe of vehicle driver primarily responsible ....

ROAD SURFACE: Tarmac/Murram/Unmade. Speed limit of .... m.p.h.
              Wet/Dry.   Street lighting—Yes/No.

Apparent Cause Code No. .... Special Features if any ....

....
....

Are Court proceedings Contemplated—Yes/No.
When a Police vehicle is involved, this form must be despatched to the Commissioner of Police and the Divisional Transport Officer within 24 hours.

Figure 5.1: The accident report form used in Kenya.

Table 5.1: Comparison of numbers of questions asked in 5 categories by the police road accident report documents of 21 developing countries with the numbers possible and the numbers in the British police booklet.

	Format: booklet =B, form /file cover=F	Admin. details & notes of action	Details of those injured	Drivers, vehicles & pass- engers	Space for state- ments	Site and statist'l info.	Total
No. of possible questions		31	58	76	5	18	188
Great Britain	B	20	19	36	5	14	94
Bahamas	F	10	10	15	2	5	42
Belize	F	14	14	14	3	4	49
Botswana	F	4	0	3	0	0	7
Cyprus	B	22	34	23	5	10	104
Fiji	F	6	1	0	0	11	18
Ghana	F	8	9	17	1	11	46
Gibraltar	B	9	14	21	4	2	50
Guyana	B	16	14	25	4	6	65
Hong Kong	F	11	4	20	4	10	49
India	F	4	7	9	0	6	26
Jamaica	B	11	21	26	4	6	68
Kenya	F						
Malawi	B	7	7	26	5	11	56
Montserrat	B	14	15	26	4	5	64
Sarawak	F	4	0	0	1	0	5
Singapore	F	12	1	18	3	7	41
Sri Lanka	F	10	3	0	0	7	20
St Helena	F	4	0	7	0	0	11
St Lucia	F	13	14	22	2	4	55
Swaziland	B	10	14	27	5	5	61
Zambia	B	12	14	27	5	5	63

ure 5.1; it has been taken from a report by Jacobs and Sayer (1976), who remark that Kenya has a high standard of road accident data collection.

Jacobs et al made up a list of questions that might be asked in a police accident report booklet. There were 188 of these, and they classified them into 5 subjects:

- Administrative details and records of immediate action.

- Details of persons injured.

- Drivers, vehicles, and passengers.

- Space allowed for statements.

- Site and statistical information.

Table 5.1 shows the numbers of questions asked by each of 20 developing countries (plus Great Britain) in each of these categories. It also shows whether the police report consisted of a booklet or a form/file cover—there tended to be more information sought when the former was used. Table 5.2 summarises the information by giving the average number of questions asked in each category as a percentage of the number in the British police booklet.

As to coded sheets similar to Stats 19, apparently only 5 countries used one at the time of this

Table 5.2: The average numbers of questions asked, expressed as percentages of the numbers asked in the British police booklet.

	Format	
	Book -let	Form/ file cover
Administrative details & immediate action	64	40
Details of persons injured	87	26
Details of drivers, vehicles, & passengers	69	27
Space for statements	87	28
Site & statistical information	46	34

Table 5.3: Comparison between the numbers of coded items used by the British Stats 19 form and those of 5 developing countries.

	Stats 19	Minimum & maximum among the developing countries
Casualties	36	7 - 21
Vehicles involved	42	3 - 112
Drivers and riders	24	0 - 28
Attendant circumstances	76	30 - 201

survey. They were much less comprehensive than the reporting documents; Table 5.3 summarises how many coded items referred to each of four subjects.

5.3 TRRL's recommendations

5.3.1 General considerations

Jacobs et al pointed out that, in designing an accident reporting system, the general desirability of a considerable amount of data must be tempered by the realisation that it stands a much better chance of being implemented—especially in a developing country—if it is not over-complicated. If only few and essential questions are asked, then it is reasonable to assume they will be answered thoroughly and accurately. But if there are many questions, there will be less readiness to complete the document.

A method simplified from the British one was suggested for adoption by developing countries. It consisted of a booklet and a coded form.

5.3.2 The booklet

The recommended booklet is illustrated at pp. 16–20 of Jacobs et al (1975). Wherever possible, for ease of completion the information required can be entered with a tick or by writing a number in a box. The front cover deals with identification of the accident by time, date, place, and severity, with the person reporting the accident, and with details of the police station and division concerned. Space is available on the inside cover and following five pages for details of 3 persons involved and (if applicable) their vehicles. There is a page for site details, including road classification and junction information, type and condition of road surface, speed limits, visibility, and weather. There is also a section for damage to other property or animals. A blank page is available for a sketch map of the site, and the remaining parts of the booklet are for statements, police officer's comments and report, and various legal and administrative matters. The booklet is simple to complete, and information can easily be found when needed. Appendix 4 of Jacobs et al (1975) gives a detailed account of the definitions of the terms used in the booklet and instructions on how to complete it.

5.3.3 The analysis form

The recommended analysis form is reproduced as Figure 5.2. It is effectively a simplified version of the Stats 19 form. All information required can be found in the completed report booklet. As with the booklet, it is divided into sections on persons involved, vehicles, site details, and identification of the accident.

Table 5.3 showed the total number of coded alternatives used by Britain and the developing countries. The newly designed analysis form uses about 34 alternatives to describe "persons involved", whereas the Stats 19 uses 36 to cover "casualties"

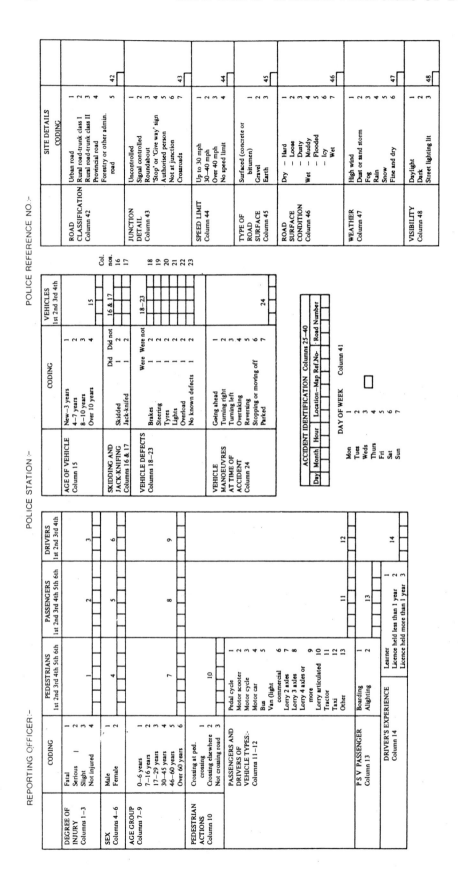

Figure 5.2: Accident analysis form recommended by TRRL for developing countries.

and 24 to cover "drivers and riders", so the former is more concise. "Vehicles involved" and "attendant circumstances and site details" are covered by 19 and 40 alternatives respectively, a balance between the extremes in the developing countries.

It was intended that the form be simple enough for the person responsible to complete without taking too much time. The completed forms would be sent monthly, or even weekly, to a central office where automated analysis could immediately be carried out. Transcription is kept to a minimum, and records needed for local use are not sent away. Appendix 6 of Jacobs et al (1975) includes a detailed account of how to complete the form and which definitions to apply to the various terms; it is of course essential that police and any other organisations involved receive adequate training in the completion of the booklet and analysis form.

5.4   An application in Egypt

5.4.1   The context

In 1980 a program of collaborative research was established between the Egyptian Ministry of Interior and Ministry of Transport on the one hand and the Overseas Unit of the TRRL on the other. Part of this work was directly concerned with reducing accidents, especially by means of low-cost remedial measures on the major inter-city highways. But part of the work was specially relevant to our present concern, the essential preliminary to improved road safety, the setting-up of an efficient system for accident reporting and processing. This had two parts to it:

- Design of an accident report booklet for the police.

- Storage and analysis of accident data using a microcomputer.

For the computing aspect, see Section 3.14.7. The process of designing the report booklet will now be described (Gaber and Yerrell, 1983, 1985).

5.4.2   Method of development

Four different designs of booklet, one of which made heavy use of symbols pictograms, were tested initially. A small group of police officers filled them in from written descriptions of accidents. Time and accuracy of completion were noted in addition to subjective ranking as regards the symbols used or writing required. As a result, two new booklets were designed, with similar content but different layout and use of symbols. Both contained space for a simple sketch plan and written account of the circumstances, in addition to concise precoded information. These booklets were tested under realistic conditions on the Cairo–Alexandria road. From examining the completed booklets, interviewing the officers involved, and visiting sites, a final single design of booklet resulted.

5.4.3   Lessons learned

The important messages to emerge from the field trials were:

- The feasibility of improving the reporting of the location of accidents.

- The need to keep data demands to a minimum and avoid items which are not normally observable or which cannot be physically measured.

- Specifically, questions on the "cause" of accidents should be avoided. (This reflects a longstanding belief at TRRL that the police cannot do this sufficiently accurately for the results to be helpful. As mentioned in Section 3.2, Britain's Stats 19 form avoids causation questions.)

5.4.4   Contents of the final booklet

The booklet has six sections:

- General information: date, time, severity, circumstances of the accident, highway and road layout details.

- Details of the vehicle and its condition; driver's age, sex, occupation, and severity of injury.

- Details of injured passengers.

- Details of injured pedestrians.

- Accident location and sketch.

- Written summary of accident.

5.5   Sri Lanka

Sayer and Hitchcock (1984) describe the accident reporting system in Sri Lanka: "All road accidents involving a vehicle, personal injury, or damage to property occurring on a public highway have to be reported. The police are responsible for reporting these accidents and detailed instructions are laid down as to how it should be done. On being informed of an accident a policeman attends the site and makes a report in his note book. On returning to his Station the notes are transferred to the Station's record book and a precoded road accident report form is filled in. These forms are sent monthly to the district Headquarters for checking before being sent to the Police Headquarters in Colombo, where the data are transferred to coding sheets in preparation for being stored on computer. Not all accidents are reported at the roadside. A significant proportion of the more seriously injured casualties attend or are taken to a hospital casualty department before the police arrive at the accident site." We now meet a new feature: "Attached to the major hospital casualty departments are hospital police posts, maintained in all major hospitals for the purpose of recording details of all casualties involving trauma. Under the agreed reporting procedure, when a road accident casualty is brought to hospital the doctor in charge of the casualty department should inform the police officer on duty in the police post. In turn, the police establish from the casualty, or persons accompanying the casualty, whether the accident has been reported by the police at the scene of the accident. If an accident has not been reported, a telephone message should, in practice, be sent from the hospital police post to the police station in the area of the accident, where a reporting officer should be assigned to the case and take the steps needed to report the accident."

5.6   Malaysia

Bin Husin and Mustafa (1985) say that the Malaysian road accident report form (Pol 27) has recently been revised, and they show the new format. A translation of the contents is given as Table 5.4. I believe the level of detail shown there to be too great for reliable routine use.

Table 5.4: Contents of the new Malaysian accident report form.

```
Time of accident
```

  • Report number and year.
  • Month of year.
  • Day of month.
  • Day of week.
  • Time of day.

```
Location of accident
```

  • Police area (contingent, district, and station).
  • Location (road number and distance).
  • Nature of locality. 4 alternatives: city; town; rural town; rural.
  • Nearby areas. 18 categories: school; offices; housing estate; hospital; shophouses; market stalls; market; night-market; factory or warehouse; bus stop; pedestrian crossing; cinema; petrol station; recreational area; religious establishment; empty space; construction site; other (specify).

```
Characteristics of accident site
```

  • Road features. 10 categories: straight; flat; slope; roundabout; bridge; turning; sharp turning; obscured turning; junction; complex junction.
  • Speed limit.
  • Road lanes. 6 alternatives: divided road; divided road without centre marking; 2-lane; 2-lane with centre marking; 2-lane with no centre marking; directed route.
  • Traffic control at intersection. 7 alternatives: lights; policed; no control; crossing with gate; crossing without gate; pedestrian crossing with lights; pedestrian crossing without lights.
  • Road surface. 4 alternatives: bitumen; concrete; stone; soil.
  • Road quality. 2 alternatives: good; bad.
  • Road surface (temporary condition). 5 alternatives: dry; wet; flooded; oily; slippery.
  • Road construction. 5 alternatives: under construction; blocked passageway; roadwork, not lighted; speed hindrance; unsurfaced road.
  • Weather. 6 alternatives: fine; dull; still; strong wind; drizzle; heavy downpour.
  • Lighting. 5 alternatives: day, good; day, bad; street lighting, good; street lighting, bad; darkness.

Table 5.4: (continued).

Particulars of vehicles

- Registration number of vehicle.
- Type of vehicle. 18 alternatives: motor car; taxi; van; jeep/Landrover; passenger bus; school bus; express bus; factory bus; communications bus; mini bus; small lorry; rigid lorry; articulated lorry with trailer; special use lorry; motorcycle, up to 250 c.c.; motorcycle, 250 c.c. or more; bicycle; non-motor vehicle.
- Make of vehicle.
- Model of vehicle.
- Engine capacity, litres.
- Ownership of vehicle. 5 alternatives: personal; welfare; governmental; police; armed forces.
- Sex of driver.
- Age of vehicle. 7 alternatives: less than 1 year; 1-2 years; 2-4 years; 4-6 years; 6-8 years; 8-10 years; more than 10 years.

Particulars of persons directly involved

- Whether driver, passenger, pedestrian, or other.
- Sex.
- Academic qualifications. 6 alternatives: primary; secondary; college; polytechnic; university; other.
- Licence status. 7 alternatives: none; learner's permit; full licence for less than 1 year; 1-5 years; 6-10 years; more than 10 years; person other than driver or passenger of motor vehicle.
- Method of gaining licence. 3 alternatives: driving school; self-taught; other.
- Age.

Particulars of casualties

- Severity of injury. 3 alternatives: fatal; incapacitating; slight.
- Total numbers of driver, passenger, motorcyclist, pedal cyclist, pedestrian, and other casualties.
- Car occupant protection, seat belt used or not.
- Motorcyclist protection, helmet used or not.
- Position in car. 3 alternatives: driver; front seat passenger; rear seat passenger.

Table 5.4: (continued).

Accident events

- Accident configuration. 9 alternatives: head-on; rear-end; side-swipe; angle; turning right; turning left; pedestrian; fixed object; other (specify).
- Vehicle manoeuvre, for each vehicle. 20 alternatives: merging lanes; diverging lanes; wrong lane; changing lanes; stopping; sudden stop; parked vehicle; starting (in traffic); starting from parked; turning right; turning left; U-turn; overtaking; following too closely; entering home driveway; avoiding moving vehicle; avoiding parked vehicle; pushing; reversing; out of control.
- Accident causation. 51 categories, in 6 groups.
  - Driver violations, 12 types: drunk; drugged; over speed limit; dangerous overtaking; following too closely; inappropriate signal; dangerous change of direction; overloaded with passengers; overloaded with cargo; inappropriate parking; carelessness while starting or entering a parking lot; other (specify).
  - Vehicle defects, 10 types: brakes; steering; wipers; bad tyre; punctured tyre; smooth tyre; faulty lights; no lights; faulty signal lights; other (specify).
  - Road defects, 11 types: undulating; boulders; slippery road surface; low shoulder; no guard rails; holes; lack of signals; lack of street lights; narrow passage; high or low man-hole; lack of road sign.
  - Weather, 7 types: misty; drizzling; heavy downpour; gale; flood; erosion; other (specify).
  - Pedestrian causes, 8 types: drunk; handicapped; sick; careless; pedestrian crossing not used; walking, working, or playing in roadway; playing ball games, etc., in roadway; other (specify).
  - Animals, 3 types: buffalo; dog; other (specify).

Damage

- Vehicle ($).
- Property ($).

5.7   Thailand

A paper by Somnemitr (1986) explicitly addresses the data-capture aspect of the road safety problem in developing countries, specifically Thailand. He draws attention to the major problem of under-reporting of accidents, citing differences between Police Department and Ministry of Public Health fatality figures as in Table 2.1 of this book. He goes on to deplore poor coordination between agencies involved in road safety measures, and hopes that the establishment in 1983 of a National Safety Council in the Office of the Prime Minister will resolve this problem. Somnemitr reports that three kinds of accident report form are in use—by the Department of Highways, by the Police Department, and by the Department of Land Transport—and reproduces a new one already adopted by one Department which it is hoped may supplant the others also.

5.8   Four projects described by Ross (c. 1986)

5.8.1   Spectrum of countries

The projects to be summarised were carried out in Bahrain, Nigeria, South Korea, and Trinidad and Tobago. Introducing these case studies of his, Ross (c. 1986) remarks that they include two large and two small countries; and two with death rates per vehicle that are low compared with other developing countries (Bahrain, Trinidad and Tobago), and two whose death rates are among the highest in the world (Nigeria, South Korea).

5.8.2   Bahrain

In the 1970's, it was required in Bahrain to report all road accidents, irrespective of their severity, to the police. Even minor damage accidents required the police to attend and the vehicles were not to be moved until then. A vehicle inspection was necessary before the vehicle was released, and a certificate proving the accident had been reported to the police was required before a garage would undertake repairs. Consequently, a great deal of time was taken up in clerical processing of the records, and the quality of vehicle inspection declined as the quantity increased. No resources were available to analyse the information collected.

Accordingly, a system was devised that reduced police involvement with minor accidents, enabling greater investigation and analysis in depth of the more serious ones. Pre-coded report forms were designed, a suite of computer programs was written for processing the data, and an Accident Unit created to identify accident blackspots and devise remedial measures.

5.8.3   Nigeria

At present, information is recorded on a blank statement form—statements of those involved, of witnesses, and of the investigating police officer. Little or no systematic attempt is made to collect details of the location, the site conditions, the weather, and so on. The statements constitute a casefile; summaries are entered into a ledger; monthly returns are made to the state headquarters of the police, from where they are forwarded to national HQ.

Chief among the improvements required are the design and adoption of a pre-printed pre-coded accident report form, including the training of police officers in how to complete it; and the efficient storage and analysis of the information thereby collected. One view of what should be included in a report form is that at Appendix V of Oluwoye (1986). Mbadiwe (1986) recommends that the TRRL suggestions (Section 5.3 and Figure 5.2 above) be adopted. Other papers in the same collection as these also comment on the inadequacy of road accident statistics in Nigeria.

5.8.4   South Korea

All traffic accidents must by law be reported to the traffic police, but considerable under-reporting of damage-only accidents is suspected. In most cases, general information on site deails is noted by the attending police officer on plain paper, then transferred to a 4-page pre-printed form at the police station, where details of drivers' licences and their statements are also recorded.

Here there is much more to build upon than in Nigeria. The existing data collection document can be taken as a starting point—but it needs to be rearranged into booklet format so that it can be carried by the police officer and completed at the accident site, reducing the likelihood of omissions and errors. It also needs to include more information about the location of the accident. However, the impact of improvement in this respect will not be felt until a programme of blackspot identification is undertaken and funds are made available for remedial measures.

5.8.5 Trinidad and Tobago

The accident data system in Trinidad and Tobago, as with many former British colonies, appeared similar to that in the U.K. some 15–20 years earlier. So in principle it was sufficient to allow fairly detailed analysis—if it had been organised suitably. Unfortunately it was not organised properly because no-one used it, and it was not used because it was organised so badly (analysis cards, prepared with hand punches, being stacked on the floor, in cupboards, and in boxes, so that retrieval of any particular one was practically impossible).

Another problem was that traffic police were not regarded as specialists, and might be transferred to other duties at any moment, so it was impossible to build up a group with experience and expertise in the subject. It is doubtless the same elsewhere, too (e.g. Nigeria—Olugbemi and Adebisi, 1986).

A six-stage plan of improvement was implemented, central to which was the establishment of a Traffic Management Unit in the country.

- Summary of brief details of each personal injury accident on a data transcription form.

- Use of hardback ledgers as an accident register. Allocation of serial numbers to accidents.

- Plotting of accident locations on 1:10000 scale map.

- Recording of accident locations and serial numbers on 1:2500 scale map.

- Preparation of an accident location register, consisting of a summary of the accidents on each link of the road network.

- As locations with high accident frequencies become apparent in the plotting of the accident maps, summarise the accidents occurring at each, then follow this up with more detailed analysis of the characteristics of the crashes and what preventive measures could be undertaken.

Table 5.5: Contents of accident report form recommended at the WHO Bridgetown 1984 meeting. Particulars of accident

- Accident ID no.

- No. of vehicles involved.

- Date of accident.

- Estimated time of occurrence.

- Light conditions. 4 alternatives: dawn; day; dusk; night.

- Weather conditions. 4 alternatives: clear; overcast; light rain; heavy rain and wind.

- Accident type. 6 alternatives: vehicle-pedestrian; vehicle-vehicle; vehicle-animal; vehicle-stationary object; loss of control/skidding; other (specify).

- Road surface. 4 alternatives: tarred; gravel; dirt; other (specify).

- Road conditions. 5 alternatives: dry; wet; muddy; oily; other (specify).

- Road defects. 4 types, each to be specified as present or absent: potholes; broken edges; under repair; other (specify).

- Environment. 8 features, each to be specified as present or absent: sidewalk; traffic light; barriers; bridges; pedestrian crossings; road signs; bends/curves; other (specify).

- Artificial road lighting. 4 alternatives: none; partial; full; n/a.

- Location. Clear language description.

- Drawing of locality.

- Statement. Clear language report.

Table 5.5: (continued).
Particulars of each vehicle involved

- Type. 8 alternatives: car; minibus; omnibus; light truck; heavy truck; motorcycle; bicycle; other (specify).

- Vehicle owner. Name, address.

- Make of car.

- Weight of car.

- Model year.

- Registration no.

- Registration date.

- Insurance type. 3 alternatives: full comprehensive; third party; none.

- Insurance company.

- Insurance policy no.

- Date policy was issued.

- Date policy expires.

- Date of last inspection.

- Defects. 4 types, each to be specified as present or absent, and with regard to whether or not it contributed to the accident: tyres; brakes; lights; steering.

- Number of occupants.

- Safety devices available. 5 types, each to be specified as present, absent, or not applicable: seat belt for driver; seat belt for front passenger; seat belts in back seat; child seat; helmets.

- Damage done to vehicle. Clear language description.

Table 5.5: (continued).
Particulars of each person involved

- Name.

- Address.

- Manner of involvement. 3 alternatives: driver (including motor and pedal cyclists); passenger (including pillion riders and loaders); pedestrian.

- Age.

- Sex.

- Injury. 5 alternatives: none; injury with no treatment; treated at scene and discharged; pronounced dead at scene; admitted to medical unit.

- Was safety device being used by this person (seat belt for car or truck, helmet for cycles)? 2 alternatives: yes; no.

- For drivers, was he/she licensed? 3 alternatives: yes; no; not applicable.

- For licensed drivers, licence no.

- For licensed drivers, date of issue of licence.

- For licensed drivers, expiry date of licence.

5.9 Caribbean recommendations

A workshop on motor vehicle injuries was held at Bridgetown, Barbados, in June 1984 (WHO, 1984b). Among its recommendations were:

- That each country should designate a permanent unit to be responsible for road traffic accident data, to coordinate information from all sources (police, hospitals, insurance), and to be the source of information for all users.

- That each country should adopt a common form for data collection by the police, after it has been pretested on a sample basis. The contents of the form the workshop participants adopted are shown as Table 5.5.

There are some respects in which the proposal at Table 5.5 is very praiseworthy, and improves upon forms used in advanced countries, but I do doubt whether it is practicable for developing countries.

5.10   Microcomputers for accident analysis in developing countries

See Section 3.14.7.

5.11   Country profiles

Annex 5 in WHO (1983a) consists of brief descriptions, with statistics, of the population, means of transportation used, road accident situation, and legislation relating to road safety, of twelve countries of the Western Pacific: Australia, Brunei, China, Fiji, Hong Kong, Japan, Korea (Republic), Macau, Malaysia, Papua New Guinea, Philippines, and Singapore.

At pages 5–8 of WHO (1982b) there are brief reports on childhood accidents (not limited to those involving vehicles) in Benin, Brazil, Senegal, and Turkey.

At pages 2–3 of WHO (1983b), some description of road accidents in Bangladesh, India, Indonesia, Sri Lanka, and Thailand is given. It is said that "Major underreporting of road casualties occurs in most developing countries. This underreporting occurs in both hospital and police data sources. In Bangladesh in a casualty hospital, it was estimated that only 25% of the hospital admission cases from road crashes were recorded by the police. In Thailand a sample study suggested that police records only covered 20% of hospital cases, and in India the equivalent figure was estimated at between 30 and 40%. In Sri Lanka, on the other hand, there is minimal underreporting because of good liaison with the police at the operational level." (Concerning Sri Lanka, see also Section 5.5 above.)

Chapter 6

Comparison of six road accident statistical yearbooks

6.1 Aim of this Chapter

This Chapter examines the contents of the annual statistical publications about road accidents from six jurisdictions in the developed world. After a general guide to what they contain (Section 6.3), it makes a detailed examination of what variables are tabulated in them, and what the categories are that the variables are divided into (Section 6.4). Later Sections extend this examination to the publications from six Australian states, review a number of previous surveys of this type, and outline how a cross-national index to data tables might be developed.

The general philosophy is that it is important (i) to know how many road accidents are happening, and what are their characteristics, (ii) to communicate this knowledge by means of a statistical yearbook, as there are many agencies and organisations whose work is facilitated by such data, and (iii) to extend this communication internationally, as many of the problems are similar in a number of countries, and so may the solutions be.

6.2 The yearbooks examined

The six road accident statistical yearbooks that were studied were as follows.
Finland. Road Traffic Accidents 1984. Helsinki: Central Statistical Office.
Great Britain. Road Accidents Great Britain. 1984 edition. London: HMSO.
Japan. Road Accidents Japan. 1984 edition. Tokyo: International Association of Traffic and Safety Sciences.
New Zealand. Motor Accidents in New Zealand.

Statistical Statement. 1980 edition. Wellington: Ministry of Transport.
Norway. Road Traffic Accidents. 1984 edition. Oslo: Central Bureau of Statistics.
Saskatchewan. Saskatchewan Traffic Accident Facts. 1982 edition. Regina: Traffic Safety Engineering Branch, Saskatchewan Highways and Transportation.

6.3 General guide to their contents

There are several types of information that all six yearbooks give: historical tables showing the development of the numbers of road accidents over a period of years, and detailed tables about the features of the road accidents that occurred in the year in question, for examples. Other types of information are included by only some countries: a copy of the accident report form, for example. Table 6.1 gives an overview; there now follow some notes on the types of contents listed there.

6.3.1 Historical trends

I refer here to tables containing data for a number of years.
Finland. 10 tables, mostly from 1980 onwards, though some from 1974. Casualty rates also included.
Great Britain. 10 tables giving data from 1909 onwards. Also, calendar of historical events affecting road safety.
Japan. 11 tables, with various starting dates, the earliest being 1926.

Table 6.1: The contents of road accident statistical yearbooks from six countries. (Y = yes, this type of information is present.)

	Fin	G.B.	Jap	N.Z.	Nor	Sask
Historical trends	Y	Y	Y	Y	Y	Y
Detailed tables for year in question	Y	Y	Y	Y	Y	Y
Casualty rates	Y	Y	Y	Y	Y	Y
International comparisons	Y	Y			Y	
Explanatory notes to tables	Y	Y	Y	Y	Y	Y
Textual section	Y	Y			Y	Y
Glossary of terms and definitions	Y	Y	Y	Y	Y	Y
Details of related publications		Y				
English language translation	Y		Y		Y	
Details of relevant legislation		Y		Y		
Data collection form	Y	Y			Y	
Description of data collection methods					Y	
Subject indexes		Y				

New Zealand. 5 tables, from 1936 or 1966.
Norway. 13 tables. mostly for 1975–84.
Saskatchewan. 8 tables, 1963–82.

Norway. Historical trends, year in question, and international comparisons.
Saskatchewan. 2 historical tables.

6.3.2 Detailed tables for the year in question

Finland. 26 in number.
Great Britain. 48 main tables, plus others on selected topics which vary from year to year.
Japan. 35.
New Zealand. 35.
Norway. 32.
Saskatchewan. 35 tales and figures.

6.3.3 Casualty rates

Rates may be calculated in a number of ways, e.g. as accidents per 10000 registered vehicles, or per 100 million vehicle kilometres travelled.
Finland. Historical trends, and comparison with other Nordic countries.
Great Britain. 6 tables giving historical trends, year in question, and international comparisons.
Japan. For year in question and historical trends.
New Zealand. For historical trends, general casualty rates for year in question, and for motorcyclists.

6.3.4 International comparisons

Finland. Tables for 3 other Nordic countries.
Great Britain. Figures for the constituent parts of the United Kingdom, 21 other European countries, Australia, Canada, Japan, New Zealand, U.S.A.
Japan. No.
New Zealand. No.
Norway. Detailed tables for the Scandinavian countries only.
Saskatchewan. No.

6.3.5 Explanatory notes to tables

Generally these are insufficiently detailed, consisting only of a couple of lines per table.
Finland. Brief notes to a few tables only.
Great Britain. Comprehensive separate section. Brief notes under individual tables.
Japan. Brief notes under individual tables.
New Zealand. Separate but brief section. Brief notes under individual tables.
Norway. Separate section, referred to under individual tables.

Saskatchewan. Brief notes under tables.

6.3.6   Textual sections

These are generally too brief and not very informative.
Finland. Brief introduction. Most text not in English.
Great Britain. Preface. Comprehensive textual and tabular review of selected topics for the year in question. Calendar of events affecting road safety.
Japan. No.
New Zealand. Brief introduction.
Norway. Several informative text sections, including ones on "Survey design and implementation", "Reliability of results", "Developing trends".
Saskatchewan. Brief text throughout.

6.3.7   Glossary of terms and definitions

Generally not detailed enough, and often there are terms not understood outside the country concerned.
Finland. A few definitions only.
Great Britain. "Notes and definitions".
Japan. 1 page of definitions, and also "Classification of different motor vehicles".
New Zealand. Included in brief "Introduction and notes".
Norway. "Terms and variables", "Severity of injury", "Classification of accidents".
Saskatchewan. Definitions (half page only).

6.3.8   Details of related publications

Finland. No.
Great Britain. Reports relating to road safety from the Transport and Road Research Laboratory.
Japan. No.
New Zealand. No.
Norway. No.
Saskatchewan. No.

6.3.9   English language translation

The translations are at times obscure in meaning.
Finland.   Mainly tri-lingual, Finnish/Swedish/

English.
Japan. Wholly in English.
Norway. Bi-lingual, Norwegian/English.

6.3.10   Details of relevant legislation

Finland. No.
Great Britain. Not specifically, though some information is in "Calendar of events affecting road safety and traffic".
Japan. No. See IATSS (1986).
New Zealand. Brief listing of traffic legislation introduced since 1965.
Norway. No.
Saskatchewan. No.

6.3.11   Data collection form

Finland. Yes.
Great Britain. Yes.
Japan. No. For a listing of the main items (83 in number), see Figure 3.5.
New Zealand. No.
Norway. Yes.
Saskatchewan. No.

6.3.12   Description of data collection methods

Finland. No.
Great Britain. No.
Japan. No.
Norway. "Survey design and implementation", "Reliability of results".
Saskatchewan. No.

6.3.13   Subject indexes

Finland. No index. Contents page gives titles of tables, does not list figures.
Great Britain. Detailed subject index. Contents page lists titles of main tables and figures.
Japan. No index. Contents page gives individual table titles.
New Zealand. No index. Contents page gives individual table titles.
Norway. No index. List of titles of individual tables and figures.

Saskatchewan. No index. List of titles of tables and figures.

6.3.14 Comment

The chief thing that emerges from this comparison, and a less formal look I have taken at the comparable publications of a number of other countries and states, is the frequent omission of elementary necessities. Any collection of official statistics should include notes on how the data was captured, how it was processed, the definitions adopted, events occurring that change the numbers substantially, and preferably some discussion of what they mean; yet many yearbooks give the reader no assistance in these matters. The best that I have seen is Britain's; I do not ask that every jurisdiction include a commentary of the same high standard that is found in Road Accidents Great Britain, as this requires a level of expertise not easily found; but I do think the inclusion in yearbooks of the materials identified in this Section is both practicable and desirable.

6.4 Details of variables and their categories

6.4.1 Arrangement of this comparison

The findings are given in six Tables, containing a total of 48 headings. These Tables give the categories by which road accidents are classified in the yearbooks listed previously. The six Tables refer to the following types of variables:

- Basic facts (Section 6.4.2 and Table 6.2).

- Site of accident (6.4.3 and Table 6.3).

- Transient environmental conditions (6.4.4 and Table 6.4).

- The accident events (6.4.5 and Table 6.5).

- The vehicle and its driver (6.4.6 and Table 6.8).

- The casualty (6.4.7 and Table 6.9).

For the most part, the Tables are arranged with columns corresponding to countries. However, where every (or nearly every) country uses the same categories (e.g. the months of the year), this would be pointless, and where only one or two countries tabulate a particular factor (e.g. accidents during public holiday periods) it would be very wasteful of space, so in these cases the information is typed across the columns.

A few notes about the preparation and interpretation of the Tables:

- An exact record of each country's practice has not been attempted. Instead, the names of the factors have to a limited extent been modified, as have the names of the categories within the factors, and even the assignment of categories to factors, in order to make a Table more understandable and emphasise the similarities between countries. This was particularly necessary for the accident events.

- Categories may not be exclusive one of another.

- In addition to the categories shown, "other" and "unknown" frequently occur.

- The categories shown may in some tabulations be condensed into fewer.

- Sometimes it happens that for some particular country two similar variables fit under the same heading in a Table, or the same variable is condensed in two different ways. In this case, the two lists of categories are distinguished by Roman numerals, i.e. (i) and (ii).

- Some categories are inherently difficult to describe in a few words.

- The language used to name or describe the categories is sometimes not clear.

- More factors and categories may be available on the accident report form than are tabulated in the yearbook.

6.4.2 Basic facts

Table 6.2 shows how these are presented in the six countries' yearbooks, under the following headings:

1 Geographical location.

2 Month of year.

3 Day of week.

4 Time of day.

5 Holidays.

It is noteworthy that already we see variations between countries even in such straightforward factors as these. Thus Great Britain doesn't feel it worth distinguishing between the four days Monday, Tuesday, Wednesday, Thursday, and Japan feels that tabulating time by the 2-hour period is sufficiently precise.

6.4.3 Site of accident

The following are the headings used in Table 6.3:

1 Nature of locality.

2 Road type.

3 Speed limit.

4 Intersection.

5 Road features.

6 Road width.

7 Road surface material.

8 Street furniture and hazards.

The last is included only to refer the reader to part 4 of Table 6.5.

The urban/rural distinction is made by most of the jurisdictions, and so is some sort of classification on the basis of road type—but this latter is generally an administrative classification (reflecting such matters as who pays for its construction and upkeep), and any correlation with its engineering excellence is imperfect. I was surprised to find only two of the six yearbooks included speed limit at the accident site as a subject for tabulation.

Details of intersection design and road features I will come to in a moment; the width of the road is tabulated by Japan and Norway, and the nature of the road surface by Norway and Saskatchewan; hazards present at the site and whether any item of street furniture was struck might have been included in this Section, but will instead be considered in part 4 of Table 6.5, in context of the accident events.

Intersection design: this is classified in a variety of ways. Japan does little more than indicate whether the site was an intersection or not; Great Britain and Norway give some idea of the geometrics; New Zealand concentrates on the nature of the control present. Whether or not this variable reflects whether the accident was truly intersection-related is a big question. Relevant crashes can occur a considerable distance away from the intersection (e.g. rear-end, into a queue of vehicles held up at the junction), and crashes can occur at or close to a junction that really have nothing to do with the fact that roads meet there—especially in city centres, where there is a high density of minor lanes branching off a street.

Road features: railway crossing is a feature identifiable for four of the countries, but otherwise there is no particular pattern.

6.4.4 Transient environmental conditions

I use this term to encompass the following (Table 6.4):

1 Weather.

2 Road surface.

3 Lighting.

The Great British weather is classified as fine, rain, snow, or fog, and the road surface as dry, wet, or icy, and the other countries play minor variations on this theme.

There is a good deal of common ground with respect to lighting conditions, too. The basic categories are daylight, nighttime with street lights, and nighttime without street lights. In several countries, twilight is an additional category; it can certainly be said that to specify this is decidedly subjective, but surely the same subjective judgment would have to be exercised to classify those conditions as day or night if the twilight category were not available? Great Britain and New Zealand attempt to give some idea of the quality of street lighting.

6.4.5 The accident events

What happened in the accident and attempts to specify its cause(s) are classified in Table 6.5 under the following 13 headings:

Table 6.2: Methods of presenting basic facts.

	Finland	Great Britain	Japan	New Zealand	Norway	Saskatchewan
1 Geographical location	12 provinces Approx. 500 municipalities	66 counties/regions		34 major cities & boroughs	19 counties 67 police districts & municipalities	492 urban communities 299 rural municipalities 537 highway-control sections

2 Month of year: All use the standard 12 months. Norway also uses the 52 weeks.

3 Day of week: All except G.B. use the 7 days of the week. (Some order them from Monday to Sunday, others from Sunday to Saturday.) G.B. uses the 4 categories Monday-Thursday, Friday, Saturday, Sunday.

4 Time of day: All except Japan use the 24 hours. Japan uses 12 2-hour periods. N.Z. also uses the 8 periods 00-06, 06-09, 09-12, 12-14, 14-16, 16-18, 18-22, 22-00.

5 Holidays: N.Z. enumerates the accidents occurring in 4 holiday periods.

Table 6.3: Methods of presenting information about the accident site.

Finland	Great Britain	Japan	New Zealand	Norway	Saskatchewan
1 Nature of locality					
Built-up	Built-up	Population concentrated area	Urban	(i) Built-up Non-built-up	
Non-built-up	Non-built-up	Suburban area	Rural	(ii) Densely populated Outside densely populated area	
		Not urban area			
2 Road type					
Motorway	Motorway	National highway		Europe road	Provincial highway
Class 1 main roads	A road	National expressway		National road	Rural road
Class 2 main roads	B road	Main local road		Provincial road	Urban street
Other highway	Other	Prefectural road		Local road	Other
Local road		City, town, & village road		Private road	
Municipal road		Road for exclusive use of cars		Places, etc	
Private road		Other		Footway/cycleway	
3 Speed limit					
50 kph	30 mph		50 or less kph		
60–70 kph	40 mph		70 kph		
80–90 kph	50 mph		80 kph		
100–110 kph	60 mph				
120 kph	70 mph				
4 Intersection					
Traffic lights in action	Roundabout	Within intersection	Traffic signals	3-leg	
Traffic lights not in action	T or staggered junction	In vicinity of intersection	Stop sign	4-leg	
Priority junction	Y junction	Non-intersection	Give way sign	Other	
Stop sign	Crossroads		Pointsman or school patrol	Non-intersection	
	Multiple junction		Uncontrolled intersection		
	Private drive or entrance		Roundabout		
	Other junction		Non-intersection		
	Not at or within 20m of junction				

Table 6.3: (continued).

Finland	Great Britain	Japan	New Zealand	Norway	Saskatchewan
5 Road features					
Controlled railway level crossing	Zebra pedestrian crossing	Non-intersection (in tunnel, curve, near corner, slope)	Bridge	Access road	
Uncontrolled railway level crossing	Pelican pedestrian crossing	Non-intersection (other)	Railway crossing	Railway crossing	
	Other light-controlled pedestrian crossing	Railway crossing	Motorway on/off ramp	Non-roadway	
	Other controlled pedestrian crossing		Raised island	Pedestrian/bicycle lane or path	
			Straight road		
			Easy curve		
			Moderate curve		
			Severe curve		

6 Road width: Japan uses the categories less than 3.5, 3.5-4.4, 4.5-5.4, 5.5-7.4, 7.5-8.9, 9.0-12.9, 13.0-19.4, 19.5+ (m). Norway uses the categories less than 3.5, 3.5-4.4, 4.5-5.4, 5.5-6.4, 6.5-7.4, 7.5-8.4, 8.5-9.4, 9.5-12.4, 12.4+ (m). For Norway also, the number of lanes and whether there is physical separation of the carriageways is given.

7 Road surface material: Norway uses the 4 categories asphalt, gravel, cobblestones, concrete. Saskatchewan uses the 4 categories asphalt/oil, gravel, dirt/earth, concrete.

8 Street furniture and hazards: see part 4 of Table 6.5.

Table 6.4: Methods of presenting information about transient environmental conditions.

1 Weather

Finland	Great Britain	Japan	New Zealand	Norway	Saskatchewan
	Fine	Fine	Fine	Sight conditions:	Clear
	Raining	Cloudy	Light rain	Good, no rain/snow	Cloudy
	Snowing	Rainy	Heavy rain	Good, rain/snow	Raining
	Fog	Snowy	Snow	Poor, rain/snow	Snowing
		Foggy	Mist	Poor, fog	Sleet/freezing rain/hail
				Poor, other reasons	Fog/smoke/smog
					Drifting snow/dust
				Temperature:	Strong wind
				7 categories, from below -14 to above +14 (deg. C)	Glare

2 Road surface

Finland	Great Britain	Japan	New Zealand	Norway	Saskatchewan
Dry	Dry		Slippery (rain)	Dry	Dry
Wet	Wet/flood		Slippery (other)	Wet	Wet
Snow/ice/sleet	Snow/ice			Snow/ice	Slush
Gritted				Snow/ice (partial)	Snow
Salted				Slippery, other causes	Ice
					Loose gravel/sand
					Muddy
					Fresh oil

3 Lighting

Finland	Great Britain	Japan	New Zealand	Norway	Saskatchewan
Daylight	Daylight	Day	Bright sun	Daylight	Daylight
Dusk	Dark, street lighting 7+ m high	Night	Overcast	Twilight	Dark
Dark	Dark, street lighting under 7 m high		Twilight, bright street lights	Dark, lighted	Dusk
Dark, lighted road	Dark, no street lighting		Twilight, some street lights	Darked, unlighted	Dawn
	Dark, street lights unlit		Twilight, no street lights		Artificial light
			Dark, bright street lights		
			Dark, some street lights		
			Dark, no street lights		

1 Collision configuration (multi-vehicle accidents).

2 Collision configuration (single- or multi-vehicle accidents).

3 Norwegian detailed list of accident types.

4 Object hit or otherwise involved, and hazards present.

5 Vehicle manoeuvre.

6 Non-collision events.

7 Number of vehicles.

8 Contributory factors.

9 Human action.

10 Human condition (alcohol, drugs, fatigue, physical disability).

11 Vehicle speed.

12 Violations by driver.

13 Pedestrian location/action/violation.

Anyone who has ever studied road accidents knows that all sorts of freakish events happen now and then. Many attempts have been made to devise a helpful system of classification of accident configurations, and no consensus has yet emerged. Part of the reason for the problem is that such a variable is attempting to serve three purposes: to indicate the vehicle movements which were intended by the drivers, to describe factually what the vehicle movements actually were, and to reflect the directions of impacts received by the vehicles (particularly important with regard to secondary safety, i.e. reducing injury in crashes, as distinct from primary safety, the prevention of crashes from occurring). To give an example: with traffic driving on the left, vehicle 1 is stationary at a junction, waiting to turn right, but had started to turn before stopping, so is at an angle to the traffic. Vehicle 2, approaching from behind at too fast a speed, brakes an swerves but loses control and its nearside impacts the offside of vehicle 1. From the point of view of primary safety, one might wish to call this a rear-end crash, the angle of the impact being irrelevant to what caused it; from the vehicle damage viewpoint, "side-swipe (same direction)" best describes it; with the secondary safety of vehicle 1 in mind, one might wish to class it with right-angled collisions into offside.

Great Britain doesn't attempt to summarise the collision configuration as such, but instead gives the manoeuvres of each vehicle. If necessary, the manoeuvres of two or more vehicles can be combined and condensed so as to give a limited number of configuration categories that are appropriate for some particular purpose. Other than Great Britain, the classification is some variant of head-on/rear-end/side-swipe/right-angled, with greater or lesser degree of elaboration. See also Table 6.6, showing a proposal by Watkins (1971), intended for adoption by the Australian states, and Table 6.7, showing a 28-category system proposed by Bohlin and Samuelsson (1973). Norway employs a long list which is published in detailed form; it is reproduced in part 3 of the Table (except that cross-reference is made to part 13 for pedestrian and sledging accidents), and illustrated in Figure 6.1. So also does New Zealand, but only the totals of the detailed categories (Figure 6.2) are given, the condensed categories shown in parts 1 and 2 of Table 6.5 being used for cross-tabulations.

Three other detailed methods of classification will now be described.

- Victoria's RUM (Road User Movement) system. Figure 6.3 shows the 1981 version, taken from Andreassend (1983), in which paper there is also a lengthy Appendix defining the circumstances for the use of the codes more precisely. The first digit divides accidents into the major types (the ten columns of Figure 6.3), and the second digit is used for subdivision. The 1972 version of the RUM codes was slightly different—see Sach (1976). A version of these codes has been adopted by New South Wales (Paterson and Baxter, 1987), and they have also received a degree of support in the U.K., being included in the Accident Investigation Manual (DTp, 1986; at Appendix 6D).

- A classification system for accidents has also been developed at Calspan (Terhune, 1983). It is known by the acronym CALAX, and illustrated at Figure 6.4. At the right of that Figure is shown the most detailed level, in which 48 types of vehicles' impacts are spec-

Table 6.5: Methods of presenting information about the accident events.

Finland	Great Britain	Japan	New Zealand	Norway	Saskatchewan
1 Collision configuration (multi-vehicle accidents)					
Same direction, rear-end	(Involvement of parked vehicles is given)	Head-on, overtaking	Overtaking	Rear-end	Rear-end
Same direction, overtaking		Head-on, other	Head-on, not overtaking	Same direction of travel (other)	Right angle
Same direction, turn		Rear (while moving)	Stationary vehicle	Head-on, overtaking	Side-swipe (same direction)
Meeting accident, direct		Rear (parking/ stopping)	Rear-end	Head-on, other	Side-swipe (opposite directions)
Meeting accident, turn		Crossing collision	Intersection, vehs moving in same direction, one turning	Turning from same directions of travel	Head-on
Crossing accident, direct		Overtaking	Intersection, vehs crossing paths, turning	Turning from opposite directions of travel	Turning left head-on
Crossing accident, turn		Contact while overtaking each other	Intersection, vehs crossing paths, turning	Crossing directions of travel, without turning	Passing, left turn
		Side, turning left	Intersection, turning	Crossing directions of travel, with turning	Passing, right turn
		U-turning	Intersection, merging	(80 accident events in detailed list)	
		Reversing	Intersection, vehs moving in opposite directions, one turning right		
		Changing course	Vehicle manoeuvring		
		Parked vehicle			
		(Modified categories for expressway accidents)			
2 Collision configuration (single- or multi-vehicle accidents)					
Single-vehicle, on the road		Collision with structure (6 subdivisions)	Lost control on straight road	Pedestrian crossing roadway	Single vehicle, on the road
Single-vehicle, off-road		Running off, rolling down	Lost control on corner	Pedestrian walking along roadway	Single vehicle, to the left ditch
Pedestrian		Running off, other	Obstruction	Sledges etc involved	Single vehicle, to the right ditch
Animal		Overtaking	Pedestrian crossing road	Single vehicle ran off road	Train
		Railway crossing (4 subdivisions)	Pedestrian, other	Single vehicle overturning in roadway, collision with animal, parked vehicle, etc	
		Pedestrian (10 subdivisions)	Train	(80 accident events in detailed list)	
		(Modified categories for expressway accidents)	Into water/river/sea		

Table 6.5: (continued).

3 Norwegian detailed list of accident types. Sometimes they are condensed into the 10 numbered categories, sometimes into the 12 lettered groups.

1 Same direction of travel:
(B) Overtaking
(B) Changing lane to left
(B) Changing lane to right
(B) Parallel lanes
(A) Rear-end
(B) Starting from stopped or parked position
(B) Uncertain sequence

2 Head-on:
(D) Straight road section
(D) Curve
(C) Overtaking, straight road
(C) Overtaking, right curve
(C) Overtaking, left curve
(D) Passing stopped or parked vehicle
(D) Starting from stopped or parked position
(D) Uncertain sequence

3 (E) Turning from same direction of travel:
Rear-end with right-turning vehicle
Other collisions with right-turning vehicle
Rear-end with left-turning vehicle
Other collisions with left-turning vehicle
U-turn
Collision with driver from footway/cycleway by right-turning vehicle
Collision with driver from footway/cycleway by left-turning vehicle
Uncertain sequence

4 (E) Turning from opposite directions of travel:
Left turn in front of vehicle in opposite direction of travel
Turning into same direction
Turning into opposite direction
U-turn in front of vehicle in opposite direction of travel
Right-turning before driver in opposite direction from footway/cycleway
Left-turning before driver in opposite direction from footway/cycleway
Uncertain sequence

5 (F) Crossing directions of travel without turning:
Crossing directions of travel
Overtaking to left at intersection
Overtaking to right at intersection
Driver from footway/cycleway crossed roadway on nearside of intersection
Driver from footway/cycleway crossed roadway on farside of intersection
Driver form footway/cycleway crossed roadway outside intersection
Uncertain sequence

6 (F) Crossing directions of travel with turning:
Right turn in front of veh. in same direction of travel
Right turn in front of veh. in opp. direction of travel
Right turn in front of left-turning vehicle
Left turn in front of vehicle in same direction of travel
Left turn in front of vehicle in opp. direction of travel
Both vehicles making left turns
Both vehicles making right turns
Uncertain sequence

7 (G if pedestrian, I if person sledging) Pedestrian (etc) crossing roadway: see 4.15

8 (H if pedestrian, I if person sledging) Person walking (etc) in or along roadway: see 4.15

9 (J) Single vehicle running off road:
To the right on straight road
To the left on straight road
To the left in right curve
To the right in left curve
To the right in right curve
To the left in left curve
Upon turning at intersection
Running into traffic island
Uncertain sequence

10 Other accidents:
(K) Animal involved
(K) Collision with fixed obstacle in roadway
(K) Road surface defects
(K) Single vehicle overturning in roadway
(K) Collision with parked vehicle on right side of road
(K) Collision with parked vehicle on left side of road
(K) Collision with parked vehicle upon overtaking
(K) Other collisions with parked vehicle
(L) Uncertain sequence

Table 6.5: (continued).

4 Object hit or otherwise involved, and hazards present

Finland	Great Britain	Japan	New Zealand	Norway	Saskatchewan
Animal	Dog on road		Animals, driven or accompanied	Animal	Animal action (deer)
	Other animal on road		Wild animals, stray, or out of control		Animal action (other wild)
					Animal action (domestic)
					Delineator posts
					Fire hydrant
	Lamp post/telegraph pole hit	Light pole	Traffic signals or signal bollards	Light pole, column, or signpost	Light standard
		Road sign	Pole	Fixed obstacle in roadway	Parking meter
					Power pole
					Signpost
					Signal stand
			Tree	Tree	Tree/bush
			Fence, letterbox, hoarding etc	Fence, guardrail	Crash cushion
		Guard fence etc	Guide or guardrail		Fence
					Guard rail
		House/wall	House/building	Wall/building	Building/wall
			Roadworks/sign/drums		Traffic barricade
					Construction zone
		Bridge pier	Bridge abutments, hand or approach rails		Bridge structure
		Central reserve/pedestrian island	Traffic island/ median	Traffic island	Median barrier
			Kerb		
			Upgight cliff/bank		Culvert
			Ditch		Kerb
			Over edge of bank		Ditch
			Visibility limited	Rock, rockcut	Rockcut
			Road surface potholed	Road surface defects	View obstructed/limited
					Defective driving surface
					Shoulders defective
					Lane markings inadequate
			Debris, boulder, or object dropped from vehicle		Construction machinery
			Landslide/washout/ floodwaters		Farm machinery
					Maintenance machinery
					Approach
					Gravel pile
					Obstacle/debris
Involvement with previous accident					Traffic control device not working

Table 6.5: (continued).

	Finland	Great Britain	Japan	New Zealand	Norway	Saskatchewan
5 Vehicle manoeuvre	Reversing	Reversing		See part 1 of this Table: which vehicle was doing what is identifiable		Reversing
	Overtaking	Parked				Changing lanes
	Turning	Stopping				Entering parked position
	Straight	Starting				Going straight ahead
		U-turning				Merging
		Turning left or waiting to				Overtaking
		Turning right or waiting				Slowing/stopping
		Straight ahead but held up				Starting from parked
		Overtaking moving or stationary vehicle				Starting in traffic
		Going ahead (other)				Stopped in traffic
						Turning left
						Turning right
						U-turning
6 Non-collision events		Skid	Overturn		Single vehicle overturning in roadway	Fire/explosion
		Jack-knife				Overturn
		Overturn				Skid/slide
						Submersion
						Jack-knife/ trailer swing

7 Number of vehicles: G.B. uses (i) the 7 categories 1 vehicle, 2, 3, 4, 5, 6, 7+ vehicles, and also (ii) the 8 categories 1 vehicle only (car), 1 vehicle only (other), pedestrian and 1 vehicle (car), pedestrian and 1 vehicle (other), 2 vehicles (both cars), 2 vehicles (other), 3 vehicles, 4+ vehicles.

8 Contributory factors: N.Z. uses the 8 main groups attributed to drivers and motorcyclists, attributed to pedal cyclists and bicycle faults, attributed to passengers, vehicle faults, attributed to pedestrians, road, weather, miscellaneous. Saskatchewan uses the 4 main groups human condition, human action, vehicle condition, environmental condition.

Table 6.5: (continued).

Finland	Great Britain	Japan	New Zealand	Norway	Saskatchewan

9 Human action: Japan uses the following 20 categories of violation by driver: disregarded signal; traffic lane etc; speed limit offence; crossing/U-turn/reversing; driving too close to vehicle ahead; overtaking; failure to stop at railway crossing; illegal right turn; illegal left turn; impeding priority driving; unsafe driving at intersection; inpeding pedestrian etc; too fast; failure to stop; improper steering; careless driving; looking aside; faulty judgment; failure to watch; failure to keep safe speed. (There are modified categories for expressway accidents.) New Zealand uses the following 12 main categories of driver faults contributory: too fast (4 subdivisions); failure to give way (5); failure to keep left (7); failure to signal in time; overtaking (3); too close in line of traffic etc; did not stop (3); sudden action (3); did not check adequately (4); inexperienced (5); parked or stopped incorrectly. Saskatchewan uses the following 11 categories of human action contributory: failure to yield; traffic control device disregarded; following too close; too fast for conditions; exceeding speed limit; turning improperly; passing or improper lane usage; reversing unsafely; driver inattention; driver distraction; driver inexperience/confusion.

10 Human condition (alcohol, drugs, fatigue, physical disability)

Great Britain	Japan	New Zealand	Saskatchewan
Under influence	Drunken driving	Alcohol suspected	Had been drinking
(blood test)	Fatigued	Screen test negative	Driving while
(other proof)		Screen test positive	impaired
(suspected)		Drugs suspected	Prescription
Breath test not		Drugs proven	medication
required		Drowsy/fell asleep	Drugs (illegal)
Breath test required		(lack of sleep)	Extreme fatigue
but not failed		Drowsy/fell asleep	Fell asleep
Breath test failed		(other)	Lost consciousness
		Physical defect	Physical disability
			Illness

11 Vehicle speed: N.Z. uses the 12 categories 10 kph and under, 11-30, 31-40, 41-50, 51-60, 61-70, 71-80, 81-100, 101+ (kph), reversing, stopped, parked.

12 Violations by driver: Japan uses the categories in part 9 above and part 3 of Table 6.8. Saskatchewan uses categories similar to those in part 9 above, plus the 10 others unregistered vehicle, inadequate brakes, no driver's licence, not using seat belt, dangerous driving, driving while disqualified, criminal negligence, failure to remain at scene, refusal of breath test, 24 hour suspension.

Table 6.5: (continued).

Finland	Great Britain	Japan	New Zealand	Norway	Saskatchewan
13 Pedestrian location/action/violation On crossing Crossing road Walking with traffic Walking against traffic Pedestrian island	In carriageway, not crossing On footway or verge On refuge/central reservation Masked by stationary vehicle-on pedestrian crossing -within 50 m of crossing -elsewhere Otherwise crossing road-on pedestrian crossing -within 50 m of crossing -elsewhere	(i) Walking facing vehicle Walking parallel to vehicle Crossing (in the vicinity of) pedestrian crossing Crossing in the vicinity of pedestrian bridge Crossing elsewhere Playing on road Working on road Stopping at footpath/verge Walking on verge Walking on footpath (ii) Violation by pedestrian: Disregarded signal Crossing, by parked vehicle Crossing, other Drunkenness, loitering Playing on road Jumping into traffic	Pedestrian faults contributory: Crossing road, walking heedless of traffic Crossing road, stepping out from behind parked car Crossing road, running heedless of traffic Crossing road, other Affected by alcohol or drugs	Pedestrian (etc) crossing roadway: On farside of intersection On near side of intersection At intersection in front of right-turning vehicle At intersection in front of left-turning vehicle At crosswalk outside intersection Outside intersection and crosswalk Behind car parked/standing on right Behind car parked/standing on left Hit by reversing veh Uncertain sequence Pedestrian (etc) walking in roadway On right side On left side On sidewalk By overtaking vehicle Pedestrian was in roadway Hit by reversing vehicle Children playing in roadway Uncertain sequence	Crossing-marked crosswalk -midblock or roadway -against signal -with signal -no signal or crosswalk Masked by parked vehicle Hitch-hiking Lying on roadway On/off school bus On/off other vehicle On sidewalk/shoulder Playing on roadway Running into roadway Walking against traffic Walking with traffic Walking on roadway Working on roadway Working on/pushing vehicle Pedestrian error/confusion

Table 6.6: Classification of road accidents into fourteen types, as proposed by Watkins (1971). The classification is by means of the initial event.

Eight types of single-vehicle accident

- Struck pedestrian.
- Struck animal.
- Struck object on road. (Includes striking overhead bridge.)
- Ran off road and struck object. (Includes striking pedestrian, animal, or vehicle.)
- Ran off road, no object struck. (Without overturning, either.)
- Overturned on road, without striking object. (Includes riders of two-wheeled vehicles falling off.)
- Person fell from moving vehicle.
- Other.

Six types of vehicle-vehicle collision

- Rear end. (Vehicles travelling in same direction on same road before collision. Can involve a turning vehicle.)
- Sideswipe, same direction. (Vehicles travelling in same direction on same road before collision. Can involve an overtaking vehicle, or a turning one, but the impact must be along the side of one of the vehicles. Includes cyclist striking open car door.)
- Head-on. (Vehicles travelling in opposite directions on same road. One or both vehicles may be turning.)
- Sideswipe, opposite directions. (Vehicles travelling in opposite directions on same road, impact being along the sides of the vehicles. One or both vehicles may be turning.)
- Angle. (Vehicles travelling on different roads, or one vehicle leaving a private driveway. Includes also collisions involving U-turning or angle-parked vehicles.)
- Other.

ified; there are 11 types of accident defined by the first two digits, and 6 by the first only. Another way of condensing the 48 basic types, in this case preserving the role of specific vehicles, is:

Single-driver forward impact: Types 121, 122, 124

Side departure: 111, 112, 113

Rear-end strike: 211, 213, 215, 217, 221

Rear-end struck: 212, 214, 216, 218, 222

Opposite direction strike: 311, 321

Opposite direction struck: 312, 322

Turn across path: 411, 413, 415

Cut-off: 412, 414, 416

Turn into path: 421, 423, 425, 427

Intruded upon: 422, 424, 426, 428

Intersecting strike: 511, 513

Intersecting struck: 512, 514

Backing: 611, 612

Other: 118, 223, 313, 323, 515, 711, 996

Unknown: 998

The U.S. National Accident Sampling System (see Section 3.12) uses a version of the CALAX method. Nash and McDonald (1985) mention that a more extensive pre-crash coding scheme is being developed.

- Belgium's 86-category method of classification is shown as Figure 6.5.

Part 1 of Table 6.5 deals with configurations which necessarily involve at least two vehicles, and part 2 turns to ones that usually concern only a single vehicle—whether it struck a pedestrian, whether it overturned, whether it ran off the road. Part 3 is the Norwegian classification system, as mentioned previously, and part 4 compares the lists of hazards each jurisdiction tabulates—hazards either in the sense of objects struck or which might have been concerned in the causation of the crash. Part 5 is similar to part 1, but the emphasis is on describing the manoeuvre of a particular vehicle, rather than the configuration of the accident as a whole. The most frequently available of the non-collision event categories (part 6) is overturning, then in part 7 we come on to the number of vehicles in the accident, tabulated only by Great Britain.

Contributory factors, broadly classified, are the subject of part 8, and are presumably only used by two of the jurisdictions because of the subjective judgment involved. More detail on human mistakes is given in parts 9 and 12. In connexion with

Table 6.7: Classification of vehicle movements into twenty-eight types, as proposed by Bohlin and Samuelsson (1973).

Three types of collision with pedestrian (or large animal)

- Pedestrian crossing the road.
- Pedestrian walking on the roadside.
- Miscellaneous.

Four other types of single-vehicle accident

- The driver of the case vehicle, in trying to avoid an obstacle, lost control of the vehicle, which ran off the road.
- The driver of the case vehicle lost control of the vehicle, which ran off the road.
- Collision with an obstacle in the road.
- Miscellaneous.

Eight types of collision between vehicles travelling in the same direction

- While the case vehicle was overtaking another vehicle it swerved to the left, whereupon the vehicles collided.
- Collision between an overtaking vehicle and the case vehicle swerving to the left.
- Collision between the case vehicle and a vehicle which suddenly changed lane.
- Collision between the case vehicle and a vehicle in front of it, which suddenly braked.
- Collision between the case vehicle and a stationary vehicle.
- Case vehicle braking, struck from behind.
- Case vehicle stationary, struck from behind.
- Miscellaneous.

Table 6.7: (continued).

Six types of collision between vehicles travelling in opposite directions

- Collision between the case vehicle and an approaching vehicle on a collision course.
- Collision between an approaching vehicle and the case vehicle which was out of control.
- Collision between the case vehicle when overtaking and an approaching vehicle.
- Collision between an approaching vehicle and the case vehicle making a left turn.
- Collision between the case vehicle and an approaching vehicle making a left turn.
- Miscellaneous.

Seven types of collision at junctions

- Collision between the case vehicle and one approaching from the left.
- Collision between the case vehicle and one approaching from the right.
- Collision between the case vehicle entering a motorway and an approaching vehicle on the motorway.
- Collision between the case vehicle on a motorway and a vehicle entering the motorway.
- Collision between the case vehicle driving into a traffic circle and a vehicle coming from the left.
- Collision between the case vehicle driving in a traffic circle and a vehicle entering.
- Miscellaneous*.

* This category does not actually appear in Bohlin and Samuelsson (1973), but there is a gap in the numerical sequence where it would be.

the long list of driver faults contributory tabulated by Japan, it is relevant that "Japanese drivers are, by law, held more responsible for traffic accidents than U.S. drivers ... By Japanese custom and law, a person (usually the vehicle driver) is charged with a traffic violation if an accident occurs" (Tomike et al, 1982). Part 10 concerns the involvement of alcohol, drugs, fatigue, and physical disability in the accident. Of the six yearbooks considered, only that of New Zealand tabulates an estimate of vehicle speed; there must be a large element of guesswork in this.

Part 13 relates to pedestrian accidents only, and compares the seven jurisdictions' classifications of pedestrian actions.

6.4.6 The vehicle and its driver

Variables relating to the vehicle and its driver are organised in Table 6.8 as follows:

1 Vehicle type.

2 Vehicle mix.

3 Vehicle condition contributory.

4 Towing.

5 Driver age and sex.

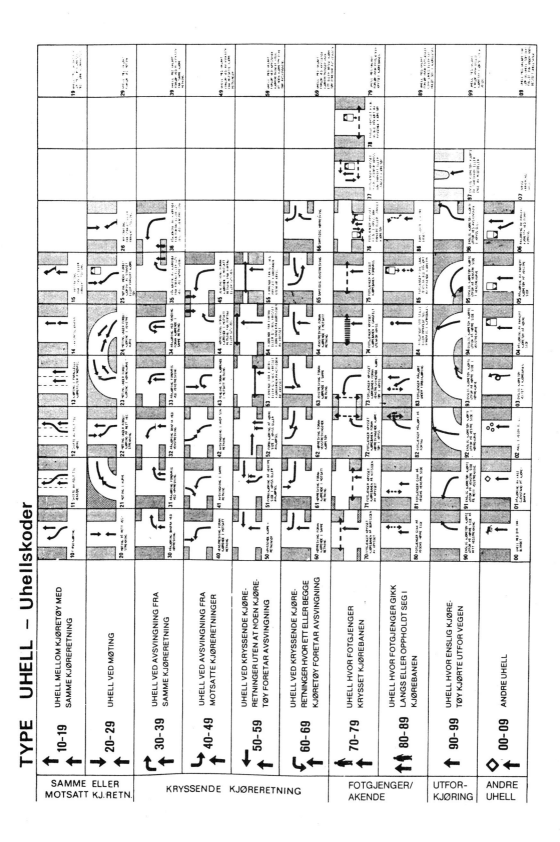

Figure 6.1: The Norwegian method of classifying vehicle movements in accidents.

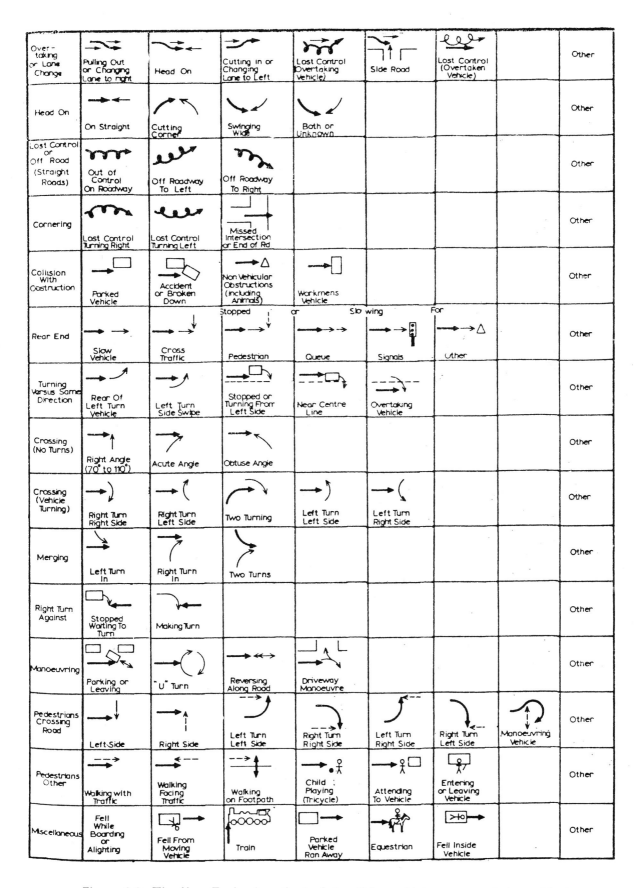

Figure 6.2: The New Zealand method of classifying vehicle movements in accidents.

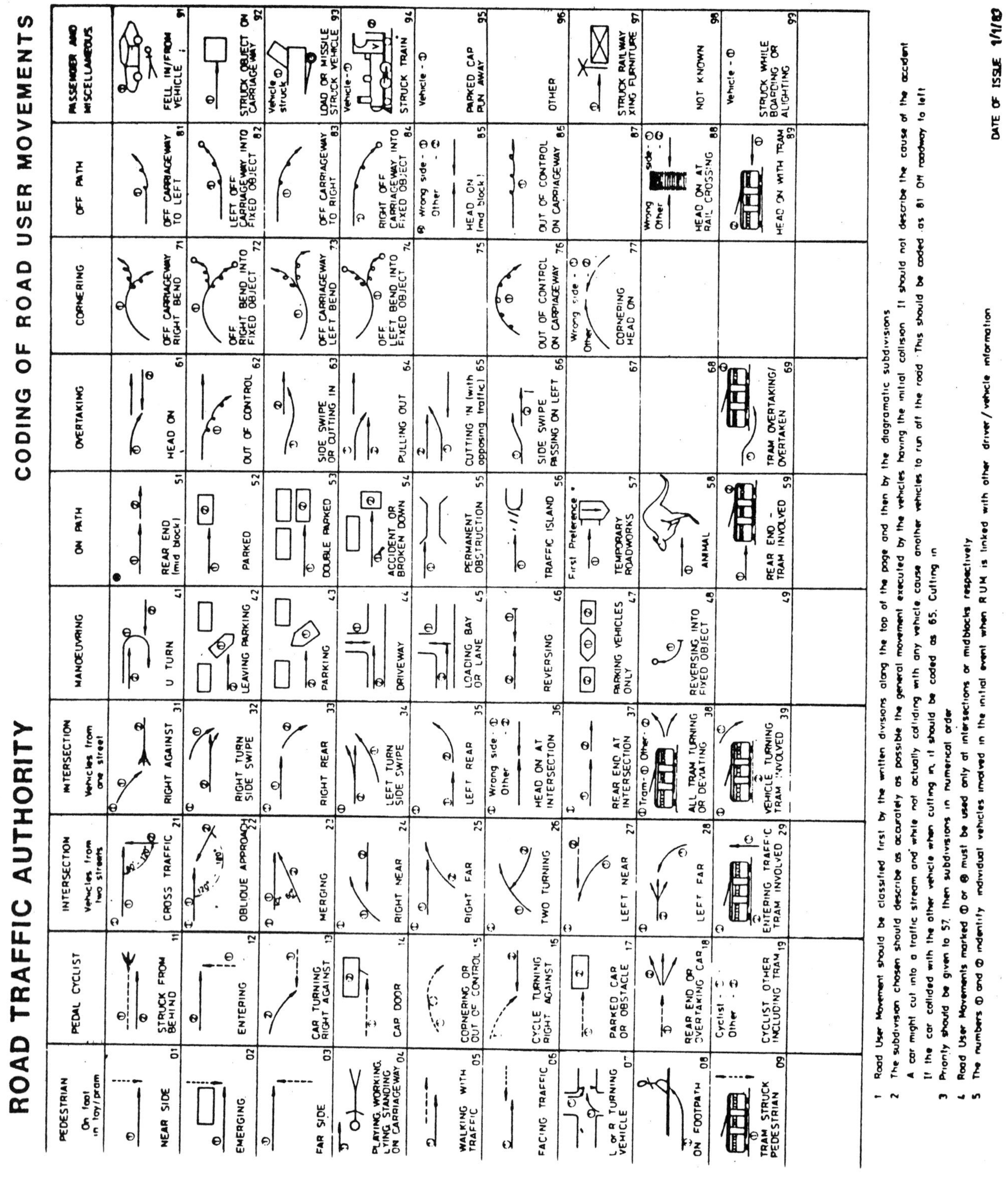

Figure 6.3: The RUM codes used in Victoria, Australia.

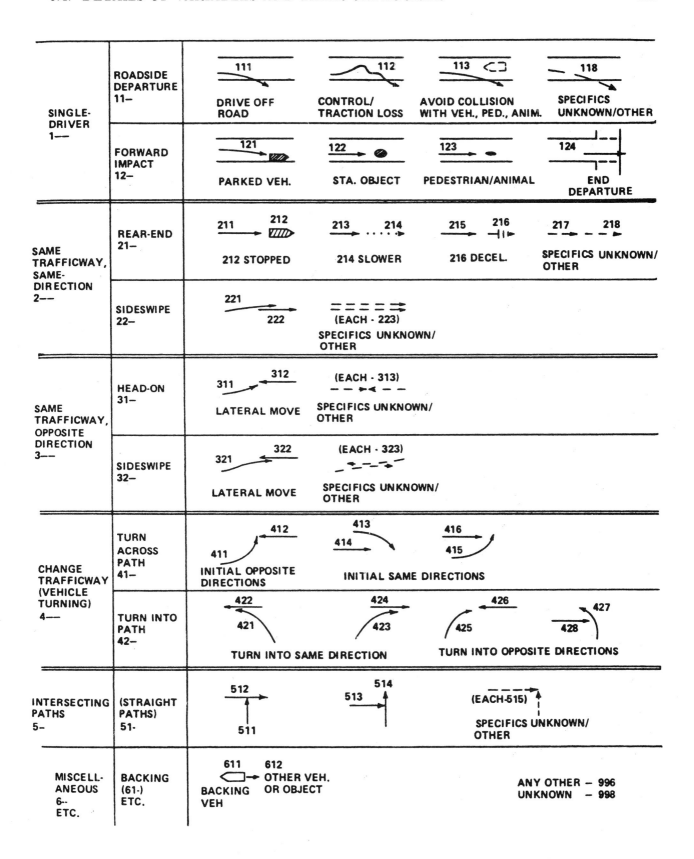

Figure 6.4: The CALAX system for coding accident configuration.

TYPES D'ACCIDENTS

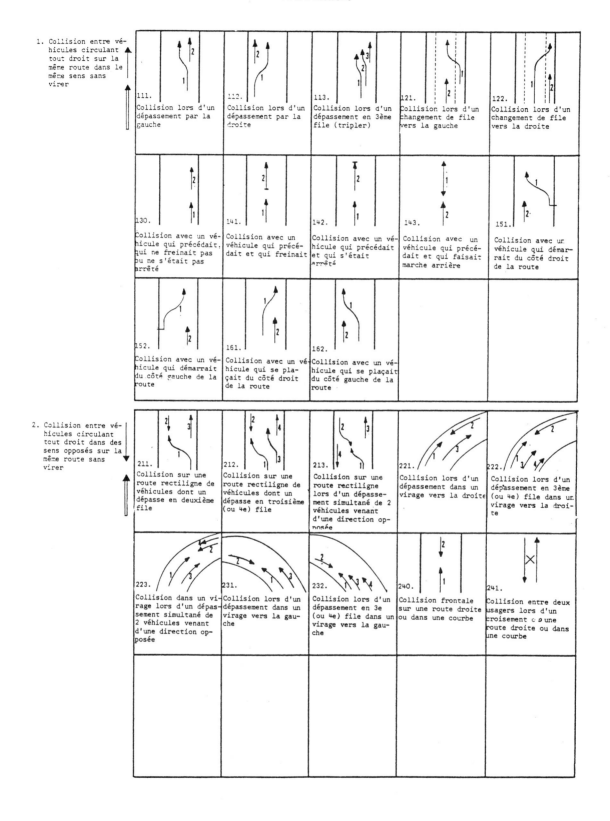

Figure 6.5: The Belgian method of classifying vehicle movements in accidents.

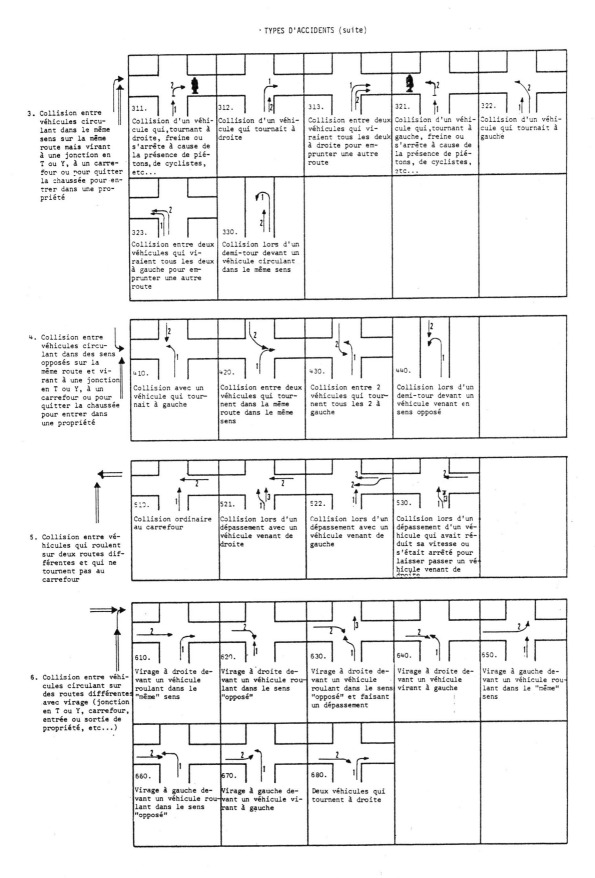

Figure 6.5: (continued).

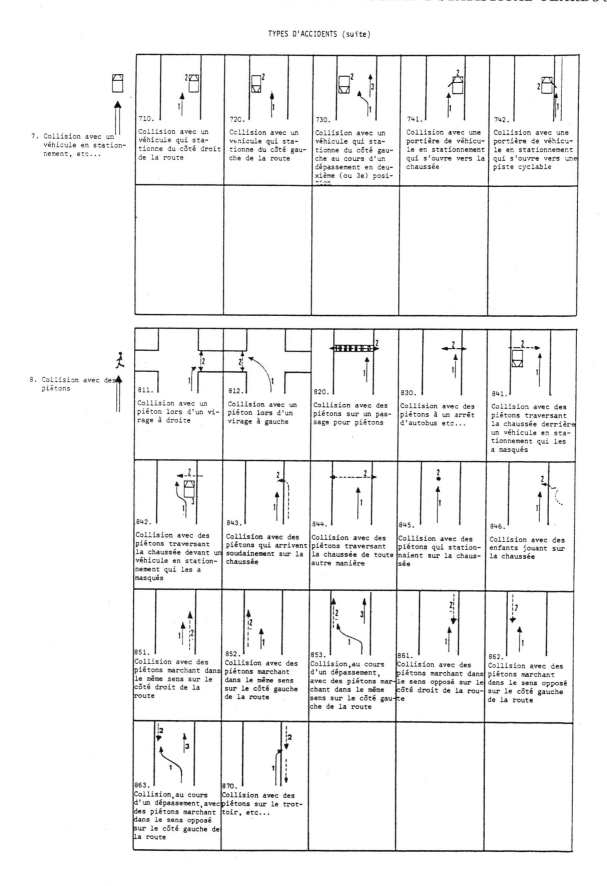

Figure 6.5: (continued).

TYPES D'ACCIDENTS (suite)

9. Collision sur la piste cyclable

911.
Collision lors d'un virage à droite avec un usager circulant dans le sens opposé sur la piste cyclable

912.
Collision lors d'un virage à droite avec un usager circulant dans le même sens sur la piste cyclable

913.
Collision lors d'un virage à gauche avec un usager circulant dans le sens opposé sur la piste cyclable

914.
Collision lors d'un virage à gauche avec un usager circulant dans le même sens sur la piste cyclable

921.
Collision à la sortie d'un carrefour avec un usager venant de droite sur la piste cyclable

922.
Collision à la sortie d'un carrefour avec un usager venant de gauche sur la piste cyclable

923.
Collision à l'entrée d'un carrefour avec un usager venant de droite sur la piste cyclable

924.
Collision à l'entrée d'un carrefour avec un usager venant de gauche sur la piste cyclable

931.
Collision entre deux usagers sur la piste cyclable lors d'un dépassement par la gauche

932.
Collision entre deux usagers sur la piste cyclable lors d'un croisement

0. Accidents n'impliquant qu'un seul véhicule

011.
Accident d'un véhicule sur une route rectiligne vers la droite dans le sens de la marche

012.
Accident d'un véhicule sur une route rectiligne vers la gauche dans le sens de la marche

021.
Accident d'un véhicule dans ou après une courbe à droite

022.
Accident d'un véhicule dans ou après une courbe à gauche

030.
Accident d'un véhicule au cours d'un virage à une jonction, entrée, etc...

040.
Accident d'un véhicule faisant marche arrière ou demi-tour

051.
Collision avec des animaux sur la chaussée

061.
Collision avec des obstacles, etc... sur la chaussée

Figure 6.5: (continued).

6 Driver experience.

7 Licence status.

Not surprisingly, there is a good deal of common ground in part 1, showing the various ways vehicle types is classified. There is much variation in the details, however, a number of terms are used whose meanings are far from obvious (e.g. "special car"), and the classifications are sometimes an uneasy mixture of the construction features of the vehicle and the use to which it is put. (A similar comment, arising from a comparison of the accident report forms of the Australian states, was made by Andreassend, 1984.)

Other vehicle variables are tabulated by only a few countries each: the combinations of vehicles in two-vehicle accidents by Great Britain, the contribution vehicle defects made to the causation of the accident by Japan, New Zealand, and Saskatchewan, and whether the vehicle was towing (Great Britain).

The FARS data in the U.S.A. (see Section 3.13) subdivides the car category, and does this both according to size (as measured by wheelbase) and as follows: Convertible; 2-door sedan/hardtop/coupe; 3-door/2-door hatchback; 4-door sedan hardtop; 5-door/4-door hatchback; Station wagon; Hatchback (doors unknown); Other automobile; Automobile (unknown type); Automobile-based pickup; Automobile-based panel truck (FARS, 1987).

The concept of passenger car size has recently been reviewed by a subcommittee of the (U.S.) Transportation Research Board's Traffic Records Committee. The subcommittee's report is summarised by Marsh (1985). It recommended that the two most suitable dimensions were wheelbase (to the nearest inch) and curb weight (to the nearest 100lb.); and also made specific recommendations as to how to divide these dimensions into 3 or 6 categories. Much more importantly, this subcommittee said that these groups were merely to serve as a common basis for data presentation and discussion—they were not to be used in the field for on-site coding. Instead, specific vehicle identification (ideally, the VIN) should be recorded, to be later decoded into vehicle model, vehicle weight, etc.

Marsh's paper is also interesting for updating information about the use of the VIN in acci-

dent records beyond the account in Section 3.11.3 above:

- VIN's are now in a standardised format and location on all recent model cars. In some states, they are even included on vehicle registration forms carried by each vehicle or driver.

- VIN's now have a check digit to verify accuracy.

- A recent survey by the Insurance Institute for highway safety found that two-thirds of the states provide for recording VIN's on police accident reports, while only one-third code the VIN's into their master accident data file.

- There is 70% recording accuracy of VIN's in Texas, while Michigan has a 90% accuracy rate. Texas does not process the VIN into computer files, whereas Michigan does.

- If vehicle licence plate number be recorded on-site instead of VIN, the latter could be added by reference to state vehicle registration files. The ease of doing this varies vary much from state to state.

Andreassend (1984) compared the vehicle classes used on the accident report forms of the Australian states. He reported that in South Australia, the Australian Capital Territory, and Tasmania, there was space on the form for vehicle type to be recorded but no categories were listed; in New South Wales also, no list was given, but in this state the coders translated the description into one of the following categories:
Car; Station wagon; Utility (car-based); Panel van (car-based); Taxi-cab; Hire car; Light truck; Four-wheel-drive light vehicle; Rigid tanker; Articulated tanker; Large lorry; Semi-trailer; Low loader; Omnibus; Self-propelled plant; Ambulance; Fire brigade vehicle; Blood bank vehicle; Police vehicle; Tow truck; Other emergency service vehicle; Unspecified motor vehicle; Non-motorised vehicles—trailers, caravans, agricultural implements; Motorcycles, motor scooters; Pedal cycles, pedal cars; Animal ridden; Animal drawn; Motorised wheel chair; Railway vehicles; Other type; Unknown.
Only in Queensland and Victoria did a list of vehicle types appear on the report form, as follows.
Queensland: Car, station wagon; Utility, panel

Table 6.8: Methods of presenting information about the vehicle and its driver.

1 Vehicle type

Finland	Great Britain	Japan	New Zealand	Norway	Saskatchewan
Moped	Pedal cycle	Bus		Train	Ambulance/fire/ police
Motorcycle	Moped	Minibus		Tramcar	Auto
Passenger car	Motor scooter	Car		Bus	Bicycle
Bus	Motor cycle	3-wheeled and 4-wheeled light car		Taxi	Construction/ maintenance equipment
Light lorry	Motor cycle combination	Truck (large-sized special)		Car	Farm equipment
Heavy lorry	Car, four wheel	Truck (large)		Van	Inter-city bus
Tractor and semi-trailer	Taxi	Truck (trailer)		Lorry	Motorcycle
Lorry and trailer	Other car	Truck (ordinary, 3-wheeled)		Other automobile	Motorhome
Special automobile	Bus/coach	Truck (van light)		Tractor	Off-highway vehicle
Emergency vehicle	Lights goods vehicle	Truck (3-wheeled and 4-wheeled light)		Light motorcycle	Other bus
Agricultural tractor	Heavy goods vehicle (rigid, 2 axles)	Special vehicle (large)		Other motorcycle	Power bicycle
Agricultural tractor and trailer	Heavy goods vehicle (rigid, 3 axles)	Special vehicle (small)		Moped	School bus
Other motor vehicle	Heavy goods vehicle (rigid, 4+ axles)	Special vehicle (agricultural)		Other motor vehicle	Semi-trailer power unit
Tram	Heavy goods vehicle (articulated, 3 axles)	Motorcycle		Cycle	Snowmobile
Train	Heavy goods vehicle (articulated, 4 axles)	Light motorcycle		Horsedrawn vehicle rider	Transit bus
Other vehicle	Heavy goods vehicle (articulated, 5+ axles)	Moped 2nd class		Other vehicle	Truck over 5000 kg
	Other motor vehicle	Moped			Truck 5000 kg and under
	Other non-motor vehicle	Bicycle			Van 5000 kg and under
		Streetcar			
		Train			
		Light non-motor vehicle other than bicycle			

Table 6.8: (continued).

Finland	Great Britain	Japan	New Zealand	Norway	Saskatchewan

2 Vehicle mix: for G.B., the combinations of vehicles in two-vehicle accidents are given.

3 Vehicle condition contributory: Japan uses a single category defective vehicle. N.Z. use the 7 categories lights and reflectors, brakes, tyre (puncture or blowout), tyre (worn tread), tyre (other), windscreen or mirror, other. Saskatchewan uses the 12 categories brakes, lights, vision obstruction/obscured, steering, suspension, suspension/wheel failure, tyre, tow hitch/connexion, engine/power train, hood/door opening, vehicle colour/dirty, jack-knife/trailer swing, modifications.

4 Towing: G.B. enumerates the accidents in which the vehicle was towing (a caravan) and towing (other).

5 Driver age and sex

Finland	Great Britain	Japan	New Zealand	Norway	Saskatchewan
	0-16	0-15	0-15		0-15
	17-19	16	16		16
	18-20	17	17		17
	21-24	18	18		18
	25-28	19	19		19
	29-34	20-69 in 5-year	20-69 in 5-year		20
	35-54	categories	categories		21-25
	55-64	70+	70+		26-65 in 10-year
	65+				categories
	(Other groupings				66+
	are also used)				

Male
Female

6 Driver experience: Japan uses the 7 categories less than 1 year, 1-2, 2-3, 3-4, 4-5, 5-9, 10+ year. N.Z. uses the 10 categories none, 1-5 months, 6-11 months, 1 year, 2, 3, 4, 5-10, 11-20, 20+ years.

7 Licence status: Finland uses the 3 categories driving licence, other permit, no licence. Japan enumerates unlicensed drivers.

van; Truck; Articulated vehicle; Omnibus; Motorcycle; Tractor; Other motor vehicle; Bicycle; Pedestrian; Animal; Railway vehicle; Other.
Victoria: Car; Station wagon; Taxi; Utility; Panel van; Articulated vehicle; Truck (excl. semi.); Bus/coach; Minibus (12 seats or less); Motorcycle, moped, scooter; Bicycle; Horse-drawn/ridden horse; Tram; Railway train/trolley; Emergency service on call (specify type); Other vehicle (specify type); Unknown.

Turning now to the paper by Croft (1984), the tone of this (whether or not it is intended by the author) comes over as a rather pessimistic one. He says: "The needs of a traffic safety authority span the whole range of vehicle characteristics. These needs are not constant but vary widely depending on the matter at hand. Often, a very broad categorisation of vehicle body type will suffice, but on occasion one needs considerable detail within a particular body type." The implication is that the traffic safety analyst's irregular but frequent desire for detailed vehicle information is not likely to be met in the foreseeable future. Croft compares the types of vehicle characteristics (dimensions, performance, etc.) that are of use to various types of user (e.g. registration and licensing authorities, road design and construction authorities, etc.), and concludes that general body type is the central characteristic: "Efforts aimed at achieving consistency, if not uniformity, in vehicle classification categories should be concentrated initially on determining a commonly acceptable classification of general body types, rather than on more detailed characteristics involving vehicle dimensions, capacity, axle configurations, etc." Consequently, "data collection...must firstly cater for categorisation by general body type; and secondly, must include some vehicle identification which will allow further categorisation by more detailed characteristics." Registration numbers are not always correctly recorded in accident reports (see Section 4.3.1), and even if they were, automatic matching of accident and registration records is often difficult; therefore, accident report forms and subsequent coding procedures should be designed so as to identify as closely as possible the general body types of the vehicles involved.

Proceeding with consideration of Table 6.8, as to characteristics of the driver of the vehicle, his or her age is tabulated in five of the yearbooks, though the ways this is grouped differ. This is understandable in the teenages, because the minimum age for holding a driving licence varies in different countries, but a greater degree of standardisation ought to be possible above age 20. The driving experience of the driver is tabulated by Japan and New Zealand, and whether the driver was unlicensed is given by Japan.

6.4.7 The casualty

This Section, and Table 6.9, is concerned with the casualties injured in the accident:

1 Category of road user.

2 Position within car.

3 Age and sex.

4 Severity of injury.

5 Location of injury.

6 Car occupant protection.

7 Motorcyclist protection.

8 Pedestrian protection.

9 Ejection and other causation of injury.

10 Number of casualties.

11 Purpose of journey.

12 Distance from home.

The basic list of road user categories is pedestrian, pedal cyclist, motorcyclist, motor vehicle occupant. Both the latter two categories may be subdivided according to whether the casualty was the driver or a passenger, and according to vehicle type (e.g. moped, motor scooter, or motorcycle proper; car, truck, bus).

Age of the casualty is tabulated in all six yearbooks, albeit by no two of them in the same way.

Severity of injury: methods of classifying this are described in detail in Chapter 8. Saskatchewan subdivides fatalities according to the time elapsing between accident and death. Location of injury: again, see Chapter 8; of the six jurisdictions considered here, only Japan tabulates this variable (see Chapter 12).

Table 6.9: Methods of presenting information about the casualty.

Finland	Great Britain	Japan	New Zealand	Norway	Saskatchewan
1 Category of road user					
Drivers and passengers separately:	Drivers and passengers separately:	Drivers and passengers separately:	Drivers and passengers separately:	Automobile driver	
Passenger car	Motor scooter user	Motor vehicle	Car	Automobile passenger	
Motorcycle	Motorcycle user	Motorcycle	Rental	Light motorcycle rider	
Moped	Car (4-wheeled) occupant	Moped	Taxi	Other motorcycle rider	
Cycle	Bus/coach occupant (passengers boarding/alighting and those not are given separately)	Bicycle	Van	Moped rider	
Bus		....	Truck	Cycle rider	
Light lorry		Pedestrian	Articulated truck	Pedestrian	
Heavy lorry		Other vehicle	Bus	Persons sledging/ skiing	
Tractor	Lights goods vehicle	Other person	....	Drivers of tractor etc	
Other motor vehicle	Heavy goods vehicle		Motorcyclist		
....	Other vehicle		Pedestrian		
Pedestrian	....		Pedal cyclist		
Tram	Pedestrian		Other		
Train	Pedal cyclist				
Semi-trailer	Moped user				
Special automobile	Motorcycle combination user				
Emergency vehicle	Invalid tricycle user				
Tractor and trailer	Taxi user				
	Minibus user				
	Also as: each of 9 casualty types in collision with each of 11 vehicle types				

Table 6.9: (continued).

	Finland	Great Britain	Japan	New Zealand	Norway	Saskatchewan
2 Position within car	Driver Front Rear	Front Rear			Driver Front seat passenger Rear seat passenger Passenger elsewhere	Driver Passenger (5 subdivisions of location)
3 Age and sex	0-5 6-9 10-14 15-17 18-20 21-24 25-64 in 10-year categories 65+	0-4 5-9 10-14 15 16 17-19 20-69 in 10-year categories 70+ (Pedestrians: 0-84 in 5-year categories, 85+)	0-6 7-12 13-15 16-19 20-69 in 5-year categories 70+ (Schoolchild grade is also given)	0-69 in 5-year categories 70+ (Child pedestrians and pedal cyclists in 1-year categories)	0-29 in 1-year categories 30-79 in 5-year categories 80+	0-5 6-10 11-15 16-20 21-30 31-40 41-50 51+
			Male Female		Male Female	
4 Severity of injury	Killed Injured	Killed Serious Slight	Fatal (within 24 hours) Serious Slight	Killed Serious Minor	Killed Dangerously injured Serious Slight	Fatal (at scene or on arrival at hospital) Fatal (within 48 hours) Fatal (within 30 days) Major injury Moderate Minor

5 Location of injury: Japan uses the 7 categories head, face, neck, chest, abdomen, waist, and spinal column, arm and feet.

Table 6.9: (continued).

Finland	Great Britain	Japan	New Zealand	Norway	Saskatchewan
6 Car occupant protection					
Seat belt used	Seat belt worn			Seat belt	Lap belt
Seat belt not used	Seat belt fitted but not worn			Child safety seat	Lap and shoulder belt
	Seat belt not fitted to vehicle			No protection	Lap belt and air bag
					Air bag
					Passive seat belt
					Child restraint
					None available
					Available, none used

7 Motorcyclist protection: Finland, Norway, and Saskatchewan distinguish between those wearing and those not wearing a helmet.

8 Pedestrian protection: Finland includes the use of a reflector or lamp; Norway gives whether a protective disk was worn.

9 Ejection and other causation of injury: Norway gives whether car occupants were thrown out, and in addition uses the three categories injured against interior, fire, drowned. Saskatchewan uses the 2 categories ejected or partially so, not ejected.

10 Number of casualties: G.B. uses the 13 catgories 4+ fatalities, 3 fatalities, 2 fatalities, 1 fatality and 2+ serious, 1 fatality and 1 serious, 1 fatality and 0 serious, 4+ serious, 3 serious, 2 serious, 1 serious and 1+ slight, 1 serious and 0 slight, 2+ slight, 1 slight.

11 Purpose of journey: Japan uses the 2 categories (for children) to/from school, playing. Norway uses the 5 categories to/from work, at work, to/from school, to/from shop etc, visit/leisure time journey.

12 Distance from home: Japan uses the 5 categories (for children): less than 50 m, 50-100, 100-500, 500-1000, 1000+ m.

Parts 6–8 of Table 6.9 examine the tabulation of the use of protective devices, for car occupants, motorcyclists, and pedestrians; in the first two cases, secondary safety is the concern, but for pedestrians it is their usage of reflectorised accessories to make themselves more conspicuous. Related to seat belt wearing (part 6) is whether the vehicle occupant was ejected or not, and this is given (part 9) by Norway and Saskatchewan. Norway also enables the numbers burned or drowned to be found. The number of casualties in the accident is classified in a fairly elaborate fashion by Great Britain.

Finally, Japan gives the purpose of journey and the distance from home of child casualties, and Norway gives journey purpose for all casualties.

6.5 Supplement: The Australian states

This Section adds to the earlier part of this Chapter by giving comparable information for the six Australian states.

6.5.1 The serials examined

The six road accident statistical serials that were studied were as follows.
New South Wales. Road Traffic Crashes in New South Wales. Statistical Statement, Year Ended December 31st, 1984. Traffic Authority of N.S.W.
Queensland. Road Traffic Accidents 1985. Brisbane: Australian Bureau of Statistics.
South Australia. Road Traffic Accidents, South Australia, 1981. Adelaide: Australian Bureau of Statistics.
Tasmania. Road Traffic Accidents Involving Casualties, Tasmania, Year Ended 31 December 1985. Hobart: Australian Bureau of Statistics.
Victoria. Road Traffic Accidents Involving Casualties, Victoria, 1985. Melbourne: Australian Bureau of Statistics.
Western Australia. Road Traffic Accidents Involving Casualties Reported to the Police Department, Western Australia, 1985. Perth: Australian Bureau of Statistics.
(For South Australia, the 1981 edition is the latest published. There has been a hiatus because of the reorganisation of road accident data processing there.)

6.5.2 General guide to their contents

Table 6.10 and the notes following it give an overview of what is in the road accident statistical serials for the Australian states.

6.5.3 Details of variables and their categories

Tables 6.11–6.16 classify the information published for the Australian states in the same way used in the earlier Tables.

6.6 Seven previous surveys

6.6.1 WHO (1972)

For a broad view of official statistical information on accidents, the report by the WHO (1972) is still of use. Member governments of the World Health Organization were asked what information they were collecting and publishing about accidents. Transport, work, home, and other accidents were included. The agencies collecting the data included the police, hospitals, out-patient clinics, insurance services, and others. The replies (from 61 countries) revealed substantial differences in the methods of collection and the definitions in use. The report concluded with a succinct justification for the statistical method in this field, that "improved statistical systems...are an essential step for developing useful programmes for prevention, provision of medical care and of compensation and, taken over time, for the evaluation of the success of such programmes".

6.6.2 Jacobs et al (1975)

Regarding the practice of road accident reporting by the police in developing countries, an excellent source of information is the report by Jacobs et al (1975), which gave the results of a questionnaire survey (replies from 34 countries) to determine the methods used. Based upon that and upon British experience, they printed their suggestion of a booklet to be used by police in developing countries to record and report details of road accidents, and also a suggested form for accident analysis. See Sections 5.2–5.3 for more information.

Table 6.10: The contents of the road accident statistical serials of the six Australian states. (Y = yes, this type of information is present.)

	N.S.W.	Qld	S.A.	Tas	Vic	W.A.
Historical trends.	Y	Y	Y	Y	Y	Y
Detailed tables for year in question	Y	Y	Y	Y	Y	Y
Casualty rates	Y	Y	Y	Y	Y	Y
International comparisons	Y					
Interstate comparisons	Y				Y	
Explanatory notes to tables	Y	Y	Y	Y	Y	Y
Textual section	Y				Y	
Glossary of terms and definitions	Y	Y	Y	Y	Y	
Details of related publications		Y	Y	Y	Y	Y
Details of relevant legislation						
Data collection form		Y				
Description of data collection methods	Y					
Subject indexes						

Notes amplifying some aspects of the above Table:

Historical trends. NEW SOUTH WALES: 3 tables and 2 figures, mainly for the period 1961–1984. QUEENSLAND: 2 tables, including 1 for the period 1941–1985, and 1 figure. SOUTH AUSTRALIA: 1 table for the period 1976–1981. TASMANIA: 3 figures for the period 1975–1985, 2 tables for the period 1965–1985. VICTORIA: 5 tables, mostly for the period 1980–1985; 8 figures, mostly for the period 1965–1985. WESTERN AUSTRALIA: 10 tables, 2 being for the period 1964–1985, the others for the period 1980–1985.

Detailed tables for year in question. NEW SOUTH WALES: 31 tables and 2 figures. QUEENSLAND: 13 tables and 2 figures. SOUTH AUSTRALIA: 10 tables. TASMANIA: 13 tables and 1 figure. VICTORIA: 11 tables and 6 figures. WESTERN AUSTRALIA: 12 tables and 2 figures.

Casualty rates. NEW SOUTH WALES: Fatality rate (per 10,000 population; 10,000 licences on issue; 10,000 registered motor vehicles; 100,000,000 vehicle km). QUEENSLAND: Fatality rate, injury rate (per 10,000 vehicles and per 10,000 population). SOUTH AUSTRALIA: Accident rates (per 100 licences; 100,000 motor vehicles registered; 100,000 population). TASMANIA: Accident and casualty (fatality and injury) rates (per 10,000 motor vehicles and per 10,000 population). VICTORIA: Accident and casualty (fatality and injury) rates (per 100,000 population and per 10,000 motor vehicles registered). WESTERN AUSTRALIA: Accident and casualty (fatality and injury) rates (per 10,000 motor vehicles registered and per 10,000 mean population).

International comparisons. NEW SOUTH WALES: 1 table comparing Australia with 5 western countries having a similar high level of motorisation. The table gives the number of deaths per 100,000,000 vehicle kms.

Interstate comparisons. NEW SOUTH WALES: 1 table comparing the number of deaths per 100,000,000 vehicle kms in the Australian states, the Northern Territory, and the Australian Capital Territory. VICTORIA: 1 table showing Victoria as a percentage of Australia.

Textual section. NEW SOUTH WALES: Descriptive text is given at the beginning of each section. VICTORIA: 6 pages of text including figures.

Description of data collection methods. NEW SOUTH WALES: Criteria for reporting and recording crashes are described.

TABLE 6.11

Table 6.11: Methods of presenting basic facts, in the six Australian states.

New South Wales	Queensland	South Australia	Tasmania	Victoria	Western Australia
1 Geographical location					
13 stat'l divs	11 stat'l divs	Adelaide	8 stat'l sub-divs	12 stat'l divs	139 local gov. areas,
178 local gov. areas	32 local gov. areas	Rest of state	47 local gov. areas	11 rural regions	26 of which comprise the
218 sections of					Perth stat'l div
freeway/state highway					

2 Month of year: All except South Australia use the standard 12 months. S.A. uses the quarters.

3 Day of week: All use the 7 days of the week.

4 Time of day: All except Tasmania and Western Australia use 12 2-hour periods. Tasmania uses 24 1-hour periods. W.A. uses both 6 4-hour periods and 12 2-hour periods.

Table 6.12: Methods of presenting information about the accident site, in the six Australian states.

New South Wales	Queensland	South Australia	Tasmania	Victoria	Western Australia

2 Road type: New South Wales uses 2 categories freeways, state highways.

3 Speed limit: New South Wales uses the categories 60 or less, 80, 100, 110 (kph).

4 Intersection

New South Wales	Queensland	South Australia	Tasmania	Victoria	Western Australia
Crossroads	Police		Crossroads	Crossroads	3-way
T junction	Traffic light		T junction	T junction	4-way
Y junction	Other/no control		Roundabout	Y junction	Multiple
Multiple				Multiple	
Roundabout				Roundabout	
Traffic signal					
Stop or give way sign					
Other control					
No control					

5 Road features

New South Wales	Queensland	South Australia	Tasmania	Victoria	Western Australia
Pedestrian controls:	Level crossing:		Straight	Straight	Straight
Marked crossing with signal	Unguarded		Curve	Curve	Curve
Marked crossing with no signal	Gates, booms, lights, other		Bridge, culvert, causeway	Bridge, culvert, causeway	Bridge, causeway
Other control	Steep hill		Level crossing	Level crossing	Railway crossing
No control	Top of hill			Roadworks	Median opening
Unknown	Bridge, culvert, causeway			Divided road	
Level crossing:	Straight road			Driveway	
Signal, gate, flagman	Bend or curve, open view				
No control	Bend or curve, obscured view				
Other or unknown					
Divided roadway					
Two-way street					
One-way street					
Straight alignment					
Curved alignment					

7 Road surface material: for Tasmania, accidents in which the road surface is loosely gravelled are enumerated.

8 Street furniture and hazards: see part 4 of Table 6.14.

TABLE 6.13

Table 6.13: Methods of presenting information about transient environmental conditions, in the six Australian states.

New South Wales	Queensland	South Australia	Tasmania	Victoria	Western Australia

1 Weather: Western Australia uses 2 categories clear, raining.

2 Road surface

Submerged, flooded			Wet and slippery		Dry
Wet, not submerged					Wet
Ice covered					
Snow					
Dry					

3 Lighting: New South Wales uses the 3 categories daylight, street lighting, dark. Western Australia uses the 4 categories daylight, night time (lights on), night time (no lights), other (including dawn/dusk).

Table 6.14: Methods of presenting information about the accident events, in the six Australian states.

	New South Wales	Queensland	South Australia	Tasmania	Victoria	Western Australia
1 Collision configuration (multi-vehicle accidents)			Moving vehicle Parked vehicle	Angle Rear end Head-on Side-swipe (same direction) Side-swipe (opposite directions)	Vehicles in traffic Parked vehicle Ran off carriageway and struck vehicle	Vehicles in traffic Parked vehicle Vehicle-vehicle collision off carriageway
2 Collision configuration (single- or multi-vehicle accidents)		Pedestrian Controlled animal Straying animal	Pedestrian Fixed object	Pedestrian Animal Fixed object Obstruction in road	On and off carriageway separately: Pedestrian Animal Object	On and off carriageway separately: Pedestrian Animal Object

4 Object hit or otherwise involved, and hazards present: New South Wales uses the 11 categories utility pole, tree, boulder or embankment, bridge/tunnel/underpass, guide post, fence or railing, building, kerb/traffic island/median dome, sign post/traffic light post/parking meter, creek/river/water, loose or falling object.

5 Vehicle manoeuvre: Tasmania use the 7 categories reversing, pulling out from kerb, turning, swerving to avoid vehicle, swerving to avoid animal, stopping suddenly to avoid collision, overtaking.

	New South Wales	Queensland	South Australia	Tasmania	Victoria	Western Australia
6 Non-collision events		Overturn Passenger accident Other non-collision	Overturn/leave carriageway	Overturn/leave roadway Passenger accident	Overturn Fall from moving vehicle	Overturn Falling (including some motorcycle accidents)

TABLE 6.14   139

Table 6.14: (continued).

New South Wales	Queensland	South Australia	Tasmania	Victoria	Western Australia

9 Human action: Tasmania uses the following 15 categories: speeding; failing to keep left; failing to give right of way; right turn without due care; inexperience; inattentive driving; improper overtaking; infirmity of driver; reversing without due care; following too closely; asleep or drowsy; pulling out from kerb without due care; failing to observe traffic sign or signal; failure to signal intention to turn or stop; hit-run.

10 Human condition (alcohol/drugs/fatigue/physical disability)

New South Wales
Blood alcohol
(N.S.W. Dept. of
Health data)
Nil
<.05
.05-.079
.08-.149
.15+

Breath test
Positive
Negative

Queensland
Blood alcohol
Negative
.01-.04
.05 to .14 in
intervals of .01
.15+

Tasmania
Blood alcohol
.01-.04
.05 to .10 in
intervals of .01
.11 to .24 in
intervals of .02
.25+

Driver was obviously
affected by alcohol,
but:
Refused blood test
Test facilities
unavailable
Test result unavailable

Infirmity, drowsiness:
see part 9 above

Victoria
Blood alcohol
Nil
.001-.05
.051-.15
.15+

12 Violations by driver: for Tasmania, see part 9 above.

13 Pedestrian location/action/violation: Tasmania uses the 7 categories blood alcohol level .05 or greater, other alcohol-related, crossing without due care, passing behind/in front of moving/stationary vehicle/object, child not under proper control, running across roadway, stepping off kerb without due care.

Table 6.15: Methods of presenting information about the vehicle and its driver, in the six Australian states.

New South Wales	Queensland	South Australia	Tasmania	Victoria	Western Australia
1 Vehicle type					
Car	Motorcar/station wagon		Motor vehicle		Motor car
Rigid truck	Utility/panel van		Motorcycle		Station wagon
Articulated truck	Rigid truck		Pedal cycle		Utility
Motorcycle	Articulated vehicle				Panel van
	Bus				Rigid truck
	Motorcycle				Articulated truck
	Tractor etc				Bus
	Pedal cycle				Tractor
	Railway vehicle				Motorcycle, scooter, moped
					Pedal cycle
					Trailer, incl. semi-trailer

2 Vehicle mix: for Queensland, the combinations of vehicles in two-vehicle accidents are given.

3 Vehicle condition contributory: Tasmania uses the 3 categories defective steering, brakes, tyres. N.S.W. uses the 10 categories brakes, steering, tyre failure, smooth tyre, wheel/axle/suspension, towing coupling, loose or projecting load, vehicle overloaded, lamp fault, other fault.

New South Wales	Queensland	South Australia	Tasmania	Victoria	Western Australia
7 Driver age and sex					
0-14		0-15	5-16		
15-19		16-29 in 1-year categories	17-20		
20-24			21-24		
25-29		30-79 in 5-year categories	25-29		
30-69 in 10-year categories		80+	30-59 in 10-year categories		
70+			60+		
Male		Male			
Female		Female			

8 Driver experience: Tasmania uses the 8 categories less than 1 year, 1, 2, 3, 4, 5-9, 10-19, 20 or more years.

9 Licence status: Tasmania uses the 5 categories learner, provisional, ordinary, interstate/international, no licence.

TABLE 6.16

Table 6.16: Methods of presenting information about the casualty, in the six Australian states.

New South Wales	Queensland	South Australia	Tasmania	Victoria	Western Australia
1 Category of road user					
Drivers and passengers separately:	Motor driver	Motor driver	Drivers and passengers separately:	Motor driver	Motor driver
Car	Motor cyclist	Motorcyclist	Motor vehicle	Motorcyclist	Motorcyclist
Rigid truck	Pedal cyclist	Passenger	Motorcycle	Pedal cyclist	Pedal cyclist
Articulated truck	Pedestrian	Pedal cyclist	Pedal cycle	Passenger (incl. on motorcycle)	Passenger (incl. pillion rider)
Motorcycle	Passenger	Pedestrian	....	Pedestrian	Pedestrian
Pedal cycle			Pedestrian		
....					
Pedestrian					

2 Position within car: New South Wales uses the 7 categories right, centre, or left of front or rear seat, goods area. South Australia uses the 11 categories driver, passenger in 5 seating positions, in rear of open utility or truck, in rear of enclosed van, in multi-seat vehicle, child nursed in front seat, child nursed in rear seat.

New South Wales	Queensland	South Australia	Tasmania	Victoria	Western Australia
3 Age and sex					
0-4	0-4	0-4	0-4	0-4	0-4
5-7	5-6	5-7	5-16	5-16	5-6
8-9	7-16	8-15	17-20	17-20	7-16
10-29 in 5-year categories	17-20	16-17	21-24	21-25	17-20
30-69 in 10-year categories	21-24	18-20	25-29	26-29	21-24
70+	25-29	21-24	30-59 in 10-year categories	30-59 in 10-year categories	25-29
	30-59 in 10-year categories	25-74 in 5-year categories	60+	60+	30-59 in 10-year categories
	60+	75+			60+
Male	Male	Male	Male	Male	Male
Female	Female	Female	Female	Female	Female
4 Severity of injury					
Fatal	Killed	Killed	Killed	Fatal	
Admitted to hospital	Injured	Admitted to hospital	Injured	Serious (i.e. admitted to hospital)	
Treated but not admitted		Treated by doctor		Requiring medical treatment	
No treatment		Treated at hospital			
Tow-away accident					

5 Nature of injury: Queensland uses the 20 categories fractures or lacerations of head and face, spine and trunk, lower limb, or upper limb, internal injuries, intracranial injuries, nerve and spinal cord lesions, crushing injuries, blood vessel injuries, foreign matter in orifice, burns, dislocations, sprains and strains, abrasions, contusions, shock.

6.6.3 Benjamin (1984)

A survey was conducted in thirteen developed countries. This included the extent of accident sampling at intermediate levels of detail; the importance of underreporting and misreporting of personal injury accidents; the availability of data on damage-only accidents. Benjamin analysed the contents of the accident report forms, in particular those throwing light on accident causation, but his results are chiefly a list of the number of options available for specifying the cause, the contributory factors, and the manoeuvres, i.e. there is not so much detail as in Sections 6.4 and 6.5 above. He remarked that "Although the purposes to which data collected in accident report forms are put can scarcely be very different as between countries, the contents of the forms used are extremely diverse, particularly with regard to the amount of detail for which they make provision."

6.6.4 Australian Bureau of Statistics

In May 1973, the Australian Bureau of Statistics prepared an analysis of the data items on the road traffic accident report forms used in the Australian states at that time. This was included in a submission to the House of Representatives Select Committee on Road Safety. It is here referenced under Commonwealth Bureau of Census and Statistics (1973). In format, it was similar to the Tables in Sections 6.4 and 6.5; in contrast with those Tables, it showed both what categories were listed on the report forms and what the categories were in published statistics. A short extract, referring to the differing treatments of parking areas, of head-on collisions, and of what constitutes an intersection, was shown as Table 5 of Bagley (1978).

6.6.5 Armour (1984)

A more recent Australian survey is that by Armour (1984), though this concentrates on variables relevant to rural road design.

According to her, the situations in which an accident must be reported to the police may be summarised as follows. Casualty accidents must be reported and recorded in the computerised database in all states. As to damage-only accidents, these must be reported if estimated damage exceeds $300 (South Australia, Western Australia), $500 (New South Wales), or $1000 (Queensland); reporting of damage-only accidents is not required in Tasmania; it is required in Victoria if the owner of damaged property is not present or a driver leaves the scene without providing his name and address to others. (Except for increases in monetary values, there does not appear to have been much change since Table 2 of Bagley, 1978, was prepared.) The damage-only accidents which, having been reported to the police, are recorded in the computerised database are: all reported accidents including those not required to be reported—Victoria, Western Australia; all reported accidents (by implication, excluding those not required to be reported)—Queensland, South Australia, Tasmania; those in which a vehicle had to be towed away—New South Wales. (Searles et al, 1986, mention that shortly all reported crashes will be included in the N.S.W. statistics. Also in their paper, the N.S.W. police accident report form is reproduced.)

The states also differ in their methods of describing the locations of accidents not at intersections:

New South Wales—distance and direction from identifying object plus a road section number.

Queensland—road name and local government district only.

South Australia—distance (in 100m) and direction from Permanent Reference Point.

Victoria—names of two intersections, one on either side of accident site.

Western Australia—distance (in 10m) from start of road; also, in terms of Permanent Reference Points.

Another summary of Australian states' practices with regard to the legal requirement to report accidents, their inclusion in a database, and the method of specifying location (intersection and mid-block), is at Tables 4.2–4.4 of Sanderson et al (1985); it is mostly, but not completely, in accord with the above account.

The extent of the injury sustained by casualties is classified as follows. In Queensland, Victoria, and Western Australia, the categories are fatal, admitted to hospital, requiring medical attention, not

Table 6.17: Five ways of describing what happened in an accident, as specified in the data bases of the Australian states.

- Accident configuration (multi-vehicle accidents only).
  Categories: vehicles travelling in same direction; vehicles travelling in opposite directions; vehicles travelling at or near right angles to each other.
  This classification may be obtained for all states except N.S.W. with no manipulation of the data. For N.S.W., vehicle-vehicle impacts are classified as rear-end, head-on, right-angle, or other, and it is necessary to obtain direction of travel from the vehicle information and combine it with the accident information.

- Object struck (single-vehicle accidents only).
  Categories: parked car; animal; object; non-collision.
  This classification may be obtained for all states. In some cases it is given directly, in others it is necessary to use the "unit type" and "vehicle manoeuvre" variables.

- On or off carriageway (single-vehicle accidents only).
  For all single-vehicle accidents in most states, and for most such accidents in all states, it is possible to make this distinction; however, in N.S.W. and South Australia, there are some cases where it may be ambiguous.

- Intersection or non-intersection.
  This information is given for all states. However, it does not necessarily reflect whether the intersection was relevant: for most states, "intersection accident" simply means the accident occurred within a specified distance of an intersection.

- Overtaking or not overtaking.
  For all states, those accidents in which the overtaking vehicle is involved in an impact are identifiable. But it is more difficult to identify those in which the overtaking vehicle is not involved in an impact (e.g. if an opposing vehicle swerves and runs off the road, this may be coded as a single-vehicle run-off-road accident).

requiring medical attention. In the other states, they are worded slightly differently:

New South Wales—dead on arrival, admitted to hospital, treated at hospital, treated at scene or by a doctor in his surgery, not treated or admitted; fatal or non-fatal is also specified (thus those who died in hospital are known).

South Australia—fatal, admitted to hospital, treated at hospital, treated by private doctor, not treated.

Tasmania—fatal, admitted to hospital, received medical attention, first aid only.

Armour's examination of how accident types are classified is summarised in Table 6.17, and the road features she found coded by each database are in Table 6.18.

Armour goes beyond the state mass accident databases and also evaluates some other sources of information:

- Police accident report forms used in the Australian states; Armour concentrates on what additional information there is beyond that which gets into the database (location of accident, sketch of accident site, narrative description of what happened, additional items

Table 6.18: Road features specified on the data bases of the Australian states*. (Y = yes, it is specified.)

	N.S.W.	Qld	S.A.	Tas	Vic	W.A.
Surface sealed/unsealed	Y	Y	Y		Y	Y
Divided road	Y	Y	Y		Y	
Freeway	Y		Y			
Horizontal alignment	Y	Y	Y	Y	Y	Y
Vertical alignment		Y	Y	Y		Y
Intersection (and type)	Y	Y	Y	Y	Y	Y
Median opening		Y			Y	Y
Merging lane		Y				
Railway crossing	Y	Y	Y	Y	Y	Y
Bridge, culvert, or causeway		Y	Y		Y	Y
Roadworks	Y		Y		Y	

* However, it is not clear whether the features are always mentioned if present, or only if they appear to be relevant to the accident.

which are not coded).

- Inquest reports on fatal accidents.

- Fatal accident reports by State Road Authorities.

6.6.6 Rotman (1967)

This author obtained accident report forms from 18 large North American cities and 6 states. He made some comparisons of the information they contained, and how it was organised, and went on to propose his own design, incorporating what he thought were the best features from the whole set.

6.6.7 Zegeer (1982)

This author surveyed methods of accident reporting, processing, and analysis in six U.S. states—Alabama, California, Illinois, Michigan, West Virginia, and Wisconsin. The results are in Appendix A of his report. A summary of the subjects dealt with is given in Table 6.19.

6.7 Cross-national indexing

6.7.1 The need

I hope that the Tables in Sections 6.4 and 6.5 are useful as they stand. (I know of no other cross-national comparison in such detail.) One can dis-

cover from it that to find out (for instance) about location of injury one can go to a Japanese source.

But such Tables would be very much more useful if they were extended in three ways:

- By including more countries.

- By improving their ease of use, so that the required information could be accessed directly through the name of a variable, or even the name of a category within a variable, rather than needing to understand the method of classification into 6 Tables and 48 parts that has been used.

- By indicating which variables are cross-tabulated with which other ones. For instance, in the Japanese publication, is location of injury cross-tabulated with severity of injury? With category of road user? With both these factors simultaneously in a three-way table?

In this Section, a suggestion is given as to how to create and organise an index that will enable the user to easily find what cross-tabulations of which items of data are published for a number of countries.

6.7.2 Indexing

An index consists of a set of words or phrases, called headings, usually arranged in alphabetical

Table 6.19: Subject-matter of the survey by Zegeer of six U.S. states.

- What is the accident reporting threshold?

- Is it the same for all counties and urbanised areas in the state?

- What types or severities of accidents are used in safety analysis?

- What highway location reference method is used?

- Questions on the precision with which accident locations are reported.

- Have any studies ever been made to test the accuracy of location reporting?

- Questions on the methods of locating accidents and of identifying high-accident spots.

- Is there a statewide uniform accident report form?

- What variables are recorded by the police officer for each accident?

- Which items are not currently needed?

- Are important data items missing?

- What data items are routinely coded incorrectly?

- Are accident data stored and maintained by computer? For how long?

- Software packages used for analysis.

- Is the accident file merged with any other highway or traffic information?

- What type of computer facility is used?

- Are statewide accident summaries produced?

- Is there close contact between engineers and police?

- Do police officers see any of the results from their accident reports?

- How many accidents are reported per year? Estimate how many go unreported.

- Resources utilised in processing accident data per annum.

- Problems with processing highway-related data.

order. There may be sub-headings, and cross-references from one heading to another may also be present. Each heading or sub-heading is associated with a citation to the location within a body of literature of information that is in some way relevant to that heading. An index is therefore a signpost to the information a user seeks, and it should also provide some basis for screening or selection before the page or document containing the information is actually retrieved.

Closely-related headings may become widely scattered in an alphabetical index, and it is a lengthy and error-prone task to search all possibilities (e.g. Rider of Motorcycle, Driver of Motorcycle, Operator of Motorcycle, Motorcycle Rider, ...). The solution to this is for the indexer to use a controlled vocabulary when preparing the index, and provide cross-references for the user who at-

```
Line
No.
1  JAPAN  A  1984  35
2  CASUALTIES
3  CATEGORY OF ROAD USER
4    PEDESTRIAN, PEDAL CYCLIST, MOTORCYCLIST, VEHICLE OCCUPANT
5  INJURY SEVERITY
6    FATAL, SERIOUS, SLIGHT
7  INJURY NATURE
8    HEAD, FACE, NECK, CHEST, ABDOMEN, SPINE, LIMBS
```

Figure 6.6: Example of a summary of a data table as it might be input to a computer.

tempts to find a term not in the controlled vocabulary (e.g. Rider of Motorcycle: see Motorcyclist).

The process of indexing may be divided into three parts:

- Analysis of the text to be indexed to select the concepts likely to be of interest to the users of the index.

- Translation of the concepts into a standard or controlled vocabulary, and development of a thesaurus to point the user to which of several synonyms is the index heading.

- Arrangement of the entries according to some set of filing rules.

As will become evident below, the index envisaged is a large and detailed one, and a computer will be needed to help process all the information. For each table in the yearbooks of several countries, the first stage would be to summarise what data can be found in it; then the second stage would be to use a computer program to process the summary into several different entries that would go into the eventual cross-national index.

6.7.3 Information to be processed

It would be desirable to carry the process of indexing beyond the headings of the tables, beyond even the factors constituting the table, to the separate categories that the factors are classified into. Such an ambitious undertaking implies the use of a computer to systematically permute and combine the elements which the user may wish to access.

The information to be input to the automatic indexing system will now be described; see Section 6.7.4 for the arrangement of the output.

Figure 6.6 gives an example of what a summary of a data table might look like. Explanation of lines in Figure 6.6:

- Line 1 indicates the data is in Table 35 of Publication A from Japan, 1984 Edition. (Bibliographical details about Publication A would be listed elsewhere.)

- Line 2 tells us that the table gives the numbers of casualties (rather than the numbers of accidents, or vehicles, etc.).

- Lines 3, 5, and 7 name the factors by which the table (in this case, a three-way one) is arranged.

- Lines 4, 6, and 8 list the categories into which the previously-named factors are divided.

An important feature that is not immediately evident is the use of a controlled vocabulary. For instance, "Bicycle" in the original table appears as "Pedal cyclist" in the summary, and "Main part of body injury" appears as "Injury nature".

6.7.4 Arrangement of index

I can envisage six types of entry in the index. Examples of the first five of them are shown in Figure 6.7. Brief explanations will now be given:

- First type of entry. Most of the index would consist of permutations of the factors included in a particular table. For the example

```
(i)      CATEGORY OF ROAD USER
            INJURY NATURE
               INJURY SEVERITY          JAPAN  A  1984  35


(ii)     INJURY NATURE    JAPAN  A  1984  35    HEAD, FACE, NECK, CHEST,
                                                ABDOMEN, SPINE, LIMBS


(iii)    MOTORCYCLIST    SEE    CATEGORY OF ROAD USER    JAPAN  A  1984  35


(iv)     RAILWAY CROSSING ACCIDENTS    FINLAND  A  1983  PAGE 27


(v)      BICYCLIST    SEE    PEDAL CYCLIST
```

Figure 6.7: Examples of five of the types of index entry.

in Section 6.7.3 the first one (by alphabetical order) would be as at (i) in Figure 6.7, telling the user that a cross-tabulation of the three factors mentioned may be found in Publication A from Japan, 1984 Edition, Table 35. There would be five further entries with the factors listed in different orders.

- Second type of entry. To find what categories of nature of injury are given in Table 35 of Publication A from Japan, 1984 Edition, there must be an entry like that at (ii) in Figure 6.7. There would be two similar entries, for category of road user and injury severity, also.

- Third type of entry. The user may wish to find out about motorcyclists, for instance. When he or she looks this up, the entry at (iii) in Figure 6.7 will be found, transferring attention from the particular category (motorcyclist) to the factor (category of road user). There would be three similar entries, referring to pedestrians, pedal cyclists, and vehicle occupants, for this factor, three more for the injury severity factor, and seven more for the injury nature factor.

- Fourth type of entry. "CASUALTIES" is too common a subject for enumeration to be worth including in the index, but suppose the subject matter of the table had been the numbers of accidents at railway crossings. Then there would be an entry like that at (iv) in Figure 6.7.

It would probably be best to arrange the above four types of entry in a single alphabetical sequence. There would be two other types, probably to be arranged in distinct sequences.

- Fifth type of entry. A thesaurus for directing the user to the controlled vocabulary, e.g. as at (v) in Figure 6.7.

- Sixth type of entry. Bibliographical details of the publications referred to.

6.7.5 Two concluding notes

(i) A rough estimate of the size of the resulting index suggests that it would be a little too big to publish as ink on paper, and that microfiche would be preferable.

(ii) Although concern is chiefly with road accident data that is routinely collected and published, there is no reason why such an index should not be extended to tables prepared and published in research studies. The method of summarising a table would often remain appropriate, and so would the method of presenting the index.

Chapter 7

A miscellany of data tables

7.1 Introduction

This Chapter simply presents some data from routine statistical sources which I consider interesting. The chief criteria for selection have been the importance of the subject, and it being unusual to be found in routine statistics. A few relevant research studies have been drawn upon, too.

I should know better than to attempt a Chapter like this: I would normally be chary of analysing a dataset without thoroughly researching its peculiarities and deficiencies, so as to appreciate what distortions might result from any particular cross-tabulation. I have felt able to break this rule because the tabulations to be given are fairly simple ones (moreover, are ones appearing in official yearbooks and thus having some degree of backing from people who do know the dataset), because I have not gone beyond the tables into fitting some sophisticated statistical model, because in some cases such as the protection afforded by seat belts and crash helmets other evidence strongly supports that given here, and because this book is aimed at a readership knowlegeable about these matters.

In part because of the limited information available to me about the data, and in part because the primary purpose of the Chapter is to merely point to the existence of certain tables in certain sources, rather than to examine the issues for their own sakes, I shall not give detailed attention to any explanations that are alternatives to the obvious ones. Suffice it to say that an apparent conclusion is only a valid one under the condition of "other things being equal"—for example, we can only conclude that seat belts reduce injury if we can assume that those wearing and those not wearing are similar as to age (and hence impact tolerance), are driving cars of similar sizes, are having crashes at similar speeds, and so on.

7.2 Seat belts

Evidence from many directions—mathematical theory of occupant movements during a crash, experimental measurement of forces exerted on a dummy during crash tests, observations of injuries in the course of in-depth studies of accidents—points to the seat belt being an effective means of preventing death and reducing injury. Does mass data add to this evidence?

Table 7.1 shows data from five U.S. states and four European countries. The K, A, B, C, 0 codes refer to the U.S. police system for classifying injury severity—K meaning the casualty is killed, 0 that he or she is uninjured, and A, B, C denoting decreasing levels of non-fatal injury. For a fuller description, see Section 8.10. Despite the differences in data collection—in particular, whether any uninjured occupants were recorded—all eight areas have one thing in common: it is clearly the case that people wearing seat belts tend to be less seriously injured than those who are unrestrained. (However, the reporting of whether a seat belt was worn can never be fully reliable—there is a tendency for people to say they used one even when they didn't, and there is a further danger that a police officer, knowing that on average injuries are reduced by belts, will in cases of severe injury be likely to guess that they weren't worn and in cases of slight injury that they were worn, when there is doubt. Such a bias, if substantial, would entirely negate the value of the evidence.)

Ohio data shows that belts work in all sizes of car (Table 7.2), Norwegian data that they work for both drivers and passengers (Table 7.3), and Finnish and British data that they work whatever the speed limit (Tables 7.4 and 7.5).

See Tables 14.12 and 14.13 for Swedish insurance data on seat belt effectiveness.

Table 7.1: Percentage distribution of severity of injury, comparing front seat vehicle occupants wearing or not wearing seat belts.

	U.S.A. 1985*		Washington state 1983			New Mexico 1983		Ohio 1984		Delaware 1983		Texas 1983		
	None	Belt	None	Lap	Lap/shoulder	None	Belt	None	Belt	None	Belt	None	Lap	Lap/shoulder
K	53	28	0.4	0.1	0.1	0.8	0.2	0.2	0.05	1.4	0.7	1.6	0.4	0.5
A	17	17	4	2	2	8	4			12	8			
B	10	13	12	8	8	17	12	24	19	47	46	98	100	100
C	4	9	12	11	13	25	28			40	46			
O	16	33	72	80	77	49	56	76	81	–	–	–	–	–
Total number	21055	4880	119639	16234	12656	4919	34456	108031	433588	769	5089	3266	137847	7996

	Norway 1984		Gt. Britain 1985		Switzerland 1984		Finland 1984	
	None	Belt	None	Belt	None	Belt	None	Belt
Fatal	5	2	7	1	7	2	9	4
Dangerous	2	2						
Serious	13	10	30	17	43	33	91	96
Slight	80	86	63	82	51	65		
Total number	1429	3078	3002	104718	3222	8177	587	2566

* Drivers only, fatal accidents only.
Sources:
Finland. Road Traffic Accidents 1984. Helsinki: Central Statistical Office of Finland.
Great Britain. RAGB (1986).
Norway. Road Traffic Accidents 1984. Oslo: Central Bureau of Statistics.
Switzerland. Strassenverkehrsunfalle in der Schweiz 1984. Bern: Bundesamt fur Statistik.
U.S.A. FARS (1987).
Delaware. 1983 Annual Report and Statistical Analysis. Delaware State Police Traffic Section.
New Mexico. New Mexico Traffic Accident Data 1983. Traffic Safety Bureau, New Mexico Transportation Department.
Ohio. 1984 Ohio Traffic Accident Facts. Columbus: Ohio Department of Highway Safety.
Texas. Motor Vehicle Traffic Accidents 1983. Texas Department of Public Safety.
Washington. Data Summary & Analysis of 1983 Traffic Collisions. Washington Traffic Safety Commission.

Table 7.2: Percentages killed and injured, according to wearing of seat belt or not, disaggregation of Ohio data by car size.

	None	Belt
(a) Percentages killed		
Subcompact	0.3	0.1
Compact	0.2	0.05
Mid-size	0.2	0.06
Full size	0.2	0.03
(b) Percentages killed or injured		
Subcompact	29	21
Compact	27	20
Mid-size	24	19
Full size	21	17

Table 7.4: Percentage distribution of injury severity of drivers, according to wearing of seat belt or not, disaggregation of Finnish data by speed limit.

	None	Belt
(a) Percentages killed		
50 kph or less	2	0.3
60-70 kph	4	1
80-90 kph	10	2
100-120 kph	20	5
(b) Percentages killed or injured		
50 kph or less	47	23
60-70 kph	60	43
80-90 kph	69	53
100-120 kph	82	61

Table 7.3: Percentage distribution of injury severity, according to wearing of seat belt or not, disaggregation of Norwegian data by seating position.

	None	Belt
(a) Drivers		
Killed	6	2
Dangerously injured	2	1
Seriously injured	13	10
Slightly injured	80	86
(b) Passengers		
Killed	5	2
Dangerously injured	3	2
Seriously injured	12	10
Slightly injured	80	86

Table 7.5: Percentage distribution of injury severity of front seat occupants, disaggregation of British data by speed limit.

	None	Belt
(a) Percentages killed		
40 mph or less	3	0.4
Higher than 40 mph	16	2
(b) Percentages killed or seriously injured		
40 mph or less	29	13
Higher than 40 mph	52	24

7.3 Crash helmets

Evidence for crash helmets reducing motorcyclists' injuries is as strong as for seat belts reducing vehicle occupants' injuries (Table 7.6), whatever the size of motorcycle (Tables 7.7 and 7.8), and whatever the age of the casualty (Table 7.9).

7.4 Effect of car size and make on injury severity

Table 7.2 showed that the larger the car, the less is the risk of death or injury to the occupants

(see also Section 14.2.3). Again from the same source as Table 7.1, Table 7.10 shows the data with injury classified by severity. But make of car does not seem to affect the probability of injury (Table 7.11). This may be because each make includes a number of different models: data for the separate models might show differences in the frequencies and types of accident. For evidence from insurance data on this, see Section 14.2.

7.5 Vehicle damage and occupant injury

Table 7.12 shows American data on severity of injury and the severity of damage to the vehicle; however, interpretation is difficult because the

Table 7.6: Percentage distribution of severity of injury, comparing motorcyclists wearing or not wearing crash helmets.

	New Mexico 1983		Ohio 1984		Texas 1981-83		Norway* 1984		France*# 1983	
	None	Helmet	None	Helmet	None	Helmet	None	Helmet	None	Helmet
K	3	1	5	2	4	2	5	2	7	2
A	26	23					6	2		
B	38	41	95	98	96	98	18	16	28	25
C	11	15					71	79	66	73
O	22	19	-	-	-	-	-	-	-	-
Total number	1553	937	3059	2713	21284	12249	218	1303	970	9457

* Naturally, the European countries do not use the U.S. categories of injury severity. The four classes in Norway are fatal, dangerous, serious, and slight.
# Urban areas only.
Sources:
As Table 7.1.
France. Les Accidents Corporels de Motocyclettes. Principales Donnees Chiffrees. Edition 1984. Paris: Direction de la Securite et de la Circulation Routieres.

Table 7.7: Percentage distribution of severity of injury, according to wearing of crash helmet or not, disaggregation of Norwegian data by size of motorcycle.

	None	Helmet
(a) Moped		
Killed	2	1
Dangerously injured	5	2
Seriously injured	16	15
Slightly injured	76	82
(b) Light motorcycles		
Killed	6	2
Dangerously injured	3	2
Seriously injured	14	15
Slightly injured	77	82
(c) Other motorcycles		
Killed	12	4
Dangerously injured	12	3
Seriously injured	25	19
Slightly injured	50	75

Table 7.8: Percentages of motorcyclists killed, according to wearing of crash helmet or not, disaggregation of French data by engine capacity of motorcycle (urban areas only).

	None	Helmet
Less than 80 c.c.	5	1
80-400 c.c.	5	2
More than 400 c.c.	10	3

Table 7.9: Percentages of motorcyclists killed, disaggregation of Texas data by age of casualty.

	None	Helmet
0-14	2.9	1.6
15-19	3.6	1.8
20-24	3.9	2.2
25-34	4.9	2.6
35+	5.5	2.5

Table 7.10: Percentage distribution of severity of injury, comparing sizes of cars, Ohio, 1984.

	Sub-compact	Compact	Mid-size	Full size
K	0.2	0.2	0.2	0.1
A	2	2	1	1
B	10	10	8	7
C	13	12	12	11
O	75	76	79	81
Total number	58679	156223	211283	213522

sample is restricted to fatal accidents.

7.6   Time till death

Belgian data divides fatalities into those dying before they were admitted to hospital, and those who succumbed later (referred to as mortally injured). Some 22% fall into the latter category. This proportion varies according to a number of other factors, such as the person's age (older people being more likely to die later), category of road user (motorcyclists, pedal cyclists, and pedestrians tending to die later than car occupants), locality

Table 7.11:   Percentages of accidents involving death or injury, by make of car, Ohio, 1984.

	Percentage
AMC	35
Buick	32
Cadillac	33
Chrysler	32
Datsun	32
Dodge	34
Ford	33
Honda	33
Mercury	33
Oldsmobile	32
Plymouth	34
Pontiac	33
Toyota	33
Volkswagen	32

Table 7.12: Percentage distribution of severity of vehicle damage, by severity of the most severely-injured occupant (fatal accidents only).

	Severity of injury				
	K	A	B	C	O
Vehicle damage:					
Severe	90	90	75	57	21
Moderate	7	9	21	31	32
Minor	2	1	4	11	36
None	1	0	0	1	11
Total number	31965	4706	4086	2707	13054

Source:
FARS (1987).

Table 7.13: Percentages of fatalities who die subsequent to admission to hospital, Belgium, 1984.

(a) By age of casualty

0-14	25
15-24	18
25-34	17
35-44	15
45-54	13
55-64	19
65+	34

(b) By category of road user

Car occupant	16
Motorcyclist	26
Pedal cyclist	27
Pedestrian	28

(c) By locality

5 cities*	33
Elsewhere	19

(d) By time of day#

2-hour period beginning:

Midnight	16
2 am	15
4 am	15
6 am	18
8 am	27
10 am	30
Noon	26
2 pm	30
4 pm	25
6 pm	24
8 pm	19
10 pm	20

* Bruxelles, Anvers, Gand, Charleroi, Liege.
# Time of day data is for 1980–84.
Source:
Accidents de la Circulation sur la Voie Publique avec Tues ou Blesses. Annee 1984. Bruxelles: Institut National de Statistique.

Table 7.14: Blood alcohol level* of driver fatalities, comparison of age groups.

	0-17	18	19	20	21-24	25-34	35-44	45-54	55-64	65+
(a) Percentage having no blood alcohol										
Illinois 1983	56	42	24	26	21	27	39	53	63	80
Wisconsin 1984	76	28	37	24	30#	31#	.	.	61#	.
U.S.A. 1985+	.	.	68	.	55	60	72	.	82	89
New South Wales 1984	.	.	57	.	58	50#	66#	70#	65#	90#
Dublin/Kildare 1977-81	.	.	29	.	16	15	.	.	39	.

(b) Percentage having a blood alcohol level of .10 or more (.08 or more for New South Wales and Great Britain)

	0-17	18	19	20	21-24	25-34	35-44	45-54	55-64	65+
Illinois 1983	31	54	59	58	68	63	55	39	31	15
Texas 1983-84@	.	28	.	52	61#	58#	55#	40#	.	10
Wisconsin 1984	14	44	59	62	59#	63#	.	33#	.	.
U.S.A. 1985+	.	.	20	.	34	32	22	.	14	7
Puerto Rico 1985+	0	.	26	.	33	30	37	40	17	12
G.Britain 1985, not mcs	.	.	27	.	39	44#	44#	22#	10#	.
G.Britain 1985, mcs	.	.	15	.	27	35#	37#	8#	16#	.
New South Wales 1984	.	.	29	.	35	38#	31#	22#	32#	10#
Dublin/Kildare 1977-81	.	.	65	.	81	77	.	.	48	.

* The proportions for which results were known were 80% (Illinois), about 70% (Texas), 81% (Wisconsin), 86% (Puerto Rico), about 70% (Great Britain), 80% (New South Wales), and 87% (Dublin/Kildare). The U.S.A. data was estimated using a complex statistical model that compensates for missing data—Appendix A of FARS (1987).

\# For Wisconsin, these age groups were 21–25; 26–35; 36 and over.
  For New South Wales, these age groups were 25–29; 30–39; 40–49; 50–59; 60 and over.
  For Texas, these age groups were 21–25; 26–30; 31–40; 41–64.
  For Great Britain, these age groups were 25–29; 30–39; 40–49; 50 and over.

+ Not driver fatalities, but drivers involved in fatal crashes.

@ Nine counties only; data includes a few fatalities from 1981–82 for four of the counties.

Sources:

Illinois. 1983 Accident Facts. Springfield: Illinois Department of Transportation.

Texas. Pendleton et al (1986).

Wisconsin. Wisconsin Accident Facts 1984. Madison: Traffic Accident Data Section, Department of Transportation.

U.S.A. FARS (1987).

Puerto Rico. FARS (1987).

Great Britain. RAGB (1986).

New South Wales. Road Traffic Crashes in New South Wales. Statistical Statement, Year Ended December 31st, 1984. Traffic Authority of N.S.W.

Dublin/Kildare. Walsh et al (1986).

Table 7.15: Percentage distribution of blood alcohol concentration in driver fatalities, comparison of males and females.

	Texas 1983-84#			Wisconsin 1984			U.S.A. 1985+	
	Male	Female		Male	Female		Male	Female
			Nil	35	68	Nil	64	79
.00-.099	45	68	.001-.049	4	5	.01-.099	8	6
.10+	55	32	.05-.099	5	3	.10+	28	15
			.10+	56	25	Estimated total		
Number of results	1018	237	Number of results	310	102	number	44821	12132

	New South Wales 1984			Dublin/Kildare 1977-81*	
	Male	Female		Male	Female
Nil	60	76	Nil	18	26
.01-.049	5	4	.001-.049	3	9
.05-.079	3	1	.05-.079	4	4
.08-.149	11	5	.08-.150	19	26
.15+	21	14	.151+	55	35
Number of results	327	78	Number of results	195	23

* Includes all fatalities, not only drivers.
# See note @ to Table 7.14.
+ See note + to Table 7.14.
Sources:
As Table 7.14.

(late deaths being relatively more frequent in cities than elsewhere), and time of day (the proportion of deaths occurring after admission being low during the night). The data is shown in Table 7.13.

7.7   Alcohol

As already mentioned in Section 4.2.7, there are difficulties with obtaining blood samples from casualties. Nevertheless, data on this is published. Table 7.14 shows the problem is especially severe among young drivers, and that it is worse in Illinois, Texas, Wisconsin, and Ireland than in the other areas listed.   Table 7.15 shows it is more severe among males than females, and Table 7.16 suggests the drinking pedestrian is as much a problem as the drinking driver.

In many U.S. states, the accident report form asks whether alcohol usage contributed to the accident. I would expect this to be a very unreliable item of information, and Pendleton et al (1986) have documented this by comparing the answers with blood alcohol concentration (BAC) test results in some counties of Texas. They found in 7% of cases in which BAC was less than the legal limit of .10, alcohol was reported as contributory, but in 68% of cases in which BAC was at least .10, alcohol was not reported as being contributory. (Though it is convenient to refer to the first group as "false positives", it is of course entirely possible for alcohol to be contributory yet the BAC to be under .10.) The proportion of cases in which alcohol was reported as contributory was noticeably lower for local police agencies than for the Department of Public Safety (24% vs. 70% when BAC was .10 or above, and 6% vs. 17% when BAC was below .10).

Table 7.16: Percentage distribution of blood alcohol concentration, according to category* of road user fatality.

	New South Wales 1984			Queensland 1985			Victoria 1984-85		British Columbia 1984	
	Drivers	Mcs	Peds	Drivers	Mcs	Peds	Drivers	Mcs	Drivers	Peds
Nil-.009	62	66	62	46	54	62	59	62		
.01-.049	5	4	6	5+	4+	8+	5+	8+	44+	58+
.05-.079	2	5	3	6+	2+	0+				
.08-.149	8	15	3	12+	13+	3+	12+	13+	21+	4+
.15+	23	11	26	31+	28+	27+	24+	18+	35+	38+
Number of results	303	102	117	154	54	37	457	117	217	53

	Delaware 1983 81-83		U.S.A.# 1985			Great Britain 1984				Dublin/Kildare 1977-81		
	Drivers	Peds	Drivers	Mcs	Peds/Pcs	Drivers	Mcs	Pcs	Peds	Drivers	Mcs	Peds
Nil-.009	40	52	68	46	58	65	61	83	65	25	24	8
.01-.049	5+	0+				6	8	5	5			
.05-.079	7+	4+	7+	13+	8+	3	4	4	2	7+	10+	15+
.08-.149	12+	7+				10	13	4	8			
.15+	37+	37+	24+	39+	34+	16	14	4	20	68+	67+	77+
Number of results	60	54	51983@	4602@	6675@	728	499	93	588	87	21	65

* "Drivers" excludes motorcyclists.

Not fatalities, but those involved in fatal crashes. Moped riders are excluded. Pedestrians and pedal cyclists are limited to those aged 14 or over.

+ For Queensland, the categories are .01-.04; .05-.07; .08-.14; .15 and over.
   For Victoria, the categories are .001-.050; .051-.150; over .150.
   For British Columbia, the categories are .000-.050; .051-.170; .171 and higher.
   For Delaware, the categories are .01-.04; .05-.09; .10-.14; .15 and higher.
   For U.S.A., the categories are .01-.09; .10 and higher.
   For Dublin/Kildare, the categories are .001-.100; .101 and higher.

@ Estimated total numbers, not the numbers of alcohol test results.

Sources:

New South Wales. As Table 7.14.

Queensland. Road Traffic Accidents 1985. Brisbane: Australian Bureau of Statistics.

Victoria. Road Traffic Accidents Involving Casualties, Victoria, 1985. Melbourne: Australian Bureau of Statistics.

British Columbia. Mercer (1987b).

Delaware. As Table 7.1.

U.S.A. FARS (1987).

Great Britain. RAGB (1986).

Dublin/Kildare. Walsh et al (1986).

Table 7.17: Cumulative percentage distribution of speeds of vehicles involved in accidents, New Zealand, 1980*.

	Car	Van	Truck	Artic truck	Bus	Motor cycle
10 kph or less	16	15	21	8	23	4
30 kph or less	36	37	44	33	50	22
40 kph or less	49	50	59	47	62	38
50 kph or less	73	73	78	62	88	75
60 kph or less	78	79	84	77	90	84
70 kph or less	86	88	96	92	98	91
80 kph or less	97	97	100	98	100	97
100 kph or less	99	99	100	100	100	99
Total number	8098	909	413	60	130	2331

* This Table excludes parked, stopped, and reversing vehicles (974, 524, and 119 in number respectively), as well as those whose speed was unknown (3269).
Source:
Motor Accidents in New Zealand. Statistical Statement. 1980. Wellington: Ministry of Transport.

Table 7.18: Cumulative percentage distribution of the speeds of errant drivers in fatal accidents, Nevada, 1983.

	Percentage
30 mph or less	7
40 mph or less	15
50 mph or less	31
60 mph or less	57
70 mph or less	81
80 mph or less	97
Total number	150

(There were 69 accidents for which the speed was unknown.)

Source:
Nevada Traffic Accidents 1983. Safety Engineering Division, Nevada Department of Transportation.

Mercer (1987b) also compared BAC and the police judgment as to whether impairment of a driver (not necessarily the fatality) was a cause. This study was in British Columbia. In 12% of cases in which BAC was .05 or less, the police cited driver impairment as a cause; in 33% of cases in which BAC was more than .05, the police did not mention driver impairment as a cause. (There was some slight evidence in this study that the cases in which BAC analysis was performed were biased towards those in which the police judged impairment to be a cause.)

7.8 Speed

Speed is very difficult to estimate even in in-depth studies of accidents, and most jurisdictions do not attempt this in their mass data, but for what it is worth, Tables 7.17, 7.18, and 7.19 give data from New Zealand, Nevada, and North Carolina respectively. If routine speed data ever means anything, it is most likely to in North Carolina, with the good liaison there between the police agencies who collect the data, the state authorities, and the Highway Safety Research Center, who use it for research. It is evident from the accident report forms reproduced in NHTSA (1986) that a

Table 7.19: Cumulative percentage distribution of the speeds of moving* vehicles in North Carolina crashes, 1985.

	Originally	At impact
5 mph or less	9	14
10 mph or less	17	28
20 mph or less	29	50
30 mph or less	46	71
40 mph or less	71	87
50 mph or less	88	96
60 mph or less	98	99
70 mph or less	99	100
80 mph or less	100	100
Total number	232244	224247

* For the original speed, 11% of vehicles' speeds were not stated; of the remainder, 5% of vehicles were stated to be not moving; for the moving vehicles, the speed distribution was as shown. As to the impact speeds, 10% were not stated; of the remainder, 10% of vehicles were stated to be not moving; for the moving vehicles, the speed distribution was as shown.
Source:
Fischell and Hamilton (1986).

few other U.S. states also collect speed information. Some years ago, Joksch (1975) found speed data in the statistics published by five U.S. states; he felt able to use it (with a great deal of caution) to demonstrate increasing accident severity with increasing speed.

7.9 Other issues

Data from Texas seems to confirm what is often suspected: that wearing dark clothing at night is dangerous, as among pedestrian casualties wearing dark colours, a higher proportion were struck at night than among those wearing light colours (Table 7.20).

The safety of children, especially as pedestrians and pedal cyclists, is understandably an emotive subject. And whether training them in appropriate behaviour on the roads is being considered, or improved design of the residential environment,

Table 7.20: Colour of pedestrian's clothing and light condition, Texas, 1983.

	Percentage of pedestrian casualties, wearing clothing of the colour shown, injured in the dark. (Figures in brackets are for fatalities.)	
Black	53	(80)
Brown	46	(77)
Green	39	(79)
Blue	38	(80)
White	33	(62)
Red	33	(45)
Yellow	28	(67)
Other	32	(71)
Not reported	36	(70)
All	36	(72)
Colour reported, total number	4826	(449)

Source:
As Table 7.1.

the questions of what they were doing and how far from home were they when injured are frequently raised. Tables 7.21 and 7.22 give some data from Japan (children, all categories of road user together). Tables 7.23 and 7.24 give data from Norway on journey purpose, the first for all ages of road user, the second distinguishing between age groups.

Table 7.21: Percentage distribution of purpose of journey, children killed or injured, Japan, 1984.

	Infant	Kinder-gartener	Elementary school student, grade		Junior high school student
			1st-3rd	4th-6th	
To/from school	0	11	24	27	46
Playing	25	21	18	16	7
Other	75	68	57	57	46
Total number	8736	10952	13178	4492	2501

Source:
Statistics '84. Road Accidents Japan. Tokyo: International Association of Traffic and Safety Sciences.

Table 7.22: Percentages of child casualties injured within various distances of their homes, Japan, 1984.

	Infant	Kinder-gartener	Elementary school student, grade		Junior high school student
			1st-3rd	4th-6th	
Within 50m	43	34	21	16	9
Within 100m	56	48	33	27	16
Within 500m	74	74	66	58	43
Within 1000m	83	85	85	80	72
Total number	8754	10958	13185	4496	2502

Source:
As Table 7.21.

Table 7.23: Percentage distribution of purpose of journey, persons killed or injured, Norway, 1984.

| | D r i v e r s | | | | | Pedest |
	Car	Other mc	Light mc	Moped	Pedal cycle	-rians
To/from work	19	10	9	12	23	9
At work	14	1	2	3	3	6
To/from school	2	2	14	11	16	14
To/from shop	6	3	3	8	9	15
Visit/leisure time	58	83	68	66	48	46
Other	0	0	2	1	12	10
Total number	2921	280	174	533	594	603

Source:
As Table 7.1.

Table 7.24: Percentage distribution of purpose of journey, Norwegian data disaggregated by age of casualty.

| | Car drivers | | | | Pedal cyclists | | | Pedestrians | | | | |
	<25	25-44	45-64	65+	<7	7-14	15+	<7	7-14	15-24	25-64	65+
To/from work	13	26	24	6	0	1	36	0	0	7	23	6
At work	9	19	16	4	0	2	4	0	0	8	16	3
To/from school	5	1	0	0	0	22	10	4	41	17	3	0
To/from shop	4	7	7	13	14	2	12	8	7	5	16	34
Visit/leisure time	67	47	53	77	29	52	38	21	36	61	44	57
Other	1	0	0	0	57	21	1	67	17	2	0	1
Total number	1139	1052	488	211	21	219	334	52	138	108	154	140

Source:
As Table 7.1.

Chapter 8

Injury classification

8.1 How this Chapter is organised

The contents of this Chapter fall into three parts. First, in Section 8.3, we shall see how the E (external cause) codes of the International Classification of Diseases (ICD) classify road casualties. Second, in Sections 8.4–8.6, we shall examine systems of classifying nature of injury, most notably the ICD N codes. Third, Sections 8.7–8.12 will discuss methods of rating severity of injury, both those which assume relatively good medical information is available (e.g. the Abbreviated Injury Scale) and those used by police forces often on the basis of very little medical information.

As already stated (Section 4.2.2), one of the major deficiencies in police data concerns what injuries were sustained by the casualty. In Britain and many other countries, the classification is: killed, seriously, slightly, un-injured. In Norway, serious casualties are subdivided into dangerously and not dangerously injured; most states of the U.S.A. use a scale (K, A, B, C, 0) that has five points when fatal and no injury are counted. A few countries divide the fatalities according to the time they survived before dying (Morocco uses four such categories). A few jurisdictions record the part of the body suffering the injury on their equivalent of the Stats 19 form; some tables of data will be given in Chapter 12. As to mortality and morbidity statistics, there is very little information about the accident circumstances, but the nature of injury sometimes is given, coded according to the ICD; in Chapters 9 and 10 some data will be examined. For reviews of other systems, including ones that attempt to grade severity rather than classify nature of injury, see Gibson (1981), Honkanen (1984), and Reinfurt et al (1978).

8.2 Two methods of classifying trauma in the ICD

For deaths and conditions requiring medical treatment that are due to external causes, the ICD provides two parallel systems of codes—E codes to describe the external cause, and N codes to describe the nature of the injury. Many countries publish the numbers of deaths registered, classified according to the E code, thus enabling the number of road accidents (for example) to be identified. Some countries code deaths according to both systems. A few cross-tabulate the E and N codes, enabling the injuries causing death in road accidents to be identified.

8.3 The ICD E codes applicable to road trauma

8.3.1 Three main groups

There are three main groups of ICD E codes applicable to road trauma: motor vehicle traffic accidents; motor vehicle non-traffic accidents (i.e. not on a public highway); other road vehicle accidents (i.e. not involving a motor vehicle; thus single-vehicle pedal cycle accidents are included here). See Table 8.1, where some other categories of interest are also shown. Table 8.2 indicates how frequently used are the various categories.

8.3.2 Details of E810–E819

Motor vehicle traffic accidents (Mvta) receive codes E810–E819:

E810 Mvta involving collision with train.

E811 Mvta involving re-entrant collision with another motor vehicle.

160

Table 8.1: Descriptions of the major (and some of the minor) categories of road vehicle deaths, with the codes they are assigned in the 8th and 9th Revisions of the ICD.

	ICD 8th Revision codes	ICD 9th Revision codes
Motor vehicle traffic accidents*	E810-E819	E810-E819 E471 AM50 AE235-AE240
Motor vehicle non-traffic accidents	E820-E823 } AE138 BE47	E820-E825 AE241
Other road vehicle accidents*#	E825-E827	E826-E829 E472 AE242
Vehicle accidents not elsewhere classifiable+	E927	E846-E848 AE245
Late effects of motor vehicle accidents	E940	E929.0
Suicide by crashing of motor vehicle	Included in E958	E958.5
Crashing of motor vehicle, undetermined whether accidentally or purposely	Included in E988	E988.5

* These two groups together are sometimes referred to as road traffic accidents.
\# Including pedal cycle accidents not involving a motor vehicle.
+ Including accidents involving powered vehicles used solely within the buildings and premises of an industrial or commercial establishment.

E812 Other mvta involving collision with another motor vehicle.

E813 Mvta involving collision with other vehicle.

E814 Mvta involving collision with pedestrian.

E815 Other mvta involving collision on the highway.

E816 Mvta due to loss of control, without collision on the highway.

E817 Noncollision mvta while boarding or alighting.

E818 Other noncollision mvta.

E819 Mvta of unspecified nature.

Apart from E814, closely equivalent to pedestrian casualties, this choice of 10 categories is unsuitable for general road safety research purposes. (Whether this will change in the 10th Revision of the ICD, I do not know; the answer may be given in Waxweiler et al, 1987, which I have not seen at the time of writing this.) Much more useful is the fourth digit of classification, but unfortunately

data is not usually published to this level of detail. The most important fourth digits are:

.0/.1 Driver/passenger of motor vehicle other than motorcycle.

.2/.3 Motorcyclist/Passenger on motorcycle.

.6 Pedal cyclist.

.7 Pedestrian.

In some countries, all (or a high proportion of) mvta casualties are coded to E819, there being insufficient information for more detailed coding.

8.3.3 Differences between the 8th and 9th Revisions

There are slight differences in the code numbers used in the 8th and 9th Revisions of the ICD. More importantly, with the 8th Revision, the usual tables published identified E810–E823 as a group, this being AE138 in the A list of 150 causes of death and BE47 in the B list of 50 causes. But as the 9th (1975) Revision has come into use in more countries, so this has changed, as the roughly corresponding group E471 in the ICD-9 Basic Tabulation List (also known as AM50 in the

Table 8.2: Certain marginal categories of motor vehicle and road accident deaths expressed as percentages of the number of motor vehicle traffic accident deaths (E810–E819).

	Motor vehicle non-traffic accidents E820-E825	Other road vehicle accidents E826-E829	Vehicle accidents n.e.c.* E846-E848	Late effects E929.0
Norway 1981	7.4	3.9		0.8
Luxembourg 1979-81	4.3	0.7		
Sweden 1974	2.9	2.2		0.5
Irish Republic 1979	2.5	1.8	0.0	
Canada 1981	2.5	0.4	0.1	
U.S.A. 1976	2.2	0.5		
Australia 1979-80	2.1	1.4	0.1	
England & Wales 1979-80	1.2	1.3		
Scotland 1979-81	0.8	0.5	0.1	
Singapore 1979-81	0.7	1.2	0.0	
South Africa 1975#	0.6	1.3		
West Germany 1979-80	0.5	1.7	0.1	0.1
U.S. states:				
Vermont 1982-83	5.1	0.0	0.0	0.0
Montana 1983	3.9	1.2		
Michigan 1982	3.3	0.5	0.1	
Indiana 1979-83	3.1	0.3	0.0	
Kentucky 1982	2.9			
Nebraska 1979-83	2.6	0.5		
Illinois 1982	2.3	... 0.3 ...		
North Carolina 1982	2.2	0.5		
Arkansas 1982	2.2	0.0	0.0	
Oklahoma 1982-83	2.1	0.4	0.1	
Louisiana 1980	1.9	0.3	0.0	
South Carolina 1982	1.8	0.4	0.0	0.5
West Virginia 1982	1.3	0.2		
Pennsylvania 1982	1.0	0.7	0.1	
Rhode Island 1982	0.0			
Australian states:				
Queensland 1982	4.9	2.3		
Victoria 1983	1.7	1.2		

* Not elsewhere classified.
\# Whites, Coloureds, and Asians only.

Sources (Table 8.2):
Countries: As Section 2.7.2 (mostly, entries coded b).
U.S. states:
Arkansas. Arkansas Vital Statistics 1982. Little Rock: Arkansas Department of Health.
Illinois. Vital Statistics, Illinois, 1982. Springfield: Illinois Department of Public Health.
Indiana. Indiana Vital Statistics 1983. Indiana State Board of Health.
Kentucky. 1982 Vital Statistics Report. Frankfort: Department for Health Services.
Louisiana. 1980 Vital Statistics of Louisiana. Department of Health and Human Resources.
Michigan. Michigan Health Statistics, 1982. Lansing: Michigan Department of Public Health.
Montana. Montana Vital Statistics 1983. State Department of Health and Environmental Sciences.
Nebraska. 1983 Annual Statistical Report of the Bureau of Vital Services. Lincoln: Nebraska Department of Health.
North Carolina. Detailed Mortality Statistics, North Carolina Residents, 1983. Raleigh: State Center for Health Statistics.
Oklahoma. Oklahoma Health Statistics 1983. Oklahoma City: Oklahoma State Department of Health.
Pennsylvania. Pennsylvania Vital Statistics. Annual Report, 1982. Harrisburg: State Health Data Center.
Rhode Island. Vital Statistics Annual Report 1982. Rhode Island Department of Health.
South Carolina. Detailed Mortality Statistics, South Carolina, 1982. Annual Vital Statistics Series, Volume II. Columbia: South Carolina Department of Health and Environmental Control.
Vermont. 1983 Annual Report of Vital Statistics in Vermont. Burlington: Department of Health.
West Virginia. West Virginia 1982 Vital Statistics. Charleston: West Virginia Department of Health.
Australian states:
Queensland. Causes of Death, Queensland, 1983. Brisbane: Australian Bureau of Statistics.
Victoria. Causes of Death, Victoria, 1982. Melbourne: Australian Bureau of Statistics.

Adapted Mortality List) includes only E810–E819. The Nordic countries have retained use of the 8th Revision, preferring the benefits of continuity to those of updating.

8.4 The ICD N codes applicable to road trauma

8.4.1 The major groups

Injury and poisoning are in Chapter XVII of the ICD, codes N800–N999. (Strictly speaking, the prefix N is omitted in the 9th Revision of the ICD.) The following are the major groups used:

AN138 Skull fracture. (This consists of: N800, fracture of vault of skull; N801, fracture of base of skull; N802, fracture of face bones; N803, other and unqualified skull fractures; N804, multiple fractures involving skull or face with other bones.)

AN139 Fracture of spine and trunk. (This consists of: N805, fracture of vertebral column without mention of spinal cord lesion;

N806, fracture of vertebral column with spinal cord lesion; N807, fracture of rib or ribs, sternum, larynx, and trachea; N808, fracture of pelvis; N809, ill-defined fractures of trunk.)

AN140 Fracture of limbs.

AN143 Intracranial injury, excluding skull fracture. (This consists of: N850, concussion; N851, cerebral laceration and contusion; N852, subarachnoid, subdural, and extradural haemorrhage following injury; N853, other and unspecified intracranial haemorrhage following injury; N854, intracranial injury of other and unspecified nature.)

AN144 Internal injury of chest, abdomen, pelvis. (This consists of: N860, traumatic pneumothorax and haemothorax; N861–N868, injury to various specified organs; N869, internal injury to unspecified or ill-defined organs.)

(These groups are those used in the 8th Revision of the ICD, not the 9th, but they have persisted.)

8.4.2 Order of preference

Many road accidents result in multiple injuries. The ICD lays down rules for selecting the underlying cause of death, including an order of preference for use where there is no clear indication on the death certificate as to which injury caused death. Unfortunately, however, several of the injuries graded equal in the order of preference are of quite different natures, e.g. fourth comes "other head injury (850–854), open wounds of neck and chest (874, 875), traumatic amputation of limbs (887, 897), and spinal cord lesion without evidence of spinal bone injury (952)" (taken from the Manual of the International Statistical Classification of Diseases, Injuries, and Causes of Death. Ninth Revision. Volume 1, p. 730, Geneva: World Health Organization). Let us consider the problem in two parts: those casualties who have suffered fatal injuries in more than one region of the body, and those whose injuries are confined to one region.

Taking the latter group first, if there is confusion between skull fracture and "other intracranial" injury, this may be deplored, but it is unlikely to have serious consequences, since both should be reduced by vehicle design or other changes aimed at protecting the head. Such confusion should not occur at the coding stage, since in the order of preference skull fracture explicitly comes before other intracranial. But at the stage of writing out the death certificate it is certainly plausible that physicians may differ in what they write, when there is damage to both the skull and brain—expertise in filling out death certificates is not something most doctors put a high priority on acquiring. There is an argument for reversing the ICD priority, in that it is presumably the associated trauma to the brain that is the cause of death in the majority of cases rather than the skull fracture itself. Indeed, as regards the diagnoses ascribed to hospital patients, this reasoning has been adopted as policy by the (U.K.) East Anglian Regional Health Authority. And it is presumably the reason for the change in coding of cause of death that occurred in Denmark in 1977 (Table 9.1).

Turning now to consider casualties with fatal injuries in more than one part of the body, similar remarks apply as regards the existence of an order of preference and its irrelevance if physicians are inconsistent. The consequences of error are more serious, however, as we certainly do want to know where to direct our priorities. The international differences and trends over time that will be discussed in Chapter 9 are so large that (assuming that a substantial part of them is not genuine) we must conclude there is something badly amiss somewhere in the system of certification, coding, tabulation, and publication, and the international coordination thereof.

It would be valuable to know to what extent differing practices with regard to the multiply-injured casualty are responsible for the variations evident in Table 9.1 below. I have not reviewed the many thousands of published detailed clinical studies of road injuries, so cannot say what consensus there is as to the frequency of casualties with two or more fatal injuries. Though it comes from a research study of post-mortem reports and clinical notes, rather than from routine statistics based solely on death certificates, data in the report by Selecki et al (c. 1981) may be of interest. The study was of 1287 deaths from neurotrauma in New South Wales in 1977; of these 1287, 495 were classified as intracranial haemorrhages, 664 as other craniocerebral injuries, and 128 as spinal injuries; 66% were road accident victims. Some data on multiple causes of death now follows:

- There were 312 cases in which more than one cranio-cerebral injury contributed to death, 104 being primarily in the non-haemorrhage group but haemorrhage contributed, 73 being the reverse, and in 135 cases the two types were of about equal importance.

- There were 279 deaths to which both head and spinal injury contributed, 128 being attributed to the spinal injury and 151 to the head injury.

- There were 395 deaths to which injuries to another part of the body contributed; the distribution of the other part of the body was 37% chest, 7% limbs, and 56% other regions.

8.5 Improving the ICD

8.5.1 Modular systems, simplification, and incorporation of severity

The ICD sometimes comes under criticism from specialists in one or other field of medicine who would like it to give more detail about their field of interest. So far as injuries and their origins are concerned, this has led to pleas for a modular system of coding. That is, one part of the code to describe the type of injury (e.g. fracture, open wound, bruise), one to describe the part of body involved (e.g. head, chest, arm), and one or more to describe the events from which the injury arose. Suggestions of this sort have been made by Heidenstrom (1979), Langley (1982), and Baker (1982).

In supporting this approach, Cryer et al (1984) assert that the ICD E codes are so unsatisfactory that their use in hospitals should not be extended, lest those who collect and use the data be discouraged and scepticism about recording and coding accident data become widespread. Philipp (1984), Ing et al (1985), and Tursz (1986) disagree.

Later in this Section I will discuss simplifications of the ICD proposed by Honkanen (1984), and the feasibility of adapting the ICD to indicate severity of injury.

8.5.2   Heidenstrom (1979)

This is what Heidenstrom has to say against the ICD: "Moreover, researchers must encounter several problems emanating from the fact that each category in the ICD system is the integration of a type of injury with a site of injury. For example, a fractured finger is coded 816, a dislocated finger 834, and a lacerated finger 883. Each category being indivisible, there is no symbol meaning fracture, dislocation, laceration, or any other given type of injury; nor is there a symbol for finger, toe, elbow, or any other body site. So, for example, in preparing a computer program for extracting the number of back injuries, the programmer, in consultation with a skilled coder, must examine the 200 categories, one by one, to identify those that might include injury to the back and then specify each of those categories to the computer. The time required, and the likelihood of error, are considerable. At the input end, the classification and its codes are not easy for coding clerks to understand, memorise, and apply. Any tendency to avoid the time and tedium involved in searching the coding manual inevitably increases the prospect of error."

Heidenstrom goes on to describe a 5-character modular code for classifying injuries used by the New Zealand Accident Compensation Commission. The first character identifies the nature of injury, as follows:

A Amputation or enucleation (traumatic).

B Burn (for scald, see W below).

C Contusion or crushing (with intact skin).

D Dislocation (without fracture).

E Effect of foreign body entering orifice.

F Fracture (includes fracture dislocation).

G Superficial injury.

I Injury to internal organ (includes brain).

L Laceration or open wound.

N Injury to nerve or spinal cord.

P Fracture of spine with cord lesion.

S Strain or sprain (joint or adjacent muscle).

T Toxic or adverse effect.

W Scald.

O Other or unspecified.

The second and third characters identify the body site. The codes for the second character are:

H Head (19 subdivisions at third-character level).

N Neck (4 subdivisions).

T Trunk (25).

U Upper limb except digits (15).

D Digit, dominant hand (24).

F Digit, nondominant hand (24).

L Lower limb (13).

M Multiple (10).

X Adverse effect of medicinal agent (20).

Y Toxic substance, chiefly nonmedical (10).

Z Adverse effect of other cause.

Characters four and five record complicating factors in the injury and whether it is to left or right and dorsal or ventral.

8.5.3 Langley (1982) and Baker (1982)

Langley (1982) goes further and argues for the application of the same principle to the E codes: "There could be codes for the cause(s) of injury, products involved, place of occurrence, activity of injured person, and whether a fall was involved, to mention a few." Commenting on Langley's article, Baker (1982) suggests these components to a modular system:

- The etiologic agent: mechanical, thermal, or electrical energy, ionising radiation, chemical, or other agent (such as water, in the case of drowning) that interferes with vital processes.

- The event: fight, crash, fire, etc. in whatever detail is appropriate.

- The vector or vehicle: fist, motorcycle, burning mattress, etc. When moving people are injured, as in falls, the vector is the person; in such cases, the characteristics of the surface impacted should be coded here, unless described in a separate, additional, category.

- The apparent intent: unintentional, purposely self-inflicted, purposely inflicted by another, undetermined, etc.

Baker also makes the important general point that, however improvement may be achieved, "it should be recognised that virtually any given amount of detail will be too little for some purposes, too much for others. Ideally, a system should permit easy, logical, expansion for those who need more detail, without sacrificing the ability to collapse categories and use an abbreviated system when that is appropriate."

8.5.4 Honkanen (1984)

Introducing the Finnish Accident Registration Project, Honkanen listed a number of shortcomings of accident registration in Finland, among them the following:

- Sloppy use of the E code in hospitals makes the differentiation of traffic accidents, nontraffic accidents, and intentional injuries problematic. (Distinction between industrial, home, and other nontraffic accidents is in any case impossible with the ICD.)

Table 8.3: Categories of transport accidents used at a Helsinki hospital, and their percentage frequencies among 33098 patients.

Category	Percentage
Aircraft	0.0
Watercraft	0.0
Motor vehicle, single car	2.2
Motor vehicle, multiple car	3.7
Motor vehicle, motorcycle	0.8
Motor vehicle, other vehicles	0.7
Motor vehicle, pedestrian	1.5
Railway	0.1
Tram	0.2
Non-motor vehicle	1.6
Other transport	1.6

- There is no national accident registration system for injuries treated in ambulatory care.

- The E code has been designed for the classification of violent death, and is not necessarily applicable in ambulatory care settings where slight injuries predominate. Due to its illogical structure and detailed classification it is difficult to use.

- The N code has five digits in the Swedish-Finnish version of ICD-8, and is too detailed for ambulatory care.

- The validity and reliability of the E and N codes have not been evaluated.

- Health care statistics have no adequate indicators for severity and social consequences of injury.

Honkanen reports on the use of a simplified E code for out-patients and in-patients at the Department of Orthopaedics and Traumatology, University Central Hospital of Helsinki. So far as transport accidents are concerned, Table 8.3 shows the categories used, and their percentage frequencies of occurrence among 33098 fresh injury cases seen in the casualty department in 1976 (Honkanen and Michelsson, 1980). Two slightly different schemes of simplification are in Appendix 21 of Honkanen (1984). The only comment I want to make about all of them is that I would want to

Table 8.4: A simple scheme for classifying injury by its type and the part of body injured.

Injured body region
1 Eye
2 Head and neck, except eye
3 Trunk
4 Hand
5 Other upper extremity,
     including wrist
6 Foot
7 Other lower extremity,
     including ankle

Injury type
01 Fractures (N800-N829)
02 Luxations (N830-N839)
03 Distensions (N840-N848)
04 Intracranial injuries (N850-N854)
05 Internal injuries (N860-N869)
06 Wounds (N870-N897)
07 Superficial injuries (N910-N919)
08 Contusions (N920-N924)
09 Foreign bodies (N930-N939)
10 Combustions (N940-N949)
11 Drug poisonings (N960-N979)
12 Alcohol poisoning (N980)
13 Other poisonings (N981-N989)
14 Congelation (N991)
15 Other injuries (N900-N909,
     N950-N959,N990-N999)

make sure that the definition of "car" was clear and used consistently. Table 8.4 is Honkanen's suggestion for simplified coding of nature of injury. Honkanen goes on to say "It can be concluded that the use of unabridged E code is not applicable in practical hospital work. Doctors are not motivated to use it. The use of the unabridged E code should be discontinued and the abridged version adopted."

8.5.5   Incorporation of severity

Perhaps the most important advance would be to include a severity code (e.g. AIS, see Section 8.7 below). Brismar et al (1982) put it in these words: "Supplementation of the diagnostic statistics as classified by the ICD system with an assessment

of the degree of severity of an accident case in accordance with the AIS and ISS classifications will substantially increase the possibility of making valid comparisons between different patient materials with respect both to therapeutic results and to medical care consumption. The importance of different factors for the degree of severity of an injury can also be elucidated more easily, as can the effect of different measures for prevention of injuries." A recommendation of a World Health Organization meeting recognises that both the N and the E codes of the ICD need revision, and that "consideration should be given to the development of particular sub-modules of these codes for the purpose of identifying indicators related to the severity of impairment and lesions" (WHO, 1982a).

Instead of waiting for changes to the ICD codes, what of the feasibility of a conversion table for getting an AIS score from an N code? Garthe (1982) gave an indication of this, and her results are summarised in Table 8.5. (Further development of this project was reported by MacKenzie and Garthe, 1983; Petrucelli, 1984a, gives updated figures on the success of ICD to AIS conversion, and these are included in Table 8.5.) Whether it matters that so many of the ICD codes are not easily converted to AIS scores naturally depends crucially on how frequently they are used in practice. This was one of the issues addressed by MacKenzie et al (1986), after developing their own conversion table. Before going on to describe this study, it should be pointed out that both it and Garthe's used the NCHS's Clinical Modification of ICD-9, which is more detailed than ICD-9 itself, this being in part accomplished by adding a fifth digit subclassification.

MacKenzie et al note that in the early 1980's, three ICD-to-AIS conversion systems were independently developed. When these were compared, substantial differences were found: the highest agreement (greater than 80%) was for extremity fractures, sprains and strains, and superficial injuries; intermediate levels (around 50%) occurred for injuries to the head, neck and spinal cord, and burns; and the lowest (below 20%) were for abdominal and thoracic injuries and injuries to blood vessels. Such low levels of agreement are obviously cause for concern. MacKenzie et al went on to ask members of the Committee on Injury Scaling of the AAAM (American Association for Automotive

Table 8.5: Numbers of codes in the 800.0—959.9 range of ICD-9-CM* that are or are not compatible with AIS, according to Garthe (1982) and Petrucelli (1984a).

	Garthe (1982)	Petrucelli (1984a)
Compatible with AIS descriptions and therefore easily converted to AIS scores	612	1165
Not compatible	1487	979
Unspecified injuries#	727	565
Late effects, noninjuries	74	74
No code available in AIS manual	112	85
Burn injuries	273	
Other problems+	301	255

* The clinical modification of the 9th Revision of the ICD, developed by the (U.S.) National Center for Health Statistics.
# ICD-9-CM codes used when only limited information is available.
+ For example, lack of qualifying information in the ICD descriptions, injuries of different severities being classified under a single ICD rubric, illogical descriptions in the ICD, definitional differences between AIS and ICD.

Medicine) which AIS code was most appropriate for each ICD code. Each conversion was reviewed by two committee members. Levels of agreement between them varied according to body region, as follows:

Abdomen and thorax 84%

Extremities 83%

Head/neck 72%

External/burns 65%

Spinal cord/nerves 57%.

The disagreements were discussed and resolved by the full Injury Scaling Committee. (Let's not quibble that discussion and resolution of disagreements does not, linguistically, mean the same as arriving at correct decisions.) As a result, of the 2072 ICD-9-CM injury-related rubrics, 89% had an AIS score assigned; 5% had two alternative AIS scores, differing by 1, assigned (most of these were head injuries); and the remaining 6% resulted in AIS=unknown. Thus considerable progress beyond Garthe's work had been achieved—but let's not forget that the data presented in Table 8.5, the disagreements between the three conversion

systems, and the disagreements between the Injury Scaling Committee members, all point to a considerable degree of inherent ambiguity.

MacKenzie et al went on to determine the frequency with which the unknown or one-point-range AIS codes resulted when processing trauma discharges from acute care hospitals in Maryland in 1983: 4% and 1% of cases respectively.

Baker (1983b) had been pessimistic about getting AIS scores from ICD codes: "Except for a small minority of injuries, it is not possible to develop a valid conversion system for translating most ICD information (even if it's coded using ICD-9-CM) into AIS codes." Whether she is convinced of the utility of the table developed by MacKenzie et al, I haven't heard. I would guess she would take the same line I would: a sensible ICD to AIS conversion is much better than nothing, but considerably less satisfactory than would be the organic incorporation of severity in the ICD.

In Britain, ICD-to-AIS conversion was made in course of the TRRL project that matched Scottish police and hospital in-patient data (see Section 13.3, Stone, 1984, and Tunbridge, 1987). Details of the recoding scheme were not given, however.

Dalkie and Mulligan (1987) report the conversion of ICD codes to AIS scores in a hospital admissions dataset from Manitoba; their paper includes

Table 8.6: The Occupant Injury Classification.

I. Body region
H Head (skull, scalp, ears)
F Face (forehead, nose, eyes, mouth)
N Neck (cervical spine, C1-C7)
S Shoulder (clavicle, scapula, joint)
X Upper extremity (whole limb, or
   part unspecified)
A Arm (upper)
E Elbow
R Forearm
W Wrist-hand (fingers)
B Back (thoraco-lumbar spine,
   T1-T12, L1-L5)
C Chest (anterior and posterior ribs)
M Abdomen (diaphragm and below)
P Pelvis-hip
Y Lower extremity (whole limb, or
   part unspecified)
T Thigh (femur)
K Knee
L Leg (below knee)
Q Ankle-foot (toes)
O Whole body
U Unknown region

II. Aspect
R Right
L Left
C Central
A Anterior/front
P Posterior/back
S Superior/upper
I Inferior/lower
W Whole region
U Unknown aspect

III. Lesion
A Abrasion
B Burn
C Contusion
D Dislocation
E Severance, transection
F Fracture
G Detachment, separation
K Concussion
L Laceration
M Amputation
N Crush
P Perforation, puncture
R Rupture
S Sprain
T Strain
V Avulsion
O Other
U Unknown lesion
Z Fracture and dislocation

IV. System/organ
A Arteries, veins
B Brain
C Spinal cord
D Digestive
E Ears
G Urogenital
H Heart
I Integumentary
J Joints
K Kidneys
L Liver
M Muscles
N Nervous system
O Eye
P Pulmonary, lungs
Q Spleen
R Respiratory
S Skeletal
T Thyroid, other endocrine
   glands
V Vertebrae
W All systems in region
U Injured, unknown systems
   or organ

Table 8.7: The New York State Injury Coding Scheme, NYSICS.

Location of most severe physical complaint	Type of physical complaint	Victim's physical and emotional states
1 Head	1 Amputation	1 Apparent death
2 Face	2 Concussion	2 Unconscious
3 Eye	3 Internal	3 Semi-conscious
4 Neck	4 Minor bleeding	4 Incoherent
5 Chest	5 Severe bleeding	5 Shock
6 Back	6 Minor burn	6 Conscious
7 Shoulder/upper arm	7 Moderate burn	
8 Elbow/lower arm/hand	8 Severe burn	
9 Abdomen/pelvis	9 Fracture/dislocation	
10 Hip/upper leg	10 Contusion/bruise	
11 Knee/lower leg/foot	11 Abrasion	
12 Entire body	12 Complaint of pain	
	13 None visible	

some examples of the assumptions made and conventions adopted.

An alternative to obtaining AIS from ICD is to convert ICD to a survival probability, empirically calculated using some convenient large database. The RESP (Revised Estimated Survival Probability) index was developed in this way from U.S. National Hospital Discharge Survey statistics (Levy, Goldberg, and Rothrock, 1982). A further feature of the RESP index is the method it uses for scoring multiply-injured casualties: it multiplies the survival probabilities for the individual injuries.

Goldberg et al (1984) studied how well the RESP index predicted such matters as death or survival, length of hospital stay, and whether intensive care was required. They did this for 242 patients treated at three Chicago area hospitals in 1977–79 who had one or more of a certain defined set of injuries (not necessarily resulting from road accidents). Their conclusions were:

- The RESP index does correlate with the chosen criteria.

- However, it does not correlate as strongly as does the ISS (Injury Severity Score, derived from the AIS, see Section 8.7.1).

- The RESP index and the ISS are together better predictors than the ISS alone.

- The RESP index needs to be based on ICD codes that are assigned by an experienced coder on the basis of the full medical record or at least the written face sheet; the ICD codes routinely written on the face sheet are not sufficiently accurate.

The same group of workers also gave another method for obtaining the combined effect of several injuries: logistic regression of survival probability on the survival probabilities for the most serious injuries (Levy, Goldberg, Hui, et al, 1982).

Some examples of single-condition survival probabilities (with the effect of age having been smoothed by regression) may also be of interest:

- Closed fracture of base of skull (N801.0)— 0.99, 0.95, and 0.92 for the three age groups under 45 years, 45–64, 65 and over.

- Cerebral laceration and contusion (N851.0)— 0.93, 0.89, and 0.86 for the same three age groups.

- Closed fracture of pelvis (N808.0)—1.00, 0.96, and 0.93.

- Injury to other and unspecified intra-abdominal organs with open wound into cavity (N868.1)—0.98, 0.62, 0.41.

(These figures were given in both of the 1982 papers by Levy and colleagues.)

Table 8.8: Accuracy of the combination of location and type of injury in the NYSICS, subdivided according to AIS.

```
          Percentage of injuries for
         which the NYSICS code agreed
          with the physician's diagnosis

AIS 1                52
    2                50
    3-6               27
Overall              48
```

8.6 Other methods of classifying nature of injury

8.6.1 The Occupant Injury Classification (OIC)

This is a four-component system using letter codes. It is used by the (U.S.) National Accident Sampling System. The components are:

I Body region.

II Aspect.

III Lesion.

IV System/organ.

The categories of each are shown in Table 8.6. The AIS (see Section 8.7) is used to code the severity. For a fuller account of the OIC, see Marsh (1972).

8.6.2 Detailed coding of head and neck injuries

In the same style as the OIC is the method of classifying head and neck injuries described by Ouellet et al (1984). There are six alphanumeric components: the first three are injury locators (region, side, aspect), the fourth defines the lesion type, the fifth describes the tissues affected, and the sixth assigns a severity score. It was developed for use with very detailed postmortem reports on motorcyclists, but the authors claim "The data sources that can be used range from simplest observation of surface injuries to the complex procedures used in the University of Southern California study of motorcycle fatalities. All levels of complexity can

Table 8.9: Accuracy of coding of location of injury in the NYSICS.

```
                           Percentage
                            correct
All locations:
    AIS 1                      78
        2                      83
        3-6                    72

All AIS levels:
    Head                       88
    Face                       89
    Eye                        87
    Neck                       79
    Chest                      75
    Back                       61
    Shoulder/upper arm         67
    Elbow/lower arm/hand       86
    Abdomen/pelvis             78
    Hip/upper leg              58
    Knee/lower leg/foot        90
    Entire body                 8

Overall                        78
```

be handled." And they evidently envisage that not all users will be Professors of Pathology: "Users of the system need at least some general acquaintance with the anatomy of the head and neck, or at least access to a textbook on general anatomy."

Ouellet et al also have some interesting things to say on injury severity: see D.F in Section 8.7.3.

8.6.3 The New York State Injury Coding Scheme (NYSICS)

A three-fold scheme of classifying injury was proposed by Spence (1975a, b). The three fields are location of most severe physical complaint, type of physical complaint, and victim's state (see Table 8.7). Spence recognises that it is unrealistic to expect a medically exact description from a police officer, and that any codes must be usable on the basis of what he sees and hears at the collision site, perhaps with a quick follow-up call to the hospital. Spence (1975b) gives a table for converting the classification to an AIS score.

On the basis of a sample of 2000 injuries, Baum

Table 8.10: Accuracy of coding of type of injury in the NYSICS.

	Percentage correct
All types:	
AIS 1	57
2	70
3-6	57
All AIS levels*:	
Concussion	46
Internal	39
Minor bleeding	67
Severe bleeding	83
Fracture/dislocation	77
Contusion/bruise	57
Abrasion	50
Complaint of pain	55
None visible	54
Overall	60

* Four types of injury omitted from list because of small frequencies.

(1978) concludes that this scheme "appears to be a viable approach to obtaining useful police reported data. It has the obvious advantages of being inexpensive to implement and not requiring any specialised medical training by the user. Moreover, the NYSICS has been demonstrated to be more effective in predicting AIS than the more widely used K-A-B-C scale." However, Baum found a substantial degree of inaccuracy when the NYSICS codes were compared with hospital medical reports—his results are summarised in Tables 8.8–8.10.

States using schemes similar to New York's may be identified from Table 8.23 below. British Columbia uses a similar one, too.

8.6.4 Ambulance crews' reports

Some ambulance services document trauma patients. The chief purpose is to assist the casualty officer when the hospital is reached, but McLean (1984) sees the information having value as a supplement to police reports, because of what it says about the injury. The report form used by the St. John Ambulance in South Australia is shown as

Table 8.11: Site and nature of injury—St. John Ambulance Service, South Australia.

Body region affected
1 Head
2 Neck
3 Chest
4 Abdomen
5 Back
6 Upper limb
7 Lower limb
8 Hand
9 Foot
0 Multiple

Type of injury
1 Central nervous system
2 Other nerve damage
3 Soft tissue injury (open)
4 Soft tissue injury (closed)
5 Internal injury suspected
6 Fracture or dislocation
7 Amputation
8 Burn

Figure 8.1. Codes for the site and nature of injury are being introduced: these are shown in Table 8.11.

8.6.5 Developing countries

Table 8.12 reproduces a proposal by the World Health Organization (WHO, 1983c) for a simple classification of injuries.

8.7 Severity: The Abbreviated Injury Scale (AIS)

8.7.1 The codes

The AIS (AAAM, 1985) is not primarily intended for routine application, but is so widely used in detailed research studies that it must be our starting point. In summary, it is as follows:

0 No injury.

1 Minor. (Such injuries are simple and may not even require professional medical treatment. Recovery is usually rapid and complete.)

CASE HISTORY
MEDICAL IN CONFIDENCE

St JOHN AMBULANCE SERVICE

ST. JOHN AMBULANCE

0 2 CASE NUMBER

SPEEDO:
- TRIP START
- PATIENT START
- PATIENT FINISH
- TRIP FINISH

TIME:
- CALL RECEIVED
- DESPATCHED
- ARRIVED SCENE
- DEPART SCENE
- ARRIVED DESTINATION
- CLEARED

NURSING HOME
MARK CARRIES
'I' INFIRMARY
'H' HOSTEL/UNIT

PRIORITY TO SCENE

PRIORITY FROM SCENE

D.O.A.

TRANSPORT FROM:
- No. & STREET
- SUBURB
- POSTCODE

PRE-ARRIVAL FIRST-AID
NIL CPR. OTH.
RENDERED BY:
OF:

TRANSPORT TO:
- No. & STREET
- SUBURB
- POSTCODE

OFFICE USE ONLY | CHARGE CODE | SERVICE CHARGE

PATIENT DETAILS

0 2 | PUNCH AS ABOVE | CASE NUMBER

2 | ACCOUNT INDICATOR (SEE CODES)

SUBY. EXPIRY DATE | SUBSCRIPTION No.

PENSION No. | TITLE (MR./MRS/MISS/ETC.)

SURNAME

INITIALS

No. & STREET

SUBURB

POSTCODE

PARENTS NAME IF PATIENT UNDER 18 | AGE

1

YES / NO | WAS CARRY THE RESULT OF V/A?

HOSPITAL ORDER No.

ACCOUNT INDICATOR CODES
- 0 - NORMAL
- 1 - SUBSCRIBER
- 2 - COUNTRY SUBSCRIBER
- 3 - INTERSTATE SUBSCRIBER
- 4 - PENSIONER
- 5 - PENSIONER SUBSCRIBER

PATIENT CODE

A B C D E (END OF, OR BREAK IN TRANSMISSION) F G H

INJURY CIRCUMSTANCES (TRAUMA CASES ONLY)

WHILE THE PATIENT WAS ENGAGED IN: __________

AT (SPECIFY PLACE): __________

SOMETHING WENT WRONG (OPTIONAL): __________

PATIENT WAS INJURED WHEN: __________

CONSULTATION WITH HOSPITAL

VOICE CONTACT
- SUCCESSFUL
- UNSUCCESSFUL

E.C.G. TELEMETRY
- SUCCESSFUL
- UNSUCCESSFUL
- NOT REQUIRED

CONDITION AT DESTINATION
- UNCHANGED
- IMPROVED
- DETERIORATED

MEDICAL INSTRUCTIONS __________

Figure 8.1: Form used by St. John Ambulance in South Australia.

CHIEF COMPLAINT & HISTORY OF THIS INCIDENT

ONSET
- ☐ SUDDEN - MINUTES
- ☐ RECENT - HOURS
- ☐ LONG TERM - DAYS

PAST MEDICAL HISTORY
- ☐ CARDIAC CONDITION
- ☐ ASTHMA/EMPHYSEMA
- ☐ DIABETES
- ☐ EPILEPSY
- ☐ C.V.A.
- ☐ HYPERTENSION
- ☐ RENAL
- ☐ OTHER

PATIENT ASSESSMENT

VITAL SIGNS	TIME	1ST:	2ND:	3RD:
RESPIRATIONS/MINUTE				
PULSE/MINUTE		☐ REGULAR ☐ IRREGULAR	☐ REGULAR ☐ IRREGULAR	☐ REGULAR ☐ IRREGULAR
BLOOD PRESSURE				

EYE OPEN.	VERBAL RESP.	MOTOR RESP.	BREATHING	PUPILS	SKIN TEMP.	SKIN COL.
☐ SPONT.	☐ ORIENTATED	☐ OBEYS COMMAND	☐ NORMAL	R SIZE REACTION	☐ COLD	☐ NORMAL
☐ TO VOICE	☐ CONFUSED	☐ PURPOSEFUL MOV.	☐ SHALLOW		☐ COOL	☐ PALE
☐ TO PAIN	☐ GROANS/ INCOMPREHENSIBLE WORDS	☐ W DRAWS TO PAIN	☐ RAPID		☐ WARM	☐ ASHEN
☐ NONE		☐ FLEXION TO PAIN	☐ LABOURED	L SIZE REACTION	☐ HOT	☐ FLUSHED
		☐ EXTENS. TO PAIN	☐ WHEEZE		☐ DRY	☐ CYANOTIC
	☐ NONE	☐ NONE	☐ OTHER		☐ MOIST	☐ JAUNDICED

UNCONSCIOUS PRIOR TO AMBULANCE ARRIVAL?
- ☐ NO   DETAILS _____
- ☐ YES   _____

DURATION _____

VOMITING	FITTING	ALLERGIES
☐ NIL	☐ NO	☐ UNKNOWN
☐ SMALL	☐ YES	☐ YES
☐ LARGE	NUMBER ____	DETAILS ____
TIME ____	TYPE ____	
TYPE ____		

1● 2● 3● 4● 5● 6● 7● 8●

INITIAL TREATMENT

- ☐ OXYGEN
- ☐ MASK
- ☐ CANNULA
- ☐ 24% VENTI MASK L/MIN ____
- ☐ AIRWAY INSERTED
- ☐ SUCTION
- ☐ VENTOLIN
  DOSE ____
  TIME ____
- ☐ GLUCAGON
  DOSE ____
  TIME ____

- ☐ ANGININE
  DOSE ____
  TIME ____
- ☐ ENTONOX
- ☐ PENTHRANE
- ☐ TRACTION SPLINT
- ☐ CARDBOARD SPLINT
- ☐ AIR SPLINT
- ☐ SPINAL BOARD
- ☐ CERVICAL COLLAR
- ☐ JORDON FRAME
- ☐
- ☐

CARDIAC ARREST & MONITORING

- ☐ OBSERVED ARREST
- ☐ UNOBSERVED ARREST
- ☐ DEFIBRILLATION
  - ON PROTOCOL
    1ST JOULES ____ TIME ____
    2ND JOULES ____ TIME ____
  - IF ORDERED
    3RD JOULES ____ TIME ____

- ☐ C.P.R. BEFORE AMBULANCE
- ☐ NO C.P.R. BEFORE AMBULANCE
- ☐ MONITOR ONLY

F FRACTURE   H HAEMORRHAGE
L LACERATION   B BURN
A ABRASION   P PAIN
S SWELLING   D DISLOCATION

CREW DETAILS
CENTRE _____
VEHICLE FLEET NUMBER _____
DRIVER _____
ATTENDANT _____

Figure 8.1: (continued).

Table 8.12: A simple scheme of classifying injuries, intended for use by lay personnel in developing countries.

```
Serious injuries (requiring
  more than dressing):
Fractures
Dislocations
Traumatic amputations
Avulsion
Haematomas
Crushing injuries
Foreign bodies in orifice
Burns
Poisoning (other than food
  poisoning)
Other serious injuries

Mild injuries (requiring
  cleaning and dressing only):
Lacerations
Punctures
Bruises
Sprains
Strains
Contusions
Abrasions
Other mild injuries
```

2 Moderate. (These almost always require treatment but are not ordinarily life-threatening or permanently disabling.)

3 Serious. (Have a potential for major hospitalisation and long-term disability but are not generally life-threatening.)

4 Severe. (Are life-threatening and often permanently disabling, but survival is probable.)

5 Critical. (Usually require intensive medical care. Survival is uncertain.)

6 Maximum. (Virtually unsurvivable.)

(The adjectives "serious" and "severe" were interchanged in some earlier versions of the AIS.)

Death may occur from any level of injury, and should be recorded separately.

As well as an overall score, separate scores may be assigned to the various distinct injuries that a person has. Indeed, these are primary in later versions of the AIS, there being a codebook for converting any of many named injuries to the appropriate AIS score, and any overall measure is a derived quantity. The codebook is arranged chiefly according to region of body: external (subdivided into skin and burns), head (subdivided into brain/cranium and face), neck, thorax, abdomen and pelvic contents, spine (subdivided into cervical, thoracic, and lumbar), extremities and bony pelvis (subdivided into upper and lower extremities). Gennarelli (1984) describes the AIS thus: "It classifies, or attempts to classify, each injury in every body region according to its relative importance on a six point ordinal scale. The AIS is anatomically based, it begins organ by organ and goes through every organ in the body. Within each organ several kinds of injury are described. Within the brain stem for instance, compressive injuries, contusions, pressure, injuries involving haemorrhage, and lacerations are described."

Besides the use of the AIS in many clinical settings, there have been some large-scale applications. Examples include about 3000 emergency room patients per annum at Odense University Hospital, over 20,000 casualties per annum in the National Accident Sampling System in the USA, and 168,000 casualties reported to the Automobile Insurance Rating Association of Japan during three months of 1979 (Tsuchihashi et al, 1981).

Having more grades, the AIS appears to be more sensitive than the British police classification (for instance). However, as will be seen in Table 8.20, grades 3, 4, and 5 are fairly rare in occurrence, thus reducing this effect. Certainly it has a much sounder clinical basis than police methods. But it is time-consuming to use, ordinarily requiring medical records and staff specially trained to code from them. Efforts have been made to see how good an AIS rating can be obtained from an ICD N code using a conversion table—see Section 8.5.5. Good overview accounts of the AIS are given by Petrucelli et al (1981), Petrucelli (1984a), and Gennarelli (1984). But there are criticisms and difficulties. These will be discussed in Section 8.7.3 below. This is what Gibson (1981) has to say: the AIS and CIS (Comprehensive Injury Scale) "are widely used throughout the world and to a greater extent than any other single index, and have exerted much influence in research and policy de-

Table 8.13: Percentage of casualties at various AIS levels who died.

	Japanese insurance data	U.S. NCSS data	U.S. NASS data	British hospital data
AIS 1	0.012	0.03	0.13	0
2	0.13	0.2	1.3	0
3	0.85	1.0	3.8	1
4	22	8	25	29
5	71	58	48	65
6	98	100	100	100
Total number	167721	21421	29063	3543

termination. It seems unlikely that their methodologic foundation is firm enough to bear that heavy burden."

Derived from the AIS is the Injury Severity Score. This is the sum of the squares of the three highest AIS scores on different body regions. It is sometimes convenient to condense the result into a small number of groups. For instance, Nygren (c. 1984) uses these:

Slight (survivors): 1-3

Moderate (survivors): 4-10

Severe (survivors): 11 or more

Fatal.

8.7.2   Probability of death as related to AIS

As has been mentioned above, with the exception that AIS 6 implies almost certain death, the occurrence of death is a distinct variable from AIS score; death can occur even at AIS 1. As will be discussed at A.B in 8.7.3 below, threat to life is the most important factor in going from a named injury to an AIS score. There remains the empirical question of what is the probability of dying at various AIS levels. Table 8.13 gives data on this question from three large studies, two American (Partyka, 1982; Ulman and Stalnaker, 1986) and one Japanese (Tsuchihashi et al, 1981). A smaller British study, of casualties attending hospital in

Reading, Berkshire, is also included (Hobbs et al, 1979).

The sampling method of the Ulman and Stalnaker study is not made clear. It is based on the National Accident Sampling System for 1979–83. However, this System results in a stratified sample, with the more serious crashes being over-represented (and this being compensated for in the estimation of national numbers). Consequently, if the data is simply a count of casualties, it will be biased towards the serious end of the scale, and this is likely to apply within any particular AIS score as well as over the whole range. This could be a reason for the higher probability of death at the lower AIS levels as compared with the other datasets. The Japanese data was taken from insurance claim files (see Section 14.7); Partyka's results were from the National Crash Severity Study, which was conducted in 8 areas of the U.S.A. during 1977–79, and included some 12000 accidents involving at least one passenger vehicle towed for damage.

The NASS data also shows what proportion died, for casualties having various combinations of AIS codes for their three most severe injuries—see Table 8.14. The fatality rate shown there is not necessarily the empirical rate for a given combination of AIS codes. Instead, a process of smoothing the data has been carried out as follows: define one combination of codes to be "certainly more severe" than another if it has at least one AIS code greater than the corresponding one in the second combination, and none smaller than the corresponding ones; if combination abc is certainly more severe than xyz, yet this is contradicted by xyz having the higher empirical probability of death, bring them together and calculate a common probability of death; repeat until all such contradictions have been eliminated. The result is the smoothed fatality rate shown.

Table 8.15 shows the probability of death as a function of both AIS score and age. The information comes from Table 3.9 of Reinfurt et al (1978), who used the Illinois Trauma Registry to prepare it. However, there are a number of limitations with this data. The most important is that it is not the probability of death as such, but the conditional probability given that death did not occur prior to the victim arriving at an initial care facility—dead-on-arrival and dead-at-scene cases, accounting for

Table 8.14: Showing how the three highest AIS codes jointly affect the probability of death.

AIS codes	Number	Died	Fatality rate*		AIS codes	Number	Died	Fatality rate*
100	7917	4	.00039		440	0	0	?
110	5031	1	.00039		441	4	3	.421
111	8845	24	.0027		442	14	5	.421
					443	47	21	.447
200	387	6	.0092		444	24	17	.708
210	527	5	.0092					
211	2359	19	.0092		500	11	4	.243
220	84	3	.014		510	3	1	.243
221	653	9	.014		511	38	8	.243
222	250	14	.056		520	2	1	.243
					521	13	3	.243
300	91	2	.014		522	7	1	.243
310	123	0	.014		530	4	2	.245
311	585	8	.014		531	14	4	.245
320	47	0	.014		532	30	6	.245
321	344	12	.031		533	50	23	.460
322	254	18	.060		540	0	0	?
330	30	3	.023		541	7	4	.400
331	147	1	.023		542	11	4	.400
332	229	11	.060		543	42	24	.554
333	198	23	.116		544	38	28	.737
					550	1	0	.245
400	16	5	.115		551	0	0	?
410	13	1	.115		552	2	0	.421
411	51	6	.115		553	14	7	.554
420	6	1	.115		554	32	24	.750
421	34	4	.115		555	22	19	.864
422	27	2	.115					
430	6	0	.115		6--	192	192	1.000
431	29	2	.115					
432	49	9	.184					
433	109	31	.284					

* "Smoothed" estimate—see text.

52% of the total, were excluded because the quality of information about their injuries was so poor. Thus the true probabilities of death are higher— roughly, twice those shown. Nevertheless, Table 8.15 does serve to give some impression of the effect of age on likelihood of dying from a certain severity of injury. Other limitations mentioned by Reinfurt et al are that it is not known to what extent the data is representative of accidents in general and automobile accidents in particular, and that since most cases were treated in trauma centres, they may have received better than average initial care, thus biasing the probabilities downwards.

8.7.3 Criticisms of the AIS, and difficulties in its use

This discussion will be organised under the following headings:

Table 8.15: Percentage of casualties at various AIS levels and of various ages who died. (Those dead-at-scene or dead-on-arrival have been excluded.)

	A g e 0-20	21-55	56-70	71+
AIS 1	. . . . 0.7 . . .			5
2	. . . . 0.6 . . .			6
3	1	2	4	8
4	. . . . . . 7			
5	. . . 17 . .		. . . 45 . .	

A. The philosophy of the AIS, in particular, the balance between the dimensions of severity.

B. Vagueness of descriptions in the AIS codebook.

C. Variability of severities within a given AIS grade.

D. Circumstances for use of the AIS.

E. Police severity data in perspective.

A. The philosophy of the AIS, in particular the balance between the dimensions of severity.

   A.A. Injuries, not outcomes.

      A.A.A. The AIS codes injuries, and not what results from them. For instance, blindness or deafness resulting from eye or ear injuries are not coded in and of themselves. Similarly, death is an outcome, and therefore not coded within AIS (except insofar as grade 6 is virtually unsurvivable), though most studies will want to record its occurrence as a separate datum. See Petrucelli et al, 1981; Petrucelli, 1982.

      A.A.B. An exception: diffuse brain injuries (commonly called concussions). In the 1980 and subsequent Revisions of the AIS, head injuries other than those to the skull are described in terms both of anatomic lesions and level of consciousness/functional alteration. Bringing in an outcome

(level of consciousness) is contrary to the general philosophy of the AIS, but was felt to be necessary to avoid losing significant brain injury data and to rectify a serious lack of consistency among AIS-76 users (Petrucelli et al, 1981; Petrucelli, 1982). It also reflects the existence of diffuse brain injuries, lesions only apparent at the microscopic level but which nevertheless can be overwhelmingly severe (Gennarelli, 1980).

A.B. Many dimensions of severity. What is the balance in AIS?

   A.B.A. History. "Severity" is a multidimensional concept. The Comprehensive Injury Scale (Committee on Medical Aspects of Automotive Safety, 1972), which was developed alongside the AIS, distinguishes four aspects: energy dissipation, threat to life, permanent impairment, and treatment period. The incidence, or frequency of occurrence, is a fifth aspect as regards severity of the problem to society, but not a measure of severity of injury to an individual. Bunketorp et al (1982) and Bull (1977) also bring out the many-faceted nature of severity, commenting that which aspect is emphasised depends on the purpose for which the rating is made. The AIS has summarised all the various aspects into a single number (hence the term "Abbreviated"). It is generally believed that threat to life has been given the greatest weight. This belief is based in part on the studies reviewed below.

   A.B.B. Comparison of AIS with CIS. Huang and Marsh (1978) showed that the AIS is essentially a threat-to-life scale: they did this by cross-tabulating the AIS for each of the 252 injury descriptions in the AIS-76 handbook with the score on the threat-to-life component of the

Comprehensive Injury Scale, and finding that a monotonic relationship accounted for all but 27 of them. By a monotonic relationship, I mean that as either AIS or threat-to-life increased, so the other one also does or at least doesn't decrease. When similar comparisons were made with the energy dissipation, permanent impairment, and treatment period components of the CIS, less correlation was found (respectively, 26%, 31%, and 32% of injury descriptions violated a monotonic relationship, as compared with the 11% for threat-to-life). A slight methodological weakness with the Huang and Marsh study is that they did not partial out (statistically control for) the effect of the other three variables when investigating the effect of the fourth one on AIS.

A.B.C. Opinions of surgeons. In studies reported by Eastham (1984, 1985) a questionnaire was mailed to a number of surgeons and emergency medicine specialists, asking for the ratings of each of a number of described injuries on each of these four dimensions of severity: mortality risk, length of stay, overall recovery period, and permanent disability/activity limitation. Other aspects of Eastham's results will be discussed at C.A below, but here it is appropriate to mention that he compared the strengths of association between AIS and the four separate dimensions of severity, and found that both threat-to-life and acute care length of stay contributed importantly to AIS. One of the statistical methods he used in his analysis was to calculate correlation coefficients between AIS and each individual severity dimension, with the effects of the other dimensions partialled out.

A.C. Is the balance right?

A.C.A. Mechanical force. Mattern et al (1979) criticised the AIS on several grounds, one of which was that it does not reflect the magnitude of mechanical force applied, e.g. both uncomplicated fracture of the femur and isolated rib fracture receive an AIS score of 2, yet the former is likely to involve a force 50 times as great; Reidelbach and Zeidler (1983) mention this point too.

A.C.B. Treatment period, disability. Reidelbach and Zeidler (1983) argue that AIS gives too much weight to mortality risk, and not enough to length of treatment period and degree of permanent impairment, and therefore that some head and body injuries currently assigned grade 3 should be downgraded to 1 or 2, thus in effect making limb injuries—with their longer treatment and disablement periods—relatively more important. On the other hand, Nathorst Westfelt (1982), in a study of children's injuries, reduced the score assigned to displaced fracture of the radius (a bone of the arm) from 3 to 2, on the grounds that such injuries were "relatively uncomplicated". And Ulman and Stalnaker (1986) express the view that "The AIS should be redefined to represent threat to life only, with a new separate code for disability." (This does not seem to me to be a logical consequence of the rest of their paper.) Petrucelli (1984b), in the course of a review of limb injuries, accepts that the AIS is a threat to life scale, and that it does not properly reflect long term disablement from limb injuries.

A.C.C. Age of casualty. Mattern et al (1979) criticised the AIS because it does not reflect the fact that an injury that a young person always survives may often prove fatal to an older one.

A.D. My views.

A.D.A. Criticism A.C.A is misguided: AIS is intended to (and should) reflect the effect on the casualty, not measure the force that produces the effect.

A.D.B. I have no strong view on the issue at A.C.B.

A.D.C. Criticism A.C.C is misguided. Some scales of threat to life (e.g. Reinfurt et al, 1978, p. v; Somers, 1981) do in fact incorporate factors other than the injury—in particular, age of the casualty, which Mattern et al (1979) want AIS to take into account. A feature of such scales which can be a disadvantage for some purposes is that if probability of death is independent of age at any particular level of the scale, then circumstances not differing in the types of trauma that result will necessarily differ in their distributions on the threat to life scale, if their age distributions are different. For most purposes, I think factors such as age are better treated as external variables in the analysis rather than being lost in the construction of the threat to life scale. In other words, threat to life should be assessed by reference to a standard person, not the person who actually has the injuries. I was pleased to see a discussion of this issue by Somers (1983). He developed two versions of a Probability of Death Score, based upon the AIS, one of which incorporates age. There is probably more that could be said on this, but his comments are a start.

A.D.D. I would like to add that I can see some case for reflecting the probable force that caused an injury by reducing the AIS for a given injury if the casualty is an elderly person. This is a different issue from the comparison of different injuries that concerns Mattern et al (1979) and Reidelbach and Zeidler (1983). It is a modification in the opposite direction to the correction for age that Mattern et al advocate. The justification for it would be that the given impact might not have resulted in the trauma that did in fact occur had instead the casualty been younger. However, see A.D.F below.

A.D.E. The main component of AIS, threat to life, depends on factors such as the medical facilities available and the age of the casualty. If a new treatment reduces the death rate from a particular injury, will the corresponding AIS be reduced? If injury x has a lower fatality rate than injury y among young people, but a higher fatality rate among the elderly (perhaps it immobilises them, resulting in some deaths from complications), should not the AIS for x be less than that for y among the young, but greater among the old?

A.D.F. One can go on multiplying philosophical subtleties such as those in A.D.D and A.D.E above. I don't think it is worth the effort. Ambiguity about what we mean by severity is less important in practice than it might seem in principle: there are usually so many other problems of availability and completeness of information facing a researcher using medical records—and even more so, a policeman coding severity at the accident scene—that this one pales into insignificance.

B. Vagueness of descriptions in the AIS codebook, and the coding difficulties that result.

B.A. Improvements incorporated in the 1980 revision. See Petrucelli et al (1981) and Petrucelli (1982); the latter paper includes some comments on the 1983 revision).

B.A.A. Part of the motivation for revising the coding of diffuse brain injury (see A.A.B above) was to improve the reliability of coding.

B.A.B. Replacement of adjectives with numbers. With regard to exter-

Table 8.16: Results from a study of the use of AIS-76 by MacKenzie et al (1978).

Comparison of emergency department record with in-patient chart as sources of information*

- Method: A single rater reviewed the emergency department records and one month later the corresponding in-patient charts.

- Sample: 50 trauma admission patients (21 vehicular trauma, 29 other causes).

- Number of injuries: 139 (from one source of information or the other).

- On the ED chart: 21% of injuries were missing, 27% were noted but there was insufficient information to assign an AIS code, 52% were coded.

- On the inpatient record: 8% of the injuries were missing, 11% were noted but couldn't be coded, 81% were coded.

- Those coded from both sources: 62 in number, 70% coded identically, 29% coded one grade higher when in-patient record was used.

Inter-rater reliability

- Method: Three raters reviewed in-patient charts. (One of the raters was a non-clinical researcher, two were nurses.)

- Sample: 98 trauma admission patients (26 had been hit by vehicles, 24 had been in vehicles, 48 had nonvehicular trauma).

- Number of injuries: 376 (noted by at least one coder); 21% were missed by two coders, 13% by one coder. 48% were either missed or couldn't be coded by at least one coder.

- Those coded by all three coders: 194 in number. Considering all possible pairs of coders, on average the codings were identical 78% of the time.

- Those coded by both nurses: 224 in number, 74% coded identically, for 22% the disagreement was only by one grade.

* See Table 10.7 for a Finnish comparison of in-patient and emergency room records—but with respect to ICD N code, not AIS.

nal injuries, AIS-76 used terms such as "deep" and "extensive" to qualify abrasions, contusions, and lacerations, leaving the interpretation of these to the coder. (Barancik and Chatterjee, 1981, complained of such generalities.) AIS-80 quantified these injuries in centimetres.

B.A.C. Overall injury severity. To assess the total effect of multiple injuries, AIS-76 suggested an overall AIS score that was a clinical judgment made by a medical coder experienced in the treatment of trauma; this being found to be much too judgmental (e.g. Mattern et al, 1979, mention finding only 80% agreement between investigators), AIS-80 recommends using the maximum of the AIS codes in a multiply-injured victim.

B.B. The adjective "crush" is used in several cases. This is not a description of a lesion, but of an injury mechanism (Hirsch and Eppinger, 1984).

B.C. Empirical studies of coding reliability.

B.C.A. Table 8.16 summarises a study of the reliability of coding using AIS-76 by MacKenzie et al (1978).

Table 8.17: Mean percentage mortality perceived for 25 injuries, as related to their AIS score.

	Ten neurological injuries, in four groups				Five orthopaedic injuries, in two groups		Ten thoracic cavity injuries, in four groups			
	A	B	C	D	E	F	G	H	I	J
AIS 1							2			
2				5	1	1				
3	3			31	2,11	2	5,8		9	16
4	11	47	36	40				22	16	29
5	33	66	61					44	36	

Table 8.18: The numbers of injuries (from a set of 95) having various combinations of AIS score and mean percentage mortality perceived.

	Perceived percentage mortality					
	0-5	6-19	20-39	40-59	60-79	80-100
AIS 1	9					
2	12	2				
3	13	11	2	1		
4	2	7	10	4		
5		4	4	5	6	3

B.C.B. MacKenzie et al (1981) give a preliminary description of a similar but much larger study using AIS-80.

C. Variability of severities within a given AIS grade.

C.A. Mortality risk as perceived by surgeons.

C.A.A. The following refers to the report by Eastham (1985), discussion of which was begun at A.B.C above. Each injury was reviewed by no less than 26 respondents. The injuries totalled 25 in number; they fell into three groups according to surgical speciality; each group was itself divided into subgroups according to nature of injury; each subgroup was divided according to severity. As an example, the three injuries in subgroup I were superficial laceration of lung, the same with unilateral haemothorax, and extensive lung laceration. Eastham found (see Table 8.17):

- Within each subgroup, the perceived mortality risk (averaged over respondents) was positively associated with the AIS score.

- For injuries all having the same AIS score, there is a wide variation in the perceived mortality risk.

C.A.B. In an earlier paper, Eastham (1984) had used a similar method for 95 injuries, biased towards the severe end of the spectrum, taken from the AIS codebook. Table 8.18 cross-tabulates AIS score and expected percentage deaths. As in Table 8.17, a considerable spread is seen at a given AIS level.

C.B. Mortality rate as affected by part of body. Table 8.19 has been prepared from Table 2 of the paper by Ulman and Stalnaker (1986) discussed in 8.7.2

Table 8.19: Percentage fatality rates according to AIS score and part of body. Sample sizes are shown in brackets.

		Chest		Head		Abdomen		Extremities*		Neck	
AIS	1	0	(349)	0	(1290)	0	(58)	0	(6002)	0	(1466)
	2	2	(41)	2	(265)	-	(0)	0	(829)	19	(21)
	3	4	(24)	15	(66)	0	(11)	3	(501)	22	(9)
	4	45	(11)	38	(58)	19	(21)	25	(4)	100	(1)
	5	89	(18)	47	(40)	30	(20)	-	(0)	25	(4)

* Includes shoulders and bony pelvis.

earlier. For NASS data for 1981–84, it shows the mortality rates for casualties whose three most severe injuries were all to the same part of the body. Ulman and Stalnaker claim "it is obvious that AIS does not relate the same to mortality rate in each body region". Well, it isn't obvious to me. True, a chi-squared test comparing head and chest at AIS 5 gives a statistically-significant result—but this is a selected comparison from the whole Table, not a valid procedure.

C.C. Are some AIS 5 injuries unsurvivable? In assessing the injuries in the AIS codebook with respect to their likely short and long term consequences, Hirsch and Eppinger (1984) excluded all AIS 6 injuries (because their consequence is simply death), and also 14 AIS 5 injuries because the general surgeon participating in their study considered these unsurvivable also.

C.D. Leg injuries, AIS 2 and 3, wide variation in typical treatment periods and levels of incapacity. Cesari et al (1983) comment that "the scale graduation is much too diffuse since one division includes pathological processes which are widely variable in severity." They divide grades 2 and 3 each into four subgrades (2A,...,2D, 3A,...,3D): for instance, an ankle sprain is scored 2A, and a trifocal fracture is scored 3D. The same group of workers (Farisse et al, 1983) say "It has seemed to us that the abridged and synoptic nature of the scaling method precluded its application to our experimentation, narrowly focused as this was to

lower limb injury research ... It is absolutely essential to have available a finer scale with which to evaluate progress in the tests to improve vehicle profiles."

C.E. AIS 1.

C.E.A. High incidence. In most of the studies where the AIS has been used, around 70% of casualties have had a maximum score of 1 (for some examples, see Table 8.20). To dismiss what follows on the grounds that the AIS is only ever used with samples of quite severely injured patients would not be correct, therefore. For an example of a scale that attempts to provide finer detail in the low end of the severity spectrum, see Section 8.11.3.

C.E.B. Apparent range of severities. Some examples of injuries coded as AIS 1 are given in Table 8.21. To me, losing a pint of blood due to lacerating a vein is obviously more serious than a minor (or even a moderate) abrasion. Admittedly, I don't have a medical degree, but it would take a lot of argument from the Injury Scaling Committee to convince me otherwise. I think one is entitled to doubt, too, whether a dislocated finger is truly as serious as a fracture of the vault of the skull (both are coded AIS 2).

C.E.C. The first reason for deploring the lack of discrimination in AIS 1 (and in AIS 2 also) is that distinctions between the various levels of sever-

Table 8.20: Percentage frequencies with which the AIS scores occurred to casualties in fourteen studies*.

	AIS 1	2	3	4	5	6
USA NASS, survivors 1983 (NASS, 1985)	85	10	4	...	1	...
USA NASS 1979 (Smith et al, 1981)	82	11	5	1	..1..	
Goteborg emergency room, bicyclists, 1983 (Kroon et al, 1984)	74	19	5	...	1	...
Waikato emergency room, fatalities excluded, 1980 (Bailey, 1984)	74	18	7	1	0	0
Japan, insurance data, 1979 (Tsuchihashi et al, 1981)	74	17	6	2	1	0
Western New York, vehicle occupants, pedestrians, and bicyclists, 1974 (Baum, 1978)	71	20	5	1	0	2
Odense emergency room 1978 (Jorgensen et al, 1979)	70	24	4	1	1	1
Odense emergency room 1979-81 (Odense Univ. Acc. Anal. Gp., 1983)	70	22	6	1	1	0
Washtenaw Co., Michigan, vehicle occupants, towaway crashes, fatalities excluded, 1971-75 (Sherman et al, 1976)	66	17	12	3	2	0
Southern England, vehicle occupants, late 1970's (Hobbs, 1981)	62	27	7	1	1	2
Berkshire, Southern England, casualties attending hospital, 1974-76 (Hobbs et al, 1979)	59	27	10	1	1	1
Adelaide, accidents to which an ambulance was called, 1976 (McLean, 1981)	58	26	12	2	0	2
Uppsala County, mopedists and motorcyclists attending hospital, 1976 (Engstrom, 1979)	52	30	13	3	1	1
Stockholm, bicyclists, multiple sources of registration (Lind and Wollin, 1986)	36	56	4	1	1	0

* These studies differed in many ways, in particular, in their selection of casualties. Grossly unrepresentative samples have not been included in the Table, but even so, it can only give a rough impression of the frequencies of occurrence of the AIS scores. In the study which matched police and hospital in-patient data for Scotland that will be described in Section 13.3 (Tunbridge, 1987), the relative percentages having AIS scores of 1–6 were 12, 67, 18, 2, 0.4, and 0.1. Thus in-patient data is as narrowly concentrated as studies taking a wider sample—but around AIS 2 rather than AIS 1.

ity within this code are of interest in their own right. To a doctor, having daily contact with the mortally wounded, both a superficial abrasion and a lacerated vein may be minor, but most people would prefer the former to the latter.

C.E.D. The second reason is that lumping such a range into a single grade will lead to low statistical power when AIS is used as a dependent variable.

C.E.E. The third reason is that differences within the AIS 1 grade could reflect differences occurring at a higher level of severity, but which are hard to detect because random statistical fluctuation dominates the small frequencies of occurrence. Suppose some low-severity injuries were re-coded as AIS 0.5, and some of

Table 8.21: Some injuries that are coded as AIS 1.

- Abrasion or contusion, area less than 25 sq.cm.
- Headache or dizziness.
- Closed fracture of mandible.
- Laceration of external jugular vein, bleeding less than about 1000 c.c.
- Fracture of one rib.
- Strain of cervical, thoracic, or lumbar spine.
- Laceration of brachial vein, bleeding less than about 1000 c.c.
- Sprain of wrist.
- Fracture of toe.

slightly higher severity as AIS 1.5. Then this hypothesis says that if condition x leads to proportionately more AIS 3–6 injuries than condition y, it will also lead to a higher ratio of AIS 1.5 to AIS 0.5 injuries. There are four lines of argument supporting this: (i) It can be justified on vague statistical grounds— the simplest way of describing the effect of a change from x to y is to say the mean injury severity has changed, without affecting any other property of the distribution, and this will usually produce the required result (Hutchinson, 1976a). (ii) We can appeal to a causative mechanism, e.g. by saying that condition x leads to more AIS 3–6 injuries because a greater mechanical force is being applied, and this must lead to relatively more AIS 1.5 compared to AIS 0.5 injuries, too (at least, if the distribution of injuries over the regions of the body is unchanged). (iii) The large amount of variability in such things as impact speed and tolerance of injury seems to me to be relevant too. Suppose that amount of injury is given by S+T+F+...when factor F is present, and by S+T+...when factor F is not present, S and T rep-

resenting contributions from speed and injury tolerance respectively, and various other influences being present also. Then because S and T are very variable, they automatically spread the influence of F over a wide range of injury severities. (iv) The best kind of support, however, would be empirical: here, I can point out that circumstances having a high fatality rate tend also to have a high rate of serious injury (British police definition), see Hutchinson (1976b). But this is of limited relevance to AIS and in particular to discrimination within AIS 1.

C.E.F. If the hypothesis discussed in C.E.E above is not valid, then the argument in C.E.D does not apply either—we want statistical power, but it must be directed at the right kind of differences.

D. Circumstances for use of the AIS.

D.A. The AIS is chiefly aimed at use with such information as is usually found in in-patient medical records, or perhaps emergency room registers.

D.B. Is an ICD N code sufficient information on which to base an AIS code? See Section 8.5.5 for discussion of this.

D.C. Can an AIS score be assigned within a few hours of hospital admission? (If so, there is a reasonable prospect of informing the police of it, for addition to their record of the accident.) Civil and Schwab (1986) report an experiment of this kind (though supplementing police data was not one of their motives). It used a single-page AIS chart in place of the rather clumsy codebook. The results were reasonably promising. See MacKenzie (1986) for comments on their paper. A later paper, which I have not seen at the time of writing this, is by Civil et al (1987). Owens (1983) mentions that police officers at the accident scene can use the AIS to grade the injuries of motorcyclists: "Accuracy of the scaling system recorded on the law enforcement accident report was amazingly accurate from the beginning and improved each year. The coding method not only assisted the emergency department physicians but also conserved the time in which the patients received definitive treatment."

D.D. Can a reasonably accurate AIS score be obtained by asking individuals about their injuries? A brief note on this is by Dorsch et al (1986). Their study is confined to head injuries; their sample is small; they do not give details of their methods, e.g. the average time between the accident and the enquiry made, or the wording of the questions about injury. Nevertheless, it is worth summarising their results. Of their 21 cases, the AIS code based on responses to a postal questionnaire was the same as that based on hospital records in 9 cases; differed by one grade in 9 cases; differed by two grades in 3 cases; the grade based on the questionnaire was the higher in 10 cases and was the lower in 2 cases.

D.E. Fundamentally, the AIS is a method of discarding information—of boiling down all the data relevant to severity that appears in a medical record to a briefer form. The intent is that little useful information be lost, and that this be more than compensated by the greater practicability of using what remains. It is worth raising the question, however, whether the right amount of information is thrown away at the right stage. There is a prima facie case that, having gone to all the trouble of obtaining, reading, and understanding an injured person's medical records, a more detailed account be kept than is provided for by the AIS—the obvious basis to build upon would be the ICD—and that conversion to AIS be an automated process carried out at a later stage. As well as avoiding discarding data on nature of injury, this would facilitate the use of severity measures differing from the AIS in their balance between the di-

mensions (e.g. placing greater weight on disability, less on threat to life). In the course of the Northeastern Ohio Trauma Study, assigning the AIS severity scores was separated from ascertaining the injury details. Barancik and Chatterjee (1981) have this to say: "A distinction should be made between (a) identifying and recording anatomic injury diagnoses from charts, and (b) converting these diagnoses to quantitative severity scores...Identification and recording of anatomic injuries would be best accomplished by a combination of precoded and narrative abstracting in hospitals while conversion to AIS severity codes should be completed independently in the central project office. Centralised control over severity coding is deemed essential to maintain accuracy and precision throughout an extended data collection period." Like Civil and Schwab (see D.C above), Barancik and Chatterjee reorganised and condensed the injury descriptions from the AIS manual so that they fitted onto a single page. They concluded that "The chief benefits of the single page method are increased productivity and reduced potential of coder bias. The need to exercise judgment in classification is sharply curtailed by coding all anatomic injury descriptors identified in a record...The method virtually eliminates the need to make severity coding decisions in hospitals, separates abstracting and severity coding processes, and reduces the opportunity to introduce bias in subsequent procedures. It also provides more information since the recorded codes uniquely identify specific anatomic injuries, whereas the dictionary manual method loses all such detail because only AIS values are coded."

D.F. Extension to detailed head/neck information. In the context of their detailed scheme of classifying head and neck injuries (see Section 8.6.2), Ouellet et al (1984) make these two points about the AIS:

- That most of the head/neck injuries reported in their detailed study simply are not described at all by the AIS-80.
- That many injuries scaled in the AIS-80 appear to be an aggregate of several injuries, and it is difficult to know what are the appropriate scores to give to the components.

I don't think these are really criticisms of the AIS, and I don't think Ouellet et al mean them to be: the level of detail of the data to be coded is different in the two schemes, and when trying to make one as compatible as possible with the other, compromises are inevitable.

E. Police severity data in perspective. Despite all the criticisms and difficulties in use that are mentioned above, AIS seems to be the best scheme of injury severity classification available at present. The fact that these limitations do exist, however, does put into perspective the criticisms made of grades of severity used by the police (to be discussed below). Compared with an ideal, police severity measures fall a long way short. But the ideal is unattainable: AIS, the present state-of-the-art, falls short too.

8.8 Severity classification by British police

8.8.1 The categories

In Britain, police classify casualties as fatally, seriously, or slightly injured. Additionally, there is the uninjured category, which will only be known about if someone else in the accident is injured. These categories are defined as follows:

Fatal. Death in less than 30 days as a result of the accident.

Serious. Examples are: fracture; internal injury; severe cuts and lacerations; crushing; concussion; severe general shock requiring hospital treatment; detention in hospital as an in-patient, either immediately or later as a result of the injuries; death on or after 30 days after the accident.

Slight. Examples are: sprains; bruises; cuts judged not to be severe; slight shock requiring roadside attention. (Persons who are merely shaken and who have no other injury should not be included unless they receive or appear to need medical treatment.)

Chapman and Neilson (1971) have this to say about these definitions: "Injury categories are a considerable source of variation. The four categories, fatally, seriously, slightly or not injured are barely sufficient for many purposes and the two borderlines between the last three categories are very uncertain. A fatality is precisely classified by the 30 days rule which includes only those dying within 30 days of the accident. But many injured are detained overnight in hospital because they cannot be examined until morning, because they may have suffered concussion, or even because they find themselves at a hospital and there is no alternative accommodation for the night. The result is that many of those falling within the definition of seriously injured do not necessarily have any of the injuries listed for serious injury. Again, in some police forces it is customary for the policeman at the scene to assess severity, while in others enquiry is made afterwards at the hospitals. The distinction between slight and no injury determines whether or not a Stats 19 entry is made. Many accidents of a minor nature are not seen by the police but are reported to them afterwards to comply with the legal requirement to do so by those involved. The police opinion then determines the severity rating."

It appears from the definition of serious injury, and from Chapman and Neilson's comments, that hospital admission is a sufficient condition for the injury to be counted as serious. But if that is so now, it was not always: the 1969 version of the Stats 20 booklet (Road Accidents Statistics, Instructions for the Completion of Road Accident Reports (Form Stats 19)) included this contradictory sentence in the definition of a slight injury: "Persons who appear to be only slightly injured but nevertheless are admitted to hospital as in-patients either immediately or later should be recorded as seriously injured if they are detained for more than three days." (This does not appear in the 1980 version.)

8.8.2 Evidence for variations in usage

Newby (1969) examined the proportions of casualties classified as having fatal, serious, or slight injuries in the (then) 152 British police forces. He showed that those forces with a high ratio of fatalities to fatal plus serious injuries tend to have a low ratio of fatal plus serious injuries to the total. The reason for this is the varying definition of a "serious" injury between police forces: if the boundary between slight and serious injury is at a relatively low level of severity, fatals/(fatals + serious) will be too low and (fatals + serious)/total will be too high. Newby also gives an example from one particular English town where the numbers of fatal and serious casualties remained consistent over the period (1950–67) examined, but the number of slight casualties suddenly increased in 1959 by 80% and continued to increase from the new level. Thus apparently some accidents that previously would have been classified as non-injury in that town were regarded in later years as slight injury. (See Section 8.10.2 for a report of this happening in Pennsylvania in 1977.)

A similar instance is given by Satterthwaite (1975) in which it was apparently the boundary between serious and slight injuries that moved. In one particular region of England, there occurred from 1968 to 1969 a fall from 30% to 21% in the proportion of injury accidents classified as serious.(In the rest of Great Britain, there was a tiny change in the opposite direction.) At the same time, the total number of accidents in that region remained much the same, as did the proportion of fatalities.

A further example is provided by the introduction during 1984 of a central injury severity assessment system by the Metropolitan Police (Greater London). The effect of this was to increase the number of casualties classified as serious by 2600, from about 15% to about 20% (RAGB, 1986).

Just as we shall find in Table 8.22 that there is variability between American states in the proportions of casualties whose severity is classified as A, B, or C, so there is variability between English counties in the proportions of serious injury. Considering just the seven major conurbations, the proportion of casualties killed or seriously injured in 1985 varied from 17% in Merseyside to 30% in the West Midlands. Such a wide range can hardly be genuine: there must be variability in either where the borderline between serious and slight injury is drawn, or in the proportions of slight injuries regarded as no injuries at all, and thus excluded from the statistics. Among the shire counties and Scottish regions, the proportion of fatal and serious casualties is over 40% in some cases, and fractionally below 20% in others.

Another study (Hutchinson and Lai, 1981) both provided evidence for differences between police forces in where they draw the line between serious and slight injury, and proposed a statistical method of taking account of this when analysing data from several police forces simultaneously. The dataset was a three-way tabulation of injury severity (the dependent variable), police force, and circumstances of injury. This is not the place to describe the methods used, but an indication of the results is that, considering the set of circumstances labelled as number 4, police forces 2, 3, and 4 had very similar proportions of fatalities (2.1%, 1.9%, 1.8%), but very different proportions of serious injuries (27%, 31%, 45%). So whatever was causing changes in the latter was not affecting the former. A possible explanation is different interpretations of the serious/slight distinction, and a statistical model built upon this idea was found to be successful.

Finally, an even more statistically-sophisticated approach was taken by Hutchinson (1983) with some data on injuries to the two drivers in head-on crashes. The severities were cross-tabulated, i.e. the numbers of each combination of severities were known. Expressed simply, the numbers of accidents where both drivers were seriously injured or both were slightly injured appeared too big relative to the numbers where one was seriously and one was slightly injured. This was interpreted as follows. The placing of the threshold between serious and slight injury was assumed to be the same for both drivers in the same accident (because they are both being classified by the same policeman at the same time), but was allowed to be different for different accidents. One cannot be sure how sensitive the results in Hutchinson (1983) are to the fine details of the statistical assumptions, but they received a heartening measure of support from a different dataset, in which it was the severities of injury to driver and front seat passenger in single-vehicle crashes that were cross-tabulated

(Hutchinson, 1986).

8.9 Other non-U.S. police systems

8.9.1 Those similar to Britain's

The following jurisdictions use definitions of serious injury that are virtually the same (apart from translation) as Britain's: the Irish Republic, New Zealand, Northern Ireland, Sweden, Switzerland. The definition in Statistics of Road Traffic Accidents in Europe is similar, too.

8.9.2 Those using period of hospitalisation

Several countries use simply the fact or the length of hospitalisation to distinguish serious injuries from others:

Saskatchewan, Canada: Admission.

Victoria, Australia: Admission.

Hong Kong: Admission for at least 12 hours.

Belgium: Admission for at least 24 hours.

West Germany: Admission for at least 24 hours.

Indonesia: Admission for at least 5 days.

France: Admission for at least 6 days.

South Korea: Admission for more than 21 days.

Austria: Admission for more than 21 days classifies the injury as "severe" (but see also Section 8.9.4 below).

Japan: Admission for at least 30 days (but see also Section 3.8 above).

Czechoslovakia: Admission for more than 42 days classifies the injury as "severe".

Saskatchewan divides injuries of those not admitted to hospital into moderate (injury or complaint of pain that required medical treatment but not admission to hospital) and minor (no treatment required).

Ross (c. 1986) mentions that South Korea distinguishes between "very slight" injury (less than 5 days in hospital) and "slight" injury (5–21 days in hospital).

In Britain, Hobbs et al (1979) concluded that a simple classification that closely related to clinical severity was the three-fold one, not detained, detained for less than three nights, detained for three or more nights. For Sri Lanka, Sayer and Hitchcock (1984) thought the second threshold should be one night higher, making the third category four or more nights.

8.9.3 Norway

In Norway, a distinction is made between those "dangerously" injured and those "seriously" injured. Short summary definitions are:

Dangerous injury: People for some time in real danger of life and supposed to suffer enduringly from the consequences of the injury. (Presumably it is the first of these concepts, i.e. danger to life, that is the dominant one, as it is difficult for anyone, let alone the police, to know if an injury will have enduring effects.)

Serious injury: Not in danger of life.

Slight injury: People receiving negligible scratches etc., including small fractures.

8.9.4 Austria

According to Benjamin (1984), Austria defines serious injury as one preventing work for at least 24 hours. But see also Section 8.9.2 above.

8.9.5 Denmark

According to Benjamin (1984), Denmark defines the seriously injured as all casualties other than those who are not hospitalised and have only soft tissue injury.

8.9.6 West Germany

According to Seiffert (1986), West Germany defines a severe injury as one requiring hospital treatment. But see also Section 8.9.2 above.

8.9.7 Brazil

If I understand the Portuguese correctly, the distinction between slight and severe injury is that the former does not endanger life and consists typically of general pain or slight lacerations, contusions, or abrasions, whereas the latter does present a risk to life and includes serious lacerations or avulsions with severe haemorrhage.

8.10 Severity classification by American police

8.10.1 The codes

Most American police forces use the K, A, B, C, 0 code recommended by the National Safety Council. The wording of the definitions of these codes varies in minor ways from place to place. Very brief descriptions are as follows:

K Fatal.

A Incapacitating injury.

B Non-incapacitating (evident) injury.

C Possible injury.

0 No indication of injury.

The following set of definitions, fuller than any other I have seen, is applied in Maryland (Dischinger et al, 1985):

- Fatal injury is any injury sustained in an accident, or as a result of an accident, that causes the death of the injured person within 90 days after the accident.

- Incapacitating injury is any injury, other than fatal, that prevents the injured person from walking, driving, or normally continuing the activities which he was capable of performing prior to the motor vehicle traffic accident. This includes severe lacerations, broken or distorted limbs, skull fracture, crushed chest, internal injuries, unconscious when taken from the accident scene, and inability to leave the accident without assistance, but excludes momentary unconsciousness.

- Non-incapacitating (evident) injury is any injury, other than fatal or incapacitating, which

is evident to any person other than the injured at the scene of the accident. This includes lump on head, abrasions, and minor lacerations, but excludes limping.

- Possible injury is any injury, reported or claimed, that is neither fatal, incapacitating, nor non-incapacitating injury. This includes momentary unconsciousness, claims of injuries that are not evident, limping, complaint of pain, nausea, and hysteria.

- Damage only (no injury) is any situation in which there is no reason to believe that any person suffered any bodily harm as a result of the motor vehicle traffic accident. This includes confusion, excitement, anger, and internal injuries unknown to the person until after leaving the scene.

The K, A, B, C, 0 scheme permits rapid evaluation under adverse circumstances and with minimal examination of the victim. But obviously many injuries in the A category are minor, such as superficial lacerations accompanied by moderate but easily controlled bleeding, and conversely the C category could include severe and potentially life-threatening injuries such as a ruptured spleen. Further doubt is cast on the validity of this classification by the finding (Carpenter, 1973) that insurance payments (in what was admittedly a small sample) for severity C were higher than for B which in turn were higher than for A. In the course of a wider investigation, Shinar et al (1983) found that a substantial number of injury accidents in Indiana were recorded by the police as damage-only (grade 0). See Section 4.3.3 for a description of their work.

8.10.2 Inter- and intra-state variations in usage

Carroll and Scott (1971) and Scott (1972) noticed enormous differences between states of the U.S.A. as to the proportions in which the A, B, C codes were used: the proportion of A injuries varied from 13% to 65%, and the proportion of C injuries varied from 9% to 75%, in a sample of 17 states. The authors thought that much of the variation must be attributed to non-uniformity of scale interpretation and use. I have compiled some more recent data—see Table 8.22. Though there are

Table 8.22: Percentage distribution of severity of injury in thirteen states.

	A	B	C
South Carolina 1985	36	22	42
Massachusetts 1981	32	32	36
Illinois 1983	27	26	47
South Dakota 1983	20	47	33
Idaho 1983	17	40	44
Washington 1982-83	15	41	45
Michigan 1983	14	31	55
Delaware 1983	13	48	39
Texas 1983	12	44	44
States that may not be comparable:			
Alabama 1983*	59	26	15
Arizona 1983#	20	47	33
Ohio 1984+	8	41	51
California 1983+	5	46	49

* Rural accidents only.

U.S. and state highways only.

+ These states use the term "severe" in describing the most serious category. Thus in California it is called a "severe wound", though the definition of this is very similar to the usual definition of code A: "Injury which prevents the injured party from walking, driving, or performing activities he/she was normally capable of before the accident." In the Ohio data table it is called "severe", but in the definitions it is called "serious visible injury", and is defined as "An injury other than fatal that prevents the injured person from working, driving, or continuing normal activities that he (she) was capable of performing prior to the accident."

Sources:

Alabama. Alabama Accident Summary. Statewide Rural Accidents. April-December 1983. (Plus similar report for January-March 1983.) Alabama Department of Public Safety.

Arizona. Arizona Traffic Accident Summary 1983. Arizona Department of Transportation.

California. 1983 Annual Report of Fatal and Injury Motor Vehicle Traffic Accidents. Sacramento: California Highway Patrol.

Delaware. 1983 Annual Report and Statistical Analysis. Delaware State Police Traffic Section.

Idaho. Motor Vehicle Traffic Accidents Statewide Summary.

Illinois. Summary of Motor Vehicle Traffic Accidents. Springfield: Illinois Department of Transportation.

Massachusetts. (Untitled report.) Boston: Registry of Motor Vehicles.

Michigan. Michigan Traffic Accident Facts 1983. Michigan Department of State Police.

Ohio. 1984 Ohio Traffic Accident Facts. Columbus: Ohio Department of Highway Safety.

South Carolina. 1985 South Carolina Traffic Accidents. Columbia: Department of Highways and Public Transportation.

South Dakota. 1983 South Dakota Motor Vehicle Traffic Accident Summary. Pierre: Department of Commerce and Regulation.

Texas. Summary of All Reported Accidents in the State of Texas for Calendar Year 1983. Texas Department of Public Safety.

Washington. Data Summary & Analysis of 1983 Traffic Collisions. Washington Traffic Safety Commission.

Table 8.23: Police injury coding methods, U.S. states. (Y = Yes, the method is used.)

	KABCO	Other	Categories and remarks
Alabama	Y		
Alaska		Y	As NYSICS, Table 8.7.
Arizona	Y		
Arkansas	Y		
California	Y		Code A is "severe", see Table 8.22.
Colorado	Y	Y	Head, chest, abdomen, skeletal.
Connecticut	Y		
Delaware	Y		
District of Columbia	Y	Y	Whether taken to hospital and whether admitted.
Florida	Y		
Georgia		Y	Killed, visible, complaint.
Hawaii: Honolulu	Y	Y	Condition of casualty if hospitalised: good/fair, serious/guarded, critical.
Hawaii: test form	Y	Y	Location of injury coded as by NYSICS, Table 8.7. Condition: refused treatment, released, good/ fair, serious/guarded, critical, dead on arrival, dead (other).
Idaho	Y		
Illinois	Y		
Indiana		Y	Almost identical to NYSICS, Table 8.7.
Iowa	Y	Y	Code A is "major". Location: upper torso, lower torso, internal, head, arms, legs, multiple, unknown.
Kansas	Y		
Kentucky	Y	Y	Location of injury coded similarly (not identically) to the NYSICS method, Table 8.7.
Louisiana		Y	Fatal, critical, serious, severe, moderate, minor, none - apparently an early version of the AIS, Section 8.7.1.
Maine	Y	Y	Location and type of injury coded similarly (not identically) to the NYSICS method, Table 8.7. Type: amputation, concussion, bleeding, burns, broken bones, abrasions/bruises, complaint of pain, shock, dizziness, other. Location: head, face, neck, back, arms, chest/stomach, internal, legs, entire body, other.
Maryland	Y		
Massachusetts	Y		
Michigan	Y	?	Method of coding not clear on the form, but other sources show the K, A, B, C, O system is used.
Minnesota	Y		
Mississippi	Y		
Missouri	Y		
Montana	Y		

Table 8.23: (continued).

	KABCO	Other	Categories and remarks
Nebraska	Y		
Nevada	?	Y	The "class" (presumably the severity) and the location of injury are recorded. Methods of coding not clear.
New Hampshire	Y		
New Jersey	Y	Y	Location of injury coded as by NYSICS, Table 8.7. Type of injury: amputation, concussion, internal, bleeding, burn, fracture/dislocation, contusion/bruise/abrasion, complaint of pain, none visible.
New Mexico	Y		
New York		Y	NYSICS, see Table 8.7.
North Carolina	Y		
North Dakota	Y		
Ohio	Y		See Table 8.22 for a comment on the definition of code A.
Oklahoma	Y	Y	Head, trunk (external), trunk (internal), arm/leg.
Oregon	Y		
Pennsylvania	?	?	Method of coding not clear.
Rhode Island	Y		
South Carolina	Y		
South Dakota	Y		
Tennessee	Y		
Texas	Y		
Utah	?	?	Method of coding not clear.
Vermont	Y		
Virginia	Y		
Washington	Y	?	Method of coding not clear on the form, but other sources show the K, A, B, C, O system is used.
West Virginia	Y		
Wisconsin	Y	Y	Head, trunk (external), trunk (internal), arm, leg.
Wyoming	Y	Y	Fatal (autopsy), fatal (diagnosis), fatal (not documented), hospitalised, treated and released, first aid at scene, no treatment, unknown.
Puerto Rico		Y	Killed, serious, slight.
U.S. Virgin Islands	Y		Fatals are divided into dead at scene, dead on arrival, died in hospital.

slight differences in the terms they use, it is likely that the first 10 states in the table are using the National Safety Council's codes. As the footnotes point out, however, the remaining 4 states are less comparable, 2 because the data refers to a selected sample, and 2 because they use the term "severe" in describing the most serious category.

Carroll and Scott (1971) and Scott (1972) also show that variability exists within states: specifically, for 8 heavily-populated counties of Michigan, the proportion of A injuries varied from 21% to 37%, and the proportion of C injuries varied from 38% to 58%, these differences occurring despite using the same accident report form and there being a single state accident reporting law.

In 1971 in Michigan, the definitions of the K, A, B, C, 0 categories were made more precise. As a result, the proportion of A injuries fell sharply (Scott, 1972). Sherman et al (1976) claimed to have shown that the new definitions more closely reflected AIS score than the old ones did (compare parts (a) and (b) of Table 8.26 below).

In 1977, Pennsylvania changed from a property damage accident being reportable if any vehicle sustained damage costing $200 or more to repair to a criterion of a vehicle needing to be towed away. Thus many accidents previously reportable became non-reportable. An incidental effect of this was to lower the threshold between damage-only and injury accidents. Previously, an accident resulting in cuts and bruises and substantial but not towaway damage would (or might) have been put down as damage-only. After the change, if someone wanted the accident to go on the record (for insurance reasons), it could only do so if it were labelled as an injury accident (Loukissas and Schultz, 1985).

Baldwin (1981) mentions in passing that an apparent sharp decrease in traffic accident injuries in a U.S. city was found to be the result of changing to only reporting those admitted to hospital as being injured.

8.10.3   Other U.S. police methods

Not all U.S. states use the categories described above—for instance, the New York State Injury Coding Scheme has already been described in Section 8.6.3 and Table 8.7. The report referenced at NHTSA (1986) is a published compilation of police accident report forms from all 50 states (plus the District of Columbia, Puerto Rico, and the U.S.

Table 8.24: Percentages of fatalities dying at various stages of treatment, Utah, 1979*.

	Urban	Rural
Died before treatment	28	58
Died en route to hospital	36	22
Emergency room death	13	6
Admitted to hospital	19	9
Transferred hospital	5	5
Number of deaths	154	172

* Average time from receipt of call to delivering the casualty to the emergency room was 37 minutes in urban areas and 90 minutes in rural areas.
Source:
Utah Vehicular Trauma. Injury and Death Associated with Fatal Accidents. Utah Department of Health.

Virgin Islands). From this, it is clear in most cases what codes each state is using. Table 8.23 shows the methods. In summary, the K, A, B, C, 0 codes are used by at least 44 jurisdictions, and other methods by at least 18; in some cases both the former and another method are employed.

8.11   Severity: Other methods

8.11.1   Time till death

In some countries, fatalities are distinguished according to the time they survived before dying. Some Belgian data on this was given in Table 7.13. The most elaborate such classification that I know of is that of Morocco, where four categories are used (see Section 12.15).

In the study by Reinfurt et al (1978) using the Illinois Trauma Registry, 34% of fatalities were dead at the scene, 18% were dead on arrival at hospital, 7% died within an hour, a further 9% between 1 and 6 hours, 5% between 6 and 24 hours, and 27% survived at least 24 hours. Table 8.24 shows at what stage of their treatment people died in urban and rural areas of Utah. No doubt one of the reasons for the differences evident there is the shorter time elapsing in urban areas before the casualty reaches hospital.

Table 8.25: The Injury Severity Scale developed in the Northern Metropolitan region of the N.S.W. Department of Health.

Rating	Typical time in hospital	Typical period of disability
1 Trivial	20 mins	1 day
2 Minor	90 mins	5 days
3 Moderate	1 day	14 days
4 Severe*	7 days	6 weeks
5 Very severe	4 weeks	18 weeks
6 Very severe & secondary disability	18 weeks	52 weeks
7 Dead on arrival#		
8 Died in hospital#		

* Most fractures are rated as 4. This contrasts with the AIS, where most simple fractures are rated 2.

This is how the scale appears in Jones (1984), but presumably a quick death ought to be rated more severe than one that was delayed.

8.11.2 Finland

Honkanen (1984, Section 3.5.8) mentions that in Finland, traffic insurance companies use a 6-category code for severity of injury when deciding the amount of monetary compensation for pain. It is based on the nature of injury, need of treatment, and resulting disability.

8.11.3 Injury Severity Scale (N.S.W.)

Jones (1984) describes a scale intended as a practical way of organising and comparing survey data collected on all types of presentations at hospital accident and emergency departments. It is based principally on an estimate of the approximate period of disability resulting from a patient's injury or injuries. The information used includes the part(s) of the body injured, the nature of injuries, the age and sex of the patient, the description of the accident, and the patient's treatment (including whether he or she was admitted, and, if so, for how long). I can disagree with some things in this list—the inclusion of the accident description, for example, and at A.D.C in Section 8.7.3 above I have argued that age should be disregarded—but the scale is very interesting in the attempt it makes to discriminate between levels of slight injury, which the AIS (Section 8.7) does poorly. The scale is as in Table 8.25.

Jones admits the poor methodologic basis of this scale: "There is an element of subjectivity in making the estimates, partly because guidelines for using the scale have been transmitted orally through several generations of personnel. The reliability (inter-rater or test-retest) of the scale has not been established. The scale has not been validated against similar severity measures." As discussed at C.E in 8.7.3 above, however, there is need for differentiating levels of severity within the slight injury range: it would be extremely valuable if a positive correlation could be established between (for instance) the proportion of cases having grades 2–8 on this scale and the proportion having grades 3–6 on the AIS.

8.11.4 Sheffield Children's Hospital grades

Five grades of injury have been used in studies of casualties attending Sheffield Children's Hospital. The following descriptions are taken from Illingworth et al (1981); data from the same paper will be given in Table 10.14.

Grade 1: So trivial that no treatment or follow-up needed.

Grade 2: Minor wounds and soft tissue injuries, bruises, undisplaced fractures of fingers or toes.

Grade 3: More serious wounds, undisplaced fractures for which admission was not required, minor head injury, minimally displaced greenstick fractures.

Grade 4: Fractures for which admission was essential, seriously displaced fractures which needed manipulation under anaesthesia, head injuries and concussion or fracture.

Grade 5: Injuries such as ruptured viscus or serious head injury in which there was a potential risk to life.

8.11.5 Reinfurt et al (1978)

These authors report an attempt to develop scales for threat to life, disability (financial consequences rather than functional limitations), and direct costs. Some aspects of this study have been discussed earlier in this Chapter. Mention should also be made of a grouping of the ICD codes into 43 categories (pp. 30–31 of their report), a description of 9 primary injury groups (p. 39), a listing of the categories used in the North Carolina Workmen's Compensation File (p. 63), and tables of the interrelationships between several injury coding systems (pp. 155–161).

8.11.6 Gibson (1981)

Gibson reviews a number of other indices of severity. Most of them are more clinically oriented than those we have considered. But, even so, Gibson says "the indices were found to depend on clinically subjective judgments, lacked clear or objective definitions, and offered little evidence that they could be used reliably... Only 5 of the 16 indices met even minimal methodologic criteria... It is concluded that a single severity index is neither desirable nor possible." But this is perhaps overly pessimistic: a scale that appears a poor predictor of survival on a patient-by-patient basis may nevertheless be adequate when applied in an epidemiologic context to hundreds or thousands of cases.

8.12 Severity: Some comparisons

8.12.1 American police codes and AIS

Table 8.26 gives data from three studies in which American police codes and AIS scores were cross-tabulated.

Part (a) shows results from 540 casualties attending the emergency room of a hospital in Ann Arbor, Michigan, whose injuries were coded according to the AIS (though it should be noted that the AIS has undergone substantial revisions since this study was conducted), and these scores were compared with the police codes assigned at the scene of the crash. In summary, for those at levels A, B, C, and 0, the percentages receiving AIS scores of 2 or above were respectively 36, 10, 9, and 6 (Carroll and Scott, 1971; Scott, 1972).

Part (b) of Table 8.26 is from Sherman et al (1976); the chief features of this sample were: crash location in Washtenaw County, Michigan; occupant injured in vehicle towed away from accident scene; fatalities were excluded.

A larger sample is that of Partyka (1982), using the National Crash Severity Study (see Section 8.7.2). Table 8.26(c) shows in what proportions the various AIS levels occurred for each police injury code. (For each casualty, the AIS shown is the maximum from what may be several injuries.) In this study, official medical data was required in order to assign an AIS code (except when there was no injury); this is the reason for the high missing data rate (especially among fatalities, since autopsies were not performed in many cases).

Finally, it appears that in the early days of the AIS it was intended that police codes 0, C, B, A, and K correspond with certain scores (or score ranges) of the AIS. But the evidence available to me is ambiguous as to what the intended correspondences were. The AIS chart in Fenner (1969) shows 0, 1, 2, 3–5, and 6–9, but those in the publications that first described the AIS and the Comprehensive Injury Scale (Committee on Medical Aspects of Injury Severity, 1971, 1972) both show 0, 1, 2–4, 5, and 6–9. The former is certainly more plausible.

8.12.2 British police criteria and TRRL's clinical scale

Grattan and Keigan (1975) found that of 293 casualties detained in hospital and classified as "serious" by British police criteria, 34% were regarded as having severe injury, 53% moderate, and 14% minor or no injury, when using the clinical scale developed at the Transport and Road Research Laboratory. (For this scale, see also Grattan, 1973.)

8.12.3 Administrative criteria

By this, I mean such matters as whether the casualty was admitted to hospital, the length of stay there, and the number of outpatient visits. Table 8.27 is taken from the Carroll and Scott (1971) study, and gives the percentages admitted to hospital for the various police and AIS codes; for the police codes, it includes also a sample from Detroit

Table 8.26: Percentage distribution over AIS level of casualties in the various police injury categories.

	K	A	B	C	0
		Police injury code			

(a) Carroll and Scott (1971)*

	K	A	B	C	0
AIS 0		1 (0)	2	8	22
1		62 (8)	87	83	72
2		21 (36)	7	5	6
3		11 (42)	2	5	0
4		2 (10)	1	0	0
5		1 (4)	0	0	0
Total number		302 (73)	134	86	18

(b) Sherman et al (1976)

	K	A	B	C	0
AIS 0		0	0	4	34
1		39	79	84	64
2		25	15	8	2
3		24	5	4	0
4		6	0	0	0
5		5	0	0	0
Total number		463	408	199	143

(c) Partyka (1982)

	K	A	B	C	0
AIS 0	0	0	3	17	96
1	0	33	65	63	3
2	1	28	21	12	0
3	3	25	8	7	0
4	7	9	2	1	0
5	41	4	0	0	0
6	47	0	0	0	0
Total number (above)	401	4033	4520	2632	9835
Total number (incl unknown AIS)	927	5333	6969	5146	11874

* Figures in brackets refer to casualties who were admitted to hospital. There were only 10 such cases for codes B, C, 0 combined, so the percentage AIS distribution is not shown for these.

cited by Carroll and Scott; for the AIS, both Table 8.27 and Table 8.28 (on average length of hospital stay) include also data from the 1983 (U.S.) National Accident Sampling System (NASS, 1985).

For casualties attending Battle Hospital, Reading, Grattan and Keigan (1975) cross-tabulated length of hospital stay and the categories of TRRL's clinical scale—see Table 8.29. Table 8.30 shows data on the relationship between AIS and

length of stay from Britain (Hobbs et al, 1979) and from Sri Lanka (Sayer and Hitchcock, 1984). Part (a) of Table 8.31 shows data on the relationship between Injury Severity Score and length of stay; this is from a Swedish study using insurance data, other aspects of which will be discussed in Section 14.6.1 (Nygren, c. 1984).

Like length of stay in hospital, the number of out-patient visits is a measure of severity that is

Table 8.27: Percentages of casualties admitted to hospital.

Police injury code*

A	B	C
24	5	3
(32)	(19)	(12)

AIS code#

0	1	2	3	4	5
6	2	39	79	100	100
	(3)	(36)	(76)	(97)	(100)

* Figures in brackets refer to a sample from Detroit.
# Figures in brackets refer to survivors included in the National Accident Sampling System, 1983.

Table 8.28: Average number of days in hospital of casualties admitted.

Police injury code

A	B	C
4	5	11

AIS code*

0	1	2	3	4	5
2	3	6	15	10	30
	(4)	(7)	(13)	(24)	(53)

* Figures in brackets refer to survivors included in the National Accident Sampling System, 1983.

convenient for some purposes as it relies only on administrative information, not clinical. Table 8.32 shows some data from the study by Partyka (1982) mentioned in Section 8.12.1 above.

Part (b) of Table 8.31 cross-tabulates Injury Severity Score and length of sick leave; the data is from Nygren (c. 1984).

Table 8.29: Numbers of cases classified jointly by length of stay in hospital and TRRL's clinical scale of severity (survivors only).

	Minor	Moderate	Severe
(Total cases = 291)			
0-48 hours	33	84	3
2-10 days	6	58	28
11-28 days	1	7	34
29 days - 3 months	0	2	25
Over 3 months	0	0	10

8.12.4 AIS and Glasgow Outcome Scale

For 434 patients admitted to the University of Pennsylvania Head Injury Center—this sample is much more severe than one typically encountered at an emergency room, or even among in-patients—Gennarelli (1980) reports how the AIS score for brain injury relates to the following: Glasgow Outcome Scale (see Table 8.33), Glasgow Coma Score, length of hospitalisation, days in intensive care, hospital charges.

8.12.5 ISS and consumption of hospital resources

Both Brismar et al (1982) and Lindstruom et al (1982) give some data from Goteborg on the consumption of various hospital resources by road accident patients having various severities of injury as measured by the Injury Severity Score.

8.12.6 ISS and the metabolism of the casualty

Metabolic measures of severity of injury are so distant from the central concern of this book that I will merely mention the recent paper by Winthrop et al (1987) and its references as starting points for reading.

8.12.7 How serious is the second most serious injury?

Table 8.34, taken from the studies by Partyka (1982) mentioned in Section 8.12.1 and by Ulman

Table 8.30: Numbers of cases classified jointly by length of stay in hospital and AIS score (survivors only).

	A I S				
	1	2	3	4	5
(a) Reading, U.K. (total cases = 3447)					
Not taken to hospital	43	1	0	0	0
Out-patient	1952	446	42	0	0
0 nights*	19	59	5	0	0
1 night	44	233	12	0	0
2 nights	13	78	22	0	0
3-10 nights	13	110	93	3	1
11-100 nights	1	32	181	18	5
101+ nights	0	0	11	3	7
(b) Colombo (total cases = 2510)					
0 nights*	41	140	15	1	0
1 night	22	373	54	0	2
2 nights	7	290	68	5	0
3-10 nights	9	503	387	38	6
11-100 nights	1	58	326	74	23
101+ nights	2	28	29	6	2

* Admitted as in-patients but did not stay overnight.

Table 8.31: Numbers of cases classified by length of stay in hospital, length of sick leave, and Injury Severity Score.

	(a) The length of time shown being the length of stay in hospital (car occupants, aged 15 or more, survivors only)			(b) The length of time shown being the length of sick leave (car occupants, aged 18-65, survivors only)		
	I S S			I S S		
	1-3	4-10	11+	1-3	4-10	11+
	(Total cases = 2732)			(Total cases = 2396)		
0 days	1393	459	26	636	77	2
1-7 days	108	200	82	172	28	1
8-14 days	11	61	74	162	74	6
15-30 days	5	69	72	210	142	24
31-160 days	1	49	101	133	331	146
161-365 days	0	2	13	15	73	96
366+ days	0	0	6	3	17	48

Table 8.32: Percentage distribution over numbers of out-patient visits of casualties* in the various AIS categories.

		A I S				
		1	2	3	4	5
Number	0	46	17	5	4	11
of	1	28	26	16	11	6
out-patient	2-6	20	44	52	43	26
visits	7 or more	5	13	27	42	56
Total number (above)		4236	1390	775	206	62
Total number (incl unknown number of visits)		6382	2452	1608	469	157

* In preparing this Table, fatalities were excluded. They were assumed to have made no out-patient visits.

Table 8.33: Cross-tabulation of AIS-Brain and Glasgow Outcome Scale.

		Outcome, 1 month after injury				
		Good	Moderately disabled	Severely disabled	Vegetative survival	Dead
AIS-Brain*	0	2	0	0	0	0
	1	24	0	0	0	0
	2	54	1	0	0	0
	3	110	8	10	0	3
	4	65	13	15	0	4
	5	13	13	33	19	47

* The higher score from either of the brain sections (anatomic or non-anatomic) of AIS-80 was used.

and Stalnaker (1986) mentioned in Section 8.7.2,
gives some evidence on this question.

Table 8.34: Evidence about the severity of other injuries compared with the maximum severity: Percentage distribution over the second-highest AIS code for casualties in the various maximum AIS categories.

	Maximum AIS					
	1	2	3	4	5	6
(a) Partyka (1982)						
Second-highest AIS 0	19	8	6	5	2	12
1	81	70	36	20	12	10
2	0	22	35	18	8	11
3	0	0	24	42	18	10
4	0	0	0	15	30	14
5	0	0	0	0	30	21
6	0	0	0	0	0	21
Total number	6308	2437	1611	503	371	187
(b) Ulman and Stalnaker (1986)						
Second-highest AIS 0	36	9	4	4	3	?
1	64	68	35	15	12	?
2	0	23	31	16	6	?
3	0	0	29	45	29	?
4	0	0	0	21	29	?
5	0	0	0	0	21	?
Total number	21793	4260	2048	429	341	192

Chapter 9

Data from death certificates

9.1 Introduction

Data collected and published by health authorities can supplement police data about road accidents. There are two main points at which a form is filled in and so can serve as a source of statistics—when a death certificate is made out, and when someone is medically treated, e.g. as a hospital in-patient.

This Chapter deals with data from death registration systems. The next one will turn to hospital in-patient statistics. The following will be the main issues in this Chapter:

- Comparison between different countries in the cause of death reported.

- The trends over time in the cause of death.

- The effect of road user category.

For brief descriptions of the death certification and registration process in 31 countries, see Chapter 2 of Alderson (1981). (The bulk of that book is a series of tables of causes of death in those 31 countries during the twentieth century.) As to developing countries, there is a comparison of the processing of death (and other vital) statistics in five of them in NCHS (1980). In 1976–79, the Statistical Office of the United Nations Secretariat carried out a survey of vital statistics methods; data from 105 countries is published in UN (1985). This includes a table of what items of information are collected about the death (e.g. cause, date, place) and the dead person (e.g. age, ethnic group, occupation) in the various countries. The information is not detailed enough to indicate the completeness or reliability of data for any particular cause of death, such as road accidents.

Refer to Section 8.4.1 for a fuller description of the injury groups than is given by their names. In particular, AN138 includes fractures of the face bones, as well as the skull proper; this is presumably unimportant for deaths, but certainly is important for hospital patients.

9.2 International comparisons

As I have called attention to previously (Hutchinson, 1981, 1984), there are substantial differences between countries in the proportions in which the major causes of death occur in road accidents. Thus, as shown in Table 9.1, 36% of deaths were ascribed to skull fracture in England and Wales in 1985, whereas in Denmark (1979) and South Africa (1978) the corresponding proportion was less than 10%. There is even a wide range in the ratio of head injuries (AN138 or 143) to body injuries (AN139 or 144).

9.3 Trends

Substantial changes over time can be seen in Table 9.1. As mentioned in Section 8.4.2, what happened in Denmark in 1977 was a coding change. Leaving this aside, the proportion of deaths ascribed to skull fracture approximately halved over about 20 years in Scotland, Norway, and South Africa; the proportion in AN143 (injuries within the head, skull fractures being excluded) doubled between 1958 and 1977 in Italy; and the proportion in AN144 (internal injuries of the body) more than doubled in several countries over the periods considered. (For head injuries specifically, and their trends, see Jennett and MacMillan, 1981.)

Despite the large differences between countries that have been remarked on above, there is a degree of consistency in the trends that have occurred. The decline in skull fracture and the rise in internal injuries occurs in most countries. And in

Table 9.1: Percentage distribution of the nature of injury causing death in road accidents, as shown in official statistics of eighteen jurisdictions.

	England and Wales		Scotland Note [1]		Northern Ireland		Irish Rep	Denmark Note [2]				Norway		Belgium Note [3]		Italy	
	1958	85	1961	81	1968	80	1979	1951	76	77	79	1959	80	1965	78	1958	77
Skull fracture AN138	50	36	44	23	47	31	35	60	52	7	8	48	24	58	33	68	36
Fracture of spine and trunk AN139	11	9	11	8	16	10	8	14	11	5	4	6	8	7	4	68	36
Intracranial inj, excl skull fracture AN143	11	13	30	34	13	8	13	11	11	53	52	18	30	7	24	14	32
Internal inj of chest, abdomen, pelvis AN144	13	31	9	32	19	41	32	6	20	24	24	11	17	7	4	10	20
Others AN140-142,145-150	14	11	6	4	5	10	12	9	5	11	11	17	21	21	35	8	12
Total number	5439	4914	398	718	219	287	644	423	867	838	734	307	379	2425	2583	8112	10435

	Hungary		Ontario		Saskatchewan		USA [4]	Vermont [5]	Japan Note [6]		South Africa Note [7]		Macau Note [8]	Switzerland Note [9]		Victoria [10]
	1968	81	1950	76	1950	78	1979	82-83	1958	80	1963	78		1968	80	83-86
Skull fracture AN138	57	54	47	27	40	29	21#	19#	48	34	20	9	56	42	25	14
Fracture of spine and trunk AN139	13	17	11	6	5	15			10+	10+	7	2	3	10	11	6@
Intracranial inj, excl skull fracture AN143	*	*	10	17	11	16	24	25	24	30	20	27	18	11	15	20
Internal inj of chest, abdomen, pelvis AN144	24	20	20	44	37	25	21	30	12	17	52	57	10	21	31	38@
Others AN140-142,145-150	6	9	13	6	7	15	33	27	6+	9+	2	5	13	17	17	22
Total number	1290	1687	836	1496	98	257	87065	454	8883	11752	1702	1830	165	2040	1791	6053

* For Hungary, intracranial injuries and skull fractures are shown together.

For USA and Vermont, all fractures, sprains, and dislocations, whether to the head, body, or limbs, are shown together.

+ For Japan, limb fractures (AN140) are included with fractures of the spine and trunk, not with "others".

@ For Victoria, chest fractures (N807) are included with internal injuries, not with fractures of the spine and trunk.

the two jurisdictions for which such a comparison is possible (England and Wales, and Switzerland), it occurs in all categories of road user, as will be shown below in Tables 9.2 and 9.3. There also appears to be a general trend away from fractures (both skull and body) to soft tissue injuries (both head and body).

9.4 Injuries to the several categories and ages of road user

In the tables of causes of death produced by the Office of Population Censuses and Surveys for England and Wales, the major categories of road user (motor vehicle occupants, motorcyclists, pedal cyclists, pedestrians) are distinguished, using the fourth digit of the ICD codes. I do not know of any other jurisdiction which does this, but data

Numbered notes for Table 9.1:

[1] In Scotland, there is a strong and increasing tendency for "multiple injuries" to be specified on death certificates, which is coded to AN150. The percentages given in this Table are therefore based on the total excluding the AN150 category ("All other and unspecified injuries"). The AN150 category comprised 22% of the total in 1961 and 46% of the total in 1981. Data for 1961 is for July–December only.

[2] In Denmark in 1977 there was a change in coding practice which transferred a large number of cases from AN138 to AN143 and from AN139 to AN144. Danish police data also gives nature of injury sustained by persons killed or seriously injured—see Section 12.5.1.

[3] The Belgian data includes railway fatalities. However, motor vehicle accidents account for some 99% of the figures given.

[4] The distribution shown is that of 87065 injuries to the 54479 persons killed who had motor vehicle accident mentioned on their death certificate. 952 of these had no nature of injury condition specified; for 955 of the deaths, motor vehicle accident was not the underlying cause of death.

[5] The distribution shown is that of 454 injuries to the 192 persons killed who had motor vehicle accident mentioned on their death certificate. For 187 of these, it was the underlying cause.

[6] Japanese police data also gives nature of injury sustained. See Section 12.13.1.

[7] Whites, Coloureds, and Asians only. Although registration of deaths of Blacks is not complete, figures are published, and the distribution of causes of death in road accidents in 1978 was very similar to that for other racial groups.

[8] For Macau, the data is for years 1964-79, excluding 1968, 1975, and 1977.

[9] The Swiss data is collected by the police, though they apparently consult death certificates, and is published in the road accidents annual. The injuries are cross-tabulated with the accident events and category of road user, and are given separately for seriously injured persons as well as for those killed. The ICD codes are not shown, so it was necessary to make certain assumptions in converting the categories used to approximately-equivalent ICD classes. Up to two serious injuries may be given for each casualty. Hence the total numbers shown exceed the numbers of persons killed.

[10] The distribution shown is that of 6053 injuries to the 1910 persons killed. The data comes from the insurance body, the Motor Accidents Board (see Section 14.3), not from death registration. It refers to the 3-year period ending June 1986.

Sources (Table 9.1):

England and Wales. Mortality Statistics, Accidents and Violence. Series DH4. London: HMSO.

Scotland. Annual Report of the Registrar-General Scotland. Edinburgh: HMSO.

Northern Ireland. Annual Report of the Registrar General Northern Ireland. Belfast: HMSO.

Irish Republic. Report on Vital Statistics. Dublin: The Stationery Office.

Denmark. Dodsarsagerne i Kongeriget Danmark. Kobenhavn: Sundhedsstyrelsen. (ISSN 0303 6642.)

Norway. Helsestatistikk. Oslo: Statistisk Sentralbyra. (ISSN 0332-7906.)

Belgium. Statistique des Causes de Deces. Bruxelles: Institut National de Statistique.

Italy. Annuario di Statistiche Sanitarie. Roma: Istituto Centrale di Statistica. (ISSN 0075-1758.)

Hungary. Demografiai Evkonyv. Budapest: Kozponti Statisztikai Hivatal. (ISSN 0073-4020.)

Ontario. Vital Statistics. Toronto: Registrar General of Ontario. (ISSN 0701-7170.)

Saskatchewan. Vital Statistics Annual Report. Regina: Saskatchewan Health. (ISSN 0710-670X.)

USA. Israel et al (1986). For 1978 data, see Chamblee et al (1983).

Vermont. Annual Report of Vital Statistics in Vermont. Burlington: Department of Health.

Japan. Vital Statistics Japan. Volume 3. Tokyo: Ministry of Health and Welfare.

South Africa. Report on Deaths. Pretoria: Department of Statistics.

Macau. Anuario Estatistico. Macau: Reparticao dos Servicos de Estatistica.

Switzerland. Strassenverkehrsunfalle in der Schweiz. Bern: Bundesamt fur Statistik.

Victoria. Statistics of Persons Killed or Injured. Melbourne: Motor Accidents Board.

Table 9.2: Percentage distribution of the causes of death of the several categories of road user, in five countries or states.

	England and Wales								Victoria*			
	Motor veh occupants		Motor cyclists		Pedal cyclists		Pedest'ns		M v occs	Mcs	Pcs	Peds
	1958	1985	1958	1985	1958	1985	1958	1985	1986	1986	1986	1986
Skull fracture AN138	40	32	62	36	62	50	48	39	13	15	18	15
Fracture of spine and trunk AN139	12	8	5	5	8	5	15	12	5	5	4	11
Intracranial inj, excl skull fracture AN143	8	11	12	12	11	20	12	15	18	19	33	23
Internal inj of chest, abdomen, pelvis AN144	24	36	11	36	10	18	9	24	44	42	31	29
Others AN140-142,145-150	15	13	10	11	9	8	16	10	20	19	13	22
Total number	1140	2091	1355	792	638	306	2281	1732	1459	264	67	447

	Switzerland#										Irish Rep Peds	West'n Aust'a Pedal cyc's
	Car occupants		Motor cyclists		Pedal cyclists		Pedest'ns		Others			
	1968	1980	1968	1980	1968	1980	1968	1980	1968	1980	1979	71-80
Skull fracture AN138	32	19	53	34	56	34	43	27	31	28	36	85
Fracture of spine and trunk AN139	11	12	10	11	6	10	10	12	13	12	9	7
Intracranial inj, excl skull fracture AN143	10	14	12	17	13	24	10	14	7	16	18	2
Internal inj of chest, abdomen, pelvis AN144	31	43	9	19	14	19	18	23	36	23	29	7
Others AN140-142,145-150	17	13	16	19	11	13	19	25	13	21	8	0
Total number	649	809	419	415	174	113	704	397	94	57	243	61

* Year ended June 1986. See also notes @ and [10] to Table 9.1.
# See Note [9] to Table 9.1.
Sources:
As Table 9.1; Lugg (1982) is the source of the data for Western Australia.

Table 9.3: Percentage distribution of the causes of death of motorcyclists in Switzerland.

	With crash helmet		Without crash helmet	
	1968	1980	1968	1980
Skull fracture AN138	46	26	56	32
Fracture of spine and trunk AN139	17	20	7	6
Intracranial injury, excl skull fracture AN143	10	14	14	19
Internal injury of chest, abdomen, pelvis AN144	12	20	7	18
Others AN140-142,145-150	15	21	16	24
Total number*	72	116	161	103

* The totals do not correspond to those of Table 9.2 because riders of "cyclomoteurs" ("motorfahrrad") have been excluded from this Table.
Source:
As Table 9.1.

from the Irish Republic is tabulated according to the 3-digit ICD code, thus enabling persons killed in accidents involving a collision with a pedestrian (nearly all of whom are pedestrians) to be identified. The police statistics of a few countries include information about the main injury sustained, enabling its relationship with many factors to be investigated. Such data will be examined in Chapter 12.

Table 9.2 shows the causes of death separately for the major categories of road user in England and Wales, Victoria, and Switzerland, and for single categories of road user in the Irish Republic and Western Australia. Table 9.3 shows the trend away from head injuries is not for motorcyclists a result of increased wearing of crash helmets, suggesting that neither is it the result of trends in vehicle design or accident circumstances in other categories of road user.

For England and Wales, Table 9.4 compares three age groups, within the categories of road user. A greater proportion of the elderly than of younger people succumb to survivable injuries such as limb fractures. The proportion of deaths due to head injury is correspondingly higher in the young.

9.5   Discussion

Table 9.1 shows that there are large differences between countries and over time in the nature of injury reported as causing death, and Table 9.2 shows that for at least two jurisdictions the trends are common to the separate categories of road user. There seem to be three groups of possible reasons for the differences between countries and, within countries, the trends over time, that are evident in Table 9.1:

- What it is customary to write on the death certificate and how this is coded. How those with multiple injuries are described and coded may be included here.

- The treatment of injuries, so the decline in deaths from skull fractures might be attributable to improved treatment of such injuries.

- The crash environment of casualties, so that important contributing factors will include the wearing of seat belts or crash helmets, vehicle design, and so on.

I suggest that it is highly desirable to know the relative contributions of these three groups, but I

Table 9.4: Percentage distribution of the causes of death in three age groups of road user, England and Wales, 1983–85.

		Motor veh drivers		Motor vehicle passengers			Mcs
		15-64	65+	0-14	15-64	65+	15-64
Skull fracture	AN138	34	13	51	35	13	35
Fracture of spine and trunk	AN139	7	16	9	7	21	6
Intracranial injury, excl skull fracture	AN143	10	7	13	12	7	12
Internal injury of chest, abdomen, pelvis	AN144	37	43	23	34	34	36
Others AN140-142,145-150		12	20	3	12	26	10
Total number		3084	500	210	1907	485	2583

		Pedal cyclists			Pedestrians			Total		
		0-14	15-64	65+	0-14	15-64	65+	0-14	15-64	65+
Skull fracture	AN138	54	53	44	46	44	35	49	37	29
Fracture of spine and trunk	AN139	5	5	8	10	7	15	9	7	16
Intracranial injury, excl skull fracture	AN143	21	15	17	19	12	11	18	11	10
Internal injury of chest, abdomen, pelvis	AN144	15	22	15	21	29	24	20	34	28
Others AN140-142,145-150		5	6	16	5	7	15	4	10	17
Total number		239	567	157	897	2094	2387	1349	10263	3538

Source:
As Table 9.1.

do not think definite evidence is available at the moment. Certainly it is clear from the ICD Manual that the aim is to be consistent in time and space. Writing about death statistics generally, Myers (1976) says "the value of cross-national investigations hinges basically on the comparability of the statistics utilised", and this applies as much to road trauma as to other causes.

For a discussion of some of the problems encountered in certifying a cause of death, see, for instance, Bennett et al (1979), and Harris and French (1980). There have been many studies of the validity of the cause of death stated on the death certificate, and the errors made—Glasser (1981) gives a general discussion, and Gittelsohn and Royston (1982) present an annotated bibliography of 128 items—but I have found little specif-

Table 9.5: Percentage distribution of disease conditions mentioned along with motor vehicle accident on the death certificate—U.S.A., 1978.

	Motor vehicle accident being the underlying cause of death	The disease being the underlying cause of death
Neoplasms	1	3
Mental disorders	10	2
Circulatory diseases	42	55
Respiratory diseases	20	16
Digestive diseases	4	8
Symptoms/signs/ill-defined	23	16
Total number of disease groups	7804	1487
Total number of deaths	7168	1096

Source:
Chamblee et al (1983).

ically about violent deaths. Concerning head injuries, Selecki et al (c. 1981) remark in passing that "the pathologist not uncommonly overestimates the role of small haemorrhages as the cause of death, tending to underestimate the often associated role of brain stem contusion".

Finally, a note about medical conditions not related to the trauma which are sometimes mentioned on death certificates of road crash victims: in the U.S.A. in 1978, there were 53,555 deaths to U.S. residents for which motor vehicle accident was mentioned on the death certificate. In 1096 cases, a disease rather than the motor vehicle accident was selected as the underlying cause of death; the relative frequencies of various groups of diseases are shown in Table 9.5. Among the remainder, there were 7168 deaths for which a disease condition was mentioned on the death certificate; the relative frequencies of these are also included in Table 9.5.

To supplement Table 9.5, Table 9.6 gives some data for North Carolina and Pennsylvania, and Table 9.7 does for North Carolina and Vermont. For North Carolina, another condition was mentioned in 15% of cases where the motor vehicle accident was the underlying cause; for Pennsylvania, the corresponding figure is 8%, if the 1351 other mentions of accident conditions (maybe nature of in-jury codes?) are ignored; for the USA as a whole, the figure was 14% in both 1978 (Chamblee et al, 1983) and 1979 (Israel et al, 1986). For North Carolina, deaths in which motor vehicle accident was mentioned but was not selected as the underlying cause of death were 1% of those in which it was; for Vermont, the corresponding figure is 3%; for the USA as a whole, it was 2% in both 1978 (Chamblee et al, 1983; NCHS, 1984) and 1979 (comparing the frequencies in Tables 4 and 8 of Israel et al, 1986).

Table 9.6: Frequency with which other conditions are mentioned on the death certificate when motor vehicle accident is the underlying cause of death—North Carolina and Pennsylvania.

	North Carolina 1983	Pennsyl -vania 1982
Diseases of heart	67	93
Other diseases	39	56
Alcohol	75	?
Accidents (not m.v.) & adverse effects	7	1351*
Homicide	0	1
Total deaths for which m.v.a. was the underlying cause	1282	1855

* Some quirk in the tabulating system, evidently.
Sources:
North Carolina.   Leading Causes of Mortality. North Carolina Vital Statistics 1983—Volume 2. Raleigh: State Center for Health Statistics.
Pennsylvania. As Table 8.2.

Table 9.7: Frequency with which motor vehicle accident is mentioned when another condition (as shown) is the underlying cause of death—North Carolina and Vermont.

	North Carolina 1983	Vermont 1982-83
Diseases of heart	10	5
Other	5	
Total deaths for which m.v.a. was the underlying cause	1282	183

Sources:
North Carolina. As Table 9.6.
Vermont. As Table 8.2.

Chapter 10

Nature of injury, hospital patients

10.1 Introduction

Hospital statistics systems provide useful information on the nature of injury in road crashes, and such data is the concern of this Chapter. (Nature of injury as recorded by the police or another source will be discussed in Chapter 12.) See also Nordentoft (1975) for comments on the accident information available from hospitals in the context of that from police, insurance, and other sources; and WHO (1979b) for how health information systems can be improved with respect to road accidents.

Refer to Section 8.4.1 for a fuller description of the injury groups than is given by their names. In particular, AN138 includes fractures of the face bones, as well as the skull proper.

10.2 In-patient statistical systems

10.2.1 England and Wales

In England and Wales, there is a one-in-ten survey of persons leaving hospital, known as the Hospital In-Patient Enquiry (HIPE). See, for example, Anderson (1978), Goldacre (1985), and references cited by them. The annual reports of this give some information about road accident casualties as a single group, the several categories not being distinguished. (Road accident casualties are identified through use of a single special code on the HIPE form, ICD E codes not being used.) The relative frequencies of the most common groups of injuries are shown in Table 10.1. As to trends over time, HIPE road accident data for 1962–67 has been examined in Chapter 7 of HIPE (1979) and for 1964–73 by Hutchinson and Harris (1978).

There were only slight changes over that period, though within the AN143 group of injuries (intracranial injuries, excluding skull fracture), there was a decrease in those reported as concussion (N850) and a corresponding rise in the remainder of the group (N851-N854). (For head injuries and their trends, see also Jennett and MacMillan, 1981.)

In some areas, additional information is available, albeit not routinely published. According to Philipp (1984), replying to a letter (Cryer et al, 1984) criticising his earlier paper (Philipp, 1983), E codes were at that time used for accident victims throughout seven of the Regional Health Authorities, in parts of four RHA's, but not (owing to resource limitations) in the remaining four RHA's. This use of E codes occurs as part of Hospital Activity Analysis (HAA), which applies to all patients (not 10%) at the RHA level and from which the HIPE sample is taken. Unpublished data for the East Anglian RHA and about half of the South East Thames RHA for the years 1980–81 was kindly provided to me by these RHA's; it contributes additional information in the following three respects.

- Nature of injury may be tabulated according to category of road user (Table 10.2) as well as in total (Table 10.1).

- More than one diagnosis may be given: whereas in Tables 10.1 and 10.2 only the first diagnosis is shown, Table 10.3 gives the distribution of diagnoses other than the main one (up to 4 in number in the case of the East Anglian RHA, up to 3 for the S.E. Thames RHA).

- Table 10.4 is an example of a tabulation of nature of injury to 3-digit ICD detail. The much

210

Table 10.1: Percentage distribution of the nature of serious injury in road accidents, in eleven countries or regions.

	England & Wales [1] 1984	East Angl'n RHA [2] 1980 -1981	S.E. Thames RHA [3] 1980 -1981	Scot- land [2] 1980	New Zeal'd [3] 1984	NSW [4] 1983	West'n Aust'a [3] 1985	Macau [5] 1978 -1979	Switz- erland [6] 1980	Vict- oria [7] 1986	San Marino [8] 1972 -1980
Skull fracture AN138	6	5	6	5	9	8	14	11	7	9	22
Fracture of spine and trunk AN139	8	6	7	7	9	11		6	10	8*	
Fracture of upper limb N810-819	9	7	8	7	7	10	9	54	10	16	19
Fracture of lower limb N820-829	22	18	23	18	19	19	16		15	19	23
Intracranial inj, excl skull fracture AN143	37	44	35	39	29	17	25	28	36	17	34
Internal inj of chest, abdomen, pelvis AN144	2	2	2	2	6	4	3	1	5	18*	2
Others AN141-142,145-150	16	18	18	22	22	32	33	0#	16	13*	0+
Total number	5919	7576	10585	8523	10461	14531	3864	220	22260	12399	753

* See Note [7].

See Note [5].

+ See Note [8].

Numbered notes:

[1] Data for England and Wales is a 10% sample. The data shown is actually for England only.

[2] Victims of motor vehicle traffic accidents (E810–E819), plus pedal cyclist victims of other road vehicle accidents (E826–E829).

[3] Victims of motor vehicle traffic accidents (E810–E819).

[4] For NSW, separations classified as after care (692 cases), observation (239), or other condition (i.e. not an injury, 2550 cases) have been excluded.

[5] For Macau, the data shown excludes AN141–142,145–150, of which there were 157 cases.

[6] Data for Switzerland includes deaths and serious injuries. See also note [9] to Table 9.1.

[7] Data for Victoria includes persons sustaining non-fatal injuries, year ended 30th June 1986. The data shown excludes lacerations, contusions, and abrasions (of which there were 23865 cases), and sprains and strains (12541 cases). Chest fractures (N807) have here been included with internal injuries, not with fractures of the spine and trunk. There were 22813 injured persons.

[8] For San Marino, the data shown excludes AN141–142,145–150, of which there were 1727 cases.

Sources:

England and Wales. Hospital In-patient Enquiry. Main Tables. Series MB4. London: HMSO.

East Anglian Regional Health Authority. Personal communication.

South East Thames Regional Health Authority. Personal communication.

Scotland. Personal communication from the Information Services Division, Common Services Agency, Scottish Health Services.

New Zealand. Hospital and Selected Morbidity Data. Wellington: National Health Statistics Centre of the Department of Health. (ISSN 0548-9938.)

New South Wales. Hospital Admissions Due to Motor Vehicle Accidents 1981-1983. Health Services Information Bulletin No 5, Department of Health, New South Wales. (ISSN 0812-1872.)

Western Australia. Hospital Morbidity Statistics, Short-Stay Hospitals. Series A. Perth: Public Health Department.

Macau. As Table 9.1.

Switzerland. As Table 9.1.

Victoria. As Table 9.1.

San Marino. Annuario Statistico. Volume 2. San Marino: Ufficio Statale di Statistica.

Table 10.2: Percentage distribution of the nature of serious injury in the several categories of road user, in seven countries or regions.

	East Anglian RHA 1980-81					S.E.Thames RHA 1980-81			Scotland 1980				
	M v occs	Mcs	Pcs	Peds	Oths	M v occs	Mcs	Peds	M v occs	Mcs	Pcs	Peds	Oths
Skull fracture AN138	5	4	4	5	9	6	4	6	6	3	4	6	6
Fracture of spine and trunk AN139	10	4	2	4	6	9	4	7	10	4	2	7	6
Fracture of upper limb N810-819	4	11	11	4	4	8	11	5	5	13	12	5	6
Fracture of lower limb N820-829	10	31	13	25	13	15	39	29	10	31	11	26	17
Intracranial inj, excl skull fracture AN143	45	33	53	47	36	41	25	39	41	25	56	43	38
Internal inj of chest, abdomen, pelvis AN144	3	3	1	1	3	3	2	1	2	2	1	1	2
Others AN141-142,145-150	22	14	16	13	29	18	15	13	27	20	14	13	25
Total number	2792	1947	1593	940	304	2846	1404	1476	2868	1126	575	1701	2253

	New Zealand 1984					Switzerland 1980				
	M v occs	Mcs	Peds	Oths	M v nta*	Car occs	Mcs	Pcs	Peds	Oths
Skull fracture AN138	9	5	11	11	4	5	7	9	8	5
Fracture of spine and trunk AN139	11	7	10	8	5	14	6	6	8	16
Fracture of upper limb N810-819	5	10	4	7	10	8	13	12	9	10
Fracture of lower limb N820-829	9	34	26	13	26	9	21	14	22	12
Intracranial inj, excl skull fracture AN143	34	19	27	37	19	40	31	43	33	32
Internal inj of chest, abdomen, pelvis AN144	7	4	6	5	6	7	3	2	5	6
Others AN141-142,145-150	25	21	16	20	29	16	18	13	16	18
Total number	4801	3073	1143	1444	747	9350	6561	1838	3820	591

	New South Wales 1983						Victoria 1986			
	M v occs	Mcs	Pcs	Peds	Oths	All	M v occs	Mcs	Pcs	Peds
Skull fracture AN138	8	5	16	11	4	6	10	4	10	9
Fracture of spine and trunk AN139	14	6	5	10	6	9	8	5	3	11
Fracture of upper limb N810-819	6	17	6	8	6	8	14	30	19	13
Fracture of lower limb N820-829	11	27	18	29	9	15	13	32	29	35
Intracranial inj, excl skull fracture AN143	16	10	24	18	11	13	18	7	25	17
Internal inj of chest, abdomen, pelvis AN144	4	3	0	3	2	3	23	8	6	7
Others AN141-142,145-150	41	31	30	21	63	45	15	13	7	8
Total number	5720	3063	347	1949	6933	18012	8213	1871	487	1788

* Motor vehicle non-traffic accidents.
Sources:
As Table 10.1.

Table 10.3: Percentage distribution of subsidiary diagnoses of the several categories of road accident victims, in two areas of England.

	East Anglian RHA 1980-81					S.E.Thames RHA 1980-81		
	M v occs	Mcs	Pcs	Peds	All	M v occs	Mcs	All
Skull fracture AN138	7	5	8	7	7	6	4	6
Fracture of spine and trunk AN139	13	7	5	12	11	10	5	8
Fracture of upper limb N810-819	12	23	12	15	15	7	14	10
Fracture of lower limb N820-829	10	17	9	16	13	10	31	20
Intracranial inj, excl skull fracture AN143	5	5	6	6	5	31	20	25
Internal inj of chest, abdomen, pelvis AN144	5	4	1	2	4	3	2	3
Other (serious)*	7	9	5	5	8	33	24	29
Other (slight)#	41	30	54	36	37			
Total number	2481	1403	771	762	5172	2939	2397	15630

* The following ICD codes have been included in Other (serious): N830–839,870–871,885–887,895–897,900–909,930–999.
# The following ICD codes have been included in Other (slight): N840–848,872–884,889–894,910–929.

higher ratio of face fractures to skull fractures in motor vehicle occupants than among pedestrians is credible. An implication of general interest is that if we tried to convert ICD AN codes to severity scores, AN138 ought to receive a higher score for pedestrians than for vehicle occupants, because skull fractures are more life-threatening than face fractures. This illustrates that in any conversion from injury nature to injury severity, we should consider whether the categories of the former are sufficiently homogeneous to permit a unique score to be assigned.

A high frequency of head injury without skull fracture (AN143) is evident from Tables 10.1 and 10.2. Part of the reason for this is that, on the "better safe than sorry" principle, it is common to admit any patient who has been unconscious,

however briefly, following a head injury. How necessary is this? How much are the statistics thereby distorted? Weston (1981) reports that in Nottingham, a relaxation of the policy resulted in the number of admissions for head injury being halved. After the change of policy, patients who had been briefly unconscious or amnesic (i.e. only for 1–2 minutes) were admitted if one of the following factors was also present: abnormal neurological signs or obtunded consciousness on arrival at hospital, fits, vomiting, severe headaches, or clinical or radiological evidence of a fracture of the skull; if none of these factors was present, the patient would be sent home, provided there was a responsible adult there to whom written and verbal instructions could be transmitted concerning observation and further care. While Weston's series of patients was not restricted to road casualties, it seems reasonable to use his result, and halve the intracranial

Table 10.4: Percentage distribution* of the several types of skull fractures and of intracranial injuries—East Anglian RHA, 1980–81, primary diagnosis only.

		M v occs	Mcs	Pcs	Peds	All
(a) Skull fractures (AN138)						
Vault of skull	N800	18	11	24	33	19
Base of skull	N801	12	22	21	45	22
Face bones	N802	65	43	48	14	53
Other and unqualified	N803	3	4	7	8	5
Skull or face with other bones	N804	2	0	0	0	1
Total number	N800-804	148	100	67	49	372
(b) Intracranial injury, excluding those with skull fracture (AN143)						
Concussion	N850	80	80	78	74	79
Cerebral laceration/contusion/haemorrhage	N851-853	1	2	2	3	2
Other and unspecified	N854	19	18	20	24	20
Total number	N850-854	1270	638	839	445	3300

* In parts (a) and (b), percentages are based on the numbers of skull fractures and of intracranial injuries respectively.

injury figure, if one wants to know the number that should "really" be termed "serious".

Nicholl (1980, p. 11) compared the information held in HAA data for Battle Hospital, Reading, with that on the corresponding casualties as recorded by the Transport and Road Research Laboratory. He found that (i) the primary diagnosis (ICD) in the HAA records identified the location of the most serious injury as assessed by TRRL in 87% of cases, (ii) the secondary diagnosis (ICD) identified the location of a second less serious injury in 62% of cases, (iii) in 6% of cases the same two injuries were recorded in HAA and by TRRL, but in opposite orders of importance, and (iv) casualties with minor or moderate concussion and other more severe injuries were sometimes recorded as having concussion as the primary condition resulting in admission to hospital.

10.2.2 Scotland, New Zealand, Australia, The United States

The corresponding system in Scotland (Scottish Hospital In-Patient Statistics), which is a full survey, not a 10% one, does not routinely publish data

on road accident victims, but data has been supplied by the Scottish Health Service and is included in Tables 10.1 and 10.2.

New Zealand and Western Australia have similar systems to Britain's. Data from full surveys of in-patients in public hospitals (N.Z.) or all short-stay hospitals (W.A.) have been included in Table 10.1 and (N.Z. only) also in Table 10.2. Table 10.5 shows that any changes in the nature of injuries have only been slight in recent years in these areas.

A study primarily aimed at evaluating random breath testing in New South Wales used routine hospital statistics and published some data on nature of injury (NSW, 1985). All hospitals in New South Wales (except for two under the Commonwealth Department of Veterans' Affairs) contribute to the collection of hospital in-patient statistics, providing an annual statewide source of hospital separation data. (As with the British data, a separation may be by discharge, death, or transfer to another institution.) The report cited points out that not every patient taken to hospital following an accident is actually admitted: hospitals with extensive casualty services may be able to treat quite serious injuries without requiring the patient

Table 10.5: Trends, or the absence of them, in the percentage distribution of the nature of serious injury in motor vehicle traffic accidents, New Zealand and Western Australia.

		New Zealand		W.A.	
		1978	1984	1971	1985
Fracture of skull, spine, or trunk	AN138-139	17	18	14	14
Fracture of upper limb	N810-819	6	7	6	9
Fracture of lower limb	N820-829	19	19	10	16
Intracranial injury, excl skull fracture	AN143	31	29	29	25
Internal injury of chest, abdomen, pelvis	AN144	5	6	3	3
Others	AN141-142,145-150	23	22	37	33
Total number		10330	10461	4827	3864

Sources:
As Table 10.1.

Table 10.6: Percentage distribution of nature of injury to pedal cyclists, with types of accident compared, Western Australia and the A.C.T.

		Western Australia		A.C.T.*	
		Pedal cycles alone#	With other vehs	Pedal cycles alone	With other vehs
Skull fracture, excl face	N800,801,803,804	4	12	9	21
Facial fracture	N802	3	2	9	7
Fracture of spine and trunk	N805-808,952	1	3	+	+
Fracture of upper limb	N810-819	16	6	14	8
Fracture of lower limb	N820-829	9	18	10	19
Dislocations, sprains	N830-839,840-848	2	1	+	+
Intracranial injury, excl skull fracture	N850-854	41	41	29	20
Internal injury of chest, abdomen, pelvis	N860-869	2	2	8	8
Lacerations and open wounds	N870-897	15	8	+	+
Others		10	7	21	17
Total number		3161	945	323	75
(Percentage killed)		(0.1)	(6.1)	(0.9)	(5.1)

* Excludes the 7 fatalities. Includes 11 pedestrians injured in bicycle collisions.
# These percentages add up to 103. Rounding of percentages to whole numbers is the reason.
+ Included with "others".

to be formally admitted, whereas a small country hospital would have to admit the person. Also, as with similar data from other countries such as Great Britain, the statistics count episodes of care, not patients—so those transferred to another hospital are double-counted, as are those re-admitted to the same hospital subsequent to discharge. The sample includes all separations from small hospitals, 12 large metropolitan hospitals, and all public hospitals in the Hunter region, plus 40% of those elsewhere, resulting in a statewide proportion of 60%. Published data is included in Table 10.1; some unpublished data, kindly made available by the N.S.W. Department of Health, in which road casualties are classified by their mode of transport, is included in Table 10.2.

McLean (1984) describes routine hospital records in South Australia, and reproduces the form used for data capture. The survey is nominally a full (100%) one, but McLean states that for about 10% of patients, the appropriate form is not completed or goes astray. In cases where it is applicable, the ICD E code is given as well as the N code.

Some data for Victoria is included in Tables 10.1 and 10.2, but the source is insurance claims, not in-patient statistics—see Section 10.3.3.

Using data from the Western Australian Hospital Morbidity Statistics System, Lugg (1982) conducted a study of persons admitted to hospital as a result of a pedal cycle accident. (Unlike a normal hospital sample, deaths occurring before hospitalisation were included in this study, through the co-operation of the Registrar General's Office.) The period of the study was 1971–80, the total sample size just over 4000 casualties (of whom 1.5% died). Table 10.6 shows the types of injury sustained. (As usual, only the most severe injury is included.) The similarities between pedal cyclists injured with and without another vehicle being involved are more striking than the differences. The differences are more or less confined to the relative proportions of arm and leg fractures being interchanged, and skull fractures being more common following a collision with a motor vehicle. However, nearly all the deaths involved a motor vehicle. Nature of injury causing death is shown in Table 9.2. Also included in Table 10.6 are results from a similar but smaller study in the Australian Capital Territory (Whately, 1985). The data is for the 4-year period beginning

Table 10.7: Agreement of the 3-digit N code between the casualty department and hospital discharge registers, with causes of disagreement.

	Percentages
Codes agreed	67
Codes did not agree	20
Incorrect in casualty department	8
Incorrect in discharge register	6
Incorrect in both	0
Diagnosis changed	4
Order of diagnoses changed	2
Diagnosis difficult to classify	1
Code missing from the casualty department register	2
Code missing from the discharge register	11
Total number	317

July 1979.

Other data comparing pedal cyclists injured with and without a motor vehicle being involved will be given in Table 10.15 (Massachusetts), Section 11.4.3 (Sweden), Table 12.4 (Denmark), and Table 13.4 (Scotland). For brain injuries specifically, a study in San Diego County, California, found that those resulting from a collision with a motor vehicle tended to be more severe, require longer hospital stays, and have less satisfactory outcomes, than those resulting from other causes (Krauss et al, 1987).

Hospital in-patient data for road casualties in the United States is apparently not available at present, though there is some hope it may be in the future. Statistics on diagnostic conditions for patients discharged from short-stay non-Federal hospitals are collected by the National Hospital Discharge Survey. In 1979 the E codes were used for the first time in addition to the N codes. But there was about a 50% undercount of the former, and it was obvious from the small estimates for motor vehicle accidents and accidental falls that the information required to provide E-code data on injuries was not available (McCarthy, 1982).

Table 10.8: Percentage distribution of the Odense sample by medical management after emergency room treatment.

	Car occs	Motor cycl's	Moped riders	Pedal cycl's	Pedest -rians	Others	Total
None	53	42	43	44	42	44	45
General practitioner	16	9	18	22	8	20	19
Hospital out-patient	8	19	15	18	9	19	15
Hospital admission	21	26	23	16	39	17	20
Deaths	2	4	0	0	2	0	1
Total number	578	133	376	1529	213	106	2935

Table 10.9: For the Odense sample, the percentage distribution of the part of body injured*.

	Car occs	Motor cycl's	Moped riders	Pedal cycl's	Pedest -rians	Total
Brain and cranium	12	8	9	8	14	10
Head (incl face and scalp)	31	13	19	33	22	28
Neck (incl cervical spine)	7	2	1	1	1	2
Chest (incl clavicle and shoulder blade)	13	8	8	5	8	7
Spine (thoracic spine only)	1	0	0	0	1	0
Abdomen (incl lumbar spine)	3	4	2	1	4	2
Pelvis (incl skin and external sex organs)	2	1	3	2	5	3
Arms	14	25	27	29	16	24
Legs	17	39	31	21	29	23
Total number	1076	271	658	2445	478	4928

* This Table gives the distribution of the lesions, casualties with lesions in more than one part of the body being counted more than once. Each part of the body was counted once only, even if it suffered more than one lesion.

Table 10.10: For the Odense sample, the percentage distibution of severity of injury for each combination of category of road user and part of body.

	Car occupants AIS			Motor cyclists AIS			Moped riders AIS			Pedal cyclists AIS			Pedestrians AIS		
	1	2	3-6	1	2	3-6	1	2	3-6	1	2	3-6	1	2	3-6
Brain and cranium	35	55	9	14	41	45	31	62	6	43	47	9	23	57	19
Head (incl face and scalp)	92	8	0	91	9	0	90	9	2	97	3	0	89	10	1
Neck (incl cervical spine)	89	1	9	40	0	60*	100	0	0*	84	4	12	50	0	50*
Chest (incl clavicle and shoulder blade)	64	18	17	48	30	22	43	47	9	63	32	5	54	26	21
Spine (thoracic spine only)	89	11	0*	100	0	0*	-	-	-	100	0	0*	75	0	25*
Abdomen (incl lumbar spine)	55	6	39	60	0	40*	50	10	40*	85	0	15	75	5	20
Pelvis (incl skin & ext'l sex organs)	55	45	0	67	33	0*	83	11	6*	92	8	0	71	17	12
Arms	84	12	3	72	24	4	86	12	2	78	20	2	71	20	9
Legs	89	9	7	74	13	12	80	12	8	86	8	6	63	21	16
All	77	16	7	67	18	14	76	19	5	83	14	3	64	23	13

* The total sample sizes (all AIS levels) in these cells were less than 20.

Ing et al (1985) lamented that most hospitals still did not record the information necessary to assign an E code.

10.2.3 Elsewhere

Several (perhaps most) other advanced countries have statistical systems on the diagnoses of hospital patients similar to those mentioned above, but I know of none that publish a table of the N codes for road accident casualties.

Honkanen (1984) mentions there is in Finland a register like HIPE, but including all hospital discharges, and having external cause coded according to the ICD E list; however, the E code is missing in about 30% of cases.

Honkanen also reports a comparison of ICD N codes in hospital discharge summaries and in emergency station records. This is shown as Table 10.7, but it should be noted that the patients were not all road casualties—indeed, if the sample was typical of Finland, probably only about 1-in-7 were. (See Table 8.16 for an American study using similar methodology, but concerned with comparing AIS grades.) Another study by Honkanen, at the health centre of a rural commune, found 6% disagreement when two coders used the 3-digit N code.

Hospital patients in Macau are classified according to both the E and N codes of the ICD, and data for 1978–79 is included in Table 10.1. However, this should be treated with caution as the hospitals included in the sample vary from year to year (in 1978–79 only data for the S. Januario and Kiang Wu hospitals was given), and also the numbers coded to AE138 vary more than they should (319 cases in 1978, 58 cases in 1979).

Hong Kong: see Section 12.9.2.

Table 10.11: Comparison of in-patients and out-patients with respect to Injury Severity Score and part of body injured, Goteborg (percentages).

	In-patients	Out-patients
(a) Injury Severity Score		
0-5	42	96
6-10	37	4
11-15	7	0
16+	14	0
Total number	71	137
(b) Part of body injured (as in AIS codebook)		
External	45	71
Head	15	11
Neck	0	0
Thorax	4	1
Abdomen	6	0
Spine	2	5
Extremities	28	11
Total number of injuries	254	244

Botswana: see Section 12.3.

The Statistical Annual of the tiny republic of San Marino includes more information about the accident events than is usually available to hospitals, and yet injuries are classified according to both the E and N codes of the ICD (see Table 10.1). Presumably there is good liaison between police and hospitals.

10.3 Statistical systems not restricted to in-patients

10.3.1 Emergency room data

Studies using records of patients treated in hospital emergency rooms (ER's) are at the periphery of our concern, because they are usually special research projects rather than a routine procedure. Nevertheless, it is worth mentioning some that have monitored ER patients over an extended period of time.

Table 10.12: Injuries to children in pedal cycle and moped accidents, Goteborg (percentages).

	Pedal cycle	Moped
Head/neck	47	22
Fracture	2	0
Concussion	11	7
Laceration	27	10
Contusion	8	3
Trunk	7	5
Fracture	2	2
Laceration	2	2
Contusion	3	1
Shoulder/upper arm	2	1
Fracture	1	0
Sprain/laceration/cont's'n	1	1
Elbow/forearm/wrist/hand	21	25
Fracture	6	11
Sprain	2	3
Laceration	8	8
Contusion	4	3
Hip/thigh/kneecap	4	2
Fracture	1	1
Sprain/laceration/cont's'n	4	1
Knee/lower leg/ankle/foot	18	44
Fracture	3	6
Sprain	1	5
Laceration	11	17
Contusion	4	13
Burn	0	3
Total number of injuries	1096	365
Total number of casualties	882	253

The Odense University Accident Analysis Group (1983) reports a study based on the accident statistics register kept by them. It includes all those treated at the ER of Odense University Hospital after having been involved in a road traffic accident in 1981. Since only about 20% were admitted to hospital, the sample is less seriously injured than others considered in this Chapter (Table 10.8). Table 10.9 shows how frequently the different parts of the body are injured; Table 10.10 is a three-way distribution, giving the percentages in the AIS categories 1, 2, and 3-6, separately for

Table 10.13: Percentage distribution of 524 injuries to 447 pedal cyclist casualties in Umea.

Head	34
(fracture 2%, concussion 9%,	
dental 9%, superficial 14%)	
Chest, abdomen, pelvis, spine	9
(fracture 4%,	
superficial 4%)	
Upper extremities	29
(fracture 12%, dislocation 2%,	
sprain 4%, superficial 11%)	
Lower extremities	28
(fracture 7%, sprain 4%,	
superficial 17%)	

Table 10.14: Comparison of injuries to child pedestrians and pedal cyclists, Sheffield (percentages).

		Child pedestrians	Child pedal cyclists
Sheffield	1	0	0
Children's	2	21	45
Hospital	3	35	44
grade of	4	34	9
severity	5	9	1
Total number		169	150
Percentage			
with fractures		26	22
Percentage			
with concussion		33	5

each combination of category of road user and part of body. Similar data for 1978 was presented in an English-language report at an IRCOBI Conference (Jorgensen et al, 1979).

For a sample of traffic accident victims in Goteborg, Table 10.11 compares in-patients and out-patients with respect to severity (as measured by the ISS) and part of body injured. The source of the data is Lindstruom et al (1982).

Another study in Goteborg was that of child casualties (up to age 15) by Nathorst Westfelt (1982). This included all emergency rooms and clinics receiving children with injuries, and extended over one year in 1975–76. Some results are shown in Table 10.12, comparing the injuries in pedal cycle and moped accidents. Another feature of this study was that it matched the case records with the social register; the social factors thereby added to the data were public assistance to the child's family, known alcoholism in the child's family, and whether the child was the subject of the Child Welfare Board's attention.

Among 447 pedal cyclist casualties presenting at Umea University Hospital in a one-year period (Bjornstig and Naslund, 1984), 13% resulted from collisions with motor vehicles, 7% from collisions with another bicycle or moped, and 1% from pedestrian collisions. The remainder were single-vehicle causes—collisions with kerbstones or objects on the ground (17%), falls on slippery roads

(14%), and so on. Table 10.13 shows some data from the study.

Illingworth et al (1981) report on 150 pedal cyclist casualties seen at Sheffield Children's Hospital over a six-month period. Table 10.14 compares this series with an earlier one of child pedestrians treated at the same hospital. (See Section 8.11.4 for a description of the severity grades used.)

Table 10.15 shows some data from Massachusetts. This came from a study of injuries to children and adolescents (i.e. those aged 19 or less), recorded in the ER's of 23 hospitals in 14 Massachusetts cities and towns (accounting for some 5 per cent of the population of the state), in the 1-year period commencing September 1980 (Gallagher et al, 1984). One interesting feature of the Massachusetts data is the comparison it makes between cyclists colliding with a motor vehicle and those in single-vehicle accidents. See Friede et al (1985) for a study specifically of bicyclist casualties, that used this Massachusetts dataset for a 3-year period starting September 1979. A footnote to Table 10.15 gives some of the findings. In the study in Waikato by Bailey (1984), the proportion of cyclists admitted to hospital was about twice as high for those struck by a motor vehicle as for those in single-vehicle crashes (23% of those attending the emergency department vs. 11%). See also Table 10.6, Section 11.4.3, Table 12.4, and Table 13.4.

Table 10.15: Percentage distribution of the nature of injury in the several categories of road user—an emergency room study of children and adolescents in Massachusetts.

		M v occs	Mcs	Pcs, with m.v.*	Pcs, no m.v.*	Peds	All
Skull fract, intracranial inj	N800-804,850-854	15	9	14	10	24	14
Fractures, dislocations (excl skull)	N805-839	7	24	22	16	13	12
Internal injuries	N860-869	0	6	2	1	2	1
Lacerations	N870-904,910-919	20	24	11	42	9	26
Sprains	N840-848,920-929	50	38	48	32	49	43
Other	N905-909,930-995	8	0	3	0	3	4
Total number in sample#		285	19	43	192	60	595
Estimated total number#		855	34	118	636	138	1781
Percentage admitted+		11	41	15	7	25	12

* In the 3-year study reported by Friede et al (1985), the distribution of injuries to pedal cyclists was: fracture of skull or spine 1%; fracture of face 1%; fracture of trunk 1%; fracture of upper limb 13%; fracture of lower limb 5%; sprain 8%; cerebral injury 6%; open and crushing wounds 27%; contusion, abrasion, effusion 36%; other 2%. In this study, 88% of cases did not involve a motor vehicle; 27% of those cases that did were admitted, as compared with 5% of those that did not.

The results of Gallagher et al are less clearly presented than they might be, but I believe the numbers shown to be correct. The actual sample was 25% of those treated at the emergency room only, plus all those killed or admitted to hospital. All percentages refer to what the total population of those presenting at the ER was imputed to be.

+ Those killed have been included with those admitted.

A series of papers by Agran and colleagues has documented motor vehicle injuries to children (0–14 years of age) in non-crash events: that is, sudden stops, accelerations, or swerves that cause passengers to strike the interior of the vehicle, or each other, or to be ejected. Their study is based in nine of the busiest emergency rooms in an urban Californian county. When judged by AIS or the need for hospitalisation, the results of ejections or falls from the vehicle tend to be more serious than those of other non-crash events. As to causes, in a series of 89 ejections and falls, the major ones were turns and swerves of the vehicle (39%), door opened (19%), and child opened the door (15%); among 83 other non-crash events, the major causes were sudden stops (73%) and turns and swerves of the vehicle (13%)—Agran et al (1985).

Rockett et al (1986) describe the methods used in obtaining a 25% sample of motor vehicle acci-dent victims from all ER's in the state of Rhode Island.

10.3.2   National Accident Sampling System, U.S.A.

Data from the NASS (see Section 3.12) on the frequency of occurrence of injuries of various severities and locations is given in Table 10.16 (Luchter, 1986). This refers to three years' data (1982–84), survivors only, there being an average of 35,000 casualties per annum, having 95,000 injuries, in the sample; the grossed-up figures are 3.4 million casualties and 7.9 million injuries.

Table 10.16: Frequency of injuries jointly by severity and location, per 1000 casualties* (NASS).

	AIS 1	2	3	4	5	Total#
Concussion	36	38	4	1	1	80
Head/face fracture	19	10	3	1	0	33
Vertebrae/cord injury	1	14	3	0	0	19
Other head/face/neck	11	0	0	0	0	37
Rib/pelvis fracture	13	14	3	0	0	30
Other chest	10	0	0	0	0	13
Internal injury	0	0	9	2	1	14
Extremity fracture	6	44	19	0	0	70
Joint injury	43	10	7	0	0	61
Muscle injury	237	1	1	0	0	239
Skin injury	1574	15	0	0	0	1594
Total+	1957	148	50	5	3	2329

* Five categories of specified injury have been omitted because of their small frequencies: brain injury other than concussion (total rate of 3 per 1000 casualties), throat injury (0.3), amputation (0.3), other artery/nerve (1), and burns (4).
# Including unknown AIS score.
+ Including unknown location and the five categories mentioned in note *.

10.3.3   Motor Accidents Board, Victoria

As will be discussed in Section 14.3, in the Australian state of Victoria, the Motor Accidents Board operates a no-fault accident compensation scheme, and their annual statistical publication includes some tables of the injuries of claimants. Though the source is not hospital statistics, the classification is by ICD N code, so the data has been included in Tables 10.1 and 10.2.

Chapter 11

Comparison of police and medical data

11.1 Introduction

Section 11.2 will discuss reasons why there might be discrepancies between police and certification figures of road deaths; it is concerned with their different procedures and definitions. Section 11.3 will examine empirical data on the discrepancies. Then Section 11.4 will compare police and hospital figures on those who are injured, emphasis being on the use of hospital data to check the completeness of the road accidents reported to the police.

Concerning road accident data deriving from death certificates, the first point is that it may be conveniently available (e.g. in the Demographic Yearbook or the World Health Statistics Annual) for some countries for which police-based data is hard to find (not being given in Statistics of Road Traffic Accidents in Europe or World Road Statistics). Section 2.5 gives details of these publications. The second point is that whether found in an international compilation or in a national publication it is very limited in scope—often only the total number of deaths classified as due to motor vehicle accidents is published. Some countries do subdivide the statistics according to the age and sex of the person killed, or (more rarely) the category of road user (whether pedestrian, pedal cyclist, motorcyclist, vehicle occupant), however.

But even the total is useful as serving as a check on the police data, particularly so for countries that do not adopt the usual practice of including in the police data people who die within 30 days of the accident and excluding later deaths. As to the certification data, there is no formal rigid time limit, but it is likely that deaths occurring later than one year after the accident will not be included in the figures, but be coded as late effects of acciden-tal injury. The result is that in countries using the 30-day standard, the certification figures are usually a few per cent higher than the police fig-ures. The difference is much larger for countries using a 24-hour limit. From the data given in Ta-ble 2.1, it may be calculated that the percentage difference even varies considerably between West-ern industrialised countries using the 30-day limit. In 1984-85 in Great Britain, the certification fig-ure exceeded the police figure by 4%. However, in West Germany in 1984-85 the certification figure was the smaller by 5%, and in France in 1984 the certification figure was also 5% less than that of the police. (This French data is particularly sur-prising: the police there only include those dying within 6 days of the accident, so their figure should be appreciably the smaller.) In Switzerland, there is close liaison between the two agencies, and the two figures usually agree to within a few deaths.

Previous publications in which police and certi-fication data on the numbers of fatalities are com-pared include those of Wigglesworth (1977; Aus-tralia only), Havard (1979; 8 countries), Hutchin-son and Adams (1981; 38 countries), and Chip-man (1983; Canada and its provinces). The con-sensus is that the certification statistics can be a useful supplement to the police statistics. If one compares the two figures and finds close agree-ment, one's confidence in the data increases. If a substantial difference is found, it at least warns one to look closely at the validity and accuracy of the figures. I agree with the conclusion of Chipman (1983): "Small discrepancies are prob-ably inevitable when definitions and procedures vary; large and consistent differences, however, should not be acceptable, and investigation into the causes is required."

11.2　Why police and certification data differ

11.2.1　Definitions

There are many slight divergencies in procedure which could account for the different figures published by police and by certification authorities. To discover what they might be, one might look for detailed descriptions of the two methods of data collection for each country listed in Table 2.1. But the prospect of trying to discover such precise information, especially the extent to which the rules are followed in practice, and not forgetting the language problem, is a daunting one. So what will be done below is to give a list of some of the possibilities. Not all of them will apply to all countries, of course. Some have been discussed further by Havard (1979), in his paper on road accident mortality among those aged 15–24 years, and the difficulties in classifying casualties and their injuries have also been examined by Andreassend (c. 1982). Some of the factors mentioned lead to biases (i.e. the data from one source consistently exceeds the other, as results from the police time limit), others to random fluctuations, e.g. whether the death is ascribed to the year of its occurrence or to that of the accident.

The precise definition of such terms as "road", "traffic", and "accident" is one potential area of divergence: what happened in the accident, where did it occur, what vehicle was involved? Deaths occasionally occur when people alight or fall from a vehicle. Are these included in either set of statistics? Or when a vehicle falls and crushes someone underneath it? What if the accident does not occur on a public road, but on private land? Or if the vehicle is a horse-drawn cart, or industrial plant, a moped, or a bicycle? When a car is driven into a river, or is in collision with a train, or the driver is poisoned by fumes, are these counted as road accidents? Are incidents included in which murder, manslaughter, or suicide is committed with a motor vehicle?

Table 11.1 refers to the procedures in England and Wales. It may be concluded that all differences in definitions and scope of the two systems are trivial (except the 30-day limit). Perhaps a cautionary note should be added: the table is in some respects a simplification of the rules in use, the definitive reference sources (the ICD Manual and the Stats 20 document) cannot give explicit consideration to all the possibilities that might happen, what happens in practice might diverge from what the rules specify, and what happens in other countries may be different.

11.2.2　Time limit

The time limit within which a death is ascribed to the road accident by the police is the major reason for differences between the sources, and has been discussed in Sections 2.2 and 11.1 above.

11.2.3　Relevant moment of time

It is likely that data from police sources for a particular year will refer to accidents that occurred in that calendar year, even if the person dies in the subsequent calendar year. On the other hand, it is likely that data from certification sources will refer to deaths that occurred (or, in some countries, were registered) in that calendar year. Further complications may arise because of the lengthy process of legal enquiry into the cause of death.

In some countries, more than one year-long period is used for statistical tabulation purposes (e.g. calendar, religious, and fiscal years), and the two sources may not use the same one.

11.2.4　Causation of death

If a person dies from, for instance, a heart attack shortly after or immediately before having a road accident, he or she might get included in one set of road accident statistics but not in the other.

11.2.5　Geographical area

Some countries are federal, or have statistical bureaux that are to some degree locally controlled. For example, anyone who has worked with British official statistics knows one has to remember whether they refer to England and Wales, to Great Britain (England, Wales, and Scotland), or to the United Kingdom (Great Britain and Northern Ireland). Police and certification statistics may refer to slightly different geographical areas, therefore. Furthermore, if the normal country of residence of the deceased, the country where the accident happened, and the country where death occurred are not all the same, the death might be treated differently by the two data-capture systems. Different

Table 11.1: Comparison of the certification and police systems for reporting road deaths (England and Wales).

	ICD-9	Stats 19
Nationality of victim	Irrelevant	Irrelevant
Country of residence of victim	Irrelevant	Irrelevant
Civilian/military status of victim	Irrelevant	Irrelevant
Country where accident occurred	Irrelevant	England and Wales
Country where death occurred	England and Wales	Irrelevant
Event falling in the relevant year	Registration of death	Occurrence of accident
Time limit for occurrence of death	1 year	30 days
Time limit for reporting accident	Irrelevant	30 days
Legal requirement	To register death	Though in an appreciable number of cases there is no legal requirement to inform the police of the accident, it is thought they virtually always are notified.
Crash caused by acute condition (e.g. heart attack, stroke, epileptic attack)	Excluded (the medical condition will be the underlying cause of death).	Included (but not counted as a fatality if death is not due to the accident).
Crash caused by chronic medical condition (e.g. blindness, deafness, infirmity, insanity)	Probably included, even though the condition is arguably the underlying cause.	Included
Crash caused by intoxication of the person killed	Included (code 305.0, nondependent abuse of alcohol, not being used in this context).	Included
Death caused by non-traumatic medical condition (e.g. heart attack) after crash	Included if the trauma was the underlying cause of death.	Included if the non-traumatic condition resulted from the crash.
Accidental poisoning by exhaust gas generated by motor vehicle in motion: death by poisoning	Included	Excluded
crash caused by poisoning, death arising from trauma	Included	Included
Accidental poisoning by exhaust gas from stationary motor vehicle	Excluded	Excluded
Motor vehicle driven into water, occupant drowns	Included	Included
Motor vehicle collides with train	Included	Included
Fire starting in motor vehicle while in motion	Included	Included
Object thrown into motor vehicle while in motion	Included	Included
Death of babies unborn up to the time of the accident	Included if live-born	Excluded
Boarding/alighting accidents	Included	Included
Place of accident	To be a motor vehicle traffic accident: public highway (see note at end of Table). Accidents elsewhere may be included in motor vehicle non-traffic accidents.	Public highway (see note at end of Table).

Table 11.1: (continued).

	ICD-9	Stats 19
Accidents with no motor vehicle involved, but involving a pedal cycle, an animal-drawn vehicle, or an animal being ridden	Excluded from motor vehicle accidents. Included in other road vehicle accidents.	Included
Accidents involving powered vehicles used solely within the buildings and premises of an industrial or commercial establishment	Excluded (included in E846)	Excluded
Accidents to persons repairing their vehicles on the public highway, if the injury is inflicted by that vehicle	Excluded (probably included in E919)	Included
Motor vehicle, not under its own power, being loaded on, or unloaded from, another conveyance	Excluded	Included
Passenger on board public service vehicle injured, without another vehicle or a pedestrian being hit	Included	Included
Pedestrian moves quickly to avoid being involved in an accident, is successful in that, but for example twists ankle	Probably excluded	Included
Pedestrian injures himself on parked vehicle	Probably excluded	Included
Suicide	Excluded	Excluded
Involuntary manslaughter	Included	Included
Murder and voluntary manslaughter	Excluded	Excluded

Note on meaning of "public highway":

According to ICD-9, a "public highway" is "open to the use of the public for purposes of vehicular traffic as a matter of right or custom". This includes approaches to docks, public buildings, and stations, and excludes driveways, parking lots, ramps, and roads in airfields, farms, industrial premises, mines, private grounds, and quarries. Accidents in these latter places will (if appropriate) be included in motor vehicle non-traffic accidents. Motor vehicle accidents are "assumed to have occurred on the highway unless another place is specified, except in the case of accidents involving only off-road motor vehicles, which are classified as nontraffic accidents unless the contrary is stated".

In the Stats 19 system, accidents occurring on the public highway which come to the attention of the police are to be reported, including those on the footway, on private roads to which the public have right of access, and on bridle paths or country tracks etc (which motor vehicles are lawfully allowed to use), and excluding those in car parks, picnic areas, petrol station forecourts, and motorway parking areas and service roads on motorway service areas.

Both ICD-9 and Stats 19 count accidents as being on the public highway if the vehicle runs out of control and has an accident off the public highway.

It appears, therefore, that the two definitions of "public highway" are virtually identical.

Table 11.2: Numbers of deaths as published by the two reporting systems: Comparison of some large cities with their national data.

	Certification data	Police data	Percentage difference*
Australia 1980	3555	3274	+ 9
A.C.T. 1980	43	30	+ 43
Austria 1980	1888	1742	+ 8
Wien 1981	251	141	+ 78
Denmark 1980	710	690	+ 3
Kobenhavn 1980	52	31	+ 68
England and Wales 1980	5831	5253	+ 11
Greater London 1978	884	689	+ 28
Finland 1978	633	610	+ 4
Helsinki 1978	47	26	+ 81
Norway 1981	390	338	+ 15
Oslo 1978	40	27	+ 48
Sweden 1980	910	848	+ 7
Goteborg 1976	82	29	+183
Stockholm 1983-84	71	53	+ 34
West Germany 1980	12521	13041	- 4
Hamburg 1976	324	283	+ 14
Koln 1981	89	81	+ 10
West Berlin 1981	256	231	+ 11

* Percentage by which the certification figure exceeds the police figure.

Table 11.3: Road deaths in Japan and its largest cities, according to the death registration authorities: Comparison of the numbers when tabulated by place of residence and by place of occurrence.

	By place of residence	By place of occurrence*	Percentage difference#
Japan 1978-80	35560	35560	0
Fukuoka 1978-79	154	145	+ 6
Hiroshima 1980	96	87	+ 10
Kawasaki 1978-80	247	223	+ 11
Kitakyusyu 1978-80	260	237	+ 10
Kobe 1978-80	298	315	- 5
Kyoto 1978-80	337	362	- 7
Nagoya 1978-80	545	481	+ 13
Osaka 1978-80	499	435	+ 15
Sapporo 1978-80	298	209	+ 43
Tokyo-to 1978-80	1204	972	+ 24
Yokohama 1978-80	508	486	+ 5

* Presumably place of occurrence of death, rather than of accident.
# Percentage by which the first number exceeds the second.

Table 11.4: Deaths from motor vehicle accidents in three U.S. states, tabulated by place of residence and by place of occurrence.

	By place of residence	By place of occurrence	Percentage difference*
Alaska 1982-83			
Anchorage census area	98	97	+ 1
Rest of Alaska	139	127	+ 9
South Carolina 1982#			
Three urban counties+	183	238	- 23
Rest of South Carolina	638	585	+ 9
Washington state 1982			
Three cities@	130	223	- 42
Rest of Washington	714	591	+ 21

* Percentage by which the first number exceeds the second.

Transportation accidents, E800–E848. Of these, 90% are motor vehicle traffic accidents (E810–E819).

+ Charleston, Greenville, Richland. In these counties, 84% of the population live in urban areas. In the remainder of South Carolina, 43% do so (1983 edition of South Carolina Statistical Abstract).

@ Seattle, Spokane, Tacoma.

Sources:

Alaska. Alaska Vital Statistics Annual Report 1983. Juneau: Department of Health and Social Services.

South Carolina. South Carolina Vital and Morbidity Statistics 1982. Annual Vital Statistics Series, Volume I. Columbia: South Carolina Department of Health and Environmental Control.

Washington. Vital Statistics Summary, Washington State, 1982. Olympia: Washington State Department of Social and Health Services.

arrangements may apply to military personnel from those applying to civilians. I imagine in some very small countries it is common for critically-injured casualties to be taken to hospital across the border. (Within Australia, people involved in accidents in the part of New South Wales surrounding and close to the Australian Capital Territory may be taken to hospital in the A.C.T. and die there, thus inflating the A.C.T. death certification statistics.) Accidents occurring near jurisdictional boundaries (I am thinking chiefly of provincial, rather than national, boundaries) may sometimes be separately recorded in both areas (or neither).

11.3   Observed discrepancies in sub-totals of deaths

11.3.1   Three methods of division

For some countries, it is possible to compare certification and police figures for certain subdivisions of the totality of motor vehicle fatalities. There are three methods of subdivision for which this may be possible: (i) Geographic, i.e. by province or other administrative unit. (ii) By age of the person killed. (iii) By category of road user (e.g. motor vehicle occupant, motorcyclist, pedal cyclist, pedestrian).

11.3.2   Geographic

Though the list may not be complete, I do know that the following countries publish both sets of statistics subdivided according to administrative unit of the country: Australia, Austria, Canada, Japan, Spain, Switzerland, and the U.S.A. I have not studied such figures in detail.

In addition, the comparison is possible for some major cities of a number of countries. This is shown in Table 11.2, where it is clear that there is a tendency for the certification figure to exceed the police figure by a greater percentage in large cities than in the country as a whole. It is likely that most of these countries tabulate certification

Table 11.5: Numbers of deaths as published by the two reporting systems: Comparison of large cities with statewide data (Illinois, Texas, Queensland, Victoria).

	Certification data	Police data	Percentage difference*
Illinois 1982	1796#	1671	+ 7
Chicago 1982	328#	293	+ 12
Texas 1983	3899	3823	+ 2
Dallas 1983	186	173	+ 8
Houston 1983	416	320	+ 30
San Antonio 1983	170	134	+ 27
Queensland 1983+	500	510	- 2
Brisbane stat.div.1983	180	115	+ 57
Victoria 1983+	749	664	+ 13
Melbourne stat.div.1983	449	338	+ 33

* Percentage by which the certification figure exceeds the police figure.

Certification data for Illinois is also published by place of occurrence of accident: in 1982 the numbers were 1891 (Illinois) and 295 (Chicago).

+ For Australian states, the certification data includes motor vehicle traffic accidents (E810–E819) only.

Sources:

Illinois (certification). As Table 8.2.

Illinois (police). 1983 Accident Facts. Springfield: Illinois Department of Transportation.

Texas. As Table 11.6.

Queensland. As Table 11.6.

Victoria. As Table 11.6.

data by place of residence but police data by place of accident, and that this is part of the reason why some difference might occur.

We can take this a little further by looking at certification data that is published according to both place of residence and place of occurrence. This is done for Japan, and we find that for large cities the place of residence figure exceeds the place of occurrence figure (Table 11.3). This is consistent with the certification-police comparison in Table 11.2. However, turning to data from three states of the U.S.A. (Table 11.4), we find the reverse is the case! This, at least, is easy to explain—major hospitals are usually in major cities, the gravely injured tend to be taken to major hospitals, and some of them die there. It is the Japanese data and the certification-police comparison that are puzzling. Why are more residents of London (for example) killed elsewhere than are others killed in London? Finally, in Table 11.5 a comparison of certification and police data (the former tabulated by place of residence) for two

U.S. and two Australian states follows the same pattern as Table 11.2.

11.3.3 Age group

A comparison of certification and police figures disaggregated according to age group is given in Table 11.6 for nineteen jurisdictions. The general tendency is for the certification figure to exceed the police figure by a greater amount in the elderly and in children than in other age groups. A plausible reason for the former is that the elderly are more likely to die from complications, after the end of the 30-day limit.

In Washington state, Mueller et al (1987) have noticed that the undercount of pedestrian deaths in police data is more marked for children under 5 than for other age groups—see Table 11.7. They ascribe this to a large number of non-traffic accidents (i.e. ones in such places as driveways, garages, and apartment building parking areas) being unknown to the police.

Table 11.6: Percentage by which the certification figure exceeds the police figure: By age group.

	0-14	15-24	25-44	45-64	65 & over	All
Belgium 1977-78	+ 7	+ 1	+ 7	+ 5	+ 6	+ 2
Canada 1979-80	+12	+ 6	0	+ 5	+ 8	+ 1*
Denmark 1984	-10	- 2	.. - 3 ...		+ 3	- 2
Great Britain 1984+	+ 2	+ 1	.. + 3 ...		+10	+ 4
Irish Republic 1976-80	+ 3	- 4	- 3	+ 2	+ 2	- 1
Michigan 1982	+21	+11	+11	+10	- 1	+10
Netherlands 1976-78,80	+ 7	0	- 2	+ 6	+ 5	+ 3
New South Wales 1983-84+	- 5	-12		... - 8 ...		- 9
New Zealand 1976-78,80	+14	+10	+11	+14	+16	+12
Norway 1977-81	+13	+ 1#	+ 3#	+12#	+14#	+ 7
Queensland 1983+		.. + 5 ...		... - 5 ...		0
South Africa 1977@		.. - 6 ...	- 3#	+16#	+50#	- 3*
South Australia 1984+		.. - 4 ...		... + 1 ...		- 2
Sweden 1977-81	+ 4	.. + 6 ...		+ 5	+ 9	+ 6
Switzerland 1976-80	+ 2	- 1	- 5	- 1	- 1	- 1
Tasmania 1982-83+		.. + 4 ...		... + 3 ...		+ 4
Texas 1983	+11	+ 5	- 2	+ 4	+ 8	+ 3
Victoria 1983+		.. + 8 ...		... +18 ...		+13
West Germany 1979-81	- 3	- 3	.. - 4 ...		- 1	- 3

* These figures are less than would be expected from those for the separate age groups because information on age was missing from the police data in 4% of cases (Canada) or 6% (South Africa).

\# Variations in age groups tabulated:

- Norway 15–29, 30–49, 50–69, 70 and over;

- South Africa 25–39, 40–59, 60 and over.

\+ For Great Britain and for Australian states, the certification data includes motor vehicle traffic accidents (E810–E819) only.

@ Whites, Coloureds, and Asians only.

Fife and Rappaport (1987) suggested that death registration statistics may substantially underreport injury as a cause of death for the elderly. Their evidence for this came from Los Angeles County: the Californian death certificate has a specific section on the external events associated with the person's death. For people aged 65 or more, the deaths coded as having an injury event as the underlying cause were found to be only 54% of those having an injury event mentioned; for those aged 85 or more, the proportion was 35%. The authors implied that many of the other deaths ought really to have had an injury code for the underlying cause. (This study was of all external causes of death, not specifically road accidents; underreporting of this type is likely to be less for road accidents than for falls and other events for which the initial trauma is relatively minor.)

11.3.4 Category of road user

Data disaggregated according to category of road user is presented in Table 11.8 for fourteen jurisdictions. The amount by which the certification figure exceeds the police figure tends to be greatest for pedestrians and least for riders of pedal cycles or motor cycles. Some caution is needed in interpreting this, as definitions of the road user categories by the two data sources may not be identical.

Sources (Table 11.6, U.S. and Australian states):

Michigan (certification). As Table 8.2.

Michigan (police). Michigan Traffic Accident Facts 1983. Lansing: Michigan Department of State Police.

Texas (certification). Texas Vital Statistics 1983. Austin: Texas Department of Health.

Texas (police). Motor Vehicle Traffic Accidents 1983. Texas Department of Public Safety.

New South Wales (certification). Causes of Death, New South Wales, 1984. Sydney: Australian Bureau of Statistics.

New South Wales (police). Road Traffic Crashes in New South Wales. Statistical Statement, Year Ended December 31st, 1984. Sydney: Traffic Authority of New South Wales.

Queensland (certification). Causes of Death, Queensland, 1983. Brisbane: Australian Bureau of Statistics.

Queensland (police). Road Traffic Accidents, Queensland, 1983. Brisbane: Australian Bureau of Statistics.

South Australia (certification). Causes of Death, South Australia, 1984. Adelaide: Australian Bureau of Statistics.

South Australia (police). South Australian Year Book No 21: 1986. Adelaide: Australian Bureau of Statistics.

Tasmania (certification). Deaths, Tasmania, 1983. Hobart: Australian Bureau of Statistics.

Tasmania (police). Road Traffic Accidents Involving Casualties, Tasmania, Year Ended 31 December 1983. Hobart: Australian Bureau of Statistics.

Victoria (certification). Causes of Death, Victoria, 1983. Melbourne: Australian Bureau of Statistics.

Victoria (police). Road Traffic Accidents Involving Casualties, Victoria, 1983. Melbourne: Australian Bureau of Statistics.

Table 11.7: Age-specific pedestrian annual death rates (per 100,000 population), Washington state, 1981–83: Comparison of the two reporting systems.

	0-4	5-9	10-14	15-19	20-24	25-29	30-44	45-64	65+	All
Certification	4.0	2.6	1.8	2.7	2.1	1.7	1.9	2.1	6.6	2.7
Police	1.5	2.3	1.6	3.2	2.1	1.7	1.8	1.8	5.9	2.4

11.3.5 Why? (An open question)

The reasons suggested above for the observed discrepancies are necessarily speculative. Definitive answers would need case by case consideration of several thousand deaths.

11.4 Empirical comparisons of police and hospital data

11.4.1 Birmingham

Bull and Roberts (1973) took a sample consisting of the first 100 cases in each month of 1970 resulting from road accidents occurring in the city of Birmingham and attending the Accident Hospital there. They classified them according to the standard criteria (Section 8.8.1) as killed, seriously injured, or slightly injured, and then attempted to trace the cases in police records. Overall, they found 71% of cases were known to the police. This included all the 15 fatals; how the proportion depended on whether the casualty was seriously or slightly injured, and on the category of road user, is shown in Table 11.9. The severity shown there is as assigned from hospital records; the police had recorded 14% of the serious cases as slight and 1% of the slight cases as serious. The hospital sample was one of road accidents, and a number involved no motor vehicle, only a pedal cycle; these were particularly poorly reported to the police.

Bull and Roberts point out that there is not a

Table 11.8: Percentage by which the certification figure exceeds the police figure: Comparison of road user categories.

	Vehicle occupants	Motor cyclists	Pedal cyclists	Pedest -rians	All
Canada 1977,79–81	. . .	– 1	. . .	+10	+ 1
Great Britain 1979–80	+ 7	+ 2	+ 6	+14	+ 8
New Zealand 1977–78,80	+12	+17	+ 1	+14	+13
Northern Ireland 1976–80	+ 9	–16	–10	+14	+ 7
Norway 1977–81	+ 8	– 2	+12	+19	+10
Sweden 1977–81	+ 6	– 3	–12	+24	+ 6
Western Australia 1976–79	. . .	+ 5	. . .	+ 4	+ 5
U.S. states:					
Michigan 1982	+10	– 6	– 8	+19	+10
Missouri 1983	. . . + 6 . . .			+16	+ 7
Montana 1983	?	?	?	0	– 7
Nebraska 1983	+ 6	0	?	+24	+ 7
North Carolina 1983	+ 3	–12	?	+ 3	+ 4
Texas 1983	?	?	?	+ 1	+ 2
Vermont 1983	+ 6	?	?	?	+ 2

Sources (U.S. states):
Police data, states other than Michigan. (i) Highway Safety Performance—1983. Fatal and Injury Accident Rates on Public Roads in the United States. Washington, D.C.: U.S. Department of Transportation. (Total fatalities and pedestrian fatalities.) (ii) Fatal Accident Reporting System 1983. Washington, D.C.: National Highway Traffic Safety Administration. (Total occupant fatalities and motorcyclist fatalities; hence, by subtraction, the "others" category in this Table.)
Police data, Michigan. As Table 11.6.
Certification data, states other than Missouri and Texas. As Table 8.2.
Certification data, Missouri. Missouri Vital Statistics 1983. Missouri Center for Health Statistics Publication No 4.29. Jefferson City: Missouri Department of Social Services.
Certification data, Texas. As Table 11.6.

legal requirement in England to report injury accidents to the police: "The only accidents legally required to be notified are those which involve a motor vehicle and cause injury to a person other than the driver and in which exchange of addresses and insurance information has not occurred." Thus single-vehicle accidents injuring only the driver are not notifiable, nor are many other accidents when the prescribed information has been exchanged. Nevertheless, there is a widespread belief that in cases of injury the police should be informed.

11.4.2 Reading

Grattan and Keigan (1975) collected injury data from all road traffic accident casualties brought to

Battle Hospital (in Reading, England) during a 6-month period of 1973, and then attempted to trace the same casualties in police records. In their sample were 846 casualties from 644 accidents. Overall, 36% were admitted to hospital. 76% of the casualties were reported to the police. Hobbs et al (1979) reported a larger study at the same hospital (extending over 1974–76 and including some 3641 casualties); Table 11.10 shows how the police registration of casualties depended on category of road user and severity of injury.

11.4.3 Sweden

Hansson (1974) studied those killed or injured in traffic accidents who were hospitalised or treated

Table 11.9: Percentages of hospital casualty cases known to the police, Birmingham.

	Drivers	Motor cyclists	Pedal cyclists	Pedestrians	Others	All
Serious	93	72	35*	91	90	82
Slight	71	63	19*	80	70	65

* Of the 40 seriously-injured pedal cyclists, in 26 cases no other vehicle was involved, and none of these were known to the police. And of the 114 slightly-injured pedal cyclists, 89 cases involved no other vehicle, and only 3 of these cases were known to the police.

Table 11.10: Percentages of hospital casualty cases known to the police, Reading.

	Vehicle occupants	Motor cyclists	Pedal cyclists	Pedestrians	All
Serious	91	73	41	82	79
Slight	82	54	29	60	66

as out-patients in the Central Hospital, Halmstad. (A few who did not pass through the Department of General Surgery were excluded.) Table 11.11 summarises his results. Overall, of seriously-injured casualties, 43% appeared in official police statistics as seriously injured, and another 16% as slightly injured; of slightly-injured casualties, 31% appeared in official police statistics, nearly all classified as slightly injured. Hansson also reviews a good deal of earlier Scandinavian work.

Nilsson (1984) reports that police statistics comprise 45% of the road casualties present in hospital in-patient statistics, the figure for vehicle drivers and passengers (60%) being rather higher than for pedestrians (45%) or cyclists (20%). Nilsson also mentions a study in Ostergotland in which of 55 persons treated in an emergency department following accidents involving cars, 32 were reported by the police; in addition, the police registered 16 casualties who did not appear in hospital records. Cyclist and moped riders injured in single-vehicle accidents were "very seldom" reported to the police. (See also Section 4.4.2.)

Engstrom (1979) found that the number of people injured in accidents involving mopeds or motorcycles in Uppsala County was about four times higher than appeared in official police statistics. The figures were: hospital series, 193 in a 1-year

period, 91 having an injury of severity AIS 2 or greater, plus 20 in a 3-month period treated in local medical centres, only 1 of whom was seriously injured; police statistics, 51, 27 being seriously injured.

A study similar to that of Bull and Roberts in Birmingham was carried out in Goteborg and reported by Bunketorp et al (1982). Of 1019 traffic accident casualties in Goteborg during July-December 1981 that were known to the police or to the hospital emergency departments, 386 were not reported by the police and 278 were missed by the hospital statistics. Table 11.12 shows both this data, arranged similarly to that of Bull and Roberts, and also that for 1983 (from Bunketorp and Romanus, 1985).

Another study in Goteborg, that concentrated on pedal cycle accidents, revealed the data of Table 11.13 (Kroon et al, 1984). About 30% of the pedal cyclists were admitted to hospital; another measure of their severity of injury is that 74% had AIS 1, 19% had AIS 2, and 6% had AIS 3 or greater. Single-vehicle accidents were responsible for 69% of casualties, bicycle-bicycle accidents for 8%, and bicycle-car accidents for 18%. In most jurisdictions, registration of the first two categories by the police will inevitably be poor, since no motor vehicle is involved and it is nei-

Table 11.11: Percentages of casualties treated at the Central Hospital, Halmstad, who were classified by the police as seriously or slightly injured, known to the police but not reported by them to the Central Bureau of Statistics, or not known to the police.

	Road user category, and severity in hospital records											
	Car occupants		Light mc*		Heavy mc*		Pedal cyclists		Pedestrians		All	
	Ser	Sli	Ser	Sli	Ser	Sli	Ser	Sli	Ser	Sli	Ser	Sli
Status with the police:												
Seriously injured	47	3	39	0	67	6	50	0	56	7	43	2
Slightly injured	20	43	12	21	13	19	9	39	24	7	16	29
Known but not in statistics	25	43	10	13	7	31	3	11	0	21	15	27
Unknown	7	11	39	67	13	44	38	50	20	64	26	42
Total number	138	236	49	63	15	16	32	28	25	14	288	453

* Light motorcycles and heavy motorcycles are distinguished by the weight being below or above 75 kg. Mopeds are included in the light motorcycles group.

Table 11.12: Percentages of hospital casualty cases known to the police, Goteborg.

	Car drivers	Car passengers	Motor cyclists	Moped drivers	Pedal cyclists	Pedestrians	Others	All
(a) 1981 (July-December)								
Serious	78	80		65	46	85	78	73
Slight	80	69		33	31	53	56	57
(b) 1983								
Serious	84	80	75	63	35	86	30	66
Slight	81	81	60	37	23	56	58	60

Table 11.13: Overlap between police and hospital samples, Goteborg, 1983.

	Car drivers	Car passengers	Pedal cyclists	Pedestrians
Percentage known to the police only	49	39	9	18
Percentage known to the police and to a hospital	32	41	16	51
Percentage in the hospital sample only	18	21	74	30

Table 11.14: Percentages of emergency department (ED) cases found in police records, related to various characteristics of the casualty, Northeastern Ohio, 1977.

Age*		Involved vehicle#	
Less than 16	28	Passenger car	61
16 or older	60	Other	24
Sex*		Mode of transport to ED*	
Male	53	Emergency vehicle	69
Female	57	Other	50
Hours, injury to ED#		Payment*	
Less than 4	64	Medicare@	82
4 or more	48	Self	63
		Private insurance	53
Time of injury#		Worker's compensation	50
10pm - 7am	72	Medicaid	33
Other	56		
		Residency*	
Hour of arrival at ED*		Resident	56
10pm - 7am	65	Non-resident	40
Other	51		
		Discharge status from ED*	
Role#		Admitted	74
Driver+	74	Not admitted	53
Passenger+	46		
Pedal cyclist@	43		
Pedestrian	46		
Other	14		

* Proportions of cases for which these variables were unknown were less than 10%.

\# Proportions of cases for which these variables were unknown were at least 40%.

\+ Vehicle other than motor cycle.

@ Numbers of cases were less than 50.

ther legally required nor customary to report such crashes. Consequently, it is most interesting that in this study there were only minor differences in injury severity between the different accident types. In Stockholm, Lind and Wollin (1986) found the same. Conceivably this finding could be modified if division of AIS 1 into subgrades of severity were available—it has already been remarked (at C.E of Section 8.7.3) that AIS 1 covers a wide range of injuries—but until that is done, the information must be taken at face value, and the conclusion drawn that cycle accidents not involving a motor vehicle must not be dismissed as being very minor in severity. As to nature of injury, victims of collisions with cars were relatively more likely to have a leg injury, and casualties in single-vehicle accidents were more likely to be injured in the face and arms. For similar results from routine hospital data in Western Australia, see Section 10.2.2. Data from Massachusetts in Table 10.15, from Denmark in Table 12.4, and from Scotland in Table 13.4 is also relevant. The Stockholm study (Lind and Wollin, 1986) found that injuries to the head and trunk were more common, and those to the lower limbs less common, in collisions with motor vehicles than in single-vehicle crashes. This study also evaluated the police registration of injured cyclists and concluded it grossly underestimated the total number.

Table 11.15: Percentages of emergency department (ED) cases found in Ministry of Transport records, related to various characteristics of the casualty, Waikato, 1980.

Drivers: age			Time	
19 or less	47		6pm - 9pm	49
20-24	40		9pm - midnight	53
25-44	48		Midnight - 5am	53
45+	57		5am - 6pm	46
Drivers: sex			Role	
Male	46		Driver	47
Female	52		Passenger	55
			Pedal cyclist	27
Drivers: ethnicity			Pedestrian	50
Caucasian	46			
Maori	57		Accident type	
			Car, single-vehicle	41
Drivers: blood alcohol			Two-car	64
concentration			Motorcycle,	
None	46		single-vehicle	18
.05+	57		Motorcycle, with car	59
Drivers: locale			Discharge status from ED	
Urban	50		Admitted	65
Rural	43		Not admitted	43
Drivers: vehicle driven				
Car	55			
Motorcycle	38			

11.4.4   Northeastern Ohio

The Northeastern Ohio Trauma Study collected a 1.9% sample of all visits during 1977 to the emergency departments of 41 of the 42 acute care hospitals in Cleveland and nearby areas of Ohio. An attempt was made to match each motor vehicle traffic collision victim in the hospital sample with the corresponding police report; this procedure was for the most part a computerised one (see Section 13.8). Overall, police reports were found for 55% of the cases; this figure depended on a number of demographic, social, and crash factors, as well as injury severity—see Table 11.14, taken from Barancik and Fife (1985). Furthermore, among the police-reported cases, 15% of the reports specified that the crash involved no injuries.

11.4.5   Waikato

The Waikato Hospital Road Accident Survey included motor vehicle casualties aged 12 or more attending Waikato Hospital (in Hamilton, New Zealand) during a one-year period starting in November 1979. At pages 189–193 of Bailey (1984) is some data on the proportions of casualties in the survey who were reported to the Ministry of Transport, possibly via the police. Overall, the proportion was 49%; Table 11.15 summarises how various factors affected the proportion.

There is also some data on the police coding of injury severity: among 258 cases, 47 were overestimated by the police in the sense that they were stated to be serious but were not admitted to hospital, and 30 were underestimated, being stated as slight but actually admitted. The data is not given, but this seems to correspond to a probability

Table 11.16: Percentages of hospital-registered victims also registered by the police, according to victim's mode of transport and AIS score (Odense University Hospital, 1979-81).

Pedal cycle	9	AIS 0	28
Moped	25	1	19
Motor cycle	48	2	37
Car	58	3	58
Van	49	4	82
Truck	42	5	85
Bus	1	6	97
Other	38		
Pedestrian	41		

of hospital admission of about 50% for those coded as serious, and 20% for those coded as slight.

11.4.6 Odense

The Odense University Accident Analysis Group (1983) presents data on how large a proportion of hospital-registered accident victims is known to the police. Using a computerised matching procedure, they found an overall proportion of 26%, though they say incorrect person identification numbers in the police registrations may have artificially reduced this. How this percentage depends on mode of transport and on severity of injury (AIS) is shown in Table 11.16.

11.4.7 Finland

Honkanen (1984) mentions that the coverage of the register of traffic accidents reported by the police to the Central Statistical Office of Finland, though 100% for fatal accidents, is only 25% for all accidents requiring medical attention. Presumably this figure was found by a hospital-police comparison study.

11.4.8 The Netherlands

In The Netherlands, the police accident data has a code specifying if the casualty was admitted to hospital, and the hospital statistics have the ICD code for external cause of injury. Maas and Harris (1984) compared the two datasets to find how complete and how representative a sample of hospitalised accident victims was in the police data.

They did not match casualties in one dataset with those in the other, so strictly speaking their results giving the ratios of the numbers in one dataset to those in the other only reflect the large-scale similarity (or otherwise) of the datasets—any interpretation of these ratios as proportions correctly recorded requires assumptions about the correctness of the hospital-admittance code on the police form and the ICD E code on the hospital form. Maas and Harris estimated that the police data had a coverage of 83% of all road accident inpatients; cyclists and pedestrians, particularly in the age group 0-14 years, were underreported to a significantly greater extent. Maas and Harris cite other evidence that in The Netherlands, the police record about 45% of accidents involving injuries, including minor ones.

11.4.9 Montreal

Stulginskas et al (1983) report a hospital-based study of children's traffic accidents in Montreal. For the year 1981, they found: (i) Of the 1152 children reported by the police to have been injured in motor vehicle accidents, 35% were not seen at a hospital emergency room, and thus probably had little or no injury. (ii) Of the 1234 children in the hospital records, 39% had not been reported to the police. (iii) Of those injured children that the police did not know about, almost 30% had a maximum AIS score of 2 or more, this figure being about the same as for the cases known to the police.

11.4.10 Adelaide: Pedal cyclists

A questionnaire survey of commuting cyclists found that of accidents requiring medical treatment by a doctor, 33% were reported to the police (Herzberg, 1985). Note, however, that these were cases which were said by the casualty to have been treated (not necessarily traceable in medical records) and to have been reported to the police (not necessarily traceable in their records).

11.4.11 Developing countries

See Section 5.11.

Chapter 12

Features of injury coding in individual countries

12.1 Australia

12.1.1 New South Wales, hospital in-patients

See Section 10.2.2.

12.1.2 Queensland, police

Casualties are classified according to a four-point scale of severity (dead, admitted to hospital, received medical treatment but not admitted, minor injury receiving first aid or no treatment), and also according to nature of injury (apparently using the categories of the ICD). Data on deaths and injuries separately is given in Table 12.1. This has been taken from Road Traffic Accidents (Brisbane: Australian Bureau of Statistics).

12.1.3 South Australia, police

Casualty data used to be published in Road Traffic Accidents (Walkerville: Road Traffic Board). The utility of the data is, however, limited by the high usage of the uninformative category "multiple" (Table 12.2). Responsibility for the processing of road accident data has recently changed, and I do not know what will be published in future.

12.1.4 Victoria, insurance

The Motor Accidents Board operates a no-fault accident compensation scheme, and their annual statistical publication includes some tables of the injuries of claimants (ICD codes). Table 12 of the 1985–86 edition of Statistics of Persons Killed or Injured in Road Accidents (Melbourne: Motor Accidents Board) tabulates nature of injury according to sex and category of road user (see Tables 10.1 and 10.2), and Table 13 does the same for fatal injuries (see Tables 9.1 and 9.2); a number of more detailed tables are available but unpublished. See also Section 14.3.

12.1.5 Western Australia, death certificates

Pedal cyclists only: see Table 9.2.

12.1.6 Western Australia, hospital in-patients

See Section 10.2.2.

12.2 Belgium

Death certificates: nature of injury (36 ICD N groups) is tabulated for road accident victims— Table 3 of Chapter VI of 1978 edition of Statistique des Causes de Deces (Bruxelles: Institut National de Statistique). See Table 9.1.

12.3 Botswana

Hospital in-patients: there is a hospital in-patient statistical system similar to that of England and Wales, in that patients are classified by N code, and also it is possible to identify road accident victims. Unfortunately, however, a tabulation of injuries to road casualties is not included in the annual report, Medical Statistics (Gaborone: Central Statistics Office).

Table 12.1: Percentage distribution of the nature of injury sustained by the various categories of road user, Queensland, 1984–1985.

	Motor drivers	Motor pass'rs	Motor cyclists	Pedal cyclists	Pedestrians	All
(a) Fatalities						
Fracture of skull & face	11	13	11	17	7	11
Fracture of spine & trunk	5	6	5	8	6	5
Intracranial injuries	24	33	26	50	31	29
Internal injuries	44	37	50	25	47	43
Other	17	11	7	0	9	12
Total number	393	289	151	36	138	1007
(b) Persons injured, excluding fatalities						
Fracture of skull & face	4	3	2	5	6	4
Fracture of spine & trunk	6	6	4	1	5	5
Fracture of upper limb	5	6	14	9	7	7
Fracture of lower limb	5	5	23	12	18	9
Intracranial injuries	9	8	5	12	9	8
Internal injuries	4	3	3	1	3	3
Laceration of head & face	19	16	3	14	12	15
Laceration of neck & trunk	4	4	3	3	4	4
Laceration of upper limb	3	3	4	3	3	3
Laceration of lower limb	4	5	10	7	3	5
Other*	38	40	28	34	32	36
Total number	7302	6207	2703	1180	1488	18880

* Mostly sprains and strains, abrasions, and contusions.

12.4 Canada

12.4.1 British Columbia, police

A classification similar to the NYSICS (Table 8.7) is used. Mercer (1987a) reproduces the report form, which includes the categories.

12.4.2 Manitoba, hospital in-patients

Injuries to hospital in-patients in Manitoba are assigned both E and N codes (Dalkie and Mulligan, 1987).

12.4.3 Ontario, death certificates

Nature of injury (ICD N, 13 categories) is tabulated for road accident victims—Table O of 1975–76 edition of Vital Statistics (Toronto: Registrar General of Ontario). See Table 9.1.

12.4.4 Saskatchewan, death certificates

Nature of injury (ICD N, 13 categories) is tabulated for road accident victims—Table 12 of 1978 edition (but not subsequent editions) of Saskatchewan Vital Statistics Annual Report (Regina: Saskatchewan Health). See Table 9.1.

Table 12.2: Percentage distribution of part of body injured—motor vehicle occupants and motorcyclists, South Australia, 1977–1981.

	Killed		Hospitalised		Other*	
	M v occs	Mcs	M v occs	Mcs	M v occs	Mcs
Head	28	27	26	7	20	3
Neck	2	3	2	0	16	1
Chest/body	3	0	9	7	10	6
Internal	8	10	1	1	0	0
Limbs	0	2	7	33	13	46
Multiple	53	54	47	48	27	34
Other#	6	3	8	4	14	10
Total number	906	202	10950	2913	26509	5039

* Treated by doctor; treated at hospital (not admitted); or treated at hospital (not known whether admitted or not).
# Includes shock, natural illness, and unknown injury.

12.5   Denmark

12.5.1   Police

The part of body injured is coded, for those killed or seriously injured, and the annual publication Faerdselsuheld (Kobenhavn: Danmarks Statistik) includes some tables on nature of injury according to category of road user. Table 12.3 compares fatalities with seriously-injured casualties admitted to hospital or not admitted, and Table 12.4 compares the different types of impact.

12.5.2   Death certificates

Nature of injury (ICD AN, 13 categories) is tabulated for motor vehicle accident victims—Table II F of 1979 edition (but not subsequent editions) of Dodsarsagerne i Kongeriget Danmark (Kobenhavn: Udgivet af Sundhedsstyrelsen). See Table 9.1.

12.5.3   Odense, emergency room patients

See Section 10.3.1.

12.6   England and Wales

12.6.1   Death certificates

Nature of injury (ICD N, 16 categories) is tabulated for victims of motor vehicle accidents (but in the case of pedal cyclists and pedestrians including victims of other road vehicle accidents also), cross-classified by sex, age group (8 categories), and category of road user (4th digit of ICD E)—Table 7 of 1985 edition of Mortality Statistics: Accidents and Violence (Series DH4) (London: HMSO). See Tables 9.1, 9.2, and 9.4.

12.6.2   Hospital in-patients

There is a one-in-ten survey of persons leaving hospital, known as the Hospital In-Patient Enquiry (HIPE). The annual reports give some information about road accident casualties as a group, the several categories not being separated. As the publication is in microfiche, it is practicable to produce so many tables that it would take too long to describe them all here. The main variables relevant here are the numbers of discharges (including deaths), duration of stay, diagnosis (ICD 3-digit), Regional Health Authority in which treated, and age and sex of casualty. See also Section 10.2.1.

Table 12.3: Percentage distribution of part of body injured—Denmark, 1982.

	Killed	Hospital-ised*	Not hosp-italised*
Intracranial injury, skull fracture, face, or eye injury	42	53	48
Injury of trunk (chest/abdomen)	9	5	6
Injury of spine/pelvis	1	3	1
Fracture/dislocation/severe sprain of shoulder, arm, or hand	0	7	25
Fracture/dislocation/severe sprain of hip, leg, or foot	1	20	15
Serious injuries in more than one main region	46	12	4
Total number	658	7111	1974

* Only those classified as seriously injured are included. Of those not hospitalised, 93% were treated in a casualty ward, 7% were not taken to a casualty ward.

Table 12.4: Percentage distribution of part of body injured for several categories of road user and types of impact—seriously injured casualties, Denmark, 1982.

	Drivers and passengers of 4-wheeled vehicles*							Motor cyclists#		Moped riders#		Pedal cyclists#		Pedest-rians#
	Frontal	Side	Rear	OT	Ejected	Other	Total	Fall	Struck	Fall	Struck	Fall	Struck	Struck
Intracranial injury, skull fracture, face, or eye injury	66	45	56	55	59	44	59	28	24	53	32	69	49	40
Injury of trunk (chest/abdomen)	9	14	7	5	3	9	9	4	1	2	2	1	4	2
Injury of spine/pelvis	2	5	13	6	3	2	3	3	4	1	1	2	2	3
Fracture/dislocation/severe sprain of shoulder, arm, or hand	7	11	5	14	8	14	9	20	15	15	13	12	12	11
Fracture/dislocation/severe sprain of hip, leg, or foot	8	11	11	10	6	17	10	32	44	25	42	13	22	29
Serious injuries in more than one main region	8	14	7	11	22	13	11	12	12	4	9	4	12	15
Total number	2199	532	107	498	181	510	4027	560	102	802	400	836	906	1207
In addition to the above, the number of slightly-injured	1183	303	92	357	36	603	2574	269	42	447	198	466	420	372

* The types of impact shown are more fully described as: flung against steering wheel, front panel, etc.; car hit in the side; car hit from behind; car overturned; thrown out of car; other.
# The types of impact shown are more fully described as: fall while driving; hit by vehicle. (There were a few percent falling into neither of these categories.)

Table 12.5: Percentage distribution of the part of body injured*—Hong Kong, 1982.

	(a) Fatal#				(b) Serious#					(c) Slight#				
	M v occs	Mcs	Peds	Total	M v occs	Mcs	Pcs	Peds	Total	M v occs	Mcs	Pcs	Peds	Total
Head	51	53	53	53	48	12	30	36	38	38	5	12	12	25
Upper trunk	14	19	13	14	31	12	22	18	21	26	8	11	14	20
Lower trunk	4	2	6	5	3	3	3	6	4	3	3	3	7	5
Arms	3	0	2	3	8	13	9	7	8	15	21	18	14	15
Legs	28	23	26	25	15	60	37	33	29	17	62	57	53	35
Total number	96	47	290	453	3959	1056	419	4093	9615	7602	1630	364	4430	14154

* Although any number of the five regions of the body may be specified for each casualty, it appears that in practice only one is used, as the numbers of injuries on which this Table is based correspond closely to the numbers of casualties given in Table 6 of Annual Traffic Accident Report 1982 (Royal Hong Kong Police).

Fatal: death within 30 days of the accident. Serious: detained in hospital for more than 12 hours. Slight: other injury.

12.7   Finland

The Finnish Red Cross initiated a 3-year project in 1981 aimed at the development of statistical indicators for accidents (especially those occurring at home and during other leisure activities). A report in English is given by Honkanen (1984). See Sections 8.5.4 and 10.2.3.

12.8   France

Police: one of the accident report forms (I think it is the one used by the gendarmerie, as distinct from the police) includes the most severe injury sustained. This is coded according to the part of body (head, chest, abdomen, vertebral column, upper limbs, lower limbs), and the type of injury (amputation, burn, fracture, other). I have not seen published data deriving from this source.

12.9   Hong Kong

12.9.1   Police

Casualties are classified according to severity and also as to location of injury. Some data kindly made available by the Royal Hong Kong Police is given as Table 12.5.

12.9.2   Hospital in-patients

Patients in Government hospitals are classified according to both the E and N codes, but unfortunately a cross-tabulation is not published.

12.10   Hungary

Death certificates: nature of injury (14 categories) is tabulated for road accident victims— Table 7.21 of 1982 edition of Demografiai Evkonyv (Budapest: Kozponti Statisztikai Hivatal). See Table 9.1.

12.11   Irish Republic

Death certificates: nature of injury (ICD 3-digit code) is given for road accident victims (ICD 3-digit E code, thus enabling pedestrians to be identified separately, as well as the total)—Table 19A of 1979 edition of Report on Vital Statistics (Dublin: The Stationery Office). See Tables 9.1 and 9.2.

Table 12.6: Percentage distribution of part of body injured—Japan, 1984.

	(a) Killed*					(b) Seriously injured*					(c) Slightly injured				
	4-wh veh	2-wh veh	Bic-ycle	Peds	All	4-wh veh	2-wh veh	Bic-ycle	Peds	All	4-wh veh	2-wh veh	Bic-ycle	Peds	All
Head	57	63	77	72	65	16	15	25	23	19	13	11	21	27	15
Face	1	2	1	1	1	9	3	3	2	4	9	7	8	11	9
Neck	11	11	6	6	9	20	2	2	1	7	58	4	3	2	31
Chest	18	14	8	9	13	14	9	9	6	10	3	4	4	3	3
Abdomen	8	7	5	7	7	4	1	1	1	2	1	1	1	1	1
Waist & spine	1	2	1	3	2	6	5	7	8	6	4	5	7	9	5
Arms & legs	1	1	1	1	1	30	63	54	59	52	12	68	56	47	35
Others	4	2	1	1	2	1	1	1	1	1	0	1	1	1	1
Total number	3391	2322	947	2576	9262	19262		10038		68388	293851		81450		575933
							23958		15003			130493		69381	

* Killed: died within 24 hours. Seriously injured: detained in hospital for 30 days or more (but see Section 3.8).

12.12   Italy

Death certificates: nature of injury (18 ICD N groups, though unfortunately N800–809 is shown as one group, not divided into head fractures and body fractures) is tabulated for road accident victims—Table 72 of 1979 edition (1978 data) of Annuario di Statistiche Sanitarie (Roma: Istituto Centrale di Statistica). See Table 9.1.

12.13   Japan

12.13.1   Police

Casualties are classified according to severity and also as to location of injury. Some data is shown in Table 12.6, taken from the annual publication Statistics '84 Road Accidents Japan (Tokyo: International Association of Traffic and Safety Sciences).

12.13.2   Death certificates

Nature of injury (11 ICD N groups, limb fractures being included with body fractures as one of the groups) is tabulated for motor vehicle accident victims—Table 8 of 1980 edition of Vital Statistics Japan. Volume 3 (Tokyo: Ministry of Health and Welfare). See Table 9.1.

12.14   Macau

12.14.1   Death certificates

Nature of injury (ICD AN) is tabulated for victims of motor vehicle accidents, classified by sex and age group—Table 4 of Chapter 15 of 1979 edition of Anuario Estatistico (Macau: Reparticao dos Servicos de Estatistica).

12.14.2   Hospital in-patients

Nature of injury (ICD AN) is tabulated for victims of motor vehicle accidents, classified by sex and age group—Table 3 of Chapter 15 of 1979 edition of Anuario Estatistico. However, this should be treated with caution since the hospitals included in the data vary from year to year. See Table 10.1.

12.15   Morocco

Police: there are four categories of people killed, differing in the time elapsing between the accident and the death—killed at the scene, during transfer to hospital, within the three days following the accident, within 30 days. (In 1976, the respective numbers were 1515, 433, 313, and 111.) Table 12.7 has been prepared from the 1970 edition of Accidents Corporels de la Circulation Routiere (Rabat: Ministere des Travaux Publics et des Communications). If these figures can be taken at face

Table 12.7: Percentages of fatally-injured pedestrians who died at the scene of the accident—Morocco, 1970.

Age group of pedestrain	Surete National (mostly urban areas)	Gendarmerie Royale (mostly rural areas)
0 - 6	52	79
7 - 13	51	77
14 - 19	58	82
20 - 39	49	77
40 - 69	42	74
70+	40	80

value (and not as reflecting delayed police presence at the scene, or incomplete reporting of late deaths, in rural areas), then possible explanations include more violent impact and delayed medical attention. (There is an extensive literature from research, as distinct from routine statistics, on times till death; for instance, Hutchinson, 1974, analysed some London data on the times till death of pedestrians.)

12.16   New Zealand

Hospital in-patients: nature of injury (21 ICD N groups) is tabulated for motor vehicle accident victims admitted to public hospitals—Table 9 of 1982 edition of Hospital and Selected Morbidity Data (Wellington: National Health Statistics Centre). See Tables 10.1 and 10.2.

12.17   Northern Ireland

Death certificates: nature of injury (ICD N, 13 categories) is tabulated for victims of motor vehicle accidents—Abstract 28 of 1979 edition of Annual Report of the Registrar General Northern Ireland (Belfast: HMSO). See Table 9.1.

12.18   Norway

12.18.1   Police

It has been mentioned in Section 8.9.3 that the "serious" category is divided according to whether the injury is considered "dangerous" or not. The police obtain information from the hospitals as to the nature of injury in each individual case, and distinguish dangerous from not dangerous injuries using a list. Some notes on the differences between fatality data collected through death certification and through road accident reporting are included in Veitrafikkulykker (Oslo: Statistisk Sentralbyra), including the following: "The statistics on causes of death also include Norwegian citizens temporarily living abroad and having been killed there in road traffic accidents, whereas the statistics on road traffic accidents include foreigners being killed in road traffic accidents in Norway."

12.18.2   Death certificates

Nature of injury (ICD N, 13 categories) is tabulated for victims of motor vehicle accidents—Table 78 of 1980 edition of Helsestatistikk (Oslo: Statistisk Sentralbyra). See Table 9.1. Evidently it would be possible to obtain the information for the several categories of road user separately, since another table gives category cross-classified by age and sex.

12.19   Papua New Guinea

Police: I believe that part of body injured is recorded (categorised into head, neck, trunk, arms, back, hips, legs), but I have not seen published data derived from this source.

12.20   San Marino

How the data is collected I do not know, but Table 26 of Volume 2 of Annuario Statistico 1972–1980 (San Marino: Ufficio Statale di Statistica) gives the nature of injury sustained by the 2480 victims of road vehicle accidents in 1972–80. It is unlikely that all these were hospitalised—very roughly, the two groups AN138–140,143–144 and AN141–142,145–150 can be assumed to be serious and slight respectively, and they had 753 and 1727

Table 12.8: Categories of injury used in Switzerland.

One or two of the following are chosen:

Head:
    1 Concussion
    2 Skull fracture
    3 Fracture of the jaw
    4 Other

Trunk:
    5 Fracture of the clavicle
    6 Fracture of the scapula
    7 Fracture of the ribs
    8 Fracture of the pelvis
    9 Internal injuries
    10 External injuries

Vertebral column:
    11 Fracture of the neck
    12 Fracture of the vertebral column
    13 Other

Limbs:
    14 Fracture of the upper arm
    15 Fracture of the lower arm
    16 Fracture of the kneecap
    17 Fracture of the tibia or fibula
    18 Fracture of the femur
    19 Fracture of the foot
    20 Other

Other injuries:
    21 Multiple fractures
    22 Burns
    23 Lacerations and contusions
    24 Other serious injuries

casualties in them. Brief particulars of the accident events are in the same dataset. See Table 10.1.

12.21 Scotland

12.21.1 Death certificates

Nature of injury (ICD N, 13 categories) is tabulated for victims of motor vehicle traffic accidents—Table C2.18 of 1980 edition of Annual Report of the Registrar General Scotland (Edinburgh: HMSO). However, a problem with Scottish data is that there is a strong (and increasing) tendency for the unhelpful general category "multiple injuries" to be specified on death certificates, which is coded as AN150. See Table 9.1.

12.21.2 Hospital in-patients

Although tables of data on road accident victims are not routinely published, the information is collected and some for 1980 has been kindly made available—see Tables 10.1 and 10.2.

12.22 South Africa

Death certificates: nature of injury (15 ICD N groups) is tabulated for road accident victims—Table 10 of 1979 edition of Deaths. Whites,

Coloureds and Asians (Pretoria: Government Printer) and Table 10 of Deaths of Blacks (Pretoria: Government Printer). See Table 9.1.

12.23 Switzerland

Police: along with Victoria, perhaps the best routine data on nature of injury. The accident report form used by the police has space for up to two injuries per casualty. The ICD is not used, but the categories available correspond fairly closely (Table 12.8). For fatalities, death certificates are consulted; it is not made clear how information on the others is obtained, but such detail clearly implies a high degree of cooperation from the hospitals—Strassenverkehrsunfalle in der Schweiz (Bern: Bundesamt fur Statistik). Tables 66 and 67 of the 1980 edition (but not the 1984 edition) of that publication give nature of injury and whether fatal or not, according to category of road user and type of accident. See Tables 9.1, 9.2, 10.1, 10.2. It is even possible to make comparisons of those wearing and not wearing a seat belt or crash helmet (Table 9.3). This source of data has not been extensively used (or, if it has, the results are not widely known in the English-speaking world). As far as I know, there is no horrible defect in the dataset that makes it unsuitable for research.

Table 12.9: Percentage distribution of part of body injured—Oklahoma, 1979.

| | Police injury severity code | | | | | | | |
| | K | | A | | B | | C | |
	Mun*	Hi'w's#	Mun*	Hi'w's#	Mun*	Hi'w's#	Mun*	Hi'w's#
Head	39	34	32	23	42	46	40	37
Head & internal	4	11	6	14	4	9	3	7
Head & other	20	23	29	35	26	21	13	8
Trunk-internal	9	9	7	8	3	3	14	17
Internal & other	5	6	7	8	4	5	4	5
Arm or leg	19	13	16	11	18	12	23	20
Trunk-external	3	4	2	2	4	4	4	6

* Municipal: publicly-maintained streets and highways within incorporated areas which maintain a police agency, excludes turnpikes and interstate highways.
# Highways, etc.: turnpikes and interstate highways, and all publicly-maintained streets and highways not included in Municipal.

Indeed, Dr. Walz of Zurich makes use of it in his review of pelvic fractures (Walz, 1984) without adverse comment.

12.24   U.S.A.

12.24.1   Death certificates

See Table 9.1 and the references cited there.

12.24.2   Hospital in-patients

Data not available at present, but may be in the future. See Section 10.2.2.

12.24.3   Oklahoma, police

The (U.S.) National Safety Council's Accident Facts booklet (1981 edition) includes a table from the Oklahoma Department of Public Safety giving a cross-tabulation of part of body injured with severity of injury (K-A-B-C-0 classification). Unfortunately, the injury categories are difficult to compare with those of other systems. See Table 12.9.

12.24.4   Texas, police

Some data is in Hilger and Scott (1982). However, there is no commentary in that report, and it is not self-evident what the figures mean. For instance, data is given for 13,000 drivers, whereas there were

129,000 injured altogether. The categories listed are: head, neck, trunk/torso/internal, arms, legs, head and chest, multiple parts, head and neck, head and arms/legs.

12.24.5   Other states, police

See Table 8.23.

Chapter 13

Prospects for matching police and hospital data

13.1 A Chapter mostly on British studies

If the information about nature and severity of injury that is in hospital medical records could be added to the corresponding police accident record, a considerable forward step would have been taken.

This Chapter will concentrate on the study in Britain by Nicholl (1980, 1981) of computerised case-by-case matching of casualties in the two datasets; this project did not utilise the casualty's name or any other unique identifier. Other British work (on Scottish data) will then be described, and then briefer mention made of a few other studies (from a number of countries) in which the two datasets were matched.

13.2 England and Wales

13.2.1 Methods

In principle, it should be a straightforward business to compare cases recorded in two datsets and determine which ones correspond. But the difficulty faced by Nicholl (1980) when he tried to match casualties recorded in the Hospital In-Patient Enquiry (see Section 10.2.1) with those in the Stats 19 system (see Section 3.2) was that neither name nor any other personal identifier was present in the two files. The matching therefore had to use the following information: age and sex of casualty, date, geographic area. Nicholl achieved a remarkable degree of success, but even so the error rate was a little higher than one would like and the necessary computer program a lot messier.

Before describing his project further, let me make this point: political concerns about confidentiality of personal information will always (rightly) make it difficult to obtain even one dataset with names recorded, let alone two in order to match them. But the lack of any sort of identifier makes a project like this one very difficult, and one is never quite sure that the error rate is unimportant. It is to be hoped, therefore, that the police and the hospital administrators (perhaps also death registration authorities, and insurance companies) can agree on a common factor that both could record yet which would not breach confidentiality—Nicholl's work would have been so much easier if the police data had included the name of the hospital the casualty was admitted to, or if both datasets had included just the initial letter of the casualty's surname (or their date of birth, or the number of the house they lived at, or almost anything).

In this project, the base dataset was that from HIPE, not from Stats 19. It had to be this way round because HIPE is only a 10% sample of hospital patients (so if one started with a Stats 19 casualty, there would be a 90% chance of him or her not being in the HIPE records even if he or she were admitted to hospital). The data was from 1972.

No doubt there is some small proportion of misrecorded data in both datasets. A more important source of difficulty is that frequently the age of a casualty is estimated by the police rather than enquiry made. Consequently, one must not insist that the age of a casualty who is otherwise a good match be exactly the same as in the HIPE record. The following outlines how Nicholl conducted the matching procedure:

Table 13.1: Notes on matching HIPE and Stats 19 data.

- Match data from one hospital region at a time. (For efficiency: computer processing time too long otherwise.)

- Create a file of Stats 19 records corresponding to the hospital region being processed (including the local authority areas that are around the edge of the region).

- Reformat the Stats 19 file from 1 record per accident to 1 record per casualty.

- Sort the records into chronological order.

- Determine grid references for each hospital.

- Read in a HIPE record.

- In the Stats 19 casualty file, start at 10pm on the day preceding that on which the HIPE casualty was admitted to hospital, and proceed through until midnight 26 hours later.

- Discard any record indicating the wrong sex.

- Discard any record for which the age difference from the HIPE record is too large.

- Discard any record for which the distance between the hospital location and the accident location is too great.

- For any Stats 19 casualty record passing the above three tests, calculate its mismatch score based upon these factors:

  (a) The direct distance between the accident and the nearest hospital with a casualty department.

  (b) The direct distance between the accident and the hospital to which the HIPE casualty was admitted, minus the least distance as in (a) above.

  (c) The difference in the age as recorded by the two systems.

  (d) The age difference expressed as a percentage of the age recorded in HIPE. (This is included both because the police should record ages of child casualties exactly, and on the more general grounds that police estimates of adults' ages are likely to be less accurate for older than for younger people.)

  (e) The time when the accident occurred, if it occurred on the day before hospital admission.

  (f) If the Stats 19 casualty is recorded as being slightly injured, the number of nights the HIPE casualty spent in hospital.

Table 13.1: (continued).

- Example of matching criteria for the S.W. Metropolitan area:

  - Exclude cases from accidents occurring more than 15 miles from the hospital, or differing in age by more than 10 years.

  - Mismatch score = 2 x miles from nearest hospital + 3.5 x extra miles from actual hospital + 2.5 x age difference + contributions from (e) and (f) (percentage age difference seems to have been omitted in this example).

  - Accept match if total mismatch is less than 35 and the second-lowest mismatch is at least 7 greater.

  - So a casualty differing in age by 2 years and injured in an accident 5 miles away, there being no nearer hospital, will get a score of 15 and will be accepted as a match provided no other Stats 19 casualty has a score of 21 or less.

- The formula for calculating the mismatch score, and the other parameters in the procedure, have to be adjusted for each hospital region, in particular to take account of how densely the area is served by hospitals.

- Tolerable discrepancies between corresponding items of information were decided upon. Any Stats 19 records exceeding these were discarded as possible matches for the HIPE record being considered.

- The discrepancy in each item of information was converted into a "mismatch" score, and a total mismatch obtained by summation; this was done for each of the records remaining as candidates after the first selection.

- The Stats 19 record chosen as the match was the one with the lowest mismatch score, except (i) if the lowest mismatch score was so large as to make any match doubtful, no match was made, and (ii) if the lowest mismatch score was nearly the same as the next lowest score, so it was uncertain which record was the true match, once again no match was made.

Once a match was found, the ICD N code and the length of stay in hospital were added from the HIPE record into the Stats 19 record.

Features of the procedure like the absolute limits on discrepancies, how to weight discrepancies into an overall mismatch score, the highest acceptable mismatch score, and the lowest acceptable difference between the two lowest mismatch scores,

were chosen on the basis of what was known about the accuracy of recording the data items, and a lengthy process of trial and error.

Table 13.1 gives further information about the procedure Nicholl adopted. There were quite a number of difficulties not reported there—for instance, it is by no means easy to find out exactly which hospitals had casualty departments at a time a few years before when the research was being done; and several varieties of accident location system were in use within the Stats 19 system, e.g. eight-digit grid reference, six-digit preceded by two blanks, six-digit as blank/3 digits/blank/3 digits, and link-and-node. In a sense, these are trivia, but they do add very considerably to the labour of a project like this.

13.2.2 Success rate and accuracy of matching

Nicholl reports that 50% of the HIPE records found a match with a Stats 19 record. Bearing in mind the known degree of difference between the two systems (Section 11.4), the recording errors present in both datasets, and the obvious difficulties when attempting to match a casualty in one of the frequently-occurring categories (e.g. male aged 20) when the hospital is in a major conurbation like London with a high density of hospitals, this was

Table 13.2: Percentage distribution of injuries over the parts of the body* in the matched dataset, with a comparison of the categories of road user.

	Car & van occupants	PSV & HGV occupants	Motor cyclists	Pedal cyclists	Pedestrians	All
Head	73	66	52	75	59	65
Neck	1	0	1	0	0	1
Shoulders	2	3	3	0	2	2
Arms	5	8	7	3	3	4
Chest	6	1	2	5	1	4
Spine	1	0	1	0	1	1
Abdomen	1	0	1	0	1	1
Pelvis	1	1	3	0	6	3
Hips	2	1	2	0	2	2
Thighs	3	4	7	3	9	6
Knees	2	1	2	0	0	1
Lower legs	3	8	14	9	14	9
Feet & ankles	2	5	6	3	2	3
Total number, all known locations	1378	73	521	204	1026	3785
Unspecified or multiple locations#	13	21	12	11	11	13

* For definitions in terms of ICD codes, see Appendix 3 of Nicholl (1980).
\# Expressed as a percentage of the grand total (location known, unknown, or multiple).

felt to be acceptable. Attempts at matching HIPE and Stats 19 records by hand had managed a 55% success rate.

An estimate of the fraction of wrong matches was made by carrying out the procedure on the hospital records of road casualties admitted to Battle Hospital in Reading in 1975; these casualties and the accidents they were involved in had previously been registered and investigated by the Transport and Road Research Laboratory; hence the matched Battle dataset could be compared with that at TRRL. The proportion of wrong matches was found to be 9%.

13.2.3   Results

Table 13.2 summarises a cross-tabulation of category of road user and region of body injured. This Table may be compared with Table 10.2.

Nicholl also gives several analyses that could only be carried out on his data, because they rely on correlating information from the HIPE record with that from the Stats 19 record. For exam-

ple, for vehicle occupants, Table 13.3 summarises a cross-tabulation of type of accident and region of body injured. This may be compared with Danish data in Table 12.4. Another analysis resulted in the finding that as the ratio of the mass of the other vehicle to the mass of the casualty's vehicle increased, so also did the median length of stay in hospital of the casualty.

13.2.4   Medical record linkage

Record linkage is an important field in medical informatics, being used for such purposes as monitoring the contacts with the health services that chronically-ill individuals have over a period of years (along with the progress of their disease and its treatment), and for identifying disease-disease and environment-disease associations. It is, however, of only limited present relevance, as the practicalities are very different—the name of the patient is available, for one thing, and there is nothing corresponding to accident date, for another. Nevertheless, it is worth mentioning the paper by

Table 13.3: Percentage distribution of injuries over the parts of the body* in the matched dataset, with a comparison of types of accident, for vehicle occupants.

	T y p e	o f	a c c i d e n t #			
	SV OT	SV non-OT	2-veh r-e	2-veh h-o	2-veh int	Mult veh
Head	72	74	74	65	69	69
Neck	2	1	0	1	3	0
Arms	9	6	0	5	1	6
Chest and shoulders	7	5	6	10	10	5
Spine	3	1	2	0	1	1
Abdomen, pelvis, hips	5	2	8	3	6	4
Legs	3	12	8	16	11	16
Total number	148	375	52	268	199	159

* For definitions in terms of ICD codes, see Appendix 3 of Nicholl (1980).
\# Single-vehicle overturning; single-vehicle non-overturning; two-vehicle rear-end; two-vehicle head-on; two-vehicle intersection; multiple vehicles. For definitions, see Appendix 1 of Nicholl (1980).

Smith and Newcombe (1979), because of the many similarities in methods to Nicholl's work. These include a system of scores for the various agreements and disagreements of particular items of identifying information, provision for partial agreements, the use of an empirically-tested threshold for the sum of the scores to separate probable linkages from probable non-linkages, and the acceptance of only the best match if there are several candidates.

13.3 Scotland

In Chapter 10, it was mentioned that Scottish in-patient statistics are based on a 100% sample, not a 10% one as HIPE is. Stone (1984) describes the methods used at TRRL to match Scottish in-patient and Stats 19 records, and Tunbridge (1987) gives a number of data tables that resulted.

An important difference from Nicholl's project was that the category of road user (ICD E code) was given in most of the hospital records. (It was missing in 27% of cases.)

There were differences in the methods of matching, too. A mismatch score based upon all the relevant variables was not calculated; instead, tolerances for the variables were specified, together with a series of combinations of tolerance values for which a match was considered acceptable. For

instance, level 1 of tolerance resulted when there was an exact match for the six variables (police force, sex, age, category of road user, severity, and date); and level 30 had exact matches for four variables, age differing by three years, and category of road user being missing from the hospital record. Less attention was paid to geographic location than by Nicholl: the police force code of the Stats 19 record was simply compared with that of where the hospital was, and (with two exceptions) an exact match insisted upon.

Some 69% of hospital records were uniquely matched; for 40% of those matched, all the relevant variables corresponded exactly. There were 7% of hospital records that found multiple Stats 19 matches.

Looking now at the matching rate from the other direction, 55% of Stats 19 casualties classed as seriously injured were matched, plus 16% of fatalities and 5% of the slightly-injured.

As with Nicholl's study, ICD N code and length of stay were added to the Stats 19 information. In addition, as was mentioned in Section 8.5.5, the N code was translated into an AIS score.

Among the findings were the following.

- Leg injuries assume a greater importance in motorcyclists and pedestrians than in vehicle occupants. (See also Table 10.2.)

Table 13.4: Percentage distribution of part of body injured, for several categories of road users and types of impact*—in-patients, Scotland, 1980–82.

	Car/LGV occupants			HGV/PSV occupants		Motor cyclists		Pedal cyclists		Pedest -rians
	S	C	H	S	T	S	T	S	T	S
Head	64	62	60	49	50	41	27	82	62	52
Spine	7	4	4	6	3	4	3	2	2	1
Chest	6	9	9	4	5	3	2	1	2	2
Abdomen	2	2	3	2	3	4	3	1	1	2
Upper limbs	8	7	8	12	10	18	15	9	10	7
Lower limbs	13	17	15	28	28	30	51	5	23	36
Total number	3338	3027	672	254	119	945	1798	129	666	5301

* Abbreviations: LGV = light goods vehicle, HGV = heavy goods vehicle, PSV = public service vehicle (i.e. bus), S = single-vehicle accident, C = collision with car or LGV, H = collision with HGV or PSV, T = any two-vehicle collision.

Table 13.5: Percentage distribution of part of body injured, effects of seating location and age, car/LGV occupants.

	Drivers		Front seat pass'rs			Rear seat pass'rs		
	14-59	60+	0-13	14-59	60+	0-13	14-59	60+
Head	62	53	76	65	51	80	65	49
Spine	4	5	2	6	6	0	8	2
Chest	9	17	0	6	13	1	5	14
Abdomen	2	2	2	2	1	3	1	0
Upper limbs	6	6	8	9	12	8	7	10
Lower limbs	17	17	12	13	17	8	14	24
Total number	4066	434	92	1888	310	238	660	83

- There is a higher proportion of leg injuries and a lower proportion of head injuries in pedal cyclists struck by motor vehicles than in those having single-vehicle accidents. This is in accord with data from Denmark (Table 12.4) and Goteborg (Section 11.4.3), but data from Australia (Table 10.6), Massachusetts (Table 10.15), and Stockholm (Section 11.4.3) present rather different pictures.

- Little difference was found between front seat occupants wearing or not wearing seat belts, in either the location or the severity of their injuries. This is a consequence of the casualties having only a limited range of severities, the slightly injured and many of those killed having been excluded because the sample was one of in-patients.

Further details of the results are given in Tables 13.4–13.6.

13.4 Coroners' data

Coroners (in England and Wales) and Procurators Fiscal (in Scotland) supply the Transport and Road Research Laboratory with information on the blood alcohol level of people aged 16 or more who die

Table 13.6: Percentage distribution of part of body injured, comparison of car/LGV occupants wearing or not wearing seat belts, and of speed limit at accident site.

	Speed limit 30 or 40 mph		Speed limit 50-70 mph	
	None	Belt	None	Belt
Head	69	61	60	53
Spine	3	7	5	7
Chest	7	10	9	9
Abdomen	1	2	2	3
Upper limbs	6	6	8	9
Lower limbs	14	14	16	19
Total number	2082	263	3036	776

within 12 hours of being injured in a road accident. It is mentioned in RAGB (1986) that computerised matching of this data with Stats 19 records is carried out.

13.5 New South Wales

The project described by Lukin and Vazey (1978) started out as an attempt to link hospital and police data on road accident victims in New South Wales. It soon became apparent to them, however, that there were problems with the suitability of the Health Commission's data system, and that these were likely to out-last the life of the project. Consequently, the project was adapted to concentrate on a sub-group of patients, those suffering a spinal injury.

This study used the name of the patient to match the records. Date of the crash and sometimes the approximate geographical area were also known. The police computerised record system was searched for accidents on the right date and at the right place, the relevant crash report numbers were printed out, and the microfilm copies of these reports examined to find which one was the right one.

The study covered traffic crash victims admitted to either of the two Spinal Injury Units in N.S.W., at the Royal North Shore Hospital and the Prince Henry Hospital, in the period 1968–74.

13.6 South Australia

McLean(1984) makes some brief comments on the feasibility and usefulness of matching various computerised datasets in South Australia. As to police and hospital data, McLean merely says that matching would be "difficult". He gives more attention to the possibility of matching police and SGIC (third party insurance—see Section 14.4) data, as (firstly) there would be greater variety of data items added to the police information (vehicle make and model as well as nature and severity of injury), and (secondly) it appears more feasible, as a copy of the relevant police accident report is (where available) kept with the claim file. (However, at present it is discarded after 12 months.) McLean recommends that the police accident report number be noted in the SGIC dataset, in case matching be attempted in the future. The ambulance crew's report mentioned in Section 8.6.4 is not computerised, but there might be enough injury information on it to make worthwhile bringing it together with the police database.

13.7 Texas

In the study by Pendleton et al (1986) of driver fatalities in Texas (see Section 7.7), it was necessary to match the mass accident data with blood alcohol data held in medical examiners' files. As in Nicholl's study, this was done without the victim's name; the age and sex of the casualty, and the date and county of the accident, were the variables used in the matching procedure.

13.8 Northeastern Ohio

The Northeastern Ohio Trauma Study collected data from a sample of visits to the emergency departments of hospitals (see Section 11.4.4 and Barancik and Fife, 1985). Emergency department reports were matched with computerised files of police reports. This was done chiefly by a computer algorithm based on the following variables: date of birth, sex, coded (Soundex) name, county of residence, approximate date of injury. Of all matched cases, 83% were identified using these (and a check showed that 95% were matched correctly). The remainder were matched by using age when date of birth was missing and by allowing minor discrepancies in age.

13.9   Quebec

13.9.1   Bourbeau et al (1981)

These authors report a study of 1008 road casualties in Quebec in 1974. The following records were linked: police accident report; hospitalisation report; case history of all medical services received; questionnaire completed by the victim or his family for the Third Party Liability Service of the Health Insurance Board. The methodology is not described, but presumably the injured person's name was available in all records.

13.9.2   Stulginskas et al (1983)

The study by Stulginskas et al (1983) of road accidents to children in Montreal (see Section 11.4.9) included a computerised cross-check between hospital emergency room and police records. Full details are not reported—presumably the child's name was available in both sets of records and this made matching easy. The police reports contained the name of the hospital to which the child had been taken, and the impression is given that this was a routine item of information, not something recorded specially for the study.

13.10   Odense and Goteborg

The calculation of how large a proportion of hospital-registered accident victims is known to the police by the Odense University Accident Analysis Group (1983)—see Section 11.4.6—appears to have been done using computerised matching of person identification numbers.

Similarly, in Goteborg, person identity numbers link specific casualties in the hospital records with the casualties reported by the police to the Traffic Planning Department (Bunketorp and Romanus, 1985).

13.11   Utah

The report on fatal traffic crashes in Utah cited in Table 8.24 was based upon the bringing together of the following sources of information: highway patrol accident report, ambulance report, paramedic report (urban areas only), emergency department log entry, autopsy report, death certificate, newspaper articles. (Not all of these were utilised in each case.)

13.12   Waikato

In the course of the Waikato Hospital Road Accident Survey (Bailey, 1984), routine hospital admission records held by the New Zealand Department of Health were matched to the specially-collected survey data. Date of admission, age, sex, and ethnic origin were the variables used for this. Bailey also raises the possibility of improving the reporting of accidents (beyond the present police/Ministry of Transport system) by including hospital, ambulance service, and Accident Compensation Commission data.

13.13   A survey by Benjamin (1987)

Part of the report by Benjamin (1987) concerns the matching of police and medical files in eleven countries. It appears that the kind of procedure described in Sections 13.2 and 13.3 is not carried out on a wide scale anywhere. However, it is anticipated that it will start in Denmark in 1988, there is an experimental linking of information about casualties hospitalised in 1982 being carried out in The Netherlands, and there is something similar being done in Sweden, too. For non-medical aspects of Benjamin's survey, see Section 3.15.

Chapter 14

Insurance data

14.1 Advantages and disadvantages

The contribution made by insurance claims data has already been touched on, in particular in Section 4.4.1 (comparing police statistics with an insurance sample) and Tables 9.1, 9.2, 10.1, and 10.2 (data on nature of injury in Victoria was from an insurance source). This Chapter will deal further with the subject, concentrating on data from the United States, Victoria, Sweden, and Japan.

The big advantages of insurance data are its volume (many insurance claims are made for crashes that are not reported to the police), the inclusion of damage-only cases, information about the vehicle characteristics (e.g. make and model of car) being known, and the injury descriptions being frequently better than in police data. The disadvantages are the time that elapses between the accident and making the claim (and thus the scope for distortions of recollection), the deliberate distortions that may be introduced by the claimant, and (in some countries) the slowness of the insurance industry to recognise the potential of the data in researching crash avoidance and injury reduction.

14.2 The HLDI and IIHS in the United States

14.2.1 Two connected institutes

The Highway Loss Data Institute (HLDI) gathers, processes, and publishes information on the injury and other insurance claims experience of various types of cars and other motor vehicles. It is funded through, and has some staff in common with, the Insurance Institute for Highway Safety (IIHS). The IIHS, in turn, receives its support from the U.S. motor insurance industry. Both organisations are based in Washington, D.C. This account is based upon HLDI (1981).

14.2.2 Data collection

HLDI calculates how many claims there are per insured vehicle year for each vehicle type, and how much these claims cost in terms of insurance payments for human injuries, vehicle damage, or theft. It is noteworthy that vehicle type is very detailed—make, model, model year, body style, and engine capacity are all available.

HLDI gets its data from major U.S. motor insurers in machine-readable form. (The companies supplying data insure about half of the private passenger vehicles in the U.S.A.) Only insurers' first-party coverage files—those under which the policyholder collects compensation from his or her own insurer, regardless of fault—are included. There are three types:

- Injury. This derives from "personal injury protection" coverage, sold in states having a "no fault" insurance system. At present this applies to 19 states, plus the District of Columbia (HLDI, 1986). Medical expenses and related losses are reimbursed without regard to who was at fault in the crash.

- Vehicle crash damage. This is from "collision" coverage, which compensates for vehicle damage.

- Vehicle theft. This derives from "comprehensive" coverage; only theft loss data is used, fire and vandalism being excluded.

Data available for each claim may be considered under two headings:

- Vehicle. The Vehicle Identification Number (see also Section 6.4.6) is the crucial item

Table 14.1: Comparison of car body styles as to crash loss experience.

	Regular 2-door	Regular 4-door	Station wagon	Sport & specialty
Relative injury claim frequency under personal injury protection coverage, for 1977-79 compacts, taking average claim frequency for all 1977-79 models as 100	100	94	85	114
Relative average loss payment per insured vehicle year under collision coverage, for 1980 subcompacts, taking average loss payment per i.v.y. for all 1980 models as 100	130	81	73	278
Relative average loss from theft per insured vehicle year, for 1980 compacts, taking the average loss from theft per i.v.y. for all 1980 models as 100	162	75	32	212

Table 14.2: Three comparisons of model pairs matched for size and body style.

Relative injury claim frequency under personal injury protection coverage, for 1977-79 2-door small subcompacts	Taking the average claim frequency for all 1977-79 models as 100, Honda Accord = 107 and Datsun 200 SX = 172
Relative injury claim frequency under personal injury protection coverage, for 1977-79 compact station wagons	Taking the average claim frequency for all 1977-79 models as 100, Oldsmobile Cutlass = 69 and AMC Concord = 102.
Relative average loss payment per insured vehicle year under collision coverage, for 1980 2-door small subcompacts	Taking the average loss payment per i.v.y. for all 1980 models as 100, Chevrolet Chevette = 93 and Volkswagen Scirocco = 203

here. It can be decoded to identify make, model (i.e. "series" in American terminology), model year, body style, and engine. Secondary sources can be used to estimate weight and power.

- Non-vehicle factors. These are the age of the insured operator, the location where the vehicle is normally garaged, the excess in force (the "deductible" in American terminology, i.e. that portion of the damage cost borne by the policy-holder), the date of the crash, and the amount of loss.

HLDI generally presents its results for vehicle comparisons after adjustment to a standard mix of driver age groups and excesses in force.

14.2.3 Some findings

- The larger the car, the lower the injury claim frequency. In itself, this is not surprising: in two-vehicle collisions, the smaller car undergoes a greater velocity change than the larger car, so a greater likelihood of injury to its occupants is to be expected. What is important is that this increased injury in small cars occurs even in collisions between two vehicles of equal size. This is at variance with British data, where no dependence of injury severity on car size is apparent under these circumstances (Grime and Hutchinson, 1979, 1982).

- Body style affects crash loss experience, with two-door cars consistently having a worse record than four-door cars and station wagons. (Not surprisingly, sport and specialty models are by far the worst.) See the first two lines of Table 14.1.

- There are large differences in crash loss experience between models, even those of the same size class and body style. Three examples of comparisons are shown in Table 14.2.

It is not credible that the number of doors a car has should be directly relevant to crash causation. The result must be due to some other factor relating to the type of person who drives it, the distance driven per year, or the traffic conditions in which it is driven. (Theft losses show the same pattern as crash losses, see the final line in Table 14.1.) Nevertheless, the finding holds true even when the effects of driver age group, vehicle use category, and vehicle density of garaging location are controlled for.

On the other hand, I am not surprised by the wide variations between models. In the late 1960's and early 1970's, make and model of car were recorded on the Stats 19 form in Great Britain. Hutchinson and Jones (1975) showed there were large differences between the types of crashes that different models had. Among a set of 12 common models, the ratio of single- to two-car crashes varied from .20 to .31 and the ratio of overturning to non-overturning in single-car accidents varied from .11 to .38 (male drivers, all ages). If the proportions vary so much, the rates with which the several types are occurring must be varying too, so it is reasonable to expect the total rate of accident occurrence to vary.

14.3   The MAB in Victoria, Australia

The Motor Accidents Board (MAB) publishes annually Statistics of Persons Killed or Injured in

Table 14.3: Average costs for fatal and major injury claimants, according to their most serious injury, and the percentage distribution of the injuries*, Victoria, year ended June 1986.

	Average cost ($'000)	Percent -age
Fatal	3	3
Spinal cord	51	0.1
Head	10	6
Internal	7	2
Other severe	10	0.4
Limb fractures	6	12
Other fractures	4	5
Whiplash and minor	2	19
Whiplash solely	2	14
Other sprains and strains	2	5
Other injuries	1	34
All (total number)	3	(23505)

* Note the different bases of this Table and the Victorian data in Table 10.1. In the latter, all injuries were included (rather than only the most serious), except that sprains, strains, lacerations, contusions, and abrasions were excluded, even if they were the most serious injury.

Road Accidents. This refers to road accident casualties in Victoria during the previous financial year (July–June), for which claims were accepted by the Board. Many of the tables of data (including those which contributed to Tables 9.1, 9.2, 10.1, and 10.2 above) are restricted to fatal and "major injury" cases only, some 42% of the total in the year ending June 1986. ("Major injury" refers to the Board having made a total payment that exceeded a certain threshold, $270 in that year.) Table 14.3 shows both the relative frequencies with which the various types of injury occurred, and the average payment made. (For minor injuries, the average amount paid was $90.)

There are a number of data tables which are not included in the statistical yearbook but which the MAB makes available to interested enquirers. Among these are cross-tabulations of injury with characteristics of the vehicle (make, body type, weight, power) and of the accident (direction of

Table 14.4: Average payment ($'000) to motorcyclists, according to their age and the engine capacity of their motorcycle. Major injuries (excluding fatalities), Victoria, year ended June 1985.

		Engine capacity of motorcycle				
		0-260 cc	261-500 cc	501-750 cc	751+ cc	All
	0-17	7.2				7.2
Age of	18-19	3.3	. . . . .	4.6	. . . . .	3.8
	20-22	4.2	3.8	4.2	3.8	4.2
casualty	23-25	3.1	4.2	3.7	6.8	4.5
	26+	4.5	3.5	3.0	4.0	3.8
	All	4.1	3.7	3.7	4.9	4.3

Table 14.5: For each of several types of accident, the percentage of cases in which a payment was made under each of several heads, and (in brackets) the average amounts paid in these cases ($'000). Major injuries (excluding fatalities), Victoria, year ended June 1984.

	Type of payment						Total number
	Hospital in-patient	Hospital out-patient	Med-ical	Ambul-ance	Loss of earnings capacity	Other	
Pedestrian and vehicle	62	66	93	72	19	44	1476
	(5.2)	(0.2)	(0.7)	(0.2)	(3.7)	(0.5)	(5.1)
Pedal cyclist and vehicle	57	64	92	73	12	30	605
	(2.5)	(0.2)	(0.4)	(0.2)	(2.1)	(0.3)	(2.4)
Intersection (vehicles from two streets)	29	58	95	55	33	56	3059
	(2.9)	(0.1)	(0.4)	(0.2)	(3.2)	(0.4)	(2.7)
Intersection (vehicles from one street)	16	44	95	30	33	71	3859
	(2.7)	(0.1)	(0.4)	(0.1)	(3.2)	(0.3)	(2.2)
Vehicle manoeuvring	24	47	94	40	32	64	1038
	(2.5)	(0.1)	(0.4)	(0.2)	(3.3)	(0.3)	(2.4)
Vehicle proceeding	23	47	92	36	33	65	1408
	(2.5)	(0.2)	(0.4)	(0.2)	(2.9)	(0.3)	(2.2)
Vehicle overtaking	39	50	94	53	33	61	313
	(3.6)	(0.1)	(0.6)	(0.2)	(4.0)	(0.4)	(3.7)
Vehicle proceeding off path	56	58	94	67	33	43	2363
	(3.2)	(0.2)	(0.6)	(0.2)	(3.6)	(0.4)	(4.0)
Passenger accidents, misc., and unknown	51	51	89	36	36	41	642
	(2.5)	(0.2)	(0.5)	(0.3)	(2.4)	(0.4)	(3.0)
Total	37	54	94	51	31	55	16423
	(3.2)	(0.2)	(0.5)	(0.2)	(3.2)	(0.4)	(3.0)

Table 14.6: Percentage distribution of nature of injury to vehicle occupants*, according to the direction of impact sustained by the occupied vehicle. Major injuries (excluding fatalities), Victoria, three years ending June 1980.

	Front	Rear	Right side	Left side	Roll over	Total
(a) Percentages based on the total excluding sprains, strains, lacerations, contusions, and abrasions						
Fractured skull	3	3	3	3	3	3
Fractured face bones	11	4	5	4	4	9
Fractured vertebrae (no spinal cord lesion)	3	6	2	3	8	4
Fractured vertebrae (spinal cord lesion)	0.2	0.0	0.2	0.3	1.1	0.3
Fractured pelvis	3	2	8	7	3	4
Fractured upper limbs	14	9	15	14	20	14
Fractured lower limbs	16	6	10	9	8	13
Dislocations	3	5	3	3	6	3
Intracranial injuries	17	29	19	18	24	19
Injuries to chest and contents	15	10	22	25	11	17
Injuries to abdomen	5	3	5	6	3	5
Open wounds of eye and orbit	3	2	2	2	1	3
Injuries to nerves	1	3	1	1	3	1
Other injuries	5	19	6	6	6	6
Total number above	10407	799	2242	2063	1315	16826
(b) Percentages based on the total including sprains, strains, lacerations, contusions, and abrasions						
The injuries above	41	15	39	36	41	37
Sprains and strains (other than neck)	3	11	4	5	3	5
Sprains and strains (neck)	6	39	8	8	4	10
Lacerations, contusions, abrasions	50	36	49	51	53	48
Total number	25450	5406	5775	5654	3199	45484*

* The total number of vehicle occupant casualties was 25402. However, the number included in this table is somewhat smaller, as cases for which the direction of impact was unknown have been excluded.

impact, RUM code).

The tables that are included vary from year to year. Thus for year ending June 1985, there is a table of the costs and numbers of payments to motorcyclists, according to age of casualty and engine capacity of motorcycle; I have calculated the average costs shown in Table 14.4. For the year ending June 1984, the costs associated with each of several crash configurations (as represented by the Road User Movement code, see Section 6.4.5 and Figure 6.3) are given—see Table 14.5. For the year ending June 1980, the nature of injury to vehicle occupants is cross-tabulated with the direction of impact sustained by their vehicle—see Table 14.6.

14.4 The SGIC in South Australia

This description is based upon Section 2.3 of McLean (1984). All claims for personal injury that

Table 14.7: The categories of accident types used by the SGIC, South Australia.

Thirteen types of mid-block pedestrian collision

- Pedestrian crossing from driver's left.

- Pedestrian crossing from driver's left, struck by overtaking vehicle.

- Pedestrian crossing from driver's right.

- Pedestrian crossing from driver's right, struck by vehicle overtaking on left.

- Pedestrian standing in road.

- Pedestrian standing in road, struck by overtaking vehicle.

- Pedestrian walking in road in direction of traffic.

- Pedestrian walking in road, against direction of traffic.

- Pedestrian playing, working, or lying in road.

- Pedestrian emerged from behind stationary vehicle.

- Pedestrian struck by reversing vehicle.

- Pedestrian on pedestrian crossing.

- Other.

Eleven types of pedestrian collision at intersection

- Eight types: each combination of pedestrian direction (from driver's left or right) and vehicle movement (approaching intersection, leaving intersection having passed straight through, turning right, turning left).

- Pedestrian crossing diagonally.

- Pedestrian playing, working, or lying in road.

- Other.

Four other types of pedestrian collision

- At roadworks or warning barrier.

- Consequence of prior accident not involving pedestrian.

- Other than elsewhere specified.

- Circumstances not known.

Seventeen types of mid-block pedal cyclist collision

- Cyclist alone.

- Cyclist into parked vehicle.

- Cyclist into animal or object.

- Cyclist into car door opening.

- Cyclist into car drawing away from kerb.

- Cyclist struck from behind.

- Head-on.

- Cyclist into rear of other vehicle.

Table 14.7: (continued).

- Opposite direction side-swipe.

- Side-swipe, vehicle overtaking cyclist.

- Cyclist moving to right, struck by vehicle travelling in same direction.

- Cyclist moving to right, struck by vehicle travelling in opposite direction.

- Cyclist crossing from driver's right.

- Cyclist crossing from driver's left.

- Vehicle overtakes cyclist and cuts in to left to enter driveway.

- Oncoming vehicle turns right in front of cyclist to enter driveway.

- Other.

Fourteen types of pedal cyclist collision at intersection

- Pedal cyclist proceeding straight, other vehicle proceeding straight, from cyclist's left.

- Pedal cyclist proceeding straight, other vehicle comes from left, turns left.

- Pedal cyclist proceeding straight, other vehicle proceeding straight, from cyclist's right.

- Pedal cyclist proceeding straight, oncoming vehicle turns right.

- Pedal cyclist proceeding straight, other vehicle overtakes cyclist and cuts in to turn left.

- Pedal cyclist turning right, other vehicle oncoming.

- Pedal cyclist turning right from left of road, other vehicle overtaking.

- Pedal cyclist turning right from centre of road, other vehicle impacts from rear.

- Pedal cyclist turning right, other vehicle comes from left.

- Pedal cyclist turning right, other vehicle comes from right.

- Pedal cyclist turning right, oncoming vehicle turns left.

- Pedal cyclist turning left, other vehicle comes from right.

- Pedal cyclist turning left, oncoming vehicle turns right.

- Other.

Four other types of pedal cyclist collision

- At roadworks or warning barrier.

- Consequence of prior accident not involving cyclist.

- Other than elsewhere specified.

- Circumstances not known.

Table 14.7: (continued).

Twenty-five types of mid-block accident

- Eight types: rollover or spin (slide down for motorcycle), on carriageway or off carriageway to left or off carriageway to right, and run off road to left or right.
- Collision with roadside obstacle where road narrows.
- Collision with animal or object in road.
- Collision with parked vehicle.
- Sideswipe with parked vehicle.
- Collision with parked vehicle on offside of road.
- Collision with car door opening.
- Head-on.
- Rear-end.
- Same direction side-swipe while passing on right.
- Same direction side-swipe while passing on left.
- U-turning, collision with vehicle from behind.
- U-turning, collision with vehicle from ahead.
- Collision with vehicle entering carriageway from left.
- Collision with vehicle entering carriageway from right.
- Collision with vehicle leaving parking space.
- Rear-end collision with reversing vehicle.
- Other.

Twenty types of collision at intersection

- Four types: rollover or spin, on carriageway or off carriageway.
- Vehicle proceeding straight, other comes from right.
- Vehicle proceeding straight, other comes from right, turns left.
- Vehicle proceeding straight, other comes from left, turns left.
- Vehicle proceeding straight, other comes from right, turns right.
- Vehicle proceeding straight, other comes from left, turns right.
- Vehicle proceeding straight, oncoming vehicle turns right.
- Into rear of same-direction vehicle proceeding straight.
- Into rear of same-direction vehicle turning left.

Table 14.7: (continued).

- Into rear of same-direction vehicle turning right.
- Collision with same-direction vehicle turning right from inner lane.
- Collision with same-direction vehicle turning left from outer lane.
- Turning right, collision with oncoming vehicle turning left.
- Turning right, collision with oncoming vehicle turning right.
- U-turning.
- Left road by proceeding straight ahead from leg of T-junction.
- Other.

Six other types of collision not involving a pedestrian or pedal cyclist

- At road works or warning barrier.
- Consequence of prior accident.
- Collision with tram.
- Fell from vehicle (not motorcycle).
- Other than elsewhere specified.
- Circumstances not known.

are processed under the compulsory third party insurance scheme in South Australia are recorded in a computerised database maintained by the State Government Insurance Commission (SGIC). The claims relate to persons (not driving an unregistered or uninsured vehicle) injured in road accidents in which at least some of the blame lies with another person. Thus the claims do not include single vehicle accidents involving injury only to the driver.

Information in this database that is not available in that deriving from police reports in South Australia includes:

- Make, model, and year of manufacture of vehicle.

- Engine capacity, if a motorcycle.

- Carrying capacity (not for cars).

- Accident type.

- Point of impact on vehicle.

- Estimated percentage liability for accident.

- Occupation of driver.

Table 14.8: Relative frequency* of injured (or killed) drivers according to car weight and age of driver (percentages).

	Small (<950 kg)	Medium	Large (1250+ kg)
15-20	6.4	3.7	3.3
21-24	4.3	2.8	2.1
25-60	3.1	2.4	2.0
61-70	3.5	2.7	2.2
71+	4.6	2.8	1.6

* It appears that the denominator was not the number of drivers in a certain age group who were involved in accidents, but the number of car owners of that age group.

- Injury, using a three-component code classifying site of injury, nature of injury, and long term outcome.

- Whether seat belt worn.

For comparison with the classification methods in Chapter 6, Table 14.7 shows the 114 accident types in the coding scheme used by the SGIC.

14.5 Searles' study in Sydney, N.S.W.

For a description of this study (Searles, 1980), which was chiefly oriented to studying how the sample of crashes in official statistics related to the larger number reported to an insurance company, see Section 4.4.1.

Some more general comments on the potential value of insurance data in monitoring the accidents at individual sites, the principal advantage over police records being the greater numbers known to insurance companies, are made by Searles and Jamieson (1983): "As the official statistics comprise only a small proportion of the crash population, significant time periods may elapse before hazardous sites are recognised, before crash trends can be established, or before sufficient crash costs can be predicted to justify a countermeasure. Early recognition of hazardous locations and implementation of appropriate countermeasures are desirable to produce savings in crash losses and hu-

Table 14.9: The effect on injury of car weight and year in which production of the model was started.

	Small	Medium	Large
(a) Frequency of injured (or killed) drivers, percentages			
1966 or before	4.4	3.0	2.4
1967-1971	3.3	2.4	2.2
1972-1976	2.8	2.2	1.8
1977 or later	2.8	2.4	1.7
(b) Percentages of injured drivers whose ISS was 4 or more (or who died)			
1966 or before	39	38	34
1967-1971	29	32	33
1972 or later	29	33	31

Table 14.10: Percentage of injured drivers whose ISS is 4 or more, or who die, related to car weight and speed limit at the accident site.

	Small	Medium	Large
50 kph or less	26	24	24
51-70 kph	36	36	32
71 kph or more	45	47	43

man suffering. Avoidable crashes may be occurring at locations while hazardous features remain unrecognised and countermeasures not installed." Certainly it is true that unavoidable statistical variation makes blackspot detection difficult: thus Wood (1981), in the U.S. context, argued it would be false economy for states to eliminate damage-only accidents from their accident records, because the fewer numbers would lengthen the time before hazardous locations were identified. Despite this, it is mentioned by TRC (1985, p. 8) that the percentage of damage-only and minor injury accidents reported by the police has declined rapidly in recent years. Searles and Jamieson also point out that before and after analysis of crash countermeasures may be distorted by the biases in what types of crash get reported to the police (Table 4.7): "For example, a countermeasure such as 'Stop' sign control may alleviate the incidence of right-

Table 14.11: For occupant fatalities, aged 15 or over, the average numbers of injuries of each combination of severity and location, per 100 such cases.

	AIS						
	1	2	3	4	5	6	Total
Skull/brain	0	2	3	8	44	15	72
Cervical spine	0	0	4	0	3	10	16
Face	2	6	9	4	4	0	25
Chest	0	5	6	7	46	2	67
Abdomen	0	0	4	10	27	0	41
Arm	1	11	13	1	0	0	27
Leg	1	9	8	9	0	0	26
External	1	10	22	0	0	4	37
Total	6	43	68	39	124	29	310

angle type crashes but increase the incidence of rear-end types. As a lower proportion of the population of rear-end type crashes appears in the official data, the 'after' crash situation will be underestimated with respect to the 'before' situation."

Searles et al (1986) reproduce the claim form used by the insurance wing of the National Roads and Motorists' Association.

14.6 Swedish studies

14.6.1 Nygren (c. 1984)

Nygren (c. 1984) reports a study of car accidents reported in a 5-year period (1976–1981) to Folksam, the largest motor insurance company in Sweden, with a 27% market share. There were some 340,000 private cars involved in the accidents, with 9000 drivers and 6000 passengers killed or injured. The data had details of the vehicles and the casualties—including medical information (hospital records or doctor's certificate).

Being an insurance sample, the consequences of the accidents were usually much less severe than in a typical police or hospital sample—thus, under 3% of the car drivers were injured. This fraction depended on driver age and size of car (Table 14.8). Apropos the issue raised in Section 14.2.3 above regarding the effect of car size on injury when the two colliding vehicles are of equal size, the frequencies of driver injury in collisions between two small cars, two medium cars, and two large

cars were in the relative proportions 4:3:3. Modern cars are associated with a lower injury frequency (Table 14.9). As is often found with police data, the higher the speed limit, the more severe the injury (Table 14.10). (ISS is Injury Severity Score, see Section 8.7.1.)

Autopsy reports were available on 456 (89%) of the fatally injured occupants. The injuries were cross-tabulated by their severity (AIS score) and the part of the body (presumably counting each part of the body no more than once). In Table 14.11 the figures have been converted to percentages by dividing by 456 and multipling by 100.

Tables 14.12 and 14.13 give Nygren's data on how seat belt usage affects injury severity and location. Seat belt usage is not easy to ascertain; Nygren discusses this at some length, and concludes that his data is probably reliable. It is the case, however, that among the less seriously injured casualties, seat belt usage is likely to be reported as unknown. It is also clear that there is something peculiar about this aspect of the data: the proportions killed, especially among the unbelted, are too high to be credible. Taken in conjunction with the low overall rate of injury, it may be suggested that some of those recorded as uninjured in this study would have been called slightly injured in others. There are two other unexpected features of Table 14.12: (a) that unbelted drivers appear to be more seriously injured than unbelted passengers— the reverse should be the case, the steering wheel and column to some extent reducing the driver's

Table 14.12: Percentage distribution of severity of injury for drivers and front seat passengers, according to seat belt usage.

| | | Drivers | | | Passengers | | |
		None	Belt	Unknown	None	Belt	Unknown
Injury	1–3	33	62	72	41	57	68
Severity	4–10	31	29	22	34	32	26
Score	11+	15	6	4	14	8	4
	Killed	21	3	2	11	3	2
Total number		522	3173	4897	254	1509	1803

Table 14.13: Percentages of surviving front seat occupants having an injury to the various body regions, by seating position, size of car, and seat belt usage.

| | Drivers | | | | | | Passengers | | | | | |
| | Small | | Medium | | Large | | Small | | Medium | | Large | |
	None	Belt	None	Belt	None	Belt	None	Belt	None	Belt	None	Belt
Skull/brain	46	25	45	24	42	21	37	20	39	22	37	18
Cervical spine	10	22	12	24	14	25	9	23	11	19	7	20
Face	40	19	32	18	34	17	37	19	34	15	39	12
Chest	22	28	22	26	17	27	20	37	21	35	20	35
Back	6	8	7	9	8	10	7	10	12	9	5	11
Abdomen	10	5	7	3	3	3	9	5	5	6	5	4
Arm	31	18	21	21	17	21	28	19	20	20	29	18
Leg	46	34	36	27	35	25	35	23	33	21	29	20
External	13	10	10	9	5	9	11	8	14	9	12	9
All regions	225	169	193	160	174	159	191	164	189	155	183	147
Total number	78	624	217	1516	77	812	46	264	125	776	41	449

injury; (b) that belted drivers appear to be less seriously injured than belted passengers—the reverse should be the case, as there is more space in front of the passenger for the belt to operate in.

14.6.2 Lindgren and Armyr (1983)

The Ansvar group of insurance companies accepts as policy-holders only those who abstain totally from alcoholic beverages. It has carried out statistical research that demonstrates that such people have a lower frequency of motor accidents than the general population. However, life-style studies show that abstinence from alcohol is associated with various other attitudes and behaviours that together ensure that (in the words of Lindgren and Armyr, 1983) "total abstainers as a group differ advantageously from non-abstainers as a group for insurance purposes". Consequently, the interpretation of motor claims statistics is not straightforward. Lindgren and Armyr report that, concerning compulsory third-party insurance, in 1981 Ansvar's claims frequency was less than that of all Swedish motor insurance companies by 8%. But this was after standardisation for various factors in which Ansvar's policy-holders differ from the norm—and one such factor was the entitlement to a no claims bonus. In that this entitlement may be presumed to be in part a consequence of temperance, it is arguable that the figure of 8% is an understatement of the effect. As to cost per claim, this is the same for property damage in Ansvar as in other companies, but tends to be less for personal injury.

14.6.3 Nilsson (1984)

See Section 4.4.2.

14.7 Japan

In Japan, compensation claims are handled not by the individual insurance companies, but by the Automobile Insurance Rating Association. Tsuchihashi et al (1981) report a study of some 168,000 casualties reported to this Association during February–April 1979. Some data has already been included in Tables 8.13 (percentage of deaths, as related to AIS) and 8.20 (relative frequencies of the AIS categories). Table 14.14 shows the distribution of injuries over the parts of the body, for all road users together, and Table 14.15 compares the separate categories. The extraordinarily high frequency of minor neck injuries in car occupants is evident in Japanese police data, too (Table 12.6).

Table 14.14: How all injuries are distributed over the parts of the body, similarly for serious* injuries, similarly for fractures, and showing also the percentage of injuries for each part of the body that are serious.

	Percentage of injuries	Percentage among the serious injuries	Percentage among the fractures	Percentage of injuries that are serious
Head and face	22	38	13	10
Neck	29	5		1
Chest	5	15	34	17
Abdomen	2	10		24
Back and pelvis	6	2		2
Upper extremities	10	7	15	4
Lower extremities	18	23	38	7
Entire body	7	1	-	1
Total number	271175#	16439#	38597#	

* "Serious" here means an AIS score of 3 or greater.
# That is, an average of 1.6 injuries per person, 0.10 serious injuries per person, 0.23 fractures per person, and 1.2 serious injuries per person who had at least one serious injury. (For brevity, injured region has been abbreviated to injury here.)

Table 14.15: Percentage distribution of injured regions of the body, according to casualty's means of transport.

	Automobile drivers	Automobile passengers	Motorcyclists	Pedal cyclists	Pedestrians
Head and face	14	24	18	25	31
Neck	57	41	11	11	7
Chest	5	6	5	5	5
Abdomen	1	1	2	3	5
Back and pelvis	4	5	5	8	8
Upper extremities	6	8	15	14	10
Lower extremities	8	10	31	25	26
Entire body	3	4	11	10	8
Total number of injured regions	68863	64205	46731	39626	51080
Total number of casualties	50143	42779	25054	21918	27394
Injured regions per casualty	1.4	1.5	1.9	1.8	1.9
Percentage of casualties with AIS 3 or greater	4.1	5.6	13.2	10.1	15.3

References

The Section or Sub-section (S), Figure (F), or Table (T) where each reference is cited, or which uses the reference as a source, is shown in square brackets.

AAAM (1985). The Abbreviated Injury Scale. 1985 revision. Morton Grove, Illinois: American Association for Automotive Medicine. [S8.7.1]

ACRUPTC (1978). A common core of road traffic accident data items. Report from the Advisory Committee on Road User Performance and Traffic Codes, Commonwealth Department of Transport, Australia. [S3.6, T3.2, T3.3, T3.4]

Agran, P F, Dunkle, D E, and Winn, D G (1985). Motor vehicle childhood injuries caused by noncrash falls and ejections. Journal of the American Medical Association, 253, 2530–2533. [S10.3.1]

Alderson, M (1981). International Mortality Statistics. London: Macmillan. [S9.1]

Anderson, H R (1978). The epidemiological value of hospital diagnostic data. In A E Bennett (Editor), Recent Advances in Community Medicine. Number 1, pp. 175–193. Edinburgh: Churchill Livingstone. [S10.2.1]

Andreassend, D C (c. 1982). Road accident definitions—Death and injury. Report from the Transport Section, Department of Civil Engineering, Monash University. [S11.2.1]

Andreassend, D C (1983). Standard accident definitions: Primary accident classes and accident types. Australian Road Research, 13, 10–24. [S6.4.5, F6.3]

Andreassend, D C (1984). Some comments on vehicle classification and accident studies. In C J Hoban (Editor), Vehicle Classification—What Are the Requirements? Proceedings of a Workshop Held at the Australian Road Research Centre, pp. 59–63. Nunawading: Australian Road Research Board. [S6.4.6]

Armour, M (1984). Sources of Australian accident and road inventory data. ARRB Internal Report 1120-2, Australian Road Research Board, Vermont South. [S6.6.5, T6.17, T6.18]

Bagley, F D (1978). The role of the Australian Bureau of Statistics. Proceedings of the Road Accident Information Seminar, held in Canberra, March 1974, pp. 16–28. Canberra: Australian Government Publishing Service. [S3.6.1, S6.6.4, S6.6.5]

Bailey, J P M (1984). The Waikato Hospital Road Accident Survey. Volume 2. Analysis and interpretation. Report No. CD 2352, Chemistry Division, Department of Scientific and Industrial Research, New Zealand. [S10.3.1, S11.4.9, S13.12, T8.20]

Baker, S P (1979). Motor vehicle occupant deaths in young children. Pediatrics, 64, 860–861. [S1.3]

Baker, S P (1982). Injury classification and the International Classification of Diseases codes. Accident Analysis and Prevention, 14, 199–201. [S8.5.3]

Baker, S P (1983a). Medical data and injuries. American Journal of Public Health, 73, 733–734. [S4.3.4]

Baker, S P (1983b). Contribution to panel discussion of the current status of trauma severity indices, p. 199. Journal of Trauma, 23, 185–201. [S8.5.5]

Baldwin, D M (1981). Classification and analysis of traffic accident records. International Highway Safety Conference, Belgrade, Yugoslavia. Miscellanies-Technical Papers, pp. 729–745. Ljubljana: Council of Republican and Provincial Road Organizations, and Washington, D.C.: Institute of Transportation Engineers. [S8.10.2]

Barancik, J I, and Chatterjee, B F (1981). Methodological considerations in the use of the Abbreviated Injury Scale in trauma epidemiology. Journal of Trauma, 21, 627–631. [S8.7.3 (B.A.B, D.E)]

Barancik, J I, and Fife, D (1985). Discrepancies in vehicular crash injury reporting: Northeastern Ohio Trauma Study IV. Accident Analysis and Prevention, 17, 147–154. [S11.4.4, S13.8, T11.14]

Baum, A S (1978). An alternative injury code for police reporting: An evaluation of the New York State Injury Coding Scheme. In D F Huelke (Editor), Proceedings of the American Association for Automotive Medicine 22nd Conference and the International Association for Accident and Traffic Medicine VII Conference, vol. 1, pp. 210–220. Morton Grove, Illinois: AAAM. [S8.6.3, T8.8, T8.9, T8.10, T8.20]

Benjamin, T (1984). Les systemes d'informations sur les accidents. Transport Environnement Circulation, No. 62, 22–24. [S6.6.3, S9.9.4, S8.9.5]

Benjamin, T (1987). Linking of data on road accidents with those from complementary files. Practices and prospects in twelve countries. Report from the International Drivers' Behaviour Research Association, Paris. [S3.15, S13.13, T3.7]

Bennett, G D, Hendrickson, D W, and Gierke, L W (1979). Filling out a death certificate. Journal of the American Osteopathic Association, 78, 121–130. [S9.5]

Bin Husin, M, and Mustafa, M S (1985). Road traffic safety and the road authorities. In Proceedings of National Workshop on the Prevention and Control of Road Traffic Accidents in Malaysia, pp. 147–157. Kuala Lumpur: Ministry of Health. [S5.6, T5.4]

Bjornstig, U, and Naslund, K (1984). Pedal cycling accidents—Mechanisms and consequences. A study from Northern Sweden. Acta Chirurgica Scandinavica, 150, 353–359. [S1.1, S10.3.1, T10.12]

Bohlin, N, and Samuelsson, L-E (1973). A methodology for coding accident configuration. In E E Flamboe and S N Lee (Editors), Proceedings of the International Accident Investigation Workshop, pp. 19–23. Washington, D.C.: National Highway Traffic Safety Administration for the NATO Committee on the Challenges of Modern Society. [S6.4.5, T6.7]

Bourbeau, R R, Laberge-Nadeau, C, Latour, R, and Maag, U (1981). Road crashes and injuries in Quebec (1974): Patterns among many variables. Accident Analysis and Prevention, 13, 349–355. [S13.9.1]

Brismar, B, Aldman, B, Bunketorp, O, Holmgren, E, Romanus, B, Lindstrom, L, and Stalhammar, D (1982). Injury evaluation—Registration of injuries and medical care consumption. In B-E Dahlgren, P Lovsund, and E Attebo (Editors), Proceedings of the First Nordic Congress on Traffic Medicine, pp. 90–92. Linkoping: Svensk Trafikmedicinsk Forening. [S8.5.5, S8.12.5]

Brown, D B, and Colson, C W (1983). Application of microcomputer technology to local accident problem identification. Transportation Research Record, No. 910, 14–18. [S3.14.7]

Bruhning, E, von Fintel, K-U, and Nussbaum, M (1987). Datenbank internationaler Verkehrs- und Unfalldaten. Bergisch Gladbach: Bundesanstalt fur Strassenwesen. [S2.6.4]

Bull, J P (1977). Measures of severity of injury. Injury, 9, 184–187. [S8.7.3 (A.B.A)]

Bull, J P, and Roberts, B J (1973). Road accident statistics—A comparison of police and hospital information. Accident Analysis and Prevention, 5, 45–53. [S11.4.1, T11.9]

Bunketorp, O, Nilsson, W, and Romanus, B (1982). Traffic accident registration and analysis in Goteborg. Proceedings of the VIIth International IRCOBI Conference on the Biomechanics of Impacts, pp. 61–75. Bron, France: International Research Committee on the Biokinetics of Impacts. [S8.7.3 (A.B.A), S11.4.3, T11.12]

Bunketorp, O, and Romanus, B (1985). Hospital-based system for analysis and follow-up of traffic accidents and casualties in Goteborg, Sweden. Traffic Operations and Management, Proceedings of Seminar M held at the PTRC (Planning and Transport Research and Computation) Summer Annual Meeting, pp. 269–279. London: PTRC Education and Research Services. [S11.4.3, S13.10, T11.12]

Burr, M A, and Brogan, H (1976). West Midlands accident analysis system. The Highway Engineer, 23(2), 8–14. [S3.2, S4.2.5]

Campbell, B J (1978). The information system in North Carolina. Proceedings of the Road Accident Information Seminar, held in Canberra, March 1974, pp. 135–145. Canberra: Australian Government Publishing Service. [S3.11]

Campbell, B J (1981). The use of the accident report form's computerized narrative description to study the contribution of vehicle defects to accident occurrence. In Three Studies of North Carolina Accident Data, Report HSRC-PR101, Highway Safety Research Center, University of North Carolina. [S3.11.5]

Carpenter, K (1973). Injury reporting reliability. Report from the New York State Department of Motor Vehicles, Albany. [S8.10.1]

Carroll, P S, and Scott, R E (1971). Acquisition of information on exposure and on non-fatal crashes. Volume II—Accident data inaccuracies. Report from the Highway Safety Research Institute, University of Michigan. [S4.3.6, S8.10.2, S8.12.1, S8.12.3, T8.26, T8.27, T8.28]

Cesari, D, Cavallero, C, Farisse, J, Bonnoit, J, Seriat-Gautier, B, Brunet, C, Daon, N, Lang, O, Billault, P, and Bourret, P (1983). A detailed injury severity scale for lower limbs based on analysis of injuries sustained by pedestrians. Proceedings of the 27th Stapp Car Crash Conference, pp. 329–349. (SAE Paper No. 831628.) Warrendale, Pennsylvania: Society of Automotive Engineers. [S8.7.3 (C.D)]

Chamblee, R F, Evans, M C, Patten, D G, and Pearce, J S

(1983). Injuries causing death: Their nature, external causes, and associated diseases. Journal of Safety Research, 14, 21–35. [S9.5, T9.1, T9.5]

Chapman, D P, and James, F J (1973). The Stats 19 road accident data procedure and its research applications. Supplementary Report 11UC, Transport and Road Research Laboratory, Crowthorne. [S3.2]

Chapman, D P, and Neilson, I D (1971). Notes for users of national accident data (Stats 19). Unpublished note, Transport and Road Research Laboratory, Crowthorne. [S8.8.1]

Chipman, M L (1983). Motor vehicle accident fatality statistics: An investigation of reliabilty. Canadian Journal of Public Health, 74, 381–384. [S11.1]

Civil, I D, Kauder, D R, and Schwab, C W (1987). Use of a single page scaling chart (CAIS-85) in clinical practice. To be presented at the 31st Annual Meeting of the American Association for Automotive Medicine. [S8.7.3 (D.C)]

Civil, I D, and Schwab, C W (1986). Use of a single page Abbreviated Injury Scale in clinical practice. Proceedings of the 30th Annual Conference of the American Association for Automotive Medicine, pp. 163–174. Morton Grove, Illinois: AAAM. [S8.7.3 (D.C)]

Committee on Medical Aspects of Automotive Safety (1971). Rating the severity of tissue damage, I. The abbreviated scale. Journal of the American Medical Association, 215, 277–280. [S8.12.1]

Committee on Medical Aspects of Automotive Safety (1972). Rating the severity of tissue damage, II. The comprehensive scale. Journal of the American Medical Association, 220, 717–720. [S8.7.3 (A.B.A), S8.12.1]

Commonwealth Bureau of Census and Statistics (1973). Submission to the House of Representatives Select Committee on Road Safety. Attachment 1—Analysis of data items extracted from road traffic accident report forms for statistical purposes. [S6.6.4]

Computer Power (1986). Report and recommendations of a study into the computing requirements of the Road Safety Division. Working Paper 10/86, Road Safety Division, Department of Transport, South Australia. [S3.3.2, S3.11.5]

Corben, B F, and Ashton, N R (1984). Road accident information and its use. In K W Ogden and D W Bennett (Editors), Traffic Engineering Practice. 3rd Edition, pp. 438–456. Clayton, Victoria: Department of Civil Engineering, Monash University. [S3.4]

Croft, P G (1984). Vehicle classification needs from the traffic safety viewpoint. In C J Hoban (Editor), Vehicle Classification—What Are the Requirements? Proceedings of a Workshop Held at the Australian Road Research Centre, pp. 53–58. Nunawading: Australian Road Research Board. [S6.4.6]

Cryer, C, Carpenter, L, and Donnelly, P (1984). Inadequacies of the ICD E code. Community Medicine, 6, 163–164. [S8.5.1, S10.2.1]

Daffin, C, Duncombe, P, Hills, M G, North, P M, and Wetherill, G B (1986). A microcomputer survey analysis package designed for the developing countries. The Statistician, 35, 505–523. [S3.14.7]

Dalkie, H S, and Mulligan, G W N (1987). The use of an injury information data base to evaluate the effectiveness of mandatory motorcycle helmet use legislation in Manitoba. Proceedings of the Canadian Multidisciplinary Road Safety Conference V, pp. 270–279. Calgary: Injury Research Unit, University of Calgary.

[S8.5.5, S12.4.2]

Daltrey, R (1983). Accident data: The report form. In D C Andreassend and P G Gipps (Editors), Traffic Accident Evaluation. Papers Presented at an Esso-Monash Civil Engineering Workshop. Clayton, Victoria: Department of Civil Engineering, Monash University. [S4.3.7]

Datta, T K, and Rodgers, R J (1980). Computerized street index for Michigan accident location index system. Transportation Research Record, No. 706, 20–22. [S4.2.5]

Dischinger, P C, Shankar, B S, Kochesfahani, D, Turney, S Z, Clark, B, Bailey, T, and Cowley, R A (1985). Automotive collisions involving serious injury or death: An analysis of trends over time (1980–1983) in Maryland. Proceedings of the 29th Annual Conference of the American Association for Automotive Medicine, pp. 287–297. Morton Grove, Illinois: AAAM. [S8.10.1]

Dorsch, M M, Somers, R L, and Woodward, A (1986). Measuring severity of head injury by mail questionnaire. Accident Analysis and Prevention, 18, 439–440. [S8.7.3 (D.D)]

DTp (1986). Accident Investigation Manual. Birmingham: Royal Society for the Prevention of Accidents (for the Department of Transport). [S3.2, S6.4.5]

Eastham, J N (1984). A construct validity analysis of the Abbreviated Injury Scale. Proceedings of the 28th Annual Conference of the American Association for Automotive Medicine, pp. 155–171. Morton Grove, Illinois: AAAM. [S8.7.3 (A.B.C, C.A.B), T8.18]

Eastham, J N (1985). The effects of AIS manual injury severity qualifiers on subjective estimates of injury severity. Proceedings of the 29th Annual Conference of the American Association for Automotive Medicine, pp. 353–363. Morton Grove, Illinois: AAAM. [S8.7.3 (A.B.C, C.A.A), T8.16]

Engstrom, A (1979). Causes and consequences of moped and motorcycle accidents. A prospective and retrospective study of clinical series. Scandinavian Journal of Social Medicine, Supplement 15. [S11.4.3, T8.20]

Farisse, J, Bonnoit, J, Seriat-Gautier, B, Daou, N, and Lang, O (1983). Evaluation of pedestrian lower limbs injury severity: Proposals for a detailed scale. In Pedestrian Impact Injury and Assessment, pp. 191–203. (SAE Paper No. 830188.) Warrendale, Pennsylvania: Society of Automotive Engineers. [S8.7.3 (C.D)]

FARS (1987). Fatal Accident Reporting System 1985. Washington, D.C.: National Highway Traffic Safety Administration. [S3.13, S6.4.6, F3.8, T7.1, T7.12, T7.14, T7.15, T7.16]

Faulkner, C R (1968). Accident debris and reported accidents at roundabouts. Laboratory Report 202, Transport and Road Research Laboratory, Crowthorne. [S4.5, T4.8]

Fenner, H A (1969). Development of a medically acceptable injury scale. In Proceedings of the Collision Investigation Methodology Symposium, pp. 632–646. (Discussion, 647–653.) Buffalo, New York: Cornell Aeronautical Laboratory (now Calspan). [S8.12.1]

Fife, D, and Rappaport, E (1987). What role do injuries play in the deaths of old people? Accident Analysis and Prevention, 19, 225–230. [S11.3.3]

Fischell, T R, and Hamilton, E G (1986). Single variable tabulations 1982–1985, North Carolina accidents. Report from the Highway Safety Research Center, University of North Carolina. [S7.8, T7.19]

Friede, A M, Azzara, C V, Gallagher, S S, and Guyer, B (1985). The epidemiology of injuries to bicycle riders. Pediatric Clinics of North America, 32(1), 141–151. [S10.3.1, T10.14]

Gaber, M A, and Yerrell, J S (1983). Road safety research in Egypt. Presented at the 9th Congress of the International Association for Accident and Traffic Medicine, held in Mexico City. [S5.4]

Gaber, M A, and Yerrell, J S (1985). Analysing the road safety problems in Egypt. Presented at the 10th Congress of the International Association for Accident and Traffic Medicine, held in Tokyo. [S5.4]

Gallagher, S S, Finison, K, Guyer, B, and Goodenough, S (1984). The incidence of injuries among 87,000 Massachusetts children and adolescents: Results of the 1980–81 Statewide Childhood Injury Prevention Program surveillance system. American Journal of Public Health, 74, 1340–1347. [S10.3.1, T10.14]

Garthe, E A (1982). Compatibility of ICD-9-CM with AIS-80. American Association for Automotive Medicine Quarterly/Journal, 4(1), 42–46. [S8.5.5, T8.5]

Gennarelli, T A (1980). Analysis of head injury severity by AIS-80. Proceedings of the 24th Conference of the American Association for Automotive Medicine, pp. 147–155. Morton Grove, Illinois: AAAM. [S8.7.3 (A.A.B), S8.12.4, T8.33]

Gennarelli, T (1984). An overview of injury severity scaling systems. In G Vimpani (Editor), Injury Severity Scaling Systems. A National Workshop, pp. 5–12. Melbourne: Child Accident Prevention Trust. [S8.7.1]

Gibson, G (1981). Indices of severity for emergency medical evaluative studies: Reliability, validity, and data requirements. International Journal of Health Services, 11, 597–622. [S8.1, S8.7.1, S8.11.6]

Gittelsohn, A, and Royston, P N (1982). Annotated bibliography of cause-of-death validation studies: 1958–1980. Vital and Health Statistics, Series 2, No. 89 (DHHS Publication No. (PHS) 82-1363), National Center for Health Statistics, Hyattsville, Maryland. Washington, D.C.: U.S. Government Printing Office. [S9.5]

Glasser, J H (1981). The quality and utility of death certificate data. American Journal of Public Health, 71, 231–233. [S9.5]

Goldacre, M J (1985). Collection, analysis and dissemination of vital and health statistics. In A Smith (Editor), Recent Advances in Community Medicine. Number 3, pp. 231–248. Edinburgh: Churchill Livingstone. [S10.2.1]

Goldberg, J L, Goldberg, J, Levy, P S, Finnegan, R, and Petrucelli, E (1984). Measuring the severity of injury: The validity of the Revised Estimated Survival Probability index. Journal of Trauma, 24, 420–427. [S8.5.5]

Grattan, E (1973). Some comments on the illustration and classification of injury data relating to the NATO CCMS collision analysis report form. In E E Flamboe and S N Lee (Editors), Proceedings of the International Accident Investigation Workshop, pp. 133–141. Washington, D.C.: National Highway Traffic Safety Administration for the NATO Committee on the Challenges of Modern Society. [S8.12.2]

Grattan, E, and Keigan, M E (1975). Patterns and severity of injury in a hospital sample of road traffic accident casualties. Presented at the 5th International Conference of the International Association for Accident and Traffic Medicine, held in London. [S8.12.2, S8.12.3, S11.4.2, T8.29]

Grime, G, and Hutchinson, T P (1979). Vehicle mass and driver injury. Ergonomics, 22, 93–104. [S14.2.3]

Grime, G, and Hutchinson, T P (1982). The influence of vehicle weight on the risk of injury to drivers. Ninth International Technical Conference on Experimental Safety Vehicles, held in Kyoto, pp. 726–741. Washington, D.C.: National Highway Traffic Safety Administration. [S14.2.3]

Hall, J W (1984). Deficiencies in accident record systems. Transportation Planning and Technology, 9, 199–208. [S4.3.4]

Hambley, J (1978). Report of workshop 3, data processing systems. Proceedings of the Road Accident Information Seminar, held in Canberra, March 1974, pp. 104–105. Canberra: Australian Government Publishing Service. [S3.1]

Hansson, P G (1974). Road traffic casualties in a surgical department. Acta Chirurgica Scandinavica, Supplementum 442. [S11.4.3, T11.11]

Harris, K W, and French, D K (1980). A methodological study of quality control procedures for mortality medical coding. Vital and Health Statistics, Series 2, No. 81 (DHEW Publication No. (PHS) 80-1335), National Center for Health Statistics, Hyattsville, Maryland. Washington, D.C.: U.S. Government Printing Office. [S9.5]

Havard, J D J (1979). Mortality from motor vehicle accidents in the 15–24 year age group. World Health Statistics Quarterly, 32, 225–241. [S11.1, S11.2.1]

Heidenstrom, P N (1979). Recording accidental injury diagnoses: An improved method. Journal of Safety Research, 11, 156–161. [S8.5.2]

Herzberg, S (1985). Adelaide cycle survey. September 1985—The journey to work in Adelaide. Preliminary data report. Report from the Faculty of Architecture and Planning, University of Adelaide. [S11.4.10]

Hilger, B A, and Scott, E S (1982). Single variable tabulations of 1981 accidents in the state of Texas. Report from the Operations Research and Systems Analysis Program, Texas Transportation Institute. [S12.24.4]

Hills, B L, and Elliott, G J (1986). A Microcomputer Accident Analysis Package and its use in developing countries. Presented at the Indian Road Congress Road Safety Seminar, held in Srinagar. [S3.14.7, S4.2.5]

Hills, B L, and Kassabgi, M (1984). A microcomputer road accident analysis package for developing countries. Presented at the Summer Meeting of Planning and Transport Research and Computation. [S3.14.7]

HIPE (1979). Hospital In-Patient Enquiry. Patterns of Morbidity 1962–1967. London: HMSO. [S10.2.1]

Hirsch, A E, and Eppinger, R H (1984). Impairment scaling from the Abbreviated Injury Scale. Proceedings of the 28th Annual Conference of the American Association for Automotive Medicine, pp. 209–224. Morton Grove, Illinois: AAAM. [S8.7.3 (B.B, C.C)]

HLDI (1981). The Highway Loss Data Institute. Washington, D.C.: HLDI. [S14.2, T14.1, T14.2]

HLDI (1986). Insurance injury report, 1983–1985 models. Research Report HLDI I85-1, Highway Loss Data Institute, Washington, D.C. [S14.2.2]

Hobbs, C A (1981). Car occupant injury patterns and mechanisms. Supplementary Report 648, Transport and Road Research Laboratory, Crowthorne. [T8.20]

Hobbs, C A, Grattan, E, and Hobbs, J A (1979). Classification of injury severity by length of stay in hospital. Laboratory Report 871, Transport and Road Research Laboratory, Crowthorne. [S8.7.2, S8.9.2, S8.12.3, S11.4.2, T8.13, T8.20, T8.30, T11.10]

Honkanen, R (1984). Finnish Accident Registration Project (FARP). Publications of the National Board of Health in Finland, No. 50. [S8.1, S8.5.4, S8.11.2, S10.2.3, S11.4.7, S12.7, T8.3, T8.4, T10.7]

Honkanen, R, and Michelsson, J-E (1980). Construction of the computerized accident registration system in a casualty department. Scandinavian Journal of Social Medicine, 8, 33–38. [S8.5.4]

Howard, B V, Young, M F, and Ellis, J P (1979). Appraisal of the existing traffic accident data collection and recording system—South Australia. Report No. CR6, Office of Road Safety, Commonwealth Department of Transport. [S3.3.1, S4.3.1, S4.3.2, T4.1, T4.2]

Huang, L C, and Marsh, J C (1978). AIS and threat to life. In D F Huelke (Editor), Proceedings of the American Association for Automotive Medicine 22nd Conference and the International Association for Accident and Traffic Medicine VII Conference, vol. 1, pp. 242–254. Morton Grove, Illinois: AAAM. [S8.7.3 (A.B.B)]

Hutchinson, T P (1974). Factors affecting the times till death of pedestrians killed in road accidents. Injury, 6, 208–212. [S12.15]

Hutchinson, T P (1976a). Statistical aspects of injury severity. Part I: Comparison of two populations when there are several grades of injury. Transportation Science, 10, 269–284. [S8.7.3 (C.E.E)]

Hutchinson, T P (1976b). Statistical aspects of injury severity. Part II: The case of several populations but only three grades of injury. Transportation Science, 10, 285–299. [S8.7.3 (C.E.E)]

Hutchinson, T P (1981). Causes of death in road crashes: Evidence from the routinely-published statistics of several countries. American Association for Automotive and Traffic Medicine Quarterly/Journal, 3(1), 39–40. [S9.2]

Hutchinson, T P (1983). A bivariate normal model for intra-accident correlations of driver injury with application to the effect of mass ratio. Accident Analysis and Prevention, 15, 215–224. [S8.8.2]

Hutchinson, T P (1984). Medical statistics on road accident injury in several countries. In S Yagar (Editor), Transport Risk Assessment, pp. 43–76. Waterloo, Ontario: University of Waterloo Press. [S9.2]

Hutchinson, T P (1986). Analysis of the joint distribution of injury severities, with special reference to drivers and front seat passengers in single-vehicle crashes. Accident Analysis and Prevention, 18, 157–167. [S8.8.2]

Hutchinson, T P, and Adams, V (1981). International statistics of road fatalities. Transport Reviews, 1, 393–397. [S11.1]

Hutchinson, T P, and Harris, R A (1978). Recent trends in traffic injury. Injury, 10, 133–137. [S10.2]

Hutchinson, T P, and Jones, I S (1975). The separation of the effects of driver and of vehicle on type of accident. 5th International Conference of the International Association for Accident and Traffic Medicine, held in London. [S14.2.3]

Hutchinson, T P, and Lai, P W (1981). Statistical aspects of injury severity. Part III: Making allowance for differences in the assessment of level of trauma. Transportation Science, 15, 297–305. [S8.8.2]

IATSS (1986). Review on road safety in Japan. IATSS Research, 1986 Special Issue. Tokyo: International Association of Traffic and Safety Sciences. [S3.8, S6.3.10, F3.5]

IHT (1986). Guidelines for accident reduction and prevention.

London: Institution of Highways and Transportation. [S3.2, S4.2.5]

Illingworth, C M, Noble, D, Bell, D, Kemn, I, Roche, C, and Pascoe, J (1981). 150 bicycle accidents in children: A comparison with accidents due to other causes. Injury, 13, 7–9. [S8.11.4, S10.3.1, T10.13]

Ing, R T, Baker, S P, Eller, J B, Frankowski, R R, Guyer, B, Hollinshead, W H, Pine, J, and Rockett, I R H (1985). Injury surveillance systems—Strengths, weaknesses, and issues workshop. Public Health Reports, 100, 582–586. [S8.5.1, S10.2.2]

Israel, R A, Rosenberg, H M, and Curtin, L R (1986). Analytical potential for multiple cause-of-death data. American Journal of Epidemiology, 124, 161–181. [S9.5, T9.1]

Jacobs, G D, Bardsley, M N, and Sayer, I (1975). Road accident data collection and analysis in developing countries. Laboratory Report 676, Transport and Road Research Laboratory, Crowthorne. [S3.2, S5.2, S5.3, S6.6.2, F5.2, T5.1, T5.2, T5.3]

Jacobs, G D, and Sayer, I A (1976). An analysis of road accidents in Kenya in 1972. Supplementary Report 227UC, Transport and Road Research Laboratory, Crowthorne. [S5.2, F5.1]

Jarvis, J R (1986). The NAASRA fatal accident report form. Proceedings of the 13th Australian Road Research Board and 5th Road Engineering Association of Asia and Australasia Joint Conference, Part 9, pp. 191–204. Nunawading: ARRB. (There were also ARRB Internal Reports by Jarvis in 1978–79 describing the early stages of this work.) [S3.7, F3.4]

Jennett, B, and MacMillan, R (1981). Epidemiology of head injury. British Medical Journal, 282, 101–104. [S9.3, S10.2.1]

Johinke, A K (1978). Uniform data collection. Proceedings of the Road Accident Information Seminar, held in Canberra, March 1974, pp. 35–43. Canberra: Australian Government Information Service. [S3.6.1]

Joksch, H C (1975). An empirical relation between fatal accident involvement per accident involvement and speed. Accident Analysis and Prevention, 7, 129–132. [S7.8]

Jones, J (1984). The Injury Severity Scale. In G Vimpani (Editor), Injury Severity Scaling Systems. A National Workshop, pp. 31–33. Melbourne: Child Accident Prevention Trust. [S8.11.3, T8.25]

Jorgensen, K, Kruse, T, Somers, R L, and Weeth, R (1979). Description of 3225 victims of road-traffic-accident trauma according to type of accident, severity of injury, and nature of lesions sustained. Proceedings of the IVth International IRCOBI Conference on the Biomechanics of Trauma, pp. 13–23. Bron, France: International Research Committee on Biomechanics of Impacts. [S10.3.1, T8.20]

Kahane, C J, Fell, J C, and Smith, R A (1977). The National Accident Sampling System—A status report. In D F Huelke (Editor), Proceedings of the 21st Conference of the American Association for Automotive Medicine, pp. 412–434. Morton Grove, Illinois: AAAM. [S3.12]

Keeling, J W, Golding, J, and Millier, H K G R (1985). Non-natural deaths in two health districts. Archives of Disease in Childhood, 60, 525–529. [S1.3]

Kelsh, W E (1983). Microcomputer-based traffic records system for small police agencies. Transportation Research Record, No. 910, 29–36. [S3.14.7]

Kroon, P-O, Bunketorp, O, and Romanus, B (1984). Bicycle accidents in Goteborg, Sweden 1983. Proceedings of the 1984 International IRCOBI Conference on the Biomechanics of Impacts, pp. 37–46. Bron, France: International Research Committee on Biokinetics of Impacts. [S11.4.3, T8.20, T11.13]

Krauss, J F, Fife, D, and Conroy, C (1987). Incidence, severity, and outcomes of brain injuries involving bicycles. American Journal of Public Health, 77, 76–78. [S10.2.2]

Lane, J C (1972). Statistical information in relation to accidents. Papers Presented at the National Road Safety Symposium (Canberra, 14–16 March 1972), pp. 42–51. Canberra: Commonwealth Department of Shipping and Transport. [S3.6.1]

Langley, J (1982). The International Classification of Diseases codes for describing injuries and the circumstances surrounding injuries: A critical comment and suggestions for improvement. Accident Analysis and Prevention, 14, 195–197. [S8.5.3]

Levy, P S, Goldberg, J, Hui, S, Rothrock, J, Iverson, N, and Hosmer, T (1982). Severity measurement in multiple trauma by use of ICDA conditions. Statistics in Medicine, 1, 145–152. [S8.5.5]

Levy, P S, Goldberg, J, and Rothrock, J (1982). The Revised Estimated Survival Probability index of trauma severity. Public Health Reports, 97, 452–459. [S8.5.5]

Lind, M G, and Wollin, S (1986). Bicycle accidents. Acta Chirurgica Scandinavica, Supplement 531. [S11.4.3, T8.20]

Lindeijer, J E (1987). A trial linkage of the road accident and vehicle registration files. Accident Analysis and Prevention, 19, 91–104. [S3.9]

Lindgren, A, and Armyr, G (1983). Total abstainers' lower insurance risk. In S Kaye and G W Meier (Editors), Alcohol, Drugs and Traffic Safety. Proceedings of the Ninth International Conference, pp. 865–873. Washington, D.C.: National Highway Traffic Safety Administration. [S14.6.2]

Lindstruom, L, Nygren, A, Stalhammar, D, Holmgren, E, Aldman, B, Brismar, B, Bunketorp, O, Romanus, B, Lindstrom, L, and Nygren, A (1982). Traffic injuries in Goteborg—Registration of accidents, injuries, and medical costs. Ninth International Technical Conference on Experimental Safety Vehicles, pp. 751–758. Washington, D.C.: National Highway Traffic Safety Administration. [S8.12.5, S10.3.1, T10.11]

Loukissas, P J, and Schultz, L C (1985). Handling changes in highway accident data reporting: The case of Pennsylvania's towaway criterion. Transportation Quarterly, 39, 73–92. [S8.10.2]

Luchter, S (1986). Traffic related disabilities and impairments and their economic consequences. In Crash Injury Impairment and Disability: Long Term Effects, pp. 93–113. (SAE Paper No. 860505.) Warrendale, Pennsylvania: Society of Automotive Engineers. [S10.3.2, T10.15]

Lugg, M M (1982). Pedal cycle accidents, Western Australia 1971–1980. Hospital Morbidity Statistics Special Studies, Series B, No. 1, Statistics Branch, Department of Public Health, Western Australia. [S10.2.2, T9.2, T10.6]

Lukin, J, and Vazey, B (1978). Integrated injury and traffic crash data system. Research Report 7/78, Traffic Accident Research Unit, New South Wales Department of Motor Transport. [S13.5]

Maas, M W, and Harris, S (1984). Police recording of road accident in-patients. Investigation into the completeness, representativity and reliability of police records of hospitalized traffic victims. Accident Analysis and Prevention, 16, 167–184. [S3.9, S11.4.8]

MacKenzie, E J (1986). Discussion of "Use of a single page Abbreviated Injury Scale in clinical practice" by I D Civil and C W Schwab. Proceedings of the 30th Annual Conference of the American Association for Automotive Medicine, pp. 175–178. Morton Grove, Illinois: AAAM. [S8.7.3 (D.C)]

MacKenzie, E J, and Garthe, E A (1983). Compatibility of the ICD-9-CM and AIS 80: An update. American Association for Automotive Medicine Quarterly/Journal, 5(2), 25–27. [S8.5.5]

MacKenzie, E J, Garthe, E A, and Gibson, G (1978). Evaluating the Abbreviated Injury Scale. In D F Huelke (Editor), Proceedings of the American Association for Automotive Medicine 22nd Conference and the International Association for Accident and Traffic Medicine VII Conference, vol. 1, pp. 55–66. Morton Grove, Illinois: AAAM. [S8.7.3 (B.C.A), T8.16]

MacKenzie, E J, Shapiro, S, Eastham, J, and Whitney, B (1981). Reliability testing of the AIS'80. Proceedings of the 25th Annual Conference of the American Association for Automotive Medicine, pp. 271–279. Morton Grove, Illinois: AAAM. [S8.7.3 (B.C.B)]

MacKenzie, E J, Steinwachs, D M, Shankar, B S, and Turney, S Z (1986). An ICD-9CM to AIS conversion table: Development and application. Proceedings of the 30th Annual Conference of the American Association for Automotive Medicine, pp. 135–151. Morton Grove, Illinois: AAAM. [S8.5.5]

Marsh, J C (1972). Existing traffic accident injury causation data recording methods and the proposal of an Occupant Injury Classification scheme. Proceedings of the 16th Conference of the American Association for Automotive Medicine, pp. 44–61. Morton Grove, Illinois: AAAM. [S8.6.1, T8.6]

Marsh, J C (1985). Recommended passenger car size definitions and the need for vehicle identification in traffic accident data. In Field Accidents: Data Collection, Analysis, Methodologies, and Crash Injury Reconstructions, pp. 7–17. Warrendale, Pennsylvania: Society of Automotive Engineers. [S3.11.3, S6.4.6]

Mattern, R, Barz, J, Schulz, F, Kallieris, D, and Schmidt, G (1979). Problems arising when using injury scales in the biomechanical investigation with special consideration of the age influence. Proceedings of the IVth International IRCOBI Conference on the Biomechanics of Trauma, pp. 223–231. Bron, France: International Research Committee on Biokinetics of Impacts. [S8.7.3 (A.C.A, A.C.C, A.D.C, A.D.D, B.A.C)]

Mbadiwe, I U (1986). Accident data collection: Experience in two states in Nigeria. In J O Asalor, E A Onibere, and G C Ovuworie (Editors), Road Traffic Accidents in Developing Countries. Volume 1, pp. 187–195. (Proceedings of the First International Conference, held in Benin.) Lagos: Joja Educational Research and Publishers. [S5.8.3]

McCarthy, E (1982). In-patient utilization of short-stay hospitals by diagnosis. Vital and Health Statistics, Series 13, No. 69 (DHHS Publication No. 83-1730), National Center for Health Statistics, Hyattsville, Maryland. Washington, D.C.: U.S. Government Printing Office. [S10.2.2]

McGuire, F L (1973). The nature of bias in official accident and violation records. Journal of Applied Psychology, 57, 300–305. [S4.3.5]

McLean, A J (1981). The severity and consequences of injuries in urban traffic accidents. Proceedings of the VIth International IRCOBI Conference on the Biomechanics of Impacts, pp. 12–19. Bron, France: International Research Committee on Biokinetics of Impacts. [T8.20]

McLean, S (1984). Road accident data in South Australia. Position Paper prepared for the Transport Planning Division, S.A. Department of Transport, by Nicholas Clark and Associates. [S8.6.4, S10.2.2, S13.6, S14.4, T14.7]

Mercer, G W (1987a). Coroner and police (MV104) accident cause frequencies, British Columbia, 1984. In CounterAttack Traffic Research Papers 1986, pp. 106–153. British Columbia: CounterAttack Program, Ministry of Attorney General. [S3.1, S4.3.4, S12.4.1]

Mercer, G W (1987b). The measurement of the contribution of alcohol to fatal traffic accidents, British Columbia, 1984. In CounterAttack Traffic Research Papers 1986, pp. 154–164. British Columbia: CounterAttack Program, Ministry of Attorney General. [S7.7, T7.16]

Mueller, B A, Rivara, F P, and Bergman, A B (1987). Factors associated with pedestrian-vehicle collision injuries and fatalities. Western Journal of Medicine, 146, 243–245. [S1.3, S11.3.3, T11.7]

Myers, G C (1976). Mortality statistics. In M Pflanz and E Schach (Editors), Cross-National Sociomedical Research: Concepts, Methods, Practice, pp. 82–97. Stuttgart: Thieme. [S9.5]

Nash, C E, and McDonald, S T (1985). New technologies and techniques for NASS accident investigations. In Field Accidents: Data Collection, Analysis, Methodologies, and Crash Injury Reconstructions, pp. 417–425. (SAE Paper No. 850245.) Warrendale, Pennsylvania: Society of Automotive Engineers. [S3.12, S6.4.5]

NASS (1985). National Accident Sampling System 1983. A Report on Traffic Accidents and Injuries in the U.S. Washington, D.C.: National Highway Traffic Safety Administration. [S3.12, S8.12.3, T8.20, T8.26, T8.27]

Nathorst Westfelt, J A R (1982). Environment factors in childhood accidents. A prospective study in Goteborg, Sweden. Acta Paediatrica Scandinavica, Supplement 291. [S8.7.3 (A.C.B), S10.3.1, T10.12]

NCHS (1980). Vital registration systems in five developing countries: Honduras, Mexico, Philippines, Thailand, and Jamaica. Vital and Health Statistics, Series 2, No. 79 (DHHS Publication No. (PHS) 81-1353), National Center for Health Statistics, Hyattsville, Maryland. Washington, D.C.: U.S. Government Printing Office. [S9.1]

NCHS (1984). Multiple causes of death in the United States. Monthly Vital Statistics Report, 32, No. 10, Supplement (2), National Center for Health Statistics, Hyattsville, Maryland. [S9.5]

Newby, R F (1969). Proposed classification of national road accident statistics by severity of injury. Presented at a Symposium organised by Planning and Transport Research and Computation, London. [S8.8.2]

NHTSA (1986). State accident report forms catalogue 1985. Washington, D.C.: National Highway Traffic Safety Administration. [S7.8, S8.10.3, T8.23]

Nicholl, J P (1980). The use of hospital in-patient data in the analysis of the injuries sustained by road accident casualties. Supplementary Report 628, Transport and Road Research Laboratory, Crowthorne. [S10.2.1, S13.1, S13.2, T13.1, T13.2, T13.3]

Nicholl, J P (1981). The usefulness of hospital in-patient data for road safety studies. In H C Foot, A J Chapman, and F M Wade (Editors), Road Safety: Research and Practice, pp. 19–25. Eastbourne: Praeger. [S13.1]

Nilsson, G (1984). Methods and data in order to describe the traffic safety situation. Presented at the International Workshop on the Methodology of Modelling Road Accident and Injury Patterns, organised by the International Drivers' Behaviour Research Association, held at the University of Sussex, 9th–10th July 1984. [S4.4.2, S11.4.3]

Nordentoft, E L (1975). Co-ordinated data collection. Relevance and validity of medicostatistical data. In E L Nordentoft, J A Wallin, and H V Nielsen (Editors), Traffic Speed and Casualties. Epidemiology of the Effects of Traffic Speed and Speed Limitations, pp. 134–142. Odense: Odense University Press. [S10.1]

NSW (1985). Hospital admissions due to motor vehicle accidents 1981–1983. Health Services Information Bulletin No. 5, Department of Health, New South Wales. [S10.2.2, T10.1]

Nygren, A (c. 1984). Injuries to car occupants—Some aspects of the interior safety of cars. A study of a five-year material from an insurance company. Acta Oto-Laryngologica, Supplement 395. [S8.7.1, S8.12.3, S14.6.1, T8.31, T14.8–T14.13]

Odense University Accident Analysis Group (1983). Statistical report. Road-traffic-accident injuries treated at the emergency room, Odense University Hospital. (In Danish with English translations.) [S10.3.1, S11.4.6, S13.10, T8.20, T10.8, T10.9, T10.10, T11.16]

Olugbemi, O A, and Adebisi, C (1986). Factors inhibiting objectives achievement of road accidents monitoring programmes in a developing country. In J O Asalor, E A Onibere, and G C Ovuworie (Editors), Road Traffic Accidents in Developing Countries. Volume 1, pp. 45–55. (Proceedings of the First International Conference, held in Benin.) Lagos: Joja Educational Research and Publishers. [S5.8.5]

Oluwoye, J O (1986). Design of an injury and traffic crash accident record system for use in Nigeria. In J O Asalor, E A Onibere, and G C Ovuworie (Editors), Road Traffic Accidents in Developing Countries. Volume 1, pp. 119–133. (Proceedings of the First International Conference, held in Benin.) Lagos: Joja Educational Research and Publishers. [S5.8.3]

Ouellet, J V, Hurt, H H, and Rehman, I (1984). A system for coding detailed head and neck injury data. Proceedings of the 28th Annual Conference of the American Association for Automotive Medicine, pp. 189–207. Morton Grove, Illinois: AAAM. [S8.6.2, S8.7.3 (D.F)]

Owens, J C (1983). Contribution to panel discussion of the current status of trauma severity indices, p. 200. Journal of Trauma, 23, 185–201. [S8.7.3 (D.C)]

Park, F T (1980). Accident data analysis and use. In Road and Bridge Engineering 1980 (Australian Development Assistance Course, Reference Papers), Vol. 1: Road Planning and Design, pp. 329–347. Walkerville: Highways Department of South Australia. [S3.3.1]

Partyka, S (1982). An estimated MAIS for NCSS via case replication. In National Center for Statistics and Analysis Collected Technical Studies. Volume III: Accident Data Analysis Results and Methodology, pp. 277–320. Report No. DOT HS-806-403, National Center for Statistics and Analysis, National Highway Traffic Safety Administration, Washington, D.C. [S8.7.2, S8.12.1, S8.12.3, S8.12.7, T8.13, T8.26, T8.32, T8.34]

Paterson, R, and Baxter, D (1987). 1986 Coding Manual for Traffic Accident Information. Rosebery, N.S.W.: Traffic Authority of New South Wales. [S6.4.5]

Pendleton, O J, Hatfield, N J, and Bremer, R (1986). Alcohol involvement in Texas driver fatalities: Accident reports versus blood alcohol concentration. In Alcohol, Accidents, and Injuries, pp. 1–9. (SAE Paper No. 860037.) Warrendale, Pennsylvania: Society of Automotive Engineers. (Same authors, same year, same title: Transportation Research Record, No. 1068, 65–70.) [S7.7, S13.7, T7.14, T7.15]

Petrucelli, E (1982). The Abbreviated Injury Scale in perspective. American Association for Automotive Medicine Quarterly/Journal, 4(4), 39–43. [S8.7.3 (A.A.A, A.A.B, B.A)]

Petrucelli, E (1984a). Injury scaling and some considerations of disability consequences. In B Aldman and A Chapon (Editors), The Biomechanics of Impact Trauma, pp. 7–23. Amsterdam: Elsevier. [S8.5.5, S8.7.1, T8.5]

Petrucelli, E (1984b). Limbs: Anatomy, types of injuries, and future priorities. In B Aldman and A Chapon (Editors), The Biomechanics of Impact Trauma, pp. 311–326. Amsterdam: Elsevier. [S8.7.3 (A.C.B)]

Petrucelli, E, States, J D, and Hames, L N (1981). The Abbreviated Injury Scale: Evolution, usage and future adaptability. Accident Analysis and Prevention, 13, 29–35. [S8.7.1, S8.7.3 (A.A.A, A.A.B, B.A)]

Pfefer, R C, and Reischl, B E (1983). Application of small computers to traffic records systems in small communities. Transportation Research Record, No. 910, 48–56. [S3.14.7]

Philipp, R (1983). Monitoring accidents and seat belt legislation: HAA data and the use of E codes in England and Wales. Community Medicine, 5, 235–237. [S10.2.1]

Philipp, R (1984). HAA and accident codes. Community Medicine, 6, 320. [S8.5.1, S10.2.1]

RAGB (1986). Road Accidents Great Britain 1985. The Casualty Report. London: HMSO. [S8.8.2, S13.4, T7.1, T7.5, T7.14, T7.16]

Reidelbach, W, and Zeidler, F (1983). Comparison of injury severity assigned to lower extremity skeletal damages versus upper body lesions. Proceedings of the 27th Annual Conference of the American Association for Automotive Medicine, pp. 141–155. Morton Grove, Illinois: AAAM. [S8.7.3 (A.C.A, A.C.B, A.D.D)]

Reinfurt, D W, Stewart, J R, Hall, R G, Dutt, A K, Stutts, J C, Li, L K, and Markley, J B (1978). Injury scaling research. Report No. DOT-HS-7-01539, Highway Safety Research Center, University of North Carolina. [S8.1, S8.7.2, S8.7.3 (A.D.C), S8.11.1, S8.11.5, T8.15]

Rockett, I, Hollinshead, W H, and Lieberman, E (1986). A statewide motor vehicle injury surveillance system. Rhode Island Medical Journal, 69, 67–70. [S10.3.1]

Ross, A (c. 1986). Accident data recording and analysis systems in developing countries. Report from the Department of Civil Engineering, University of Newcastle upon Tyne. [S5.8, S8.9.2]

Rotman, M (1967). Proposal for a uniform traffic accident report. Traffic Quarterly, 21, 419–434. [S4.2.5, S6.6.6]

Sach, N D (1976). The Victorian road accident location system. Proceedings of the 8th Annual Conference of the Australian Road Research Board, Part 5, Session 27, pp. 7–19. [S4.2.5, S6.4.5]

Sanderson, J T, Cameron, M H, and Fildes, B N (1985). Identification of hazardous road locations: Final report. Report No. CR37, Federal Office of Road Safety, Federal Department of Transport, Australia. [S6.6.5]

Satterthwaite, S P (1975). A note on the classification of accidents by severity. Report from the Traffic Studies Group, University College London. [S8.8.2]

Sayer, I, and Hitchcock, R (1984). An analysis of police and medical road accident data: Sri Lanka 1977–81. Supplementary Report 834, Transport and Road Research Laboratory, Crowthorne. [S5.5, S8.9.2, S8.12.3, T8.30]

Scott, R E (1972). Evaluation of severity codes in accident data. HIT Lab Reports, March 1972. (Highway Safety Research Institute, University of Michigan.) [S8.10.2, S8.12.1, T8.25]

Searles, B (1980). Unreported traffic crashes in Sydney. Proceedings of the 10th Conference of the Australian Road Research Board, Part 4, pp. 62–74. [S4.4.1, S14.5, T4.6, T4.7]

Searles, B, Booth, M, and Jamieson, J (1986). Source, reliability and interpretation of available crash information and future needs. In A Practical Approach to Road Safety. (Proceedings of a one-day discussion forum, organised by the Australian Institute of Traffic Planning and Management.) Sydney: National Roads and Motorists' Association. [S4.4.1, S6.6.5, S14.5]

Searles, B, and Jamieson, J (1983). Accident data: Other sources. In D C Andreassend and P G Gipps (Editors), Traffic Accident Evaluation. Papers Presented at an Esso-Monash Civil Engineering Workshop. Clayton, Victoria: Department of Civil Engineering, Monash University. [S4.4.1, S14.5]

Seiffert, U W (1986). Discussion on Paper 860505. In Crash Injury Impairment and Disability: Long Term Effects, pp. 127–136. Warrendale, Pennsylvania: Society of Automotive Engineers. [S8.9.6]

Selecki, B R, Ring, I T, Simpson, D A, Vanderfield, G K, and Sewell, M F (c. 1981). Injuries to the head, spine, and peripheral nerves. Epidemiology of neurotrauma in New South Wales, South Australia, and the Australian Capital Territory, 1977. Report on a study. Report from the Trauma Subcommittee of the Neurosurgical Society of Australasia. [S8.4.2, S9.5]

Sherman, H W, Murphy, M J, and Huelke, D F (1976). A reappraisal of the use of police injury codes in accident data analysis. Proceedings of the 20th Conference of the American Association for Automotive Medicine, pp. 128–138. Morton Grove, Illinois: AAAM. [S8.10.2, S8.12.1, T8.20, T8.26]

Shinar, D, Treat, J R, and McDonald, S T (1983). The validity of police reported accident data. Accident Analysis and Prevention, 15, 175–191. [S4.3.3, S8.10.1, T4.3, T4.4, T4.5]

Skelton, N (1973). The use of the OSIRIS package in the analysis of accident data. Presented at a Symposium organised by Planning and Transport Research and Computation, London. [S3.14.1]

Smith, M E, and Newcombe, H B (1979). Accuracies of computer versus manual linkages of routine health records. Methods of Information in Medicine, 18, 89–97. [S13.2.4]

Smith, R A, Fell, J C, Smith, S R, and Hart, S A (1981). The national accident picture—1979. Proceedings of the 25th Annual Conference of the American Association for Automotive Medicine, pp. 347–367. Morton Grove, Illinois: AAAM. [T8.20]

Somers, R L (1981). The Probability of Death Score: An improvement of the Injury Severity Score. Proceedings of the 25th Annual Conference of the American Association for Automotive Medicine, pp. 281–290. Morton Grove, Illinois: AAAM. [S8.7.3 (A.D.C)]

Somers, R L (1983). New ways to use the Abbreviated Injury Scale: A guide to evaluating threat to life. American Association for Automotive Medicine Quarterly/Journal, 5(2), 31–33. [S8.7.3 (A.D.C)]

Somnemitr, T (1986). Road traffic accident prevention in Thailand. Proceedings of the 13th Australian Road Research Board and 5th Road Engineering Association of Asia and Australasia Combined Conference, Part 2, pp. 140–154. Nunawading: ARRB. [S5.7]

Spence, E S (1975a). A proposed injury code for automotive accident victims. Report from the New York State Department of Motor Vehicles, Albany. [S8.6.3, T8.7]

Spence, E S (1975b). Validity test of New York State Injury Coding Scheme (NYSICS). Report from the New York State De-

partment of Motor Vehicles, Albany. [S8.6.3, T8.7]

Stenzel, W W (1983). The promise of new technology: Implications for traffic record systems. Transportation Research Record, No. 910, 43–48. [S3.14.7]

Stone, R D (1984). Computer linkage of transport and health data. Laboratory Report 1130, Transport and Road Research Laboratory, Crowthorne. [S8.5.5, S13.3]

Storms, D (1983). Data sources and injury epidemiology. Proceedings of an International Course organised by the Johns Hopkins University School of Hygiene and Public Health and the World Health Organization, held in Baltimore, June 1983, pp. 28–39. [S4.1]

Stulginskas, J V, Pless, I B, and Frappier, J-Y (1983). A total population survey of traffic accidents among children. Proceedings of the 27th Annual Conference of the American Association for Automotive Medicine, pp. 169–177. Morton Grove, Illinois: AAAM. [S11.4.9, S13.9.2]

Terhune, K W (1983). CALAX: A collision taxonomy for research and traffic records. Journal of Safety Research, 14, 13–20. [S6.4.5, F6.4]

Thompson, E J (1985). Statistics and safety—Collecting and interpreting the data that matter. Presented at the 2nd Biennial Symposium on Road Safety and the Road User, held at the University of Salford, September 1985. [S3.2]

Tomike, T, Mori, H, and Foust, D R (1982). Traffic accidents in Japan—The 1980 statistics. Proceedings of the 26th Annual Conference of the American Association for Automotive Medicine, pp. 279–296. Morton Grove, Illinois: AAAM. [S3.8, S6.4.5, T3.5, T3.6]

TPR (Traffic Planning and Research Pty. Ltd.) (1973). A review of mass data in relation to road safety. Report NR/21, Australian Department of Transport. Canberra: Australian Government Publishing Service. [S3.6.1]

TRC (1985). Introduction to Comprehensive Computerized Safety Recordkeeping Systems. Transportation Research Circular, No. 293. [S3.15, S14.5]

Tsuchihashi, M, Nishikawa, S, Mii, K, and Okamura, M (1981). Road traffic accidents and the Abbreviated Injury Scale (AIS) in Japan. Accident Analysis and Prevention, 13, 37–42. [S8.7.1, S8.7.2, S14.7, T8.13, T8.20, T14.14, T14.15]

Tunbridge, R J (1987). The use of linked transport-health road casualty data. Research Report 96, Transport and Road Research Laboratory, Crowthorne. [S8.5.5, S13.3, T8.20, T13.4, T13.5, T13.6]

Turner, D S, and Mansfield, E R (1983). Variability in rural accident reporting. Transportation Research Record, No. 910, 8–14. [S4.3.8]

Tursz, A (1986). Epidemiological studies of accident morbidity in children and young people: Problems of methodology. World Health Statistics Quarterly, 39, 257–267. [S8.5.1]

Ulman, M S, and Stalnaker, R L (1986). Evaluation of the AIS as a measure of probability of death. Proceedings of the 1986 International IRCOBI Conference on the Biomechanics of Impacts, pp. 105–119. Bron, France: International Research Council on Biokinetics of Impacts. [S8.7.2, S8.7.3 (A.C.B, C.B), S8.12.7, T8.13, T8.14, T8.19, T8.34]

UN (1985). Handbook of Vital Statistics Systems and Methods. Volume II: Review of National Practices. (Studies in Methods, Series F, No. 35.) New York: Statistical Office, United Nations. [S9.1]

Walsh, D, Bofin, P, Sheehan, B J, O'Donnell, B, and Dean, G (1986). Road traffic accidents and alcohol, Dublin and Kildare 1977-1981. Irish Journal of Medical Science, 155, 156–159. [T7.13, T7.14, T7.15]

Walz, F H (1984). Lower abdomen and pelvis: Anatomy and types of injury. In B Aldman and A Chapon (Editors), The Biomechanics of Impact Trauma, pp. 279–287. Amsterdam: Elsevier. [S12.23]

Watkins, C J (1971). Uniform road traffic accident reporting procedures. Australian Road Research, 4, 67–91. [S3.6.1, S6.4.5, T6.6]

Waxweiler, R J, Kruse, T, and Smith, G S (1987). Proposed modifications to transportation injury codes for the Tenth Revision of the International Classification of Diseases. To be presented at the 31st Annual Conference of the American Association for Automotive Medicine. [S8.3.2]

Weston, P A M (1981). Admission policy for patients following head injury. British Journal of Surgery, 68, 663–664. [S10.2.1]

Whately, S (1985). Bicycle crashes in the Australian Capital Territory. Report No. CR 35, Federal Office of Road Safety, Federal Department of Transport. [S10.2.2, T10.6]

WHO (1972). Availability of accident statistics. World Health Statistics Report, 25, 756–778. [S6.6.1]

WHO (1979a). Crash protection in road accidents. WHO Chronicle, 33, 381–382. [S1.7]

WHO (1979b). Road traffic accident statistics. Report on a WHO ad hoc technical group, Prague, 26–28 September 1978. Euro Reports and Studies, No. 19, World Health Organization Regional Office for Europe, Copenhagen. [S10.1]

WHO (1982a). Statistical indicators for accidents. Document ICP/ADR 052; IRP/ADR 218-21, World Health Organization Regional Office for Europe, Copenhagen. [S8.5.5]

WHO (1982b). Study group on assessment of country surveys on accidents in childhood. Report on a WHO meeting, held in Ankara, November 1982. World Health Organization. [S5.11]

WHO (1983a). Report on the seminar on the prevention of road traffic accidents, held in Manila, February 1983. Manila: Regional Office for the Western Pacific of the World Health Organization. [S5.11]

WHO (1983b). National road accident control programme development. Report on a WHO meeting, held in Dhaka, November 1983. World Health Organization. [S5.11, T2.1 (footnote)]

WHO (1983c). Symposium on accident prevention in childhood. Report on a WHO/ICC/IPA meeting, held in Manila, November 1983. World Health Organization. [S8.6.5, T8.12]

WHO (1984a). Road traffic accidents in developing countries. Report of a WHO meeting. Technical Report Series, No. 703, World Health Organization, Geneva. [S5.1]

WHO (1984b). Joint HQ/PAHO workshop on the prevention and care of motor vehicle injuries in the Caribbean. Report on a WHO meeting, held in Bridgetown, June 1984. World Health Organization. [S5.9, T5.5]

Wigglesworth, E C (1977). Road trauma: Who should be counted? Medical Journal of Australia, 1977-2, 439–440. [S11.1]

Willett, P (1981). Accident data collection. Report on Project WMR 77/6, Main Roads Department, Western Australia. [S3.5]

Willis, C O, Turner, D S, and Colson, C W (1983). Evaluation of accident reporting histories. Transportation Research Record, No. 910, 19–26. [S4.3.8]

Winthrop, A L, Wesson, D E, Pencharz, P B, Jacobs, D G, Heim, T, and Filler, R M (1987). Injury severity, whole body protein turnover, and energy expenditure in pediatric trauma. Journal of Pediatric Surgery, 22, 534–537. [S8.12.6]

Wood, E M (1981). Challenge to the Conference: The FHWA perspective. Transportation Research Circular, No. 233 (Management of Accident Data Systems: Report of a Workshop), 4–5. [S14.5]

Zegeer, C V (1982). Highway accident analysis systems. National Cooperative Highway Research Program Synthesis of Highway Practice, No. 91. [S3.11, S6.6.7, T6.19]

Index

Topics are referred to by the Chapter (C), Section or Sub-section (S), Figure (F), or Table (T) in which they appear. Citations of a particular author should be traced with the Section (or other) number at the end of the entry in the list of References.